PASTORAL CHALLENGES & CONCERNS

A CHRISTIAN HANDBOOK FOR LEADERS

EDITED BY

BRENDAN GEARY
JOCELYN BRYAN

kevin mayhew

kevin mayhew

Revised edition published in 2018 by Kevin Mayhew Ltd
Buxhall, Stowmarket, Suffolk IP14 3BW
Tel: +44 (0) 1449 737978 Fax: +44 (0) 1449 737834
E-mail: info@kevinmayhew.com

www.kevinmayhew.com

9 8 7 6 5 4 3 2 1 0

ISBN 978 1 84867 937 5
Catalogue No. 1501568

Cover design by Rob Mortonson
© Image used under licence from Shutterstock Inc.
Edited by Virginia Rounding
Typeset by Angela Selfe

Printed and bound in Great Britain

Contents

Introduction to the Second Edition

It is ten years since the first edition of the *Christian Handbook of Abuse, Addiction & Difficult Behaviour* was published. The book was well received and has been used by individuals involved in pastoral leadership, as well as by lecturers and tutors in training courses for ministry, and clergy and lay formation. The opportunity to prepare a revised and expanded edition has enabled the editors and authors to bring the chapters up to date, where appropriate, with research that has taken place since the first edition. It has also provided an opportunity to add new chapters to the book. The addition of chapters on the digital world, and Asperger's and autism led to a reconsideration of the title of the book, as it would be insensitive and inaccurate to label these behaviours as 'difficult'. The revised and expanded edition has a new title: *Pastoral Challenges and Concerns: A Christian Handbook for Leaders*. This title also seemed a more appropriate way to describe the contents and target readership for the book, which works well as an academic text for people in formation for ministry and for leaders in a range of ministerial roles.

The chapter on child sexual abuse has been updated to take account of the revelations about Jimmy Savile's behaviour, the abuse that took place in Rotherham, Salford and other English cities, and the recent revelations about abuse of boys who were part of training programmes for football clubs. The chapter on adult bullying incorporates some recent data from reports as well as the recent @MeToo phenomenon where men and women have found the courage to report sexual harassment in the worlds of entertainment and politics. William Macgregor, a recently qualified lawyer, has contributed the section on the law of harassment and bullying. The chapters related to addictions have been updated regarding changes in the law and recent research.

Society's awareness of Asperger syndrome and autism has increased significantly in the past ten years. Mark Haddon's novel, *The Curious Incident of the Dog in the Night Time*, and the stage play based on the novel, brought this condition to the attention of a wider audience. There have also been moves to integrate young people with these conditions into regular schools, and to find ways to engage them in a positive way. The Revd Tracey Hume has written a sympathetic chapter about Asperger's and autism. She provides clear explanations to help readers to understand the conditions, and helps the reader to see the world and the experience of church from the perspective of people with these conditions and their families. Making use of her own pastoral experience, she focuses mostly on how to welcome people with these conditions into church. The principles she presents can also be adapted to the workplace.

Bex Lewis, Senior Lecturer in Digital Marketing at Manchester Metropolitan University, has written a thoughtful chapter on the digital age, with its challenges and opportunities, especially for people involved in church and pastoral ministry. She tries to move beyond the panic response which is common, or the attitude that 'I am too old for this'. She suggests that we no longer have a choice about whether to be involved with the internet and the digital world. For all practical purposes, it is the world in which we now live and move. She addresses the issues of addiction, online bullying and abuse, which are also addressed, where appropriate, in other chapters in the book. She suggests that we require a change of attitude, and growth in awareness of the technologies which are no longer simply a part of our lives but which increasingly define and provide the parameters for our lives.

Two chapters have been added to the second, thematic, section. Jocelyn Bryan has contributed a chapter on early relationships, to help people involved in management and ministry to understand how experiences in the early years can have such a profound effect on the development of personality and behaviours in childhood and adulthood. Brendan Geary has written a chapter on self-regulation. This chapter builds on the section on self-regulation that was published in the chapter on psychological themes (Concluding Reflections) to provide more information on this key dimension of motivation and personal behaviour. There is some repetition of this new material in the Concluding Reflections, but the editors felt it was better to leave this chapter intact than to try to remove the sections that were written for the first edition of the book.

The movement known as Positive Psychology has arguably had the most significant impact of any development in the field of psychology in recent years. It has generated creative and practical avenues of research, has attracted research funding and has changed the language of psychology. It has also affected government policy in a range of ways.[1] The chapter on psychological themes has been expanded to include some key developments related to this movement: the role of positive emotions, post-traumatic growth, neuroplasticity, and mindfulness (contributed by Dr James Walsh). Hopefully, these additions will reflect some of the significant, positive, changes that have taken place in the world of psychology in relation to difficult behaviours, and how to help people to manage their own behaviours and the challenging behaviours of others.

Jocelyn Bryan and Brendan Geary

---

1   http://worldhappiness.report/

PART I

CHAPTER ONE

Child Sexual Abuse

Brendan Geary

John was a young, personable, engaging primary school teacher. He was enthusiastic, related well to pupils, staff and parents, and was liked and appreciated by the head teacher at the church school where he taught. John's easy manner and willingness to work outside school hours on sports and social events meant he was trusted and held in high regard. He would stay with the pupils during breaks, take them for football on Saturdays, and direct school shows. Over time he got to know the parents who invited him to family events, and gratefully accepted his offers to babysit, especially for the 10 to 12-year-old boys with whom he appeared to have a particular rapport. This impressive façade came crashing down when one of the students let it be known that John had been touching him inappropriately after school when he was 'coaching' him in maths. After the first allegation the floodgates burst, 5 more students began to tell their stories, and John eventually pleaded guilty to 23 cases of sexual assault.

While John's story might not be reported in the national media, it is probably more familiar to people who work in the area of sexual abuse than the more lurid, high profile cases of child rape and assault that are presented to readers in the headlines of national newspapers. The revelations about Jimmy Savile, celebrity child abusers, the Soham murder case, Fr Brendan Smyth[2] in Ireland, and similar stories are highly charged, but are not representative of the majority of cases of sexual abuse. The revelations of sexual abuse of children – mostly boys

---

2 Fr Brendan Smyth was an Irish priest who was convicted of abusing over 100 children over a 40-year period. He died in prison in 1997. http://www.bbc.co.uk/news/uk-northern-ireland-33223162. Retrieved 13 May 2016.

– in British football clubs reveals that the sexual abuse of children has found its way into all parts of our society.[3]

The revelations of abuse in football have raised concerns about abuse in sport. A review of safeguarding cases in sport that was published in 2014 gathered data on a total of 652 cases and referenced 132 cases of alleged abuse in football between 1967 and 2002.[4] The majority of victims in this review were boys, and physical and sexual abuse was the most frequently reported. As of 16 December 2016, the National Society for the Prevention of Cruelty to Children (NSPCC) had received more than 1700 calls about alleged sexual abuse in sport to their dedicated phone line in a three-week period. Police have said that 83 potential suspects have been identified, involving 30 clubs. There have also been concerns about the extent of abuse in ethnic minority communities. Social and cultural values can prevent reporting of these crimes, as well as the effect of issues related to family honour, shame, stigma and the consequences for girls regarding their ability to find a suitable marriage partner.[5]

Child abuse arouses fear, disgust, anger, and contempt. It is a disturbing subject about which it is difficult, if not impossible, to remain dispassionate. Researchers suggest that about one in three girls and possibly one in four boys are victims of some kind of inappropriate sexual behaviour, ranging from talk about sex (or sexualised talk), through inappropriate touching, to intrusive sexual acts, at some point during their childhood. Violent sexual acts on children involving penetration are not the norm. It would appear that the more intrusive the violation, the younger the age, and the more frequent the abuse, the more damage tends to be done. It has also been shown that abuse committed by trusted family members or friends tends to leave deeper psychological scars. The high prevalence rates mean that, knowingly or not, many of us will have contact with someone who, at some time during his/her life, has suffered from abuse.

---

3   http://www.bbc.com/sport/football/38211167. Retrieved 15 December 2016.
4   Rhind, D., McDermott, J., Lambert, E. and Koleva, I. (2014). A review of safeguarding cases in sport. *Child Abuse Review* 24: 418–26.
5   Duffy, Judith. (9 October 2016). Survivors speak out about the 'hidden' child sexual abuse in ethnic minority communities. *The Herald*, p. 30.

The exposure of cases of paedophilia and ephebophilia, and even rape, has led to changes in the canon law of the Catholic Church,[6] and the setting up of the Nolan Commission (2001)[7] and the Cumberlege Commission (2007)[8] in the Catholic Church in England and Wales, the McLellan Commission (2015)[9] which reviewed the safeguarding policies and practices of the Catholic Church in Scotland, and an independent review to uncover historic cases of sexual abuse in the Church of England.[10] The Ryan (2009)[11] and Murphy (2009)[12] reports revealed the extent of child sexual abuse by clergy in Ireland. Since that time the National Board for Safeguarding Children of the Catholic Church in Ireland[13] has undertaken audits of safeguarding practice of every diocese and religious order in Ireland and these reports have been published online, often causing considerable embarrassment to dioceses and religious orders whose history in the area of protection of children did not meet acceptable standards. The film *Spotlight*, which won the Academy Award for best film in 2015, highlighted the extent of abuse in the Archdiocese of Boston and the systematic cover-up of the abusive behaviour of 87 priests. The international coverage given to this film raised people's awareness of this issue once more.

This chapter will begin by exploring what is meant by abuse and will then describe briefly the effects of abuse on victims. There will then be sections on the different types of child abuse, with examples from clinical experience. The issue of celebrity abuse and cases where there are multiple abusers will be discussed. This will be followed by a discussion of the issues related to child sexual abuse and the churches. A discussion of approaches to treatment will be offered, followed by a section on the churches and abuse, and a reflection from a Christian perspective.

---

6   *On More Grave Delicts Reserved*, Vatican City, 2001.
7   *A programme for action: Final report of the independent review of child protection in the Catholic Church in England and Wales*. (2001). London: Catholic Bishops' Conference of England and Wales.
8   http://www.cumberlegecommission.org.uk/. Retrieved 13 May 2016.
9   https://www.bcos.org.uk/Portals/0/McLellan/363924_WEB.pdf
10 Butt, R. (22 October 2007). Church pledges to root out decades-old child abuse cases. *The Guardian*.
11 http://www.childabusecommission.ie/. Retrieved 13 May 2016.
12 http://www.justice.ie/en/JELR/Pages/PB09000504. Retrieved 13 May 2016.
13 http://www.safeguarding.ie/. Retrieved 13 May 2016.

Definitions

The NSPCC offers the following definition of child sexual abuse:

> Sexual abuse occurs when an adult exploits their power, authority or position and uses a child sexually to gratify their own needs.[14]

A sex offender is someone who engages in sexual behaviours that are considered illegal. This is important, as laws regarding age of consent vary in different countries and may be different for boys and girls. Researchers, as a rule of thumb, will use 16 as a cut-off point, with the perpetrator being at least 5 years older than the victim. It is important to bear in mind that child sexual abuse involves touching and non-touching behaviours. Showing pornography to a child, exposing genitals, watching a child undress or use the bathroom, or initiating an unwelcome conversation about sexual development or adult sexual topics, also constitute abuse, as they invade the private world of the child.

The rapid development of the internet has given rise to new categories of abuse. Children can be groomed over the internet, with perpetrators arranging meetings in the real world. With video cameras, it is possible to invite or pay children to take off their clothes or perform sexual acts in front of the camera. It is more correct to talk about child abusive images rather than child pornography, as any involvement of children in sexual activity via the internet involves abuse and exploitation. One member of a religious order was arrested in February 2016 for taking images of naked adult models from the internet and digitally adjusting the images to make them look like children.[15] This also constitutes abuse.

Statistical data on sexual abuse

Statistical data are a prerequisite of serious study in any area, particularly when it can have an effect on public policy and law. Having said that, it is particularly difficult to obtain reliable data where child abuse is concerned.

---

14   NSPCC. *Keeping Children Safe: A child protection awareness programme.*
15   http://www.brokenrites.org.au/drupal/node/364. Retrieved 13 May 2016.

Authors agree that most crimes go unreported, and victim reports, for various reasons, may not be as objective and reliable as a researcher would like. Despite their limitations, statistics can be instructive.

A British study undertaken in 2011 found that 24.1% of adults had experienced sexual abuse (both contact and non-contact) during their childhood by another child or an adult. The prevalence of contact offences was 11%.[16] Until recently, it was accepted that women were perhaps three times more likely to have been victims of sexual abuse than men. However, recent research suggests that there are more male victims than was previously thought. It appears that there is a higher risk of girls being abused by a family member and that boys are more vulnerable to abuse by a stranger.[17] Males are more reluctant to report abuse than females, and this may contribute to the underreporting of these offences.

In 1995 the American Medical Association (AMA) described sexual assault as a 'silent-violent epidemic'.[18] The following statistics are offered by the National Sex Offender Public Website in the United States:

- In a 2012 maltreatment report 26% of child victims who were sexually abused were in the 12–14-year age range. 35% were younger than 9 years of age.

- Approximately 1.8 million adolescents in the United States have been victims of sexual assault.

- The Centre for Disease Control estimated that approximately 1 in 6 boys and 1 in 4 girls have been sexually abused before their eighteenth birthday.

- 69% of teen sexual assaults that were reported to the police took place in the home of the victim, the offender or another individual.

- Young people aged 16–19 years of age were 3.5 times more likely than the general population to be victims of an actual or attempted sexual assault.[19]

---

16 https://www.nspcc.org.uk/globalassets/documents/information-service/research-briefing-child-sexual-abuse.pdf (p. 3). Retrieved 13 May 2016.

17 Ibid.

18 American Medical Association. Sexual assault in America [Press release]. (6 November 1995). Quoted in Freeman-Longo, R. and Blanchard, G. (1998). *Sexual abuse in America*. Vermont: Safer Society Press.

19 https://www.nsopw.gov/en/Home/About. Retrieved 13 May 2016.

Almost 20 years ago, Freeman-Longo and Blanchard reported that as many as 17% of men in the United States were prepared to admit to having sexually abused a child.[20] They also reported that 90% of sex abuse cases do not go to trial.

The NSPCC report on child abuse for 2013–14 entitled *How Safe Are Our Children?* reported a total of 36,429 offences against children. This is the highest number for a decade. It is likely, though, that this sharp increase reflects a greater willingness of children (and others) to report abuse against children as a result of increased high profile cases and awareness of the issue of child sexual abuse.[21]

Effects of abuse

One of the consequences of media interest in sexual abuse has been an increase in the study of the effects of abuse. While some children and adults appear to be able to recover more quickly than others, not everyone shares the same psychological resilience or capacity to recover from traumatic events in a robust way. We know that many victims have suffered serious consequences as a result of abuse by others. Victims of sexual abuse often display a higher incidence of psychological problems and difficulties in social and interpersonal functioning. They can have difficulties in trusting others and often have low self-esteem, as well as feelings of powerlessness and alienation from themselves and others. One victim who was abused by her father wrote as follows about her experience:

> I was robbed of my childhood, my innocence, my ownership of my own body, and my sexuality. I withered away. Not all at once, but in one way or another, piece by piece, and finally my whole person, my body, and my soul were taken away from me.[22]

Two large studies from California and Canada present a convincing picture of the devastating effects of abuse on children. In the Californian

---

20 Freeman-Longo, R. and Blanchard, G. (1998). *Sexual abuse in America.* Vermont: Safer Society Press.

21 https://www.nspcc.org.uk/globalassets/documents/research-reports/how-safe-children-2015-report.pdf. Retrieved 13 May 2016.

22 McGlone, G.J., Shrader, M. and Delgatto, L. (2003). *Creating safe and sacred places: Identifying, preventing, and healing sexual abuse,* p. 44. Minnesota: St. Mary's Press.

study it was found that victims of sexual abuse were two and a half to four times more likely to suffer mental health problems than those who had not been abused.[23] The following problems were mentioned in the report: drug abuse or dependence, major depressive disorder and manic episodes, phobia, panic and obsessive-compulsive disorder. There appeared to be higher levels of mental illness among women than men. The study concluded that people who had experienced abuse in childhood (under 16 years of age) had significantly higher levels of mental illness than non-abused individuals.

A group of Canadian researchers investigated physical and sexual abuse and reported similar findings.[24] They also found that the men who had been sexually abused had a higher incidence of disorders than men who had been physically abused. This confirms our sense that sexual abuse is more damaging than physical abuse. It appears that a history of physical or sexual abuse increases the possibility of mental illness later in life, and this is stronger for women than for men.

Sexual abuse can also manifest itself behaviourally and can be seen in increased aggression or avoidance/dependency, substance abuse, impulsivity or delinquency. Recent research also suggests that early experiences of abuse may have permanent effects on the structure of the brain.[25]

Consequences for victims

Robert Freeman-Longo and Geral Blanchard write that 81% of sex addicts report that they were abused as children.[26] They also report an estimate that a high percentage of men and women involved in prostitution were victims of incest, physical abuse or sexual abuse. They lament that a consequence of prostitution is often arrest and involvement in the criminal system. This seldom leads to therapeutic help to deal with the abuse that led these people to prostitution in

23 Burnam, Audrey M., Stein, Judith A., Golding, Jacqueline M., Siegal, Judith M., Sorenson, Susan B., Forsythe, Alan B. and Telles, Cynthia A. (1988). Sexual assault and mental disorders in a community population. *Journal of Consulting and Clinical Psychology* 56: 843–50.

24 MacMillan, Harriet L., Fleming, Jan E., Streiner, David L., Lin, Elizabeth, Boyle, Michael H., Jamieson, Ellen, Duku, Eric K., Walsh, Christine, A., Wong, Maria Y.Y. and Beardslee, William R. (2001). Childhood abuse and lifetime psychopathology in a community sample. *American Journal of Psychiatry* 158(11: 1878–83).

25 Teicher, Martin H. (2002). The neurobiology of child abuse. *Scientific American,* March: 68–75.

26 Freeman-Longo, R. and Blanchard, G. (1998). *Sexual abuse in America.* Vermont: Safer Society Press.

the first place, but may in fact reinforce feelings of anger, bitterness, victimisation, and hopelessness.

It is also recognised that a number of men and women who sexually abuse others were victims of sexual abuse themselves. While it is noted that not every person who has been abused becomes an abuser, it would appear that up to one third of those who are abused later behave in this way themselves. Gerard McGlone, a Jesuit priest and clinical psychologist, alerts us to the need to be careful not to equate a history of abuse with becoming an abuser. In his study of sex-offending and non-offending Catholic priests, he found that 19% of normal priests (i.e. those who had not offended against children) said that they had been abused in their childhood. However, when asked, they said that they did not go on to become offenders themselves.[27]

The circles of damage perpetrated by sexual abusers radiate beyond the individual victims. Many perpetrators are themselves affected by their behaviour. While they have a powerful range of ways of justifying the abuse, the fact that they are secretive, manipulative, threatening and/or cunning, demonstrates clearly enough their knowledge that what they are doing is wrong. Many perpetrators express relief once they are caught and have the opportunity for treatment. One recovering abuser wrote:

> Twenty years ago I was a respected member of my community, publisher of our local paper, and a sexual abuser. Being arrested was the best thing that could have happened to me. I was lucky to get treatment . . . and it worked. I have now been back in society for nearly 10 years and have not abused again. I have been given a second chance and I will not throw that away.[28]

Communities also suffer: parishes, religious communities, social and neighbourhood networks, families, schools, businesses. What is the appropriate response when a former trusted employee has been

---

27 McGlone, Gerard J., S.J. (2001). *Sexually offending and non-offending Roman Catholic priests: Characterization and analysis*. Unpublished doctoral dissertation, California School of Professional Psychology, Alliant University, San Diego.

28 Freeman-Longo, R. and Blanchard, G. (1998). *Sexual abuse in America*, p. 5. Vermont: Safer Society Press.

charged, arrested and/or found guilty of child abuse? How should you respond if an employee has been using a work computer to download child pornography? It is easy to understand how a concerned employer, priest or co-worker might want to terminate the contract of an employee in order to protect children, as well as the good name of the school, parish or business. However, the problems of unemployment will only exacerbate the stress related to discovery and involvement in the legal and criminal justice systems. There are no easy answers. The number of victims of sexual abuse extends far beyond the individual who is assaulted.

Sexual abuse and the abusers

It may be instructive to take a moment to think about what kind of person comes to mind when the phrase 'child abuser' is used. It would be surprising if our mental image was not influenced by media reports of socially inept, unattractive, devious, unhappy, aggressive, predatory, manipulative white men. Many people still have the 'stranger danger' rhyme ringing in their heads. The reality is somewhat more complex. The most surprising thing about sex offenders is how ordinary they are. Men and women from all social classes and walks of life are found among sex offenders. While offenders are mostly men, there is a growing awareness of women who also abuse. In the autumn of 2007 a 44-year-old female probation officer pleaded guilty to two charges of engaging with sexual activity with a child (a 15-year-old boy)[29] and a female tennis coach was convicted of sexual activity with a 13-year-old girl.[30] In September 2015, Marie Black, a 34-year-old woman from Norfolk, was found guilty of 23 cases of child abuse. It appears that she organised sex parties where children were raffled to adults for sex.[31] An NSPCC Research Briefing (2013) reported that 17% of calls to Childline concerned an allegation against a female abuser. Analysis of calls from boys indicated that, in the 70% of calls where the gender of the abuser was specified, 34% were male and 36% were female.

---

29   Ahmed, M. (30 October 2007). Truant officer 'broke one of last taboos' by having sex with errant pupil, p. 15. *The Times*.

30   Heffernan, C. (3 November 2007). Tennis coach jailed for sex acts with 'infatuated' girl, p. 13. *The Guardian*.

31   http://www.telegraph.co.uk/women/womens-life/11899484/Female-paedophiles-Why-women-sexually-abuse-children.html. Retrieved 13 May 2016.

The comparable figures for girls were 67% male perpetrators and 6% female perpetrators.[32]

Child molesters tend to be family members or people in positions of responsibility or trust (teachers, probation officers, clergy). They seldom use force or aggression. It has been noted that they often use what are known as 'cognitive distortions' to justify their behaviour. Cognitive distortions are distorted ways of thinking that help child molesters to excuse, minimise, rationalise or deny their abusive behaviour. The following examples will help to illustrate this kind of distorted thinking:

- I was showing the child affection.

- The child came on to me. I didn't initiate this.

- He/she never told me to stop.

- I was not given any sex education and I did not want this child to grow up ignorant like me.

- She knows I did this because I love her.

These 'cognitions' (ways of thinking) enable the offenders to commit the offence without experiencing the anxiety, shame or guilt that would normally accompany these actions. One of the problems with presenting information about child molesters is that almost all of our information comes from people who have been involved in the criminal justice system. We know little about people who are attracted to children but who have never acted on their desires.

Libby Purves presents a sympathetic portrait of this kind of person in her novel *More Lives than One*. The novel focuses on Kit Milcourt, an inspirational teacher who is falsely accused of sexual abuse of a female pupil while on a school trip to Venice. Before he is told that the girl has retracted her accusation, Kit tells his wife that he could not have been guilty of abuse of a girl as he was attracted to boys. The story continues with Kit saying:

---

32 https://www.nspcc.org.uk/globalassets/documents/research-reports/how-safe-children-2015-report.pdf, p. 3. Retrieved 13 May 2016.

> If the human creature you instinctively desire is a boy of eleven, you do not deserve to live. Anybody can tell you that. I agree . . . I don't deserve to live. But here I am. A paedophile, what they call a fixed preferential paedophile, and not even a sensible one. Sensible ones jump off high buildings or drive into trees as soon as they understand what they are.[33]

Libby Purves captures the anguish, self-hatred and fear of men who find themselves attracted to children but who manage never to act on their desires. Libby Purves' novel is a salutary reminder that not every person with paedophilic desires necessarily acts on them, and that these people deserve understanding and help. How do you ask for help if your sexual desires are both abhorrent to society and, by definition, criminal?

In Germany there is now a programme for people who become aware of paedophilic desires to enable them to seek help confidentially. The Dunkenfeld (Dark field) programme started in 2005 and has since spread to ten cities.[34] So far the programme has treated 440 paedophile patients, with an average age of 37. While it is impossible to evaluate the effectiveness of the programme, it appears to be making a significant difference to the lives of the (mostly) men who participate. The programme makes use of group therapy and cognitive behavioural therapy (CBT) techniques to enable the patients to understand their desires and find strategies to manage their feelings and behaviour.

Understanding abuse and abusers

There are a number of issues to bear in mind when trying to understand child molesters:

- Is the person attracted to boys, girls or both?

- What age range is the molester attracted to/involved with?

- Has violence or aggression been a part of the abusive behaviour?

---

33 Purves, L. (1998). *More lives than one.* p. 183. London: Hodder & Stoughton.
34 https://www.theguardian.com/society/2015/oct/16/how-germany-treats-paedophiles-before-they-offend

- Does the abuser have an interest in adult sexual relations or is he/she only interested in children?

- Is the abuse restricted to family members or is the focus of desire and abuse children who are not related to the abuser?

Bearing in mind what has been written above, it is possible to consider three broad types of offender: paedophiles, familial offenders, and ephebophiles. It is important to note, however, that no system of categorisation adequately accounts for the extraordinary range of deviant sexual interests and behaviour. This categorisation is broadly useful but also limited.

Paedophilia

Mental health professionals make use of the Diagnostic and Statistical Manual of Mental Disorders, currently in its fifth edition and commonly known as DSM V.[35] This provides criteria for a range of psychiatric disorders, and is often a useful starting point for discussion of a mental health problem. The criteria for paedophilia are as follows:

A. Over a period of at least 6 months, recurrent, intense sexually arousing fantasies, sexual urges, or behaviors involving sexual activity with a prepubescent child or children (generally age 13 years or younger).

B. The individual has acted on these sexual urges, or the sexual urges or fantasies cause marked distress or interpersonal difficulty.

C. The individual is at least age 16 years and at least 5 years older than the child or children in Criterion A.

While these criteria are useful, they are not without difficulties when it comes to providing a clinical diagnosis. It is also evident that the word 'paedophile' is often used incorrectly in the media, as it is frequently used to describe any sexual behaviour involving an under-age child or adolescent. The word paedophilia comes from the Greek words for

---

35 American Psychiatric Association. (1994). *Diagnostic and statistical manual of mental disorders* (5th edition, revised). Washington, DC: Author.

'child' and 'love'. In some ways it is a misnomer, as the behaviour we are describing is not about love, but about abuse, power, and control. Bill Marshall prefers to use the term 'child molester'. It focuses on the behaviour and does not depend on strict adherence to the criteria described above. It will continue to be used for the moment in order to distinguish this group (who are sexually interested in prepubescent children to whom they are not related) from other groups.

Some paedophiles are attracted only to children. These are called 'exclusive type'. Others are attracted to adult men or women as well as children. These are known as 'non-exclusive type'. The key feature for a diagnosis of paedophilia is an attraction to children who do not have the visible characteristics related to puberty. In reality, this often involves children who are 14 years of age and younger. A second important distinction is whether or not the abuser is attracted to children in a specific age range (e.g. 10–12, as was the case with John, whose story was presented at the beginning of this chapter), or whether they have regressed in some way from a normal interest in adult partners. The word 'regressed' in this context suggests that the person is functioning emotionally and sexually at an age range that is less than his or her biological age – e.g. a 30-year-old who is relating emotionally as a child or adolescent. Those who are fixated can have very high numbers of victims, often more than a hundred. John J. Geoghan, the former priest whose exposure as a child molester led to the sex abuse crisis in Boston in 2002 which then spread to the whole of the United States, was accused of having abused an estimated 200 children.[36]

Those who are regressed tend to have fewer victims, as their sexual behaviour is often related to experiences of stress, and depends on situation or opportunity, whereas the fixated offender will often seek out opportunities and groom their victims over a period of time. This can be seen, for example, in the film *The Woodsman*, where both the main character (played by Kevin Bacon) and a subsidiary character are seen to groom potential victims by gradually getting to know them, building confidence, and showing interest, generosity and affection. It is also evident that they have a knack of choosing children who need or are starved of affection, or who have low self-esteem.

---

36 Boston Globe Investigative Staff (2016) *Betrayal: The Crisis in the Catholic Church*: The Findings of the Investigation That Inspired the Major Motion Picture. Profile Books

John, who was described at the beginning of this chapter, was given the clinical diagnosis of paedophilia. He had an older brother, a younger sister and, after his mother's second marriage, a younger stepbrother. His father was in the armed forces and his family split up while his father was serving in Northern Ireland. His older brother, Phil, who is married with two children, was also convicted of sex abuse with a young girl. John admitted that when he was an adolescent he abused his own younger brother, who was six at the time. In attempting to understand the factors that may have contributed to his deviant interest, John mentioned that during his childhood his father would sometimes rent a cottage in the country for himself and his brother. They often slept in one room, his father in a double bed and John and his brother in bunk beds. It was quite common for them to be naked together, which John found embarrassing. His father would share his pornographic magazines with his sons. This began when John was about eight years of age and his brother a little older.

It is difficult to be exact in explaining the reasons for someone's deviant sexual interest, but the fact that his brother also abused a child suggests the possibility of a genetic influence. A number of psychologists have also observed that, if a child is exposed to inappropriate sexual activity or material, this can affect normal sexual development, especially around eight years of age. Sex offenders often come from a disturbed family background, and difficulties in early attachment have been shown to be a feature of child molesters. John's family was disrupted due to his father's service in the army, so this could have been a contributing factor.

John reported that he felt like a child among adults and was more secure in the company of children. While he was outgoing and socially attractive, he felt like an imposter and inept with adults, had low self-esteem and had never attempted to have a girlfriend. While he did not complain of loneliness, this is often a feature of child molesters. He genuinely believed that the boys he molested were his friends and, after his arrest, was shocked when the victim statements were read to him and he became aware of the pain he had inflicted on these children.

Familial sexual abuse

A useful (but not absolutely clear) distinction can be made between those who abuse children outside their own families and those who abuse family members. Within the latter category it is important to distinguish between blood relatives (fathers, brothers, uncles, aunts) and relatives by marriage (stepfathers, uncles). While the word 'incest' is commonly used, 'familial offenders' is a more accurate descriptor. In situations where fathers abuse their own daughters, it has been suggested that this may be as a result of the mother/wife losing interest in sexual relations with her husband, who then turns to his adolescent daughter to have his sexual needs met. The daughter may remind the father of his wife when she was younger. In other situations, the perpetrator may be experiencing stress, and the combination of loneliness, attractiveness of the victim, power imbalance in the relationship and poor self-esteem may combine and lead to sexual abuse. Their offences tend to be more emotionally driven than the result of deviant sexual interest. Men who are involved in familial abuse are usually attracted to adult women rather than children. Their emotional pain may be in relation to feelings of anger or revenge, or a need to restore self-esteem or to be soothed, or loved, or feel close to someone.

It is not uncommon for alcohol to be a contributory factor, as it leads to people losing the inhibitions that normally put constraints on behaviour that they know to be wrong or that could lead to personal embarrassment. It should be absolutely clear that offering an explanation for familial abuse does not mean it is being condoned. Men who experience difficulties in their sexual relationships with their partners have no right to abuse or impose on their sons, daughters or stepchildren in order to attempt to have their own needs met. Billy Connolly, the Scottish comedian and actor, spoke about his sexual abuse by his father. Connolly shared a bed with his father after his mother left the family.[37] He spoke about the complexity of not wanting the abuse but finding it pleasurable. He also spoke about how the abuse affected his adult life and sexual development.

The following examples give some idea of the range of situations that fall into this category.

- Mike was a hard-working construction contractor who was divorced and recently remarried to a woman with a daughter

---

37 http://www.theguardian.com/uk/2001/sep/23/vanessathorpe.theobserver. Retrieved 13 May 2016.

from a previous marriage. Mike was often under stress. He drank heavily and had been unfaithful to his second wife. Mike woke up one day with a heavy hangover and was confronted by his stepdaughter who accused him of coming into her room the previous night and touching her inappropriately. This had happened on two occasions. Mike claimed to have no memory of the event.

- David had five children, the eldest of whom was his 15-year-old daughter. His wife had died and he was left to bring up the children himself. David had had an abusive childhood. He was often beaten by his father, belittled, deprived of food and appropriate clothing, and kept away from school. He could not read and write. He was brought up on a farm, was isolated from other children, and was often locked out at night and had to sleep in the barn. He had a profound lack of self-esteem and little self-confidence. After his wife died, he relied on his daughter not only for practicalities but also for bringing up the younger children. At some point she became his sexual partner.

- Darryl, an Afro-Caribbean man, was introduced to sex by his aunt when he was 12. It was not a positive experience, but he did not feel able to resist, and felt both ashamed and afraid to tell his mother. As an adult, he abused his own daughter.

It is difficult to find common threads in these stories; some had been abused in their own childhoods, others not; some used alcohol, others did not; some had poor self-esteem, others did not; some had adult sexual partners available, others did not. In so far as anything is common to this group, it appears that they have significantly fewer victims than men diagnosed as paedophiles. It should be said that there are some men who are paedophiles who exploit marriage to come closer to victims, while others may have paedophilic interest and exploit their family to fulfil their desires. This may have been the case with John, who abused his own stepbrother.

Ephebophiles

The word 'ephebophile' comes from the two Greek words, 'ephebos' meaning adolescent, and 'philia' meaning love. This is not a diagnostic term, but is used to describe adults who become sexually involved with adolescents in the 14–18 age range. As with paedophiles, they fall into two categories: those who are fixated and those who are regressed. The following two examples may help to illustrate the difference.

- Joe was a heating engineer in his mid-forties. He was shy, physically awkward, not particularly attractive, lacked social skills and had limited interests. He was arrested with a group of other men for making pornographic videos with adolescent boys. It was then discovered that he had spent holidays in South East Asia where he spent time with adolescent boy prostitutes. While able to be sexually aroused by adult men, his preference was for adolescent males.

- Frank is an Anglican priest in his mid-thirties. He is enthusiastic, generous, pastorally sensitive, and reliable. He runs a young adult group in his parish which attracts young people in mid to late adolescence. One young man became close to him and began to talk about his difficult family situation. On one occasion he stayed behind after a meeting at Frank's house. He was clearly distressed and Frank gave him a hug. Somewhere in the embrace the hug became stimulating and led to a sexual encounter.

These two examples are very different. Joe was predatory and exploited vulnerable young men for his own sexual gratification. Frank is probably psychosexually immature, and possibly has never come to terms with his own homosexuality. The combination of affection, dependence and attraction led to a sexual relationship. Frank's sexual awakening occurred in a situation where boundaries were not respected and a young man's trust was abused. From a psychological perspective, ephebophiles tend to have significantly fewer victims and are less fixated than paedophiles.[38]

As many as 80% of Roman Catholic priest offenders may fall into this category, although this has been questioned in recent reviews, with

---

38 Songy, D.G. (2003). Psychological and spiritual treatment of Roman Catholic Clerical sex offenders. *Sexual Addiction & Compulsivity* 10(2–3): 123–38.

one author suggesting a figure of 57%.[39] The John Jay Report identified 2512 offenders of whom 3.8% offended only against children under 10 years of age.[40] These men could be diagnosed as paedophiles. A second group, comprising 18.95% of the priests, abused only males between 13 and 18 years of age. These could be characterised as ephebophiles. A further group, comprising 30.2% of the priests, had at least one victim younger than 13 and at least one victim older than 15. A further 42.1% had victims of various ages and genders. This research highlights the challenges and difficulties of trying to make use of diagnostic or descriptive categories. That being said, such categories can be helpful in understanding different profiles and behaviours related to child sexual abuse.

It is not uncommon to hear stories of high school teachers (male and female) who become sexually involved with adolescents whom they are teaching. Whether or not the victim is under the age of consent, the behaviour constitutes a breach of trust and abuse, as there is an imbalance of power in the relationship. Problems can also occur in other situations as a result of relationships formed over the internet. Without suggesting this as an excuse, there are men who have found themselves involved in relationships with adolescents who might never have become involved before the availability of internet chat rooms. The young people themselves, of course, are victims of exploitation and deception in these relationships.

As mentioned earlier, the age of consent varies from country to country. Carol Sarler, a journalist, commenting on the suggestion of Terry Grange, Chief Constable of Dyfed-Powys in Wales, that we need greater clarity in the labelling of sex offenders, wrote:

> We cannot agree between one border and the next at what age a boy or girl is emotionally developed enough to give consent: Malta and The Netherlands think 12, Canada and Italy weigh in at 14, cautious Greece holds out for 15 and the good burghers of Iceland go as high as 17 . . .

---

39   McGlone, G.J. (2003). Prevalence and incidence of Roman Catholic Clerical Sex Offenders. *Sexual Addiction & Compulsivity* 10(2–3): 111–21.

40   http://www.usccb.org/issues-and-action/child-and-youth-protection/upload/The-Nature-and-Scope-of-Sexual-Abuse-of-Minors-by-Catholic-Priests-and-Deacons-in-the-United-States-1950-2002.pdf.

Quite why it is 16 in the United Kingdom is not clear. (*The Times*, Monday, 20 November 2006)

It is not abnormal to find a physically mature adolescent attractive, as advertisers who make use of models who look younger than their age know only too well. Our society, however, makes a judgement about the ability of young people to make an emotionally mature decision regarding their readiness for sexual relations. We also know that many adolescents start having sex at a relatively young age. However, there is a difference between sexual experimentation with someone of the same age, and becoming involved with a person who is more than five years older (speaking of adolescents). Sexual involvement of an adult with an adolescent is considered sexual abuse, as our society concludes that young people under 16 (or whatever the age of consent is) still need the protection of the law.

Celebrity cases

On 3 October 2012, the British Independent Television Company ITV broadcast *The other side of Jimmy Savile*, which contained reports of child sexual abuse by the celebrity entertainer and fundraiser Jimmy Savile. Savile had been involved in television for over 50 years with a range of pop music and light entertainment programmes. His fundraising gave him a special status, and society at large, as well as politicians and church leaders, indulged and excused his eccentric behaviour and personality. Since the programme was aired, there have been revelations of widespread abuse in hospitals where he worked as a volunteer or led charity events, at the BBC, in caravans, dressing rooms, etc. He abused boys and girls, and young women. It appears that some people were aware of his behaviour and some courageously passed on information to managers or police. Despite being questioned under caution, he was never charged with abuse.

Other celebrities were accused of abuse in the wake of the Savile revelations, leading to other men being sent to prison – for example, Rolf Harris, Stuart Hall, and Max Clifford. Savile was clearly a narcissistic man with complex relationships with his mother and other women. He had a high sexual appetite, and his work and charitable involvements provided outlets for his deviant behaviour. It appears that he was protected by a culture of deference and adulation in the BBC and other places, and that people were either afraid to report him out of fear for their own jobs and reputations, or were not prepared to believe what they heard. Dame Janet Smith undertook a report into Savile's activities at the BBC with an examination of the culture and management of the organisation. Her report revealed a culture of fear, macho sexuality and sexual harassment in the organisation which contributed to the abuse of children, and young women.[41]

Savile's celebrity and notoriety may distort our understanding of the abuse perpetrated by other figures. Many of the accusations stem from the 1950s, 60s and 70s, when there was no culture of safeguarding and children were less likely to be believed if they found the courage to report abuse. Many of the men who have been accused and found guilty of abuse came from ordinary backgrounds and suddenly found themselves the focus of adulation and admiration. They may have lacked a strong moral code, and were able to take advantage of a situation that appeared to condone their sexual activity. Rona Fairhead, a member of the BBC Trust, said, 'We turned a blind eye where we should have shone a light.'[42] Like a great deal of clerical sexual abuse, where incidents of abuse peaked in the late 1970s and then declined, it may have been partly a phenomenon of its time. As a result of the change of culture in these organisations, exposure of abuse from the past with the intervention of authorities and the law, awareness of the vulnerability of children, the introduction of safeguarding guidelines, greater confidence in children to report abuse and be believed, and changes in the law, such organisations, hopefully, will be safer places for children than was the case 50 years ago.

Multiple perpetrator sexual offending

On 21 August 2014 Professor Alexis Jay delivered her report on child sexual exploitation in Rotherham. She reported a conservative estimate of 1400 victims over a 10-year period.[43] In the first page of her report, she wrote:

---

41 http://www.bbc.co.uk/bbctrust/dame_janet_smith. Retrieved 13 May 2016.
42 http://www.theguardian.com/media/2016/feb/25/serious-failings-bbc-jimmy-savile-abuse-72-woman-children-report. Retrieved 13 May 2016.
43 http://www.rotherham.gov.uk/downloads/file/1407/independent_inquiry_cse_in_rotherham. Retrieved 13 May 2016.

In just over a third of cases, children affected by sexual exploitation were previously known to services because of child protection and neglect. It is hard to describe the appalling nature of the abuse that child victims suffered. They were raped by multiple perpetrators, trafficked to other towns and cities in the north of England, abducted, beaten, and intimidated. There were examples of children who had been doused in petrol and threatened with being set alight, threatened with guns, made to witness brutally violent rapes and threatened they would be next if they told anyone. Girls as young as 11 were raped by large numbers of male perpetrators.

The Rotherham report (along with trials and convictions related to the exploitation of children) was perhaps the most shocking of a series of such trials and revelations of abuse in England in the years between 2011 and 2015. There were similar trials and reports in Oxford, Rochester, Bristol, Telford and Derby. The perpetrators often came from Pakistan, Afghanistan, East Africa or other countries with a high Muslim population. There appears to have been a fear of reporting these crimes in case the authorities could be accused of racism. Ironically, the perpetrators often appeared to feel alienated from the dominant culture and part of the explanation offered for their behaviour was a feeling of anger and marginalisation from English/British society. Yet, paradoxically, there was a fear of naming and addressing this aspect of the abuse on the part of social work departments, the police and some politicians.

In order to understand such behaviour, it is necessary to understand the group culture that these men belonged to. It has been noted that the perpetrators may not have deviant sexual interest as part of their character, but that shared group membership, acceptance of group norms and the powerful effects of male bonding all contribute to the behaviour. It is possible that the culture these men belonged to had an elevated sense of male dominance and tolerated a lack of respect for women. White women may have been seen as deserving humiliation and abuse. Individuals can behave differently in groups from how they would normally behave as individuals. Participation in the group can neutralise the feelings of guilt and shame of the individual and can normalise behaviour that is criminal, against professed value systems and not otherwise condoned. Similar behaviour can be observed in American University Fraternities, especially during the initiation rituals known as hazing.[44]

It appears from previous studies that it is not unusual for brothers, other relatives and acquaintances, to be members of such groups, and for up to a third to have previous convictions for sexual abuse. These men hold distorted attitudes which help them to deny, minimise and justify their behaviour. Sexualised violence against women becomes acceptable to the group, enhances their sense of maleness and entitlement, and builds group bonding. The behaviour also binds the group together in a set of rituals, establishes a pecking order in the group, and requires secrecy. It is difficult to leave such groups. The men who belong to these groups behave in antisocial ways but may not meet the requirements for a diagnosis of Antisocial Personality Disorder.[45] They may also have normal sexual preferences but behave in an abusive and exploitative way when part of the group.

The number of such groups and the subsequent arrests, trials and imprisonments highlight the dangers of this kind of subculture. It is to be hoped that the reports that have emerged, along with the ensuing publicity, will lead to greater awareness on the part of the police and social services. It will also require self-examination on the part of the communities where these men live, work, worship and socialise. Like the Catholic Church, which has had to confront aspects of Catholic and clerical culture in the wake of the clergy sex abuse scandals, the Muslim and possibly other communities now need to examine aspects of their culture and traditions which may be contributing to the sexual abuse and exploitation of children.

Treatment

Society's main interest in the treatment of sex offenders is in creating a safer society to protect past and potential victims. Research has focused

---

44 Harkins, Leigh and Dixon, Louise. (2010). Sexual offending in groups: An evaluation. *Aggression and Violent Behavior* 15: 87–9.

45 http://www.theravive.com/therapedia/Antisocial-Personality-Disorder-DSM--5-301.7-%28F60.2%29.

on what factors, if any, are amenable to treatment. Researchers and those involved in the treatment of offenders consider static and dynamic risk factors separately. Static factors, as the word suggests, are those that cannot be changed, e.g. age, type of victim, number of offences, any non-sexual offences, and use of violence in criminal/sexual activities. Dynamic factors are those that, it is hoped, are amenable to treatment and can be changed. These include psychological factors such as submissiveness, aggressiveness, self-esteem, anger, empathy, locus of control, emotional congruence with children, attitude to women or children, loneliness, coping skills, and intimacy deficits, etc. There has been considerable research on how these factors contribute to offending behaviour and how, and to what extent, they can be changed, and which, when changed, demonstrably contribute to lower risk of re-offence.

Child abusers, writing about their experience, suggest that personal distress contributes to their offending behaviour. Negative emotional states can be related to poor decision making for anyone, and they are often at the root of a range of addictive or self-defeating behaviours, such as gambling, alcohol and drug abuse, over-spending and over-eating.

Offenders themselves are aware that they are more likely to act out (abuse children) when they are experiencing negative mood states. Their adherence to treatment and capacity to learn are also likely to be enhanced if they are feeling good about themselves. Lastly, an approach to treatment that attempts to enhance the quality of life of offenders, and that supports alternative goals and values that offer satisfying rewards, is more likely to be effective if the offender feels good about himself and feels that his life is getting better. This suggests that therapists, without losing sight of the primary goal of keeping children safe, should intentionally aim to enhance offenders' feelings of safety, esteem and well-being.

Sexual abuse and the churches

The topic of child sexual abuse is not new for the Church. Canon 71 of The Council of Elvira, 309 AD, specifically penalises sexual contact with boys.[46] In the Middle Ages, the Church condemned sexual involvement

---

46   http://www.awrsipe.com/patrick_wall/selected_documents/309%20Council%20of%20Elvira.pdf

with boys,[47] and a number of religious orders have had to deal with sexual abuse at various stages in their history. The topic has been given significant attention in the last 20 years as a result of media exposure of abuse in the Roman Catholic Church in particular, although other churches have also had to deal with this issue.[48]

As a result of clergy sexual abuse scandals, the Catholic Church in England and Wales appointed a Commission under the chairmanship of Lord Nolan 'To examine and review arrangements made for child protection and the prevention of abuse within the Catholic Church in England and Wales, and to make recommendations.' This resulted in the report entitled *A Programme for Action* (2001).[49] Similar commissions were established in other English-speaking countries. As a result of the Nolan report, the Catholic hierarchy established the Catholic Office for the Protection of Children and Vulnerable Adults (COPCA). Baroness Cumberlege (2007) undertook a review of the recommendations of the Nolan report. She noted the considerable progress made in child protection as a result of the work of COPCA, but made some observations and further recommendations.[50]

Perhaps the most significant point to emerge from the Cumberlege Report is the need for a change of culture in the Church. The report mentions 'an over-dependence on volunteers, the erosion of trust between priests and bishops, and a continuing resistance to change among bishops' (*The Tablet*, 21 July 2007, p. 6). COPCA made extraordinary progress in highlighting the issue of child abuse and promoting the 'paramountcy principle' – i.e. that the welfare and safety of children must have priority in the Church –, in creating systems of reporting, and in checking and training volunteers and church personnel. The Cumberlege Report makes it clear that the Church is now a safer place for children. Changing the Church's culture is a much bigger task. As with bullying and partner violence, it is the culture which supports

---

47   Richards, R. (1990). *Sex, dissidence and damnation: Minority groups in the Middle Ages.* New York: Barnes & Noble.

48   See Geary, B. (2011). Church historical records of child sexual abuse. In B. Geary and J.M. Greer (eds). *The Dark Night of the Catholic Church.* Stowmarket, Suffolk: Kevin Mayhew Ltd, pp. 19–52, for a discussion of child sexual abuse in the history of the Catholic Church.

49   *A programme for action: Final report of the independent review of child protection in the Catholic Church in England and Wales.* (2001). London: Catholic Bishops' Conference of England and Wales.

50   *Safeguarding with confidence – Keeping children and vulnerable adults safe in the Catholic Church.* (2007). The Cumberlege Commission Report. www.cumberlegecommission.org.uk.

abuse which needs to be tackled and changed. This is a far more difficult enterprise, requiring, as it does, transparency, accountability and delegation of powers from institutions (the churches) which have often developed in a secretive, hierarchical way, with few structures of accountability.

Marie Keenan, an Irish researcher, interviewed seven Roman Catholic priests and two brothers who were members of Catholic religious orders to understand the factors that contributed to clergy sexual abuse. She concluded that these men were trying to live the project of Perfect Celibate Clerical Masculinity – and failed to do so. After listening to the men whom she interviewed, she concluded that these men felt lonely and unfulfilled and had few close friends. They had status in society but felt powerless within the Church. Outwardly they lived compliant lives, but internally they struggled to manage their sexual desires and feelings. Moral reasoning was entirely intellectualised. They were 'rule-keepers', who lost their personal identity and integrity in pursuit of an ideal which was, for them, unattainable. She concluded:

> My belief is that all the men who participated in my research tried to remain good and faithful priests and brothers as they lived in a battlefield of opposing forces of denied sexuality, emotional need, learned rationality, and intellectualization of physical, sexual, and emotional life.[51]

Children became the sacrificial lambs when their attempts to live a celibate life, and their bargaining with God through prayer and renewed attempts at fidelity, failed. Keenan's research highlights aspects of the Catholic system which need to be changed in order to create a healthier culture in which men can become priests and live their celibate commitment in a healthy way.

A year after his election, Pope Francis established a Pontifical Commission for the Protection of Minors. This international Commission, under the leadership of Cardinal O'Malley of Boston, has the following task:

---

51 Keenan, Marie. (2012). *Child sexual abuse and the Catholic Church: Gender, power, and organizational culture*, p. 256. Oxford: OUP.

> The purpose of the Commission is to propose initiatives to the Roman Pontiff, according to the procedures and determinations specified in these Statutes, for the purposes of promoting local responsibility in the particular Churches for the protection of all minors and vulnerable adults.[52]

The appointment of the Commission generated high expectations among victims, and it is not always easy for them to be patient with the slow pace at which work is done in the complex Vatican bureaucracy. Peter Saunders, a victim of sexual abuse by a priest and a member of the Commission, was suspended after a vote of the Commission on 6 February 2016. It appears that members of the Commission felt that he was not able to accept the discipline and discretion required when working as part of a Commission. His resignation caused considerable embarrassment for the Vatican and the Commission. It appears that there is also resistance within the Vatican to the work of the Commission.

The Catholic Church is not the only religious organisation that has had to deal with this issue. There have been reports of cases of child abuse involving the Anglican[53] and Methodist Churches, as well as the Jehovah's Witnesses.[54] There was also a newspaper article in *The Herald on Sunday* (Scotland) which presented information about abuse within the Muslim community. The newspaper report suggested that the institutional denial, moving of perpetrators, disbelief and marginalising of victims that happened in Christian churches has also happened in the Muslim community.[55]

The Church of England's policies on child protection are outlined in the report entitled *Protecting All God's Children*, published in 2004. The stated aim is to create a 'culture of informed vigilance'.[56] As well as policies and procedures for dealing with allegations of abuse, there is a section on ministering to those who might pose a risk to children, and

---

52 http://www.news.va/en/news/statues-for-commission-for-protection-of-minors-re. Retrieved 13 May 2016.

53 http://www.theguardian.com/uk-news/2015/sep/08/former-bishop-peter-ball-admits-sexually-abusing-young-men.

54 https://www.bbc.com/news/uk-england-42025255.

55 http://www.heraldscotland.com/news/12766888.Child_abuse_in_mosques__Lifting_the_veil_of_secrecy/

56 *Protecting All God's Children*. (2004). The Child Protection Policy for the Church of England (3rd edition), p. 6. Available at: https://www.churchofengland.org/sites/default/files/2017-11/protectingallgodschildren.pdf

a helpful list of resources and websites. The Methodist Church of Great Britain issued a report in 2006 entitled *Tracing Rainbows Through The Rain*, which is a follow-up to the report *Time for Action: Sexual Abuse, the Churches and a New Dawn for Survivors*, published by Churches Together in Britain and Ireland (CTBI).[57] *Tracing Rainbows Through The Rain* emphasises the importance of listening to survivors of abuse and provides resources for ministry and preaching. The Methodist Church, which was one of the first churches to produce a report on sex offenders in the Church,[58] also has a 'Safeguarding' policy which is designed to prevent the abuse of young people and to promote their welfare.[59] A range of resources is available to support churches and groups in understanding and implementing child protection policies. Policies and reports of the Church of Scotland can be accessed at the following website: http://www.churchofscotland.org.uk/about_us/safeguarding_service. The Church of Scotland also issues a newsletter with helpful information – for example, on the implementation of the Protection of Vulnerable Groups (Scotland) Act, 2007.[60]

Bill Marshall, in a paper entitled 'A proposal for the prevention and treatment of child molestation by Catholic clergy', shares an experience from a visit to Taiwan, where he was told that a high incidence of abuse of boys in Buddhist monasteries had recently been uncovered. He comments that 'When men are placed in positions of authority over children ... some of them will take advantage of the situation to sexually molest.'[61] This appears to be true no matter the religion, culture, country or organisation. It is particularly heinous when it happens in churches or other organisations like the Scouts (or by football coaches),[62] which are dedicated to the welfare and development of children.

Child sexual abuse and institutions

A great deal of the abuse that took place in the Catholic (and other) churches took place in institutions – for example, boarding schools,

57 *Time for Action: sexual abuse, the Churches and a new dawn for survivors.* (2002). London: Churches Together in Britain and Ireland.
58 http://www.methodist.org.uk/downloads/conf-church-and-sex-offenders-2000.pdf.
59 http://www.methodist.org.uk/downloads/safe-update-3-1110-childrenandyoungpeople.pdf.
60 http://www.churchofscotland.org.uk/about_us/safeguarding_service.
61 Marshall, W.L. (2011). The prevention and Treatment of Child Molestation by Catholic Clergy, in B. Geary, and J.M. Greer, (Eds.). *The Dark Night of the Catholic Church*. Stowmarket, Suffolk: Kevin Mayhew Ltd, pp. 555-584.
62 Bentham, M. (18 September 2005). Child abusers who shame British football. *The Observer*, News, pp. 8–9.

reformatories, orphanages, schools for the deaf, clinics and hospitals. The Ryan Commission in Ireland dealt specifically with abuse in institutional settings, as will the Commission which began to investigate sexual abuse in institutional settings in Scotland in October 2015.[63] Revelations about the Boy Scouts, the BBC, child care homes in Northern Ireland,[64] sports clubs[65] and other organisations display certain common features. Richard Scorer, a lawyer who has specialised in defending personal injury lawsuits related to child sexual abuse, noted three specific themes which emerge in such cases:[66]

- A culture of hierarchy and deference can be found in each of these organisations and institutions. Clergy have an elevated position in religious organisations, and talent or sporting success brings 'untouchable' status in other contexts.

- There is a climate of fear which makes it difficult for people to report, partly as they are unlikely to be believed, and partly as revelation could bring harm to the institution. In one case, a boy who reported abuse to a senior member of staff was sent to the person against whom he complained to talk about his allegation.[67]

- A concern for the reputation or financial assets of the institution. The Catholic Church was castigated for this behaviour. The Murphy Report, which investigated abuse in the Roman Catholic Archdiocese of Dublin, noted that: 'the Dublin Archdiocese's pre-occupations in dealing with cases of child sexual abuse, at least until the mid-1990s, were the maintenance of secrecy, the avoidance of scandal, the protection of the reputation of the Church, and the preservation of its assets. All other considerations, including the welfare of children and justice for victims, were subordinated to these priorities.'[68]

---

63   http://www.gov.scot/Topics/People/Young-People/protecting/child-protection/historical-child-abuse.
64   http://www.hiainquiry.org/index/latest-news.htm.
65   https://www.theguardian.com/world/2012/oct/09/jerry-sandusky-sentenced-child-abuse.
66   Scorer, R. (5 March 2016). The stain that remains. *The Tablet* 270(9141): 4–5.
67   Personal conversation with a victim of abuse in Germany. 15 December 2015.
68   http://www.justice.ie/en/JELR/Pages/PB09000504.

Scorer makes the point that what happened in the Catholic Church was not unique, and that such behaviour can be found in all organisations. It is difficult for people who are part of systems to report colleagues, especially if those colleagues are in positions of power.[69]

Approaches to treatment

There are three main approaches to the treatment of sex offenders: psychotherapy, cognitive behavioural group therapy (CBT), and medication. Individual psychotherapy relies on a process of motivation to change and insight to lead the patient from a situation of anxiety and pain to one of greater psychological health, inner freedom and internal congruence. Berlin (1985) writes that it is impossible to work out why we have certain attractions and not others, simply by a process of self-reflection and insight. Even with a motivated patient, it is unlikely that this process can lead to the change that is considered desirable. Berlin writes, 'There is little convincing evidence to show that the traditional psychotherapies alone are invariably effective means for treating paedophilia.'[70]

Sex offender treatment is now typically conducted in groups, where the offender can experience both the support and challenge necessary to bring about behavioural change. The group process is particularly effective in helping offenders to deal with their feelings of shame and vulnerability. They can also benefit from the experience of others who have spent a longer time in therapy.

John, who was mentioned at the beginning of this chapter, was actively engaged in both individual and group therapy. A significant breakthrough happened for him when he was present at a group presentation about a young man who had been abused by his teacher. The young man was the same age as his own victims, and the similarity of the circumstances meant he could no longer minimise or deny his behaviour. Over the next few months he confronted his feelings of shame and self-loathing. This eventually led to greater self-acceptance and peace. Interestingly, just after this he began to form a relationship

---

69 Geary, B. (2011). 'A strip of white with the might of an empire behind it': Contributions of the Catholic hierarchical system to sexual abuse of children. In B. Geary and J.M. Greer (eds). *The Dark Night of the Catholic Church*, pp. 71–108. Stowmarket, Suffolk: Kevin Mayhew Ltd.
70 Berlin, Fred S. (1985). Paedophilia. *Psychiatry* 19: 79–92.

with a woman who was slightly younger than he was. This became an adult sexual relationship over time. His paedophilic desire did not disappear, but he was helped to manage this desire with medication. He was able to inform his girlfriend of his past, and she decided to remain with him, despite his history.

Reviews of recent research suggest that there are grounds for optimism regarding the value of CBT programmes, which are based on social learning theory. This theory suggests that our behaviours (and thought patterns) are learned through experience, and that subsequent rewarding experiences reinforce these behaviours and ways of thinking (cognitions). CBT programmes tend to focus on the abusive behaviour and seek to target the specific features of the abuser that are in need of change. They focus on the recognition and correction of cognitive distortions, relapse prevention (which consists of identifying the patterns of thinking and behaving that lead to abuse, and putting in place strategies to prevent further abuse), and training in empathy and other interpersonal and social skills (emotional coping, anger management, self-esteem).

This chapter began with a range of statistics related to sexual abuse. Some of these are well known and, when they are quoted, tend to provoke expressions of shock and anger. Bill Marshall, however, notes that fewer than one in five sex offenders will re-offend, and that for those who complete CBT programmes the re-offence rate is reduced to one in ten. He writes that 'Long term evaluation of these programmes has demonstrated that the rate of re-offending among treated offenders is substantially lower than among similar untreated offenders.'[71] This is borne out by the fact that, in the 17-year existence of the Wolvercote clinic (a specialist clinic in England dealing with sex offenders which has since been closed), only 13 of the men who completed the programme returned to court or prison.[72]

It is worth noting in this context that 45% of calls to the Stop it Now! helpline in the period 2002–2005 were from abusers or potential abusers concerned about their feelings or behaviour towards children.

---

71 Marshall, W.L. (1992). The social value of treatment for sexual offenders. *The Canadian Journal of Human Sexuality* 1(3): 109–14.
72 Stacey, J, Making our World a Better Place (Part 1). http://news.bbc.co.uk/2/hi/uk_news/england/2092911.stm

Donald Findlater, the manager of Stop it Now!, was quoted in *The Times'* report:

> What our analysis shows is that there are people out there, unknown to police and social services, who are troubled by what they have done or are about to do. Our job is to agree with them the different options they can take today. The challenge for us is, can we help before a child gets hurt?[73]

These data may help dispel the myth that child molesters are untreatable or not motivated to change.

The third approach to treatment is what is commonly called 'chemical castration'. This does not, of course, involve actual castration, but the use of medications (antiandrogenic, i.e. 'reducing maleness') that can lower testosterone which is related to sexual arousal and performance. The medication does not work in every case, and its success appears to be related to the level of motivation of the client, and to the avoidance of alcohol and other drugs. Programmes which combine these medications with group and/or individual therapy appear to have good levels of success in preventing recidivism.

We can conclude then that treatment can make a difference to child abusers, although the nature of the treatment needs to be tailored to the individual. Individual therapy on its own is seldom enough, although it can be effective when combined with group therapy using CBT principles. Antiandrogenic medications have been shown to be helpful for paedophiles and other sex offenders with deviant interests. Finally, there have been a number of studies that have shown that, where clients cooperate with treatment, recidivism can be significantly reduced.

Good Lives model[74]

The link between individual well-being and lower recidivism is central to Ward's (2002) argument for the enhancement of the lives of sex offenders, and his proposals for treatment of sex offenders. Ward proposes that, if society enables and encourages sex offenders to have

---

73 McVeigh, K. (15 May 2007). Worried paedophiles make most calls to child abuse line, *The Times*, p. 16.
74 http://www.goodlivesmodel.com/. Retrieved 13 May 2016.

their needs met in constructive pro-social ways, they will have less need to return to antisocial behaviours that are harmful to themselves and others. He argues that there will be a reduction in crime as the sex offenders will learn to have their needs met in constructive, non-criminal, ways. He writes that 'The Good Lives Model is based around two core therapeutic goals: to promote human good and to reduce risk.'[75]

Offenders themselves are aware that they are more likely to act out when they are angry, stressed or frustrated. Their adherence to treatment and capacity to learn are also likely to be enhanced if they are feeling good about themselves. An approach to treatment that attempts to enhance the quality of life of offenders, and that supports alternative goals and values that offer satisfying rewards, is more likely to be effective if the offender experiences enhanced well-being. Ward identifies a list of ten primary goals that are necessary for human well-being: life, knowledge, excellence in play and work, excellence in agency, inner peace, friendship, community, spirituality, happiness and creativity. The 'Good Lives' approach which has emerged from his thinking on this subject proposes that treatment should be oriented to take account of these basic human needs and that it will be more successful and effective as a result. A focus on human needs and well-being may lead to the ends desired by society while enhancing the lives of offenders.

A Christian Response

The combination of the Christian teaching that sexual relations should be reserved to the marital relationship and Jesus' attitude of respect for children, using them as a model of those who would enter the kingdom of God (Mark 10:13-16), significantly influenced attitudes to children over the centuries. The whole thrust of the Judaeo-Christian tradition to protect the weak has also been a factor in creating a moral context where exploitation and abuse of children is considered unacceptable.

Care for victims is also supported by the central tenet of Christianity which sees Jesus as the sacrificial victim whose suffering is redemptive

---

75   Ward, Tony. (2006). Promoting human goods and reducing risk. In PFNZ 2006: Beyond retribution: Advancing the law and order debate. *Proceedings of the 2006 Fellowship of New Zealand conference, Prison Fellowship New Zealand*, pp. 111–17.

for humanity. Within the Christian tradition, victims have a certain status and are entitled to sympathy, assistance, rescue from suffering, and recompense for deprivation of freedom, important rights, or opportunities. This may help to explain the compensation culture which has gripped the United States and is finding its way into other English-speaking countries.

While it is true that Jesus showed respect and care for children, the line in St Matthew's Gospel regarding the feeding of the five thousand – which, of course, refers to five thousand men – should also be borne in mind: 'Those who ate were about five thousand men, besides women and children' (Matthew 14:21). The shadow side of the Judaeo-Christian tradition is that in many ways it continued to accept the prevailing attitudes which marginalised women and children. In the case of children, the biblical injunction to 'spare the rod and spoil the child' (Proverbs 13:24) was often used to justify physical violence and harsh punishments which would not be tolerated today. One of the achievements of the women's movement and the various liberation movements of the 1960s and 70s was that of giving voice to women, and to other victims of violence, oppression, or abuse – especially children.

As has already been said, victims enjoy a certain status in Christianity. The victims of abuse have tragically not always been heard, and in fact were often disbelieved or punished if they dared to speak up. There has been a change in recent years with educational programmes taking the issue of sexual abuse more seriously. Organisations like Childline in the UK[76] and Stop it Now![77] have made a significant difference to the lives of many children and adults, as have the recent attempts of dioceses and religious orders to provide counselling and compensation for victims of clerical abuse. The Towards Healing organisation in Ireland offers therapy to victims of clergy sexual abuse in a way that respects the confidentiality of the people who wish to benefit from counselling.[78]

While care for the victims is paramount, care for offenders is also important from a Christian perspective. The principle of 'love the sinner but hate the sin' still has value, especially when dealing with child molesters who are unquestionably at the bottom of the heap as

---

76   http://www.childline.org.uk. Tel: 0800 11 11.

77   http://www.stopitnow.org.uk Tel: 0800 1000 900.

78   http://www.towardshealing.ie/.

far as society is concerned. Even in prisons they need special protection, as other prisoners show their contempt and anger if they are in mixed accommodation. John J. Geoghan, the former priest who abused children in the Boston archdiocese, was murdered in prison not long after his conviction.[79] There are also cases of offenders being attacked in British and Irish prisons.

Professor Fred Berlin, Director of the National Institute for the Study, Prevention and Treatment of Sexual Trauma, wrote the following:

> Almost two thousand years ago, as an outraged crowd attempted to stone to death a woman whose sexual behaviour they considered offensive, one man stepped forward to stop the retribution, speaking of revenge while espousing values such as compassion, understanding, forgiveness and reformation. He asked that persons be judged not simply by their behaviour, but with some appreciation for their humanity.[80]

As Winston Churchill said in the House of Commons in 1910, the hallmark of a civilised society is how it treats those whom it imprisons.[81] On 8 February 2016, David Cameron, at the time Prime Minister of the United Kingdom, made a speech in which he outlined a positive agenda for prison reform. He said:

> I also strongly believe that we must offer chances to change, that for those trying hard to turn themselves around, we should offer hope, that in a compassionate country, we should help those who've made mistakes to find their way back on to the right path.
>
> In short: we need a prison system that doesn't see prisoners as simply liabilities to be managed, but instead as potential assets to be harnessed.[82]

---

79 http://www.nationalcatholicreporter.org/todaystake/tt082703.htm.
80 Berlin, Fred S. (2000). The etiology and treatment of sexual offending. In D.H. Fishbein (ed.). *The science, treatment and prevention of antisocial behaviors*, Ch. 21, pp. 1–15. Kingston, NJ: Civic Research Institute.
81 James, R.R. (ed.) (1974). *Winston S. Churchill: His Complete Speeches, 1897–1963*. New York: Chelsea House Publishers.
82 https://www.gov.uk/government/speeches/prison-reform-prime-ministers-speech.

The vision offered in this speech is one that Christians should be able to support.

The Christian tradition challenges us to be inclusive of those whom we would seek to exclude from the community. Organisations like Sanctuary UK work to help churches and other groups to support sex offenders. In Sanctuary's Winter 2006 Newsletter, readers are reminded that the Probation Service started as police court missionaries, and that many church organisations are active in this area.[83]

A key challenge to Christians is in the area of forgiveness. Should victims forgive – or be expected to forgive – their abusers? Can abusers be forgiven? Should they seek self-forgiveness? This is a complex issue, but a few comments can be offered at this point. In the first place, it would be wrong to expect or put any pressure on a victim to forgive an abuser – or parents or others who showed disbelief, or sided with the abuser, as has happened often, especially if the abuser was a trusted friend or family member. Forgiveness is a difficult, demanding, although ultimately rewarding, process. Each person has to undertake this journey when he or she feels ready, with appropriate support.

It is clear from recent research that the process of forgiveness has significant psychological benefits in the area of personal well-being, and mental health, but this is a choice that has to be made by the victim in his/her own time. Secondly, it has to be said that there is no cheap grace in this area. Mark Yantzi, a Canadian Mennonite Pastor who has worked with victims and abusers, makes it clear that, before forgiveness can be extended, the abuser must face his or her behaviours squarely, and not use Christian faith as a way of avoiding the hard, searching, emotionally demanding work of therapy. He describes premature forgiveness as 'religious window dressing', and understands the fears of survivors that granting forgiveness can leave an offender feeling that he has been let off the hook.[84]

Sex offenders are often churchgoers. While this may be alarming, given the relatively high number of young children who attend churches, it can also be an asset, as many offenders return to the practice of faith or develop spiritual lives as part of their recovery. It is

---

83   Sanctuary (Winter, 2006). *News and Prayer letter.* www.sanctuaryuk.com.
84   Yantzi, M. (1998). *Sexual Offending and Restoration.* Ontario: Herald Press.

important to be cautious in this area, and suspicious of offenders trying to create a good impression or seeking avoidance of the hard work of personal therapy and confronting past abusive behaviour. However, it is at least likely that religious faith and spirituality have the potential to help sex offenders in their recovery.[85] Religious faith offers a clear set of moral guidelines, and spirituality involves a relationship with God, Jesus or a higher power.[86] These can provide comfort, security, and support. They can also be a source of challenge to inappropriate thinking and behaviours. Church communities can provide a certain amount of individual support and accountability. These should not be underestimated when trying to help a child molester change behaviour and become reintegrated into society.

The Church of England addresses this difficulty in its report, *Protecting All God's Children*. In the section entitled 'Our theological approach', the authors write:

> Because redemption and forgiveness are so central to the gospel, the Church is not only well equipped to assist in the rehabilitation of offenders, but is also particularly challenged by them. Our congregations can be a refuge for those who have perpetrated abuse but are seeking help in maintaining a non-abusive way of life. Other abusers may see church membership as an opportunity to be close to children in order to continue their abusive pattern of behaviour ... The genuine penitent will accept the need for careful arrangements for their return to church fellowship. This is in line with the Church's realistic understanding of sin and its effects.[87]

This reflection demonstrates an attempt to hold in balance the Christian values of the Church as a community of reconciliation and forgiveness,

---

85 Geary, B., Ciarrocchi, J.W. and Scheers, N.J. (2006). Sex offenders, spirituality, and recovery. *Counselling and Spirituality* 25(1): 47–71.

86 Geary, B., Robinson, T. and Robinson, G. (2011). Within our darkest night: Rekindling spirituality in the clerical offender during treatment. In B. Geary and J.M. Greer (eds). *The Dark Night of the Catholic Church*, pp. 365–400. Stowmarket, Suffolk: Kevin Mayhew Ltd.

87 *Protecting All God's Children*. (2004). The Child Protection Policy for the Church of England (3rd edition), 1.2, p. 3. Available at: https://www.churchofengland.org/sites/default/files/2017-11/protectingallgodschildren.pdf

and a realistic appraisal of the difficulties involved in offering support to an abuser.

One of the most striking and significant initiatives in recent years has been the Circles of Support and Accountability that began in the Mennonite church in Hamilton, Canada. Pastor Harry Nigh was asked to find accommodation for a repeat sex offender who was being released into the community. He was understandably uncomfortable with this request, having young children himself. However, he rose to the challenge and, out of his generosity and Christian vision, the Circles of Support and Accountability were born. The idea is fairly simple. Groups of six volunteers will form a group around a released offender. They give up some of their time each week to have coffee together, have a chat, check up on progress with job hunting, meetings with counsellors, probation officers, doctors, and so on. Once a week the whole group gathers to spend time together, have a meal, and to celebrate another week which is free of crimes against children.[88]

Gordon Stuckless, who admitted over 500 sexual acts against children while working for the Toronto Maple Leafs, left jail in 1998 and is a member of a circle. David Wilson, a British criminologist, interviewed him. Stuckless said:

> The worst thing would be to come home to nothing. No support. You just sit there and watch TV. Crazy ideas come into your head and you say, 'To hell with it.' You throw up your hands and that's when another victim happens. But if you have your circle to talk to, well there you go.[89]

According to Wilson, Britain's Prison Service sex offender treatment programme, based on the principles of treatment outlined above, claims a reduction in offending of around 10–15%. The Circles of Support and Accountability programme has been shown to cut re-offending rates by 70%. This programme has now been introduced into the UK at a number of places, under the guidance of the Home Office. Not all of the groups in the United Kingdom are run by Christian groups

---

88 Wilson, D. (18 November 2004). Quality Time with Paedophiles. http://www.guardian.co.uk/comment/story/0,,1353545,00.html
89 Ibid.

or by Christians alone.[90] Nevertheless, in its origins and its values, it clearly demonstrates the place for a Christian response to sexual abuse of children. It also shows that this is not simply the misguided care of Christian liberals, but a sound programme that shows compassion for offenders, and cuts re-offence rates.

This chapter began with John's story prior to being arrested for molesting children. During the process of discovery, arrest and sentencing, John was befriended by the minister in his church. His family was also supported by this faith community. Speaking of his church minister, John said, 'Her non-judgemental care, compassion for me and my family, and simple presence during the toughest times, convinced me that there was something in religion for me.'

Conclusion

In this chapter an attempt has been made to explain the nature of child abuse, especially outlining the devastating effects on children, and the widening circle of people who are affected by this behaviour. Three different types of child abuser have been described: paedophiles, familial (incest) offenders, and ephebophiles. It has been suggested that these different types of offender have different problems and represent different levels of danger to the public or to organisations. Celebrity abuse and abuse by multiple abusers were also discussed, along with particular issues related to abuse by clergy. Issues related to treatment and recidivism were explored. The good news is that many offenders do not want to re-offend. Those who actively participate in treatment offer a good prognosis for changed behaviour. The 'Good Lives' approach to treatment of sexual abusers offers a clinically researched approach to treatment which is based on human and Christian values. Christian teaching demands that we care for children and victims, but a mature Christian vision also challenges us to find room for offenders in society and (with appropriate protection and safeguards for children and victims) in our churches. The recent development of Circles of Support and Accountability demonstrates how friendship, support, compassion, and faith can significantly improve the lives of offenders and make society a safer place for children.

---

90   http://www.circles-uk.org.uk/

Do's and Don'ts

- DO take a child seriously if he or she tells you that something inappropriate has been done to him/her.

- DON'T rush to interfere. Do contact social services, Childline, the NSPCC helpline, or Stop it Now! for advice and information.

- DO follow the child protection procedure of your own organisation.

- DO provide supportive counselling or help for relatives, work colleagues or others who are affected.

- DO, as an employer or priest/minister, contact a lawyer before making any decisions regarding employees who have been accused or found guilty of sexual abuse.

- DO advise families to report any crime that has been committed.

- DON'T ask unnecessary questions of victims or abusers, but offer support as long as it is necessary.

- DON'T promise to keep information a secret if it involves a child who is being sexually abused.

- DON'T ostracise the perpetrator if you previously had a relationship with him or her. People who are guilty of abuse need as much support and contact as possible as they go through the stages of discovery, trial, treatment, probation and rebuilding their lives. Personal support does not mean you condone their actions.

Recommended reading

Geary, B. and Greer, J.M. (2011). *The Dark Night of the Catholic Church*. Stowmarket, Suffolk: Kevin Mayhew Ltd.

Keenan, M. (2012). *Child Sexual Abuse and the Catholic Church: Gender, Power and Organizational Culture*. Oxford: OUP.

McGlone, G.J., Shrader, M. and Delgatto, L. (2003). *Creating Safe and Sacred Places: Identifying, preventing, and healing sexual abuse*. Minnesota: St. Mary's Press.

Yantzi, M. (1998). *Sexual Offending and Restoration*. Ontario: Herald Press.

Websites

http://www.childline.org.uk	Childline
http://www.stopitnow.org.uk	Stop it Now!
http://www.elderabuse.org.uk	Action on Elder Abuse
http://www.dh.gov.uk:	The Department of Health

Church Reports

The McLellan Commission (Scotland):
http://www.bcos.org.uk/Portals/0/McLellan/363924_WEB.pdf

The Ryan Commission (Ireland):
http://www.childabusecommission.ie/

The Murphy Commission (Ireland):
http://www.justice.ie/en/JELR/Pages/PB09000504

The Church of England:

https://www.churchofengland.org/more/safeguarding
Child Protection and Protection of Vulnerable Adults
https://www.churchofengland.org/more/safeguarding

The Methodist Church:

Child protection
http://www.methodist.org.uk/for-ministers-and-office-holders/safeguarding/

Roman Catholic:

Child Protection and protection of Vulnerable Adults
www.cumberlegecommission.org.uk

The Church of Scotland:

http://www.churchofscotland.org.uk/about_us/safeguarding_service

CHAPTER TWO

Domestic Abuse

Lesley Orr

Domestic abuse is prevalent throughout the world – part of the continuum of gender and sexual violence which has blighted human history. In the UK, millions of women and their children live with the daily threat and reality of coercive controlling abuse and assault in and around their homes. Research evidence over the past 40 years shows clearly that domestic abuse cuts across class, age, religion and ethnicity, although women in particular groups or circumstances experience factors which increase the likelihood that they will be affected. Partners who conduct household regimes of abuse live in cities and towns; in tower blocks and rural communities; in salubrious villas and in the midst of poverty; their victims range from professional women to those living with disability and discrimination. People say that it happens behind closed doors – but coercive control extends into social space too, and is often hidden in plain sight. It happens to Christians. It is committed by Christians. Although the characteristic pattern of violent controlling abuse is overwhelmingly conducted by men against women, men can also experience abuse from female partners; and domestic abuse is a significant problem in same-sex relationships too. The statistical probability is that there are both perpetrators and those who experience abuse in every large organisation and in every congregation of the Christian Church, of all denominations, and in other faith traditions. We live in a society where fundamental human rights are daily violated on an alarming scale, with devastating personal, social, economic and spiritual consequences. The Church, as the Body of Christ in the world, is challenged to respond with clear-minded awareness and analysis; with theological reflection; with compassion and justice; with practical support and with self-critical examination of our own historical complicity in all that has conspired to make domestic abuse hidden, 'normal' or 'justifiable'.

Let's listen to Anna's story. She is a Christian woman living in Britain.

I was thrown into the cupboard under the stairs. Blood was pouring from wounds gouged deep into my breast by a screwdriver, and the awful insults were still ringing in my ears. I heard the key turn in the lock and I knew I would be enduring another long dark night of pain and shame, with no food or clothes. The next morning, he let me out and told me to clean myself up before ironing his shirt. Then we set out together for church. It was Easter Sunday, and that morning, as I listened to the story of Jesus alive in the garden, asking Mary to share the good news of resurrection, I realised finally that I had to break free, for the sake of my children; for the sake of the person God wanted me to be. For too long I had accepted the humiliation and the degradation. I kept thinking about the marriage service: surely if vows had been blessed by God, I should have been helped through this? It hadn't occurred to me that a Christian marriage could be abusive, and that added to the sense of failure and isolation. I was shamed into silence. My life was so compartmentalised. I was in the women's group and the choir and attended worship, but it was all separate from the hell at home. Everyone else in our respectable suburban congregation, – they seemed to live such nice, safe lives, all playing 'happy families'. Maybe some of them were living with abuse too, but I never knew. Those issues were never raised and church seemed almost the last place for honest sharing of pain and vulnerability. I really didn't think the people in church would believe what was going on. In fact I knew they wouldn't, because my husband was so well thought of and a pillar of the church. Years later I met someone from that congregation who said, 'I remember one time I saw you in a state and listened to your explanation for the bruises and bandages – now I know you were covering up for him. If only I'd thought that he might have battered you, or had simply asked if there was any problem, but it didn't even occur to me.' . . . We all lived under that tyranny of respectability. Violence against any person is destructive and isolating, and it's essential for the health of the church – and to support those who suffer – that we should find ways of breaking the silence. The violence is IN the silence . . . I long to find a church where I would be able to take a hurting friend in good faith, to find comfort and prayer and peace . . . a sea of welcoming faces and outstretched arms.

Living in an abusive relationship was fearful – like being kept in a dark, dismal, suffocating tomb. It's been traumatic, but I do believe that I am coming out of the shadows, into the light of new life. [91]

For over 20 years, Anna's husband, John – a professional man and prominent church member – chose to use escalating and increasingly frequent physical brutality and sexual degradation against her, as part of a strategy of coercive and controlling behaviour which included habitual verbal, mental and emotional abuse. Their three children were more than silent and terrorised witnesses. They lived in a state of anxiety and confusion, and sometimes blamed themselves for what was happening to their mother. John undermined and manipulated the children's relationship with her and this was a key element of his strategy of household domination. Anna and the children all amended their own behaviour to comply with his demands, or to avoid the threatened consequences. Finally, she girded her courage and fled the home in which she had invested so much love and care. Anna and her children found safety and support in a Women's Aid refuge, but struggled with poverty, dislocation and continuing physical and mental health issues as they endeavoured to rebuild their shattered lives. The terror was not over, for this seemingly good Christian man continued obsessively to threaten and pursue his ex-wife; he also used child contact arrangements to undermine their safety and well-being. Eventually, he formed a new relationship, and was remarried in their home church. He has never

---

91 Most of the personal accounts and comments of women who have experienced domestic abuse, which appear throughout the chapter, are from *Out of the Shadows: Christianity and Violence Against Women in Scotland* (2000), the report of an action-research project conducted by Lesley Orr for University of Edinburgh Centre for Theology and Public Issues

been apprehended or sanctioned for his criminal behaviour. During the years of abuse, the whole family were involved in their local church, but that Christian community did not seem equipped or encouraged to recognise or confront the situation, to support the woman whose rights were violated, or to offer appropriate support either to the woman and her children, or to the man who perpetrated the abuse.

What is domestic abuse?

> It was like a hostage situation – trapped, physically and emotionally. I never knew what would happen from day to day, or even from hour to hour. And to live with that level of terror and anticipation of damage and pain and fear, while trying to protect three small children, is obviously an impossible task. I don't know why I thought I could sustain it, but there was a desperation to try. *(Anna)*

All human beings ought to have the opportunity to live full and dignified lives, to develop their capacities and gifts, to explore and share their personhood. All persons deserve freedom from fear, harm, degradation and constraint. Political and economic systems of oppression violate these human rights around the world, and terrorism has generated new kinds of anxiety. But there are millions of women like Anna who are denied these rights in their homes and personal lives; they experience everyday terrorism and entrapment at the hands of their intimate partners.[92] It creates long-lasting fear and trauma, which reinforce the abuser's control over the abused person. It affects vastly greater numbers of people than global terrorism, and it has impacts on many aspects of society as well as on the individual. This is key to understanding the realities of domestic abuse.

For over 40 years, since grassroots groups of women in the UK highlighted the problem of 'battered wives' and created the Women's Aid movement to respond, activists, researchers, policy makers and service providers have debated this phenomenon, and the language which is used to describe it. Definitions are a vital tool to outline

---

92 See Rachel Pain. (2012). *Everyday Terrorism: How Fear Works in Domestic Abuse.* https://www.dur. ac.uk/resources/geography/downloads/EverydayTerrorism.pdf.

the scope and characteristics of the problem, and to help us respond effectively. Evidence gathering, research and analysis have become more sophisticated, but also contested, since women broke through the silence of centuries to challenge the age-old acceptance that what goes on behind closed doors is a private matter, and named domestic abuse as a serious public problem.

Domestic abuse is not an isolated incident or a fight between equal partners. It is a pattern of surveillance and domination by one partner over the other. Fear is not just a by-product, but a central tactic deployed to achieve compliance. This intimate partner violence is characterised by controlling, coercive, threatening, degrading and violent behaviour, including sexual violence, by a partner or ex-partner. A 'constellation of abuse' is deployed which impacts on all aspects of life.[93] Within this pattern of behaviour, physical violence may be virtually non-existent, or regular and 'low level', or severe and sustained. Financial control is a common and effective element of the strategy. In the large majority of cases domestic abuse is experienced by women and is perpetrated by men. Michael P. Johnson calls it *intimate terrorism*.[94]

Johnson's widely used typology of intimate couple violence makes important distinctions between intimate terrorism and other very common uses of violence between couples. Intimate partners, both male and female, sometimes use violence (verbal abuse, aggression, physical fighting) against each other in situations where arguments and disagreements flare up and escalate. This kind of couple violence is more likely to be mutual, perpetrated by both men and women, and not intended to dominate and control the other's space for action. Johnson calls this *situational couple violence*. *Violent resistance* is when a victim of intimate terrorism fights back or uses violence to defend herself or her children.

It is important to understand that violent *acts* can occur in the context of very different kinds of relationship. To a police officer arriving at the scene, it may not be immediately apparent whether the incident has been a fight which got out of hand, or part of an ongoing

93 Dobash, R.E. and Dobash, R.P. (2004). Women's violence to men in intimate relationships: Working on a puzzle. *British Journal of Criminology* 44(3).
94 Johnson, Michael P. (2008). *A Typology of Domestic Violence: Intimate Terrorism, Violent Resistance and Situational Couple Violence*. Northeastern University Press.

pattern of fear-based control and regulation by one partner over the other. When an incident of domestic violence is recorded, there is nothing to indicate whether it is the action of someone who habitually uses violence to intimidate and control; or an act of retaliation or self-defence; or the result of a one-off fight. That is why, in recent years, services, policies and legislation to tackle domestic abuse have increasingly utilised the concept of **coercive control**, to shift the focus from *acts* of violence, to purposeful *strategies* and *patterns of behaviour* exercised by one partner over the other (and extending to control of the whole household, including children). **Coercion** is the threat or use of sanctions/force to compel unwanted behaviour, or to impede the ability to do something she wishes. **Control** is about the structural patterns of behaviour and unwritten rules utilised to gain compliance and obedience indirectly, by monopolising vital resources (including finances), micro-regulating, limiting and depriving the partner's access to freedom of choice or action.

American scholar and forensic social worker, Evan Stark, is the prizewinning author of *Coercive Control: How Men Entrap Women in Personal Life* (2007). This major and influential study builds on the experiences of survivors and those who support them, as well as a substantial research literature, to argue that the key to understanding domestic abuse is not physical assault (and it is not about the fights many couples have which sometimes escalate into mutual violence), but fear-based coercion and control of intimate partners or ex-partners, which 'jeopardises individual liberty and autonomy as well as safety', and is centred on 'the micro-regulation of women's default roles as wife, mother, homemaker and sexual partner'.

Stark's conclusion is that domestic abuse as coercive control is primarily a violation of human rights, rather than a crime of assault, because it results in gender-specific infringements and prevents women from freely exercising their social, economic and political agency. He proposes a definition of domestic violence/abuse from the standpoint of its survivors, as:

> A course of calculated, malevolent conduct deployed almost exclusively by men to dominate individual women by interweaving repeated physical [and often sexual] abuse

with three equally important tactics: intimidation, isolation and control ... The primary harm men inflict is political, not physical, and reflects the deprivation of rights and resources that are critical to personhood and citizenship.[95]

Stark's analysis of the way domestic abuse works might be extended to highlight what it has in common with other manifestations of violence against women (VAW).

By focusing not on tallies of incidents, but on impact and consequences for women, we see that all kinds of abuse and violence (not just in domestic settings but wherever human beings conduct our daily lives) function to control women and girls, to constrain their freedom of action as well as safety, and thus to violate their human rights.

Violence Against Women – A global problem

Violence against women (VAW) – particularly intimate partner violence and sexual violence – is a major public health problem and constitutes a violation of women's human rights.

Recent global prevalence figures indicate that about 1 in 3 (35%) of women worldwide have experienced either physical and/or sexual intimate partner violence or non-partner sexual violence in their lifetime.

- 35% of all women will experience either intimate partner or non-partner violence.

- Intimate partner violence is the most common type of violence against women, affecting 30% of women worldwide (22.7% in high income countries, including the UK).

- 38% of female murders are committed by intimate partners or ex-partners. This is the most common form of death for women aged 16–44.

Launching this systematic meta-study of global prevalence data, World Health Organization Director-General Dr Margaret Chan said: 'These findings send a powerful message that violence against women is a

95   Stark, Evan. (2007). *Coercive Control: How Men Entrap Women in Personal Life*. Oxford University Press.

global health problem of epidemic proportions', and one of the research team commented: 'This new data shows that violence against women is extremely common. We urgently need to invest in prevention to address the underlying causes.'[96]

Ranging across domestic abuse, rape and sexual assault, commercial sexual exploitation, forced marriage and other categories of VAW, recurring themes in women's descriptions of men's violence include the use of tactics of control, humiliation and degradation, sexualised abuse, the abdication of responsibility by the male abuser and the attribution of blame to the woman. These are found regardless of the woman's relationship to the perpetrator and whether the experience is a discrete event or recurring. Indeed, significant numbers of women experience repeated victimisation or patterns of abusive behaviour and more than one type of violence over the course of their lives. For example, there is a significant correlation between working in prostitution and having experienced child sexual abuse and/or domestic abuse at home and up to 75% of women who begin working in prostitution do so before the age of 18.

Research, policy and practice have tended to consider gender-based violence in distinct 'silos', but it is vital to recognise their connections and commonalities, as part of a continuum of violence against women. This concept was introduced by Liz Kelly, who made the connections between what was defined in criminal justice and public discourse as 'violence against women', and the everyday experiences of girls and women which have the cumulative impact of narrowing their autonomy, causing anxiety and fear, limiting their freedom of movement, making them self-conscious about their bodies and appearance, affecting their self-understanding and worth, teaching them to scrutinise and police their own behaviour and socialising them to keep quiet, or to accept constraints, because that's 'just the way things are'. Where mundane violations are ignored and unchallenged, girls and boys learn powerful messages about what is acceptable, what is allowed, and who pays the price.

Understanding VAW is not just about counting up incidents, but recognising how the *context* of what happens influences meaning and

---

96   World Health Organisation press release, 20 June 2013, http://www.who.int/mediacentre/news/releases/2013/violence_against_women_20130620/en/

consequences. Cultures and institutions – including churches – which turn a blind eye to everyday sexism create conducive contexts for gender-based violence.

Despite recent public concern about institutional sexism facilitating abuse (e.g. in the BBC) there is surprisingly resilient cultural tolerance or justification for the right of men and boys to assume that such behaviour is OK. Up to one in two young men and one in three young women believe that forced sex by men against women is justifiable in certain circumstances. Harassment is habitually dismissed as trivial; misogynistic comments as jokes or banter.

The idea of a continuum of VAW should not be taken to mean that there is a hierarchy of seriousness or severity based on extent of physical force or harm, but instead that it reflects the spectrum of complex, often interlinked experiences of harassment, violation, abuse and exploitation. Individual girls and women might experience single or repeated violations; similar or different forms of abuse throughout their lives, and in a range of locations. The same men may perpetrate different kinds of abuse. Some forms of violence span the globe (domestic abuse, rape, commercial sexual exploitation) while others have a more limited geographical or cultural-contextual range (e.g. female genital mutilation, child and forced marriage, male son preference, commodification of sexualised femininity).

Men's experience of intimate partner violence

We know that men also experience abuse and violence in their relationships, from partners who may be female or male. Men are affected by domestic abuse in different ways – as perpetrators, as adult survivors of an upbringing in a household where it was occurring, and by directly experiencing abuse. To ensure safe, appropriate and effective interventions for all who are victimised, regardless of their sex, it is important to recognise the significant gender differences in prevalence, risk factors and impacts. Recent research has sought to investigate the realities behind the statistics of men subjected to abuse. To what extent are intimate terrorism and coercive control (in other words, the fear-based regime of domination identified and addressed by Women's Aid and other services) experienced by men at the hands of their partners?

This is a complex question. The fact that roughly equal numbers of men and women use physical aggression against their partners has been established in numerous surveys and meta-analyses. But this should not be interpreted as meaning that women's violence against men is equivalent in nature, scale or impact. As Johnson demonstrates, these surveys highlight situational couple violence rather than intimate terrorism. They focus on discrete acts of aggression and force and do not measure or evaluate the context, impact and 'constellation of abuse'. They disclose the reality of violence and fighting among couples as an extremely widespread and problematic phenomenon, but the causes and consequences of fighting are not the same as those of violent coercive control. However, qualitative research based on samples in contact with criminal justice, safety, health and service providers, regardless of the severity of physical violence, consistently tells a story of 'intimate terrorism' which entraps women and rarely men.

But it is important to acknowledge the realities and impacts on men who do live with aggressive and abusive partners. The national Men's Advice Line offers confidential and expert support, and can help men find the help they require: http://www.mensadviceline.org.uk/

Domestic abuse is a gendered issue

Research to explore the complex experiences and meanings of violence used by men and women provides help in understanding the 'puzzle' of apparent statistical gender symmetry. Dobash and Dobash studied 95 couples in Scotland with men and women reporting separately on violence in their relationship. They conclude that women's use of violence differs in nature, frequency, intention, intensity, injury and emotional impact. Men mostly reported women's violence as 'inconsequential' which did not affect their well-being or safety, and did not make them adapt their behaviour. Swan et al. have investigated women who used aggression against male partners. They found that moderate physical violence and emotional abuse were comparable between men and women, but that severe physical violence, injury, sexual coercion, and other controlling behaviours were mostly committed by men. Looking at factors associated with coercive control, there was weak evidence for treating partner as an inferior; trying to make him feel he was crazy; blaming partner for her problems; keeping him isolated from family. While there were high incidences of physical and psychological aggression, neither sexual violence nor jealous monitoring featured strongly. Most female violence was reactive and driven by defensive motives. When women were arrested as domestic violence offenders they were often trying to get away from a violent partner, or were trying to avoid further abuse, especially where they thought their children were in danger. Swan's team concludes that female perpetrators are more likely to be acting out of fear and desperation, while rage, surveillance, regulation and jealousy characterised the abuse committed by male partners. Women's violence is usually preceded by violence of the man towards the woman, and in order to challenge both male and female violence, traditional gender attitudes and roles must be targeted. The Dyn project in Wales, which offers support and advice to men affected by domestic abuse, also found that there were markedly different risk factors for men as victims. Perpetrators' threats to kill, commit suicide or stalking do not feature as prominently, and nor do extreme jealousy/control. Research into killing of intimate partners indicates that female partners are six times more likely to be the victims of domestic homicide, often committed by men when women separate from them, and/or driven by extreme jealousy. Risk of female perpetration is higher in self-defence, after systematic intimate terrorism, or when their partner has abused or threatened their children. Substance abuse is often implicated.

Recent qualitative research conducted in Sweden was based on interviews with 20 men who had been subjected to psychological, physical or sexual violence from partners (18 women and 2 men).[97] They reported different experiences, in severity, frequency and consequences. Some had been injured, and interviewees had experienced diverse feelings, from sadness, anger, powerlessness and worthlessness, to having been amused or not being impacted. Some described being ridiculed or belittled for not being 'manly' enough. Verbal attacks often used sexist and homophobic language. Many of the interviewees had also subjected their partners to violence, including intimidation, surveillance, control and sexual coercion. Only one man had been subjected to intimate

---

97 Nybergh, L., Enander, V. and Krantz, G. (2016). Theoretical Considerations on Men's Experiences of Intimate Partner Violence: An Interview-Based Study. *Journal of Family Violence* 31.

terrorism, and that was by his male partner. Female partners did not succeed in establishing physical or sexual control, and in general violence was not a successful control tactic for them – it did not pose a genuine or frightening threat. Some men presented as victims but seemed to rationalise and excuse their own coercive controlling violence, while magnifying that of their partners. A key difference is that men are able to use societal male privilege and expectations – as Stark argues, they lay down household rules on the basis of stereotypical female roles and micro-regulate their partner's performance. Women do not have this possibility at their disposal.

Compared with women, men are overwhelmingly involved in all types of violence. It is mostly men who commit acts of personal violence – against women and girls, as well as towards other men and boys. Men are also most often implicated in other types of 'organised' or institutional violence as victims and perpetrators of violence. Around the world, militaries are male-dominated in personnel and culture. Men own guns and weapons more than women, and are imprisoned and murdered more than women. Men are taught to use violence, and violence as a means of problem solving and control is culturally sanctioned, both implicitly and explicitly, in different ways throughout the world.

Domestic abuse is not inevitable. To get to the root of the problem, we must examine links between the individual behaviour of some men, the norms of 'masculinity' into which they are socialised, and prevailing structures and values in our society – including religious ones. It is as gendered human beings that we develop our sense of self, and our knowledge of the world. Social and institutional power structures at all levels from the interpersonal to the international support the right of some groups to exercise control over others, and the use of violence as part of that control. These unequal power relations traditionally privilege men over women, and domestic abuse both reflects and reinforces that inequality.

For men and boys the relationship between dominant social norms of masculinity and violence are important. These are features of our human relations and culture and they require urgent and critical scrutiny, for the well-being of all human beings. Men's experience of victimisation is shaped by those norms.

Explaining why men's domestic abuse of women is so common

Men's domestic abuse is a complex phenomenon, influenced by a number of interrelated factors. The historical context is of particular importance in understanding violence against women in general and domestic abuse in particular as socially accepted and even encouraged – especially to chastise or control. Legal changes over the centuries were not directed towards eliminating men's abuse, but rather to putting legal limits on how far a man could go, reflecting the belief that a husband had authority over his wife and was given the legal and moral obligation to manage and control her behaviour. The use of physical coercion was simply one of the 'legitimate' means traditionally used to achieve such control. In 1915, following an established precedent, a London magistrate ruled that a man could beat his wife so long as the stick he used was no thicker than a man's thumb.[98] Marital rape was not illegal until 1991.

Many theories have been proposed to explain why some men use violence and coercion against their female partners. Common and stereotypical notions, too often repeated in media and popular discourse, that men are somehow 'hard-wired' for violence, are erroneous and extremely unhelpful. If that were the case we would have to explain why most men are *not* violent or abusive – and also why many intimate terrorists show no inclination to use such behaviour in other aspects of their lives. Some explanations have focused on individual pathology, arguing that domestic abuse is the behaviour of deviant or psychologically disturbed men, others on attachment theory, social learning, or 'stress' factors leading to loss of control or disinhibition caused by alcohol or substance misuse. A widespread assumption is that there is a 'cycle of violence' transmitted from one generation to the next, but this is strongly contested in the literature, and although social learning theory may provide some useful insights, it is hugely unhelpful to assume that boys who grow up in an abusive household will themselves become violent partners. At the level of popular misconception and debate,

---

98 See Foyster, Elizabeth. (2005). *Marital Violence: An English Family History 1660 – 1857* Cambridge University Press, pp. 12–13 for discussion of how the 'rule of thumb', though never enshrined in legislation, became embedded in discourse, and impacted on police and court practice in England.

simplistic attempts to create categories or 'types' of men who abuse as somehow different from 'normal' men are misleading. They ignore the underlying pervasiveness of gender inequality which is embedded in the everyday experiences of women and girls, and which is supported by widespread functional violence. They also serve to separate and demonise individual men who perpetrate abuse, while failing to analyse the values, institutions and structures which so deeply shape dominant models of masculinity based on status, competition, fear of weakness, emotional detachment. Too often they are used to excuse or minimise accountability. Many of the explanations are inadequate when gender is ignored, or are based on an assumption that male violence is somehow innate, natural or uncontrollable. Researchers and practitioners continue in the endeavour to integrate valid insights from various perspectives, recognising the complexity and multidimensional nature of domestic abuse and its environmental contexts. The criteria for evaluating these should reflect our desire for outcomes which seek equality, empowerment, justice, dignity and well-being for all.[99]

Some misconceptions about domestic abuse

- *Domestic abuse only happens in poor and deprived families*

Abusive individuals come from all walks of life and social circumstances:

> It's not just a few sad, pathetic souls. It's not just drunk men coming back from the shipyards. It's not just men who are 'sick in the head'. It's not just an argument that gets out of hand. It's not about women provoking their husbands. Everyone has conflicts and disagreements. But millions of women suffer abuse because men and institutions abuse their power.

99   The Violence Reduction Unit coordinates effective anti-violence initiatives across Scotland: http://www.actiononviolence.co.uk/. Michael Kaufman, Canadian founder of the White Ribbon Campaign, has written extensively on men, masculinities and violence, http://www.michaelkaufman.com/articles/. The White Ribbon Campaign encourages men to be active in resisting violence against women, http://www.whiteribbonscotland.org.uk/.

- *Alcohol and drugs cause abusive behaviour*

Alcohol and drug use can be factors in abusive behaviour. Some abuse their partners when they have been drinking, some only do so when they are sober, and some use violence and abuse whether drunk or sober. Drinking can provide an easy excuse, but is more of a trigger than a root cause of the choice to act violently.

> He started to drink a lot, and spend too much money, and that worried me. But he shouted, 'Don't you dare tell me what to do', and I thought I mustn't turn into a nagging wife.

- *Domestic abuse happens because men fly into a rage and momentarily lose control*

Some abusive men use violence indiscriminately in different situations, against men, women and children. Many more only ever use threats and violence against their partners, and do so because it seems an effective way to dominate them. Once a man has started to abuse his partner, it is likely to continue, and to get progressively worse. It seems to provide rewards without effective sanctions to inhibit such behaviour.

> When I look back, I see that he always got his own way . . . I lived through some frightening times. If he wasn't in control he could get really nasty . . . He claimed when we saw a counsellor that it had never been real violence because he took care not to leave marks on my face. That horrified me – to think he could be so calculating.

- *Some women just 'ask for it': their actions, appearance or attitudes provoke and deserve a violent response*

Surveys and the prevailing tone of popular discourse around domestic and sexual violence suggest that such attitudes remain disturbingly common. Many young people think that there are times when it's OK to beat or have coerced sex with women and girls – especially in relationships.

As this chapter argues, coercive control is often exercised through rules, restrictions and surveillance based on the man's sense of entitlement or jealousy, while those who are on the receiving end make strenuous and fruitless efforts to avoid or allay the violence. No one, male or female, deserves to be abused, and it is always a violation of human dignity.

> Whatever I said was wrong. Whatever I suggested was unreasonable. 'How dare you presume to think you deserve that?' he would say. And if I didn't always agree with him, I just got hit. I became introverted. I totally lost my confidence. I wanted to try harder and harder all the time to be good, to be a proper wife, to please him, to stop him hurting me – and the more I tried, the worse it got. There was no 'I' left in the end – just a shadow fading into walls.

The impact on children

> No one thinks of the kids – thinks what effect it has on them. It doesn't just affect the mother – it's the kids . . . Because they're the ones that have got to see it, and hear it.

Most children are aware of the abuse their mothers experience, and often witness or hear incidents. Many such children are also direct victims of physical or sexual abuse. Recent research estimated that 29.5% of all young people under 18 have been exposed to domestic abuse, and approximately 5.7% in one year. In another study, 55% of mothers whose children were on the child protection register were themselves also being abused. There is a strong association between domestic violence and fatal child abuse in 'family wipe-outs'. These are regular incidents where men kill not only their partner/ex-partner, but also their children (and often themselves).

> [My dad] was quite an abusive partner for my mum and quite an abusive parent to his children. That's what I remember, constantly being afraid. I wasn't allowed to even be affectionate to my mum because that meant that, you know, you could be the next target, and that's a really

scary and horrible thing for a child to have to go through.
(David, recalling his experiences from the age of eight)

A core message of recent research by Emma Katz is that the children of adult victims are not just being exposed to the physical violence. They, as much as the adult female victims, are experiencing coercive control – being manipulated, confused and harmed by it. They develop coping strategies which involve policing their own speech, activities and movements. Like their mother, their radar is always on alert, trying to predict the unpredictable. Abusive partners who are also fathers (or in parental roles) frequently undermine mother-child relationships as part of their strategy to gain domination in the household. Children suffer far-reaching negative impacts on their behaviour and emotional well-being, and on their cognitive abilities and attitudes, and their neurological development. But Katz's study shows that children can also play an active and important role in promoting resilience and recovery from abuse – for themselves and their mothers – by supporting one another in a range of everyday ways. They can demonstrate remarkable resilience, especially when they are able to find appropriate supports in their families and communities.[100] Good professional support for both mothers and children, during and after domestic abuse, is often pivotal. For example, CEDAR (children experiencing domestic abuse recovery) is a group-work model inspired and adapted from an innovative Canadian model of group work for children. The model is based on core principles recognising domestic abuse is damaging to children as well as to the mother/child relationship, and the belief that mothers are best placed to support their own children in their recovery. It is about creating a safe place for children and their mothers to help each other to find the best strategies to deal with their experiences and rebuild their lives.[101]

The complex interplay of risk and protective factors reinforces the need to shift from blaming women for their 'failure to protect', to exploring strengths, the potential to create places of safety and support for survivors, and challenges to domestic abuse offenders. It is vitally

---

100   Katz, E. (2016). Beyond the Physical Incident Model: How Children Living with Domestic Violence are Harmed By and Resist Regimes of Coercive Control. *Child Abuse Review* 25(1).

101   http://www.cedarnetwork.org.uk/

important to secure realistic and adequate safe contact arrangements. Although most women who separate from abusive partners want their children to remain in touch with their father, many men use contact as an opportunity for continuing to intimidate and abuse. Concerns about children's safety and the lasting impacts of domestic abuse are routinely overlooked in arrangements for post-separation contact, and this frequently leads to children being placed at risk of further harm and abuse. While women are exhorted to leave violent partners in order to safeguard their children, the judicial system routinely ignores the stated wishes of children and requires women to facilitate contact, despite their justifiable concerns about the safety and well-being of their children. If such concerns are raised, they risk being seen as hostile and malicious. There is ample evidence that abusive men's parenting capacity is often overestimated, leading to high levels of neglectful care during contact, continued opportunities to exercise coercive control, and making it difficult for women and children to establish safe and independent lives.[102]

Young people, dating and domestic abuse

Domestic abuse is not limited to adults; there is an increasing awareness of violence and control within teen relationships.

- 1 in 5 teenage girls have been assaulted by a boyfriend.

- Young women are more likely to experience sexual violence than other age groups.

- Young women with older partners are at increased risk of victimisation.

- Recent surveys (including Zero Tolerance and End Violence Against Women campaign) reveal that approximately 40% of young people are already being subjected to relationship abuse in their teenage years. Around 25% of 14-year-olds had been forced to have sex or been coerced into unwanted sexual activity by someone they were dating.

---

102 http://rightsofwomen.org.uk/wp-content/uploads/2014/10/Picking_Up_the_Pieces_Report-2012l.pdf

Children and young people are also increasingly targeted, online and in person, for sexual exploitation, including organised prostitution and pornography. A recent project undertaken by Zero Tolerance and YWCA Scotland found that youth workers across Scotland were seriously concerned about the prevalence of teen relationship abuse, including pressure or coercion into sexual activity.[103] The non-consensual sharing of intimate images – so-called 'revenge porn' – has become a major form of abuse (and not just for teens) and has been recognised as a criminal offence. STIRitUp (Safeguarding Teenage Intimate Relationships) is a European Union Project which offers excellent resources.[104]

Leaders of church-based youth clubs and organisations may be able to provide safe and trustworthy space for discussion of the many ways gender and sexual violence impact on young people's lives, and to convey clear messages about the importance of respect and equality in relationships. Sadly, despite safeguarding and increased awareness of risk, it also continues to be the case that some predatory adults who get into positions of trust can find opportunities to groom, exploit and abuse young people.

Abuse in LGBT relationships

Domestic abuse in the lesbian, bisexual, gay and transgender community is a serious issue. About 25% of LGBT people suffer through violent or threatening relationships with partners or ex-partners. As with abuse in heterosexual partnerships, the problem is underreported. Those affected by lesbian, gay or trans domestic abuse are often afraid of revealing their sexual orientation or the nature of their relationship.

LGBT people can face discrimination and fear dismissal by police and social services, or find a lack of support from their peers who would rather keep quiet about the problem in order not to attract negative attention towards the LGBT communities. HIV status or AIDS may also play a role in keeping partners together, if one partner provides health care for the other, or if there are concerns about disclosing status. Lack of access to safe and knowledgeable support services may add to the isolation and confusion. It is good that there is now a dedicated national helpline, and local service provision is improving.

---

103   http://www.zerotolerance.org.uk/Projects/AttitudesResearch
104   http://stiritup.eu/

Because heterosexual intimate relationships are the socially acceptable norm, they shape our common understanding of what constitutes an 'ideal' relationship, while those beyond the pale of normal may be depicted as sick, deviant, comic or sinful. Homophobia increases vulnerability and compounds the abuse experienced from the partner, but it intersects with gender inequality in ways which can be exploited differently by male or female partners. Treating same-sex and heterosexual abuse as two facets of a single phenomenon does not help our understanding of the complexities, or provision of appropriate responses. The primary focus of this chapter is on men's coercive control of women in marriage or other heterosexual partnerships; but it is vital that the Church recognise the reality of same-sex domestic abuse, and be aware that homophobia is one of the key social mechanisms which keeps that reality hidden.[105]

Possible indicators of domestic abuse

The most reliable indicator is someone saying she (or he) is experiencing abuse. But because normal features and power dynamics of intimate heterosexual relationships, based on ideas about romance, protectiveness, and appropriate roles for men and women (especially provision of domestic services), can shade imperceptibly into coercive control, it is often very hard for those affected to identify or to name what is happening to them. All persons are unique and will react to their particular circumstances in their own way. The following do not always signify that abuse is occurring, but should be considered when looking at the overall picture: we cannot rely solely on signs and indicators. But it is important to be aware and sensitive to the possibility of domestic abuse. A key issue to consider is how to create the right conditions for disclosure and to offer appropriate support. Listening receptively is the key, not providing simplistic or inappropriate solutions. Helping to identify pathways and referral to Women's Aid or other services providing informed advocacy is much better than offering the wrong advice, or telling someone what they should do – however well intentioned.

---

105 http://www.galop.org.uk/ hosts the national helpline for LGBT domestic abuse.

Signs of control

> He would never allow me to visit my family on my own. And very quickly, the only friends we saw were his friends. He wrote lists of all my domestic chores, down to how I folded the towels or organised the cupboards, and went round checking obsessively when he came home. Sometimes he would take a hair from his head and leave it somewhere in the house. If it was still there when he got home, I would get hell. He really did control every aspect of my life – decided what I was doing and when; what I wore, who I talked to, whether I could spend any money. *(Jean)*

- Partner accompanies the woman, insists on staying close, and answers questions addressed to her

- Reluctance of the woman to speak or disagree in front of her partner

- Verbal insults and put-downs

- He restricts her access to family and friends

- She is prevented from working or studying

- Intense jealousy or possessiveness expressed by the partner or reported by the woman

- Lack of independent transportation, access to finances and ability to communicate freely by phone

- Harm, or threats, to pets, significant objects, children

- Mobile phone is used to track and monitor her movements and contacts.

Indicators (behavioural, physical, psychological)

> I wanted to get over the anger, which I thought wasn't the proper Christian way to feel. I had always tried to sustain myself by praying, taking sleeping pills, blocking out what was happening to me, and pushing away the sense that

things were very very wrong. I wanted to cry; I was so full of the pain inside. But I just pushed it all down and carried on and tried to deny it. That was the way I coped with it and hoped that God would make it go away. I was confused because I had been brought up to believe that God would look after me if I was good. So the only conclusion I could accept for years was that I was bad. *(Annette)*

- Inability to concentrate
- Frequent use of prescription tranquillisers and pain medication
- Sleep and appetite disturbances
- Damaging coping strategies – heavy smoking, substance misuse
- Denial or minimisation of abuse to block out the reality, and to survive from day to day
- Seeming frightened, nervous, ashamed, evasive or embarrassed
- Unexplained physical injuries, recurring or chronic poor health
- Abdominal and gastrointestinal complaints
- Chronic headaches
- Depression, anger, frustration
- Withdrawal
- Fear
- Panic attacks
- Low self-esteem and confidence
- Exaggerated sense of personal responsibility for the relationship, which includes self-blame.

The costs of domestic abuse

The effects and consequences of abuse are profound. They extend into all aspects of victims' health, well-being, economic security and sense of self. Housing is a major issue: Shelter reported that 40% of all homeless women claimed that domestic abuse was a contributing factor. Costs may include some or all of these:

- Violations of personal safety, dignity, bodily functions and space for action
- Bruises, broken bones, disability, injuries, illness, disease (including STDs and HIV/AIDS), death
- Depression and chronic anxiety
- Complex post-traumatic stress disorder (PTSD) and psychosomatic complaints
- Self-harming and suicide attempts
- Betrayal of trust and integrity
- Use of alcohol, drugs etc. as coping strategy
- Undermining of self-esteem and worth
- Shaming, dishonour and disgrace across cultural contexts
- Impacts on earning power, educational opportunities, achievements and place in society
- Spiritual devastation, loss of faith and/or faith community.

There are also economic costs in lost productivity and the impact on police, social and health services. Although only a small percentage of all those affected make use of hospital or police services, they still constitute a sizeable proportion of the entire hospital or police client population.[106] Research published in 2011 put the estimated cost of domestic violence in England at over £5.5 billion a year, as follows:

- £1.6bn for physical and mental health costs
- £1.2bn in criminal justice costs
- £268m in social services costs
- £185.7m in housing and refuge costs
- £366.7m in civil legal costs
- £1.8bn in lost economic output.

---

106 Dutton, D. G. (1995). *The Domestic Assault of Women* (Vancouver: UBC Press).

A TUC Survey, *Domestic Violence in the Workplace* (2014) detailed the enormous economic, social and personal impact on individuals and their employment, including significant time off work, transport problems, and the abuser's controlling tactics (harassing phone calls and emails, stalking) reaching beyond home and into the workplace.[107]

The cost to men and boys

Michael Kaufman, founder of the White Ribbon Campaign, argues that men and boys have been damaged by learned behaviour – historical and contemporary social constructions of 'what it means to be a man', associated with violence and aggression in sports, among friends and at schools and work, and ensuing power relations: 'We need to reach out, to mobilise men, to make them understand that violence against women is their issue. We need, as men, to work as partners with women.'[108]

The costs of men not changing

Rory Macrae has worked with offenders in Edinburgh for many years, and helped develop the award-winning Caledonian System, an accredited criminal justice intervention which provides an integrated approach to address men's domestic abuse and improve the lives of women, children and men. He says: 'Most abusing men on some level are unhappy with their behaviour and would like to change. To start the process, one needs to look at the motivation men have for using violence; what is their understanding of why they were violent, and what "benefits" do they think result from continuing to abuse? It is intentional and functional. We believe that men *can* change, and that the costs of them not changing are huge.'[109]

Interventions for change: Perpetrator Programmes

Project Mirabal (2009–2015) was a major research initiative to evaluate Domestic Violence Perpetrator Programmes (DVPP) in the UK, conducted by Professor Liz Kelly (London Metropolitan University),

---

107 https://www.tuc.org.uk/sites/default/files/Domestic_Violence_And_The_Workplace_0.pdf
108 Recorded from presentation by Michael Kaufman, 'The Costs of Domestic Abuse' conference, Edinburgh City Chambers, 2003. See article by Kaufman at https://www.theguardian.com/commentisfree/2012/mar/26/domestic-violence-against-women
109 Presentation by Rory Macrae at 'The Costs of Domestic Abuse' conference, 2003.

Professor Nicole Westmarland (Durham University) and Charlotte Watts (London School of Hygiene and Tropical Medicine). The question of what to do in response to domestic abuse has been a controversial issue in policy, practice and academia. As the Mirabal Executive Summary Report notes, there have been repeated calls for interventions that call offenders to account and endeavour to facilitate change in behaviour, but there has also been scepticism about the efficacy of either criminal justice sanctions or the community-based DVPPs. Project Mirabal used a range of innovative research methods to investigate, over a period of time, programmes across Britain (e.g. the Caledonian System) which meet the Respect national accreditation standard (and thus include provision of a support worker for women whose partners are attending the programmes). The research also located the DVPPs within the larger context of coordinated community responses to domestic abuse. Six measures of success were identified to assess 'Steps Towards Change'. These indicate key aspects of attitudinal and behaviour changes required for men to shift away from coercive control:

- Respectful communication (thinking before speaking, and choosing not to use the power men have assumed to exercise)

- Women's expanded space for action (restoring freedom denied)

- Safety and freedom from violence and abuse for women and children

- Safe, positive and shared parenting (including increased awareness of children's fears and anxieties)

- Awareness of self and others (understanding the impact of their abusive behaviour)

- Safer and healthier childhoods (better outcomes for children who have worried about their mother's safety, and been frightened of the perpetrator).

Perhaps to the surprise of the investigators, who confess to having been sceptical in the past, their extensive and varied data (from men, women and children) gave clear evidence that all indicators showed improvements, and there were dramatic reductions in physical and sexual violence. The programmes require a lot of hard work through layers of new understanding, reflection on learning and, crucially, being able to translate into changed patterns of behaviour. But the report notes some important techniques (time out, count to 10, positive self-talk . . .) which help men interrupt habitual ways of behaving. While most participants had a surface acceptance of gender equality, there were deeper ideas about masculinity which operated in their self-identity and taken-for-granted routines. The prevailing notion of man as provider and head of household who knows what is best for the family seemed to legitimise men's sense of entitlement to make decisions of all kinds – including women's freedom of dress, action, work and so on; and it was women's challenges to the unwritten rules which lay at the heart of their partners' perceived need to exercise control. When manifested in abuse, that control destroyed the very safety and security they were supposed to secure. The men who made greatest progress in DVPPs gave time and effort to rethink and remake themselves – as men and as parents. Changes women reported making for themselves likewise were about rejecting the diminished femininity into which they had been coerced.[110]

It's everybody's business . . .

Local authorities, public sector agencies, voluntary organisations, private companies and trade unions all have a vital role in ensuring that the best possible response and service is provided to anyone affected by domestic abuse. A good example is the Corporate Alliance Against Domestic Violence, a national membership charity working with employers to lessen the impact of domestic abuse in the workplace. It provides research, resources and training to facilitate awareness, good practice and safety in workplaces. All organisations have a legal responsibility to protect the health, safety and welfare of their staff but, beyond that, by raising awareness of the issue and supporting those enduring abuse, employers help to prevent it in the wider community. Domestic abuse affects attendance and presenteeism, staff turnover and mental well-being at work. It also affects workplace teams, who may be

---

110 Project Mirabal, Executive Summary Report, January 2015, https://www.dur.ac.uk/resources/criva/ProjectMirabalexecutivesummary.pdf

caught up in a member's distress or in supporting them to move on. CAADV Chief Executive, Melissa Morbeck, says: 'Employers need to remember that those dealing with domestic violence often want to stay in work because they see the workplace as a safe place, and by taking simple proactive steps the organisation can help them to disclose what is happening in their homes . . . Sometimes HR and others mistakenly believe they can save someone's life. They need to remember that they're not in the business of counselling – but they can signpost people to appropriate services that can help.'[111]

Zero Tolerance has developed an Employers' PACT (Policy, Action, Communication and Training) and Toolkit to support employers in addressing the health and safety, economic and human resources consequences of violence against women, including domestic abuse. It aims to make employers, unions and statutory bodies aware of the business reasons why a VAW policy is needed in the workplace, but also acts as a resource for employers to access free information and support for policy development.[112]

. . . including the Churches'

> The church could be a huge well of welcome and help, but we're trapped in our traditional modes of behaviour and a theology to justify it. That's not the Christianity I believe in. I think the issue should be given a higher profile, in the context of affirming dignity – not being pitied and patronised, but valued and cared about and respected as women. We could be a real sanctuary of courage and love.
> (Samantha)

Many people in different denominations are recognising that churches have a responsibility and a unique opportunity to contribute to a wider community response in countering domestic abuse and violence against women. Christians have been challenged by survivors and activists to

---

111   Quoted in https://www.personneltoday.com/hr/how-to-deal-with-the-effects-of-domestic-violence-in-the-workplace/ For more information about the Corporate Alliance see http://thecorporatealliance.co.uk/about/
112   https://www.zerotolerance.org.uk/news/blog/zt-publishes-new-guidance-for-employers-/

be faithful to the life-giving message of equality, liberation, justice, compassion and love which is at the heart of the gospel. The wellspring of our faith is the affirmation that each person is created as equal and precious in the image of a loving God. Any violation of body, dignity and autonomy is a denial of that image incarnated in humanity. So we are called to be partners in challenging domestic abuse and supporting gender justice. The human and material resources of the Church are available in every community and corner of the British Isles, no matter how isolated. Many initiatives and resources have been developed to inform and support appropriate Christian responses to the reality of domestic abuse in our churches, and in wider society. The Methodist Church's Good Practice Guidelines are a clear and practical source of information.[113] As part of its engagement with Violence Against Women as a global and national concern, in 2014 the Church of Scotland produced a substantial report which reflects from the standpoint of victims and survivors and encourages 'Living a Theology that Counters Violence Against Women'.[114] The Church, along with other faith communities in Scotland, worked in partnership with Scottish Women's Aid on a project entitled 'Domestic Abuse: Together We Can Stop It', it supports the White Ribbon Campaign, and has employed a VAW Development Worker to coordinate action across all departments and aspects of church life. The Scottish Interfaith Group on Domestic Abuse, meeting under the auspices of the Scottish Catholic Safeguarding Service, seeks to raise awareness, challenge misconceptions and stand together as people of God with those who are affected. It organises study days, conferences, exhibitions and work with children and young people, as well as raising awareness of domestic abuse within its own faith communities and it provides resources for these.[115] Initiated by an ecumenical group of Christians including survivors of domestic abuse, Churches Together in Cumbria have developed an impressive integrated programme of training, information and resources. CTiC also has a team of 18 domestic abuse and sexual violence champions across the county.[116]

---

113   Methodist Church: https://www.methodist.org.uk/media/1125/safe-update-6-1110-domestic-abuse-guidelines.pdf
114   http://www.churchofscotland.org.uk/__data/assets/pdf_file/0005/5909/domestic_abuse_may2011.pdf
115   http://ifgoda.org.uk/
116   http://www.churchestogethercumbria.co.uk/domestic-violence.html

Restored is an international Christian alliance working to transform relationships and end violence against women. It is aware of the work of many Christian organisations in responding to VAW, but asks, 'where is the church, and where are the men when it comes to ending it? Church leaders are not speaking out and challenging the attitudes and behaviours that promote violence against women. And Scripture on marriage and relationships is often misinterpreted and used to justify abuse.' Restored provides a wealth of resources, training, campaigns and projects to address these fundamental questions. Churches are encouraged to become members.[117]

Learning from the experts

> Fear is the most dominating emotion, because everything else is subject to it. I was almost paralysed by fear, and only a determination to protect my children released some energy to drag myself out of that total erosion of personhood . . . When you begin to claim your life back, of course you feel absolutely betrayed. It's as if you have been sold something romantic and beautifully wrapped, but when you open it up it's hideous and dangerous. Once I expected the Church to have answers to all my questions. But now, I think I have answers to some of the questions the Church should be asking about domestic abuse. And I know that may sound rather arrogant, but I've changed from being a victim and now I'm a survivor. I think my story – our story, all of us who have experienced violation and abuse – is a resource for the Church. *(Anna)*

For too long, public perceptions of domestic abuse – not least in the churches – have been plagued by a kind of thinking one writer describes as DIM:

> **D**enial of the reality or extent of the problem
> **I**gnorance about the character, causes, dynamics and impact of domestic abuse as coercive controlling violence
> **M**inimisation of the harm done – to women, to children, to men; of the costs to communities and society.

---

117   http://www.restoredrelationships.org/about-us/

DIM thinking has often focused on the behaviour or pathology of women who are victimised, and has denied, ignored or minimised the responsibility of the perpetrators of abuse. 'She must have done something to provoke him . . . she's crazy . . . she's vindictive . . . she deserves a good slap.' These attitudes often rely on the assumption that there are appropriate and expected female roles and behaviours – especially in the domain of marriage and personal relationships, and that when women fail to perform in that domain, they might even 'deserve' to be brought into line or chastised by their husbands. These traditional and commonplace assumptions, rooted in notions of gender inequality and male entitlement, were for centuries enshrined in church teaching and authority – even if severe beatings and cruelty might have been considered excessive assertions of patriarchal authority.

The history of all religions, including Christianity, is in part the history of legitimising and colluding with the abuse of women. Sacred writings, theologies, structures and cultural traditions have been widely misused to claim that male dominance and female submission is part of God's plan for humankind. John Calvin's advice concerning abused wives in sixteenth-century Geneva reflects an attitude that prevailed in Protestant and Catholic churches alike:

> Except where her life is in danger, she must bear with patience the cross which God has seen fit to place upon her, and meanwhile not to deviate from the duty which she has before God to please her husband, but to be faithful whatever happens.[118]

This counsel to patience, duty, obedience and fidelity has been repeated down the centuries by theologians, pastors and others (of all church traditions and theological persuasions) who have concluded that a measure of violence and control might be acceptable or even desirable in order to guard the morality of family and Church. As courageous Christian voices of survivors from around the world began to break the silence of violence, they reported a depressing litany of ignorant,

---

118 Quoted in Livezey, L.G. (28 October 1987). Sexual and family violence, A growing issue for the churches. *Christian Century*, p. 938. https://www.religion-online.org/article/sexual-and-family-violence-a-growing-issue-for-the-churches/

inappropriate and dangerous pastoral responses to abused women: of ministers and priests who did not believe them, or who blamed women for provoking their husbands; of attitudes to marriage which implied that the permanence of the institution was its highest value, even when that compromised the safety, health and well-being of women and children. These attitudes are far from dead. In 2015, a Spanish archbishop used a sermon to hold women responsible for men's domestic abuse: 'Often the macho reaction comes about because she asked for a separation.' He criticised an alleged culture of 'quickie divorces' and said that women were typically to blame for not accepting their partner.[119]

In the Old Testament of the Christian Scriptures, there are many problematic accounts of men's violence against women, described as 'texts of terror' by the biblical scholar, Phyllis Trible.[120] In these stories, women are treated instrumentally, to be used, abused, discarded, forgotten or killed. The patriarchal norms of marriage, as described in the law and history of the Jewish people, exhibited many of the same features. Men 'took' wives as part of their economic wealth. Adultery was essentially a crime against another man's property. Wives had no rights of possession over their own physical or sexual integrity. This pattern has been, and remains in many places, a widespread cross-cultural reality. This was well known by one church minister who habitually subjected his wife to degrading sexual demands, telling her, *you are my wife, and there is no such thing as rape in marriage. This is my right and you'll do as I say.*[121]

Women from traditional religious backgrounds may internalise an instrumental rather than intrinsic sense of personal identity and worth, and associate their own value almost entirely with the satisfaction of others' requirements and desires. Their sense of what it means to be a 'good wife' depends on supporting, advancing and protecting their husband's public standing and reputation, even when his private behaviour is reprehensible.

We are not all direct perpetrators of extreme or abusive behaviour; yet conventional assumptions, use of careless, exclusive and otherwise inappropriate language (in worship as well as in other social contexts),

---

119   Archbishop Braulio Rodriguez Plaza of Toledo, sermon preached 27 December 2015.
120   Trible, P. (1984). *Texts of Terror*. Philadelphia: Fortress Press.
121   Orr Macdonald, L. (2000). *Out of the Shadows*.

jokes, media portrayals and other pervasive aspects of the world we live in, all contribute to an environment which tacitly normalises or condones men's right to lay down the rules for their families, and enforce them through fear.

> In my experience, there's a kind of collusion between Church and culture that says, 'Och well, that's just what men are like.' As if that makes it all right, or as if they have to be treated like slightly wayward children. It devalues men too; it deprives them of the maturity of accepting responsibility for their choices and behaviour. I find the whole 'buddiness' rather degrading . . . Boys will be boys – 'you know he didn't mean it because he was crying to me the next day'. I don't want men to behave like that. I don't want women to be obliged to parent their partner. And I do think that the Church can be part of that. It hasn't really said: 'Men, you should have more respect for yourselves, and you should NOT treat your wives that way.' That has to be faced openly. You know, I have never ever heard a sermon that addresses the relationship between men and women realistically. I have never heard anyone talk about prevailing attitudes to male violence. *(Jean)*

Religious beliefs and values, and belonging to a church community, can be foundational features of identity, giving purpose and structure to the way we live our lives. These things can be used by abusers, who know what matters to their partner, as effective tools to secure compliance, undermine self-esteem and ability to resist. Doctrines and texts are often woven into the gendered messages women learn about themselves to undermine their worth and autonomy. They can be interpreted and internalised as disempowering stories: about submission and obedience, about sacrifice and silence.

German theologian, Dorothea Soelle, has written about the 'silent cry' of survivors – heard not in words but expressed in the body and ways of acting. This is their story and testimony to injustice. She calls the Church not only to become attuned to hear the divine cry of anguished survivors, but to lend all the resources of its own imagination to the task of giving it voice.[122]

Religious resources for resistance

For those who have experienced abuse, it can be particularly important to be given permission to develop and express a language of resistance, a transformative story to live by – especially if religious words and symbols have been implicated as tools for grooming and silence. Survivors need to be affirmed as people with the right and ability to question, to feel, to define themselves and to reinterpret their experiences, when all those things have been taken from them. The gospel promise of abundant life is for every person. The gift to imagine – and begin to hope for – different ways of being, is profoundly spiritual, and must be nurtured with care. If our churches do not serve as trustworthy and enabling communities for this difficult process, where else will survivors go? Serene Jones, president of Union Theological Seminary, writes: 'The language of faith can reach straight into the heart of the imagination. The fragmented anatomy of trauma can leave one without a world, without speech, stories, memory, community, future or a sense of self; theology's task is to re-narrate to us what we have yet to imagine.'[123]

The normalised and hidden violations which embed gender inequality in all contexts have deep roots in religious structures and interpretations. The traditions and institutions of the Church shifted away from its origins in the radical egalitarian Jesus movement, and were historically shaped to give privilege, power and proclamation to men. They exhorted women to be subordinate, serving and silent. Women of faith have struggled against these odds to find voices and words which give shape and meaning to their experiences. They have too often been denied the rights to be authors and interpreters of their own lives. Bringing the authentic story to light is hard work, for it is so often buried deep under other damaging stories women learn about themselves: stories told to them by their abusers, but often reinforced or preceded by messages absorbed at home, in the world around them – and, not least, in churches. Thank God that churches are at last

---

122   Soelle, Dorothea. (2001). *The Silent Cry: Mysticism and Resistance*. Fortress Press.
123   Jones, Serene. (2009). *Trauma and Grace: Theology in a Ruptured World*. Westminster John Knox Press.

acknowledging these things and seeking to be resources rather than roadblocks for victims of abuse.

Domestic abuse, like all forms of gender-based violence, is not simply a 'women's issue': it must be a deep and central concern for all who believe that each human being is created in the image of a loving God, and who long for wholeness and justice – in relationships and communities. Most men in the Church abhor, and neither condone nor practise, domestic abuse. They have a particular calling to stand alongside their sisters in solidarity, and to challenge any notion that it is either acceptable or particularly 'masculine' to dominate women and children. The Church has been deeply involved in shaping and sustaining the values, attitudes to sex and relationships, and customs of society in this country. And the Church, present in the midst of every community, has both a responsibility and an opportunity to understand, resist and seek to prevent this evil which distorts individual and corporate life. We are also custodians and representatives of good news: the way things are is not the way things are meant to be.

Positive sanctions and support to change behaviour can be most effective when they emerge from a community which is actively committed to counter-cultural, transforming understandings of what it means for men and women, girls and boys to be truly human. As Christians, we require imaginative efforts to develop models of human relationship and community, based on self-worth, equality, mutuality, respect, hospitality and inclusiveness. Jesus offers a challenging example of a man struggling to transcend conventions and stereotypes of male and female behaviour; He publicly confronted religious leaders, challenging their hypocrisy, and he took risks for the sake of those on the margins. He did not choose to coerce, control or dominate, or use people carelessly. He allowed the voices of the oppressed to be heard, affirming their right to space, dignity and worth. And he encouraged them to take responsibility for their own choices.

Action for Change: A gospel imperative

> The deaconess from the local church came to see me when I was at my lowest ebb. She said, 'there's a place for you in the church anytime, but only when it feels right for you'.

> She was there when I needed her, and kept me company when I felt really alone. She stuck with me and gave me courage. That woman was my companion through the wilderness. She helped restore my faith in my whole self, in the church, and in God. *(Samantha)*

In recent years, there has been an outpouring of literature and action as Christian theologians, pastors and lay people (many of them survivors of violence and abuse) grapple with the hard questions raised by the reality of domestic abuse afflicting the Body of Christ in the Church as well as in the world. Some of the most searching questions are about the nature of the Church as human community and as a sign of God's loving purpose. How can the Church fulfil its pastoral and prophetic task to resist and overcome malevolence and injustice? How can it be a source of empowerment, hope and new life? How do we act, in faith, for change?

> Church needs to be a place where women are respected, listened to, reassured they have nothing to be ashamed of. The priest might not always be the best person to speak to, but it's so important to preserve the confidence and safety of someone living with abuse. Don't feel compelled to give advice or solve the problem. Just be there on the journey, which can be long and frustrating for all concerned. And don't tell us we need marriage counselling! That just gives him another opportunity for crocodile tears and excuses and bullying, and to get the world on his side. I felt so alone until a couple in the church understood and were on MY side. *(Jean)*

Sanctuary has theological resonance, meaning a place of divine presence, and in Jewish tradition, places of sanctuary often offered refuge and protection in the midst of a worshipping community which accepted responsibility for naming a wrong, confronting it and administering justice. Many women and children affected by domestic abuse have encountered the love of God in the midst of oppression, because they have found, in the open, non-judgemental, clear-minded compassion of others, that safe and secure space (which can be physical, emotional, spiritual), offering prolonged support for refuge and encouragement. Sanctuary also has a broader quality – an intentional and public effort to stand up to domination, give it a name and a face; work with local allies to nurture the support networks which can break through the web of social entrapment.

> The Church is always good at asking victims to forgive, but not so good at challenging perpetrators to ask for forgiveness, to change their behaviour, to offer some kind of compensation for ruined lives. Until I see some evidence that justice can be done, I won't meet a God of compassion in the Church. *(Anna)*

Compassion arises from involvement. It begins with creating the conditions for speaking out (but only when it feels OK) with listening. This is hard work. It requires an open heart, a clear mind and endurance. The experience of hearing, touching, feeling and responding to pain and suffering is the key to change. The Hebrew word for compassion means 'womb love'. The mercy of God is like that – committed, passionate, protective and nourishing; yet making space to grow and mature. Sometimes it has to take risks, to be fierce and angry. And from such engaged compassion flows the justice of true sanctuary.

> When your self-esteem is rock bottom, and your pain is raw, it is very difficult to knock on the door if you have no idea who, or what, will be on the other side. You need constant, ongoing acceptance and support . . . it has to be said, loud and clear, WE'RE HERE, WE CARE, THIS IS A SAFE PLACE, ABUSE IS NOT GOD'S WILL FOR YOU, YOU ARE NOT ALONE. *(Jean)*

Practical recommendations

Action for change is a corporate responsibility. As individuals, citizens, congregations, clergy, church employees, and at every level of the Church's structures, there are many practical and creative ways to respond. Practical suggestions must be understood and implemented in full awareness of the underlying dynamics of power and privilege which are embedded in church structures and cultures. Honest critique and structural changes must happen at every level to lay the groundwork which will ensure some measure of safety and security for those who have kept silent because they have had well-founded fears of the dangers of speaking out in a compromised institution. The burden of risk cannot be placed, by well-intended church leaders or members, on those we want to 'help' or 'include'. We dare not ignore the need to address some fundamental questions about religious oppression and complicity, which have contributed to the exclusion and shaming of people suffering abuse.

Making our churches safe places
DO

- Display posters, leaflets and information about services such as Women's Aid, Rape Crisis and independent domestic violence advocates (IDVA) in church premises, and invite speakers from local groups to raise awareness or suggest practical action.

- Acknowledge domestic abuse and other forms of gender violence in the context of regular worship – in prayers of confession and intercession, in preaching, in the use of new hymns or liturgies, in symbol and action for healing and justice.

- Be sensitive and careful in use of language and image in worship. Consider the impact or effect (both helpful and hurtful) many religious words, hymns or symbols might have on those affected by abuse.

- Encourage individuals or designated groups within the congregation to be specially informed and aware of the issues, so they can be a trustworthy point of contact and referral. They might also take the lead in any church participation in local initiatives (e.g. multi-agency partnership on domestic abuse).

- Draw up a charter outlining the church's position on domestic and sexual abuse, and how it will work towards *protection, provision and prevention* in the local community. Use this as an awareness-raising exercise, perhaps to be shared with ecumenical partners. Churches Together in Cumbria have done this: http://www.churchestogethercumbria.co.uk/domestic-violence.html

Such initiatives not only raise the level of awareness and concern among church members, but contribute to the perception that this congregation/church will be a safe place where victims and survivors might share their stories and their pain, and find solidarity in their search for justice.

Advice to those with pastoral or leadership responsibility, or who want to help a friend

Evidence indicates that women experiencing abuse may appreciate being invited to disclose, if it feels safe and the listener is non-judgemental. They may turn to someone they trust, whether or not that person has an official role.

- DO try to find a quiet and private space to talk.

- DO take time to listen and believe – don't push or force disclosure, acknowledge the strength and courage they have shown.

- DO make it clear that their safety is the first priority, and perhaps help them to make a safety plan (whether they choose to stay or leave). Women's Aid, Refuge and other expert services will give guidance and information to help clarify options.

- DO ask what they want from you, or the church, and in the relationship with their partner.

- DO ask about children, if there are any, and do everything possible to ensure that children are kept informed and involved, where appropriate.

- DO take a note of what you are told, the date, the context, and other factual information, as a record.

- DON'T judge or dismiss what you are told.

- DON'T make decisions or assumptions on their behalf, or else you simply reflect the controlling behaviour of the abuser.

- DON'T ever tell a woman she just needs to pray harder, or forgive, or reconcile.

- DON'T offer to mediate or to confront the abusing partner; or put the woman, children or yourself in danger.

The kinds of question which might help to bring coercive control to light include:

- Is there someone/your partner making you afraid?

- ... making you do something/s of which you are ashamed?

- ... controlling your movement and contacts?

- Do you feel trapped or constrained by someone's behaviour towards you?

- Have you been hurt or harmed by your partner?

The church can certainly play a vital part in providing pathways and referrals to the specialist services and agencies. But it may have a particularly helpful role in offering friendship, understanding and steady support for the long haul. Leaving and recovering from domestic abuse is usually a long, slow and complicated process, and non-judgemental companionship on that journey is so important. Long after the immediate crisis is past, Christian survivors may need and want to talk about some very deep questions – Where was God in that situation? Why did we suffer? What can I do with my feelings of anger, betrayal, distress? Does being a Christian mean I have to sacrifice my own hopes and rights for the sake of my husband? – or they may be helped by having folk alongside them in the confusion and silence; or sometimes (if they ask for it) to pray with and for them.

Conclusion

It is time to say NO to domestic abuse. Governments, local authorities, public services, businesses, the media – all of us, wherever we live and work, are challenged to support specialist NGOs and become part of a coordinated community response. And it's not enough simply to provide services for those directly affected. We need to engage in tackling deep-seated attitudes and norms, so that, as a society, we prevent and eradicate abusive coercive controlling behaviour in all its forms. There have indeed been significant and positive developments, but there's a long way to go. It is good news that churches have started to listen and to act. There are growing signs of good will; informed and appropriate responses; collaboration with others in the wider community. In 1994, an ecumenical consultation on violence against women in Europe met at the Corrymeela Community's centre for peace and reconciliation in Northern Ireland. It brought together survivors, practitioners and theologians, and issued a challenge to the Christian community which is as relevant now as it was then. The Ballycastle Declaration called for churches to be a real source of encouragement and empowerment: by listening and learning from women; by acknowledging our complicity in personal and structural inequality; and by acting in solidarity with all who suffer the consequences of abuse. Let us honestly reflect and rise to the challenge. Has the Church addressed gender relations as a justice issue? Do we name domestic abuse in our prayers? Do we preach about the equal dignity and rights of women created in the image of God? Have we spoken out and campaigned for legal and social changes? Do we work with our local partners to ensure that churches and communities are safe places where everyone has space for action? How can we truly be sanctuaries of God's presence in the world if we do not recognise and honour that presence in the experiences of all women, children and men whose lives are affected by domestic abuse? Can we embody the kind of church this survivor seeks?

> I long for the church to be a supportive community. A place of celebration, hospitable, open and friendly. A community of courage, willing to challenge the causes of violence. Not a place to hide or cover up suffering in our midst, but accepting of vulnerability, pain and the messy realities of human life. A sacred space where it's safe to be just who we are, and loved by God.

CHAPTER THREE

Alcohol and Other Addictions

Christopher C.H. Cook

Introduction

Addictive disorders are encountered in contemporary life in a variety of forms. Few people can be unaware that Western society faces a serious problem with illicit drugs such as heroin, cocaine or amphetamine, even though most members of the population will never use these drugs. Popular debate continues about whether drugs like cannabis are really as dangerous as they are said to be, and whether or not they are truly 'addictive', and the use of cannabis is widespread among young people in large sections of society. Yet, addiction to the drug nicotine, in ordinary cigarettes, is already a massive and widespread problem, which contributes significantly to ill health and mortality, as well as to the economic costs carried by our health services. Alcohol, which is said to be 'our favourite drug', is consumed legally by most members of the adult population, and alcohol misuse is widely condemned, but the borderland between alcohol addiction and heavy drinking is nothing like as clear cut as most people imagine. So, we find that drug addiction involves not only the young, and not only marginalised sections of our society, but virtually all of us.

Of course, addiction is concerned not only with drugs and drug use, but also with other behaviours that show similar qualities of impaired self-control and harmfulness. Thus, many people are aware that gambling, or various kinds of gaming, can be addictive, and there is popular and journalistic interest in so-called 'shopaholism'. It is further suggested that various kinds of eating disorder, relationships, and patterns of sexual behaviour, also show addictive qualities. If the concept of addiction is extended in this way, it becomes easy either to trivialise it, or else to conclude that we are all addicted. Even if the harm generated by some of these behaviour patterns prevents us from dismissing the idea of addiction altogether, it is still easy to become confused about exactly what addiction is, and difficult to know when it is, or is not, actually encountered.

If addiction were merely confusing, perhaps it would not be worthy of inclusion in this book. However, as has already been intimated, it is in fact a very serious social problem, with a huge impact upon our society. Furthermore, it presents a significant pastoral challenge to our churches – not only because many young people in our churches have been offered drugs, or have even tried them,[124] and not only because lust and greed begin to sound like problems which involve all of us, but also because addiction is a serious social ill which should be a focus of concern for the mission of the Church. When Jesus summarises his mission in the synagogue at Nazareth, at the very beginning of Luke's Gospel, he does so in the reading of words from the prophet Isaiah which speak of setting captives free:

> 'The Spirit of the Lord is upon me, because he has anointed me to bring good news to the poor. He has sent me to proclaim release to the captives and recovery of sight to the blind, to let the oppressed go free, to proclaim the year of the Lord's favour.' *(Luke 4:18, 19)*

If addiction is a form of captivity, or oppression, which impoverishes those who are afflicted by it, then surely we must ask ourselves: 'How can we today continue the mission of Jesus, to bring good news to the poor, to proclaim release to the captives, to set the oppressed free?'

Description of the problem

As we have already seen, addiction is concerned with a wide range of different drugs – including legally available drugs such as alcohol and nicotine – as well as illicit drugs such as heroin and cocaine. It quite possibly also takes in a range of other behaviours which don't involve any kind of drug use. However, let's take alcohol first as an example.

---

124   Cook, Goddard and Westall, 1997

Alcohol as an example of the problem

Fig. 1: Standard (UK) units of alcohol[125]

The amount of alcohol that people consume is most easily measured in standard 'units' (see Fig. 1). A UK unit of alcohol represents a single glass of wine, a single measure of spirits, or a half-pint of standard strength beer. Each of these contains about 10 g of pure alcohol. However, much beer and wine exceeds these amounts, and wine is often sold in larger glasses, so it is important to be careful when calculating the number of units consumed.

Current recommendations by the Royal Colleges of General Practitioners, Physicians, and Psychiatrists, as well as by the British Medical Association, are that men should not consume more than 21 units per week, and women not more than 14 units per week.[126] Department of Health guidelines were similar – albeit expressed as daily limits: that men 'should not regularly drink more than 3–4 units of alcohol a day' and that women 'should not regularly drink more than 2–3 units of alcohol a day'.[127] However, these were revised in 2016, and the UK Chief Medical Officers now recommend, for both men and women, that 'To keep health risks from alcohol to a low level it is safest not to drink more than 14 units a week on a regular basis.'[128] The new guidance also warns about the dangers of single-episode heavy drinking.

In England, about 36% of men, and 37% of women, exceed the previously recommended 'sensible' weekly limits for alcohol consumption.[129] Men aged 45 to 64 years, and women aged 45 to 54 years

125   Institute of Alcohol Studies. 2004. IAS Fact Sheets. Alcohol and you. London: Institute of Alcohol Studies
126   British Medical Association. (1995); Royal College of Physicians, Royal College of Psychiatrists and Royal College of General Practitioners (1995).
127   Department of Health, Home Office, Department for Education & Skills and Department for Culture (2007).
128   UK Chief Medical Officers (2016).
129   These, and other statistics in this section, are taken from Health & Social Care Information Centre (2013).

were most likely to exceed recommended weekly limits, but younger people (aged 16 to 24 years) are more likely to drink heavily on a single occasion.

Research shows that, in general, alcohol-related harm is correlated with the amount of alcohol consumed. The more an individual drinks, the greater the risk that that person will sustain or cause alcohol-related harm. Some patterns of consumption (notably recurrent binge drinking) are more harmful than others, and some benefits (in relation to protection against coronary heart disease) appear to be associated with low levels of drinking.[130]

Quite apart from the human misery and suffering, the cost of all of this to the economy is considerable. It is estimated that the health and social costs of alcohol misuse, including loss of productivity in industry, amount to £21 billion per year in England and Wales.[131]

But what does all of this have to do with alcohol addiction? Isn't heavy drinking, or alcohol 'misuse', a completely different kind of problem? Surely, the very idea of addiction suggests some kind of inability to manage without alcohol – a medical problem, perhaps – which is in a completely different category to ordinary drinking? Well, in fact, this view of things is not upheld by research. It is impossible to distinguish solely on the basis of the amount of alcohol consumed between the heavy drinker and the alcohol addict. Heavy drinking simply merges into addictive drinking, without any clear cut-off between the two. As the amount of alcohol consumed increases, the risk of harm also gradually increases, and the risk of alcohol dependence (or addiction) increases but, again, there is no clear boundary between heavy drinking and harmful drinking or alcohol dependence.

There is also something of a paradox – especially with regard to alcohol. The risk of harm increases with greater levels of consumption. Thus, the person who drinks more than twice the recommended limits is at greater risk (for example) of sustaining a drink-driving accident than the person who drinks moderately. However, there are many more people who drink moderately. Thus, across the population as a whole, some forms of harm are associated mainly with moderate drinking

---

130 Babor, Caetano, Casswell, Edwards, Giesbrecht, Graham, Grube, Hill, Holder, Homel, Livingston, Österberg, Rehm, Room and Rossow (2010).
131 HM Government (2012), p. 3.

and not with very heavy drinking – simply because there are many more moderate drinkers. Taking a population view of things therefore requires that account be taken of the 'prevention paradox': in order to completely eliminate alcohol-related harm, attention has to be given not only to those who drink heavily, but also to those who drink moderately; in fact, to everyone. Alcohol policy research also suggests that measures which focus only on education about moderate drinking tend not to be effective.[132] Policy measures with the greatest research support take into account the drinking of the whole population – as, for example, with taxation, which reduces the overall consumption of the population and, thus, the associated burden of harm.

What is addiction?

Professor Jim Orford has shown that similar patterns and findings apply to gambling, drug taking, eating and sexual behaviour as to alcohol, all of which he considers to be examples of 'excessive appetitive behaviours'.[133] In each case, the behaviour can become excessive, and this is associated with harm and with features of 'addiction', but in each case it is also difficult to find any clear boundary between what is 'normal' and what is abnormal. Thus, we cannot completely separate normal drinking from alcoholism, we can only estimate how much people drink, how much harm alcohol is causing, or how addicted they are.

Up until now, the word 'addiction' has been used rather loosely and without definition. In fact, it is used relatively little now in scientific circles, as it has proved to be rather difficult to define, or at least it has meant different things to different people. If a definition were to be offered, that suggested by Professor Robert West would appear to be a good one; that is, addiction is:

> behaviour over which an individual has impaired control, with harmful consequences (West, 2001, p.3).

---

132 For a review of the evidence for different forms of alcohol policy, the reader may wish to see the World Health Organization's report *Alcohol: No Ordinary Commodity* (Babor, Caetano, Casswell, Edwards, Giesbrecht, Graham, Grube, Hill, Holder, Homel, Livingston, Österberg, Rehm, Room and Rossow, 2010).

133 Orford (2001).

However, this is a general definition and we have seen that it is not necessary to be addicted in order to sustain harm. It is also difficult to measure exactly what 'impaired control' is. If I eat rather more of a very tempting dessert than I think I should, knowing that I need to lose weight, does that make me addicted?

The dependence syndrome

A big step forward in understanding addictive behaviour was made in the late 1970s with the introduction of the concept of the 'dependence syndrome'.[134] This employs the concept of the medical 'syndrome', as a collection of signs and symptoms that seem to occur consistently together, as a better way of talking about what it means to be addicted. The dependence syndrome, originally described in relation to alcohol, but later in relation to other drugs and behaviours, also reflects the biological, psychological and social aspects of what it means to be addicted, and it is something that can be measured, so we can make an estimate of just how addicted someone is. It has become the basis of internationally employed systems of definition and classification of mental disorder.[135]

The seven elements of the alcohol dependence syndrome are as follows:

- Narrowing of drinking repertoire
- Salience of alcohol-seeking behaviour
- Increased tolerance of alcohol
- Repeated withdrawal symptoms
- Relief or avoidance of withdrawal symptoms by further drinking
- Subjective compulsion to drink alcohol
- Reinstatement of dependence after abstinence.

Not all of these elements have to be present, and each can be present in varying degree. It will be helpful now, briefly, to consider each in turn:

---

134 Edwards and Gross (1976).
135 World Health Organization (1992).

Narrowing of drinking repertoire

Most people who drink alcohol have a 'repertoire' of drinking behaviours. One day they may drink beer in a pub after work with colleagues, another day they may have wine with a family meal at home, and another day they may attend a cocktail party with friends. One day they may have several drinks, another day they may have only one, and on other days they do not drink at all. However, as dependence progresses, this repertoire becomes narrower: drinking on one day is increasingly similar to drinking on any other day in quantity, type and pattern.

Salience of alcohol-seeking behaviour

Usually, drinking is subsidiary to other priorities in life. Thus, we don't drink when driving, because we know that this puts ourselves or others at risk. If drinking causes us harm and, for example, a doctor advises us to cut down the amount that we drink, we take that advice, because we value our health and wish to avoid harm. However, as dependence progresses, drinking becomes increasingly harmful and yet it takes priority over other areas of life – it becomes the 'salient' concern. As salience increases, marriage, work, health, morality and other concerns are all sacrificed as necessary to the priority of drinking, and daily life begins to revolve increasingly around the priority of drinking.

Increased tolerance of alcohol

'Tolerance', in this context, is a pharmacological concept. The effect of most drugs is dependent upon the dose administered or consumed. The relation between dose and effect, at least for a given individual, is usually predictable. However, regular use often results in diminished effect. Thus, in order to achieve the same effect, an increased dose is required. For the drinker, this means that the amount of alcohol consumed tends to increase, so that the desired subjective experience of intoxication is maintained. Eventually, when liver damage is severe and the body is unable to break down alcohol effectively anymore, a reverse tolerance may occur, and small amounts of alcohol can have a disproportionately large effect.

Repeated withdrawal symptoms

After prolonged regular consumption of alcohol, physiological adaptation to the presence of alcohol in the bloodstream and other tissues takes place. Once this has happened, a falling level of alcohol (e.g. as a result of an admission to hospital, or during a night's sleep) results in a physiological imbalance. This is manifested in a so-called 'withdrawal syndrome', the symptoms of which are specific to the type of drug concerned. In the case of alcohol, this characteristically includes nausea, sweating and tremor. In more severe cases there may be vomiting and severe anxiety. The alcohol-withdrawal syndrome may also be complicated by fits, or by 'delirium tremens' (commonly known as 'DTs'), a potentially life-threatening confusional state associated with disorientation, delusions and hallucinations.

Relief or avoidance of withdrawal symptoms by further drinking

Withdrawal symptoms are relieved by resumed alcohol consumption and most alcohol-dependent individuals therefore learn that the discomfort of withdrawal is easily treated by having another drink. This can lead, for example, to early morning drinking in order to relieve the discomfort of withdrawal that has begun while asleep the night before.

Subjective compulsion to drink alcohol

The subjective experience of being dependent upon alcohol – or other drugs and behaviours – is that of feeling a strong inner drive to engage, and re-engage, with drinking (or drug use, etc.). This can be experienced as 'craving' – a strong desire for alcohol – or impaired control of drinking, such that it exceeds pre-determined limits. Most dependent individuals can stop drinking for a time without too much trouble. Remaining abstinent for the longer term is much more difficult.

Reinstatement of dependence after abstinence

The establishment of dependent drinking usually takes a number of years. Typically, it takes place gradually over a period of time. However, re-establishment, or 're-instatement', of the dependent pattern of drinking is typically much more rapid. Furthermore, it can occur many years later. Thus, someone who imagines that they have overcome their alcohol dependence, as a result of several years of complete abstinence from alcohol, may start drinking again, imagining that there will be no further problem. In these circumstances, a dependent pattern of drinking can be resumed very quickly – from within a few hours, to a few days, weeks or months. So striking is this phenomenon that it appears to be exceedingly unusual that anyone who has once become severely dependent can ever return to a moderate pattern of social drinking.

The causes of dependence

What are the causes of dependence? On the one hand, it is clear that there are genetically determined biological differences between people, which render some of us more vulnerable than the rest to dependence upon one drug or another. On the other, it is also clear that the environment in which we live is hugely important. People do not use drugs that are not available to them and, even if a particular drug is available, the decision whether or not to use it will also be influenced by the attitudes of others – or the 'acceptability' of drug use within that culture or community. In addition to this, other stresses and events might further predispose some individuals to increase their use of a drug – for example, as a means of managing distress or anxiety. In general, the more often someone uses a drug, and the more of it that they use, the more likely they are to become dependent on it.

As we have already seen in the case of alcohol, the harms resulting from the use of a particular substance are directly proportional to the extent to which that substance is used, or consumed, within a given population. Among these harms we might identify dependence as being a particular concern, as it makes discontinuation of the drug less likely, even where harm is caused, and it tends to further escalate the extent of use by the dependent person.

Of course, the nature of the drug or behaviour which becomes the focus of addiction is also important. Up until this point, alcohol has been used as the main example, as it is widely and legally consumed, socially accepted, and yet also potentially highly dangerous because of its effects on human behaviour and its potential to cause organ damage (to the brain, liver, and pancreas, but also to many other organs). However, alcohol is only one substance about which we need to be concerned.

People do not generally become addicted to a drug unless it has some mood-altering, or other mind-altering, property. Even then, some drugs appear to be more 'addictive' than others. In the case of LSD, for example, the development of tolerance is so rapid as to make true dependence relatively rare. Continued regular use is increasingly ineffective. However, this does not mean that intermittent use of LSD does not cause significant harm – just that the harm is less related to dependence and more related to the particular mind-altering and other effects of the drug.

The legal, and more or less socially acceptable, drugs which can cause dependence include alcohol, nicotine and caffeine. Prescribed drugs which can lead to dependence include various kinds of tranquillisers, and especially the benzodiazepine group (including drugs like Valium, Librium and Ativan). Controlled drugs, possession, sale and use of which are regulated under the Misuse of Drugs Act 1971,[136] include heroin, cocaine, amphetamines, cannabis, Ecstasy, and LSD. Solvents, although not controlled under the Act, are also both harmful and mood altering. Commonly misused by school-age children, their sale is restricted in the UK on the basis of age.[137] Hallucinogenic mushrooms are also widely used by young people, but possession of these mushrooms, which grow in the wild, is not illegal.[138] It is not possible to go into detail here concerning the effects of all of these drugs and the type and extent of harm that each causes. However, the interested reader may wish to consult one or more of the helpful reports or reference works produced by various organisations.[139]

It has been mentioned that behaviours, as well as drugs, can be associated with patterns of dependence. Mostly, these behaviours are not the subject of legislation, although of course concerns with gambling, one of the first behavioural patterns not involving drug/substance use to be recognised as a form of addiction,[140] have led to legal regulation

---

136 This Act is subject to various subsequent amendments, including, for example, the Drugs Act (2005).

137 Only persons age 18 years or above may purchase solvents, including gas lighter refills, certain types of adhesive and aerosol, paints and petroleum-based products, etc. Alcohol sales are similarly regulated. Tobacco products and National Lottery tickets/scratchcards are restricted to those age 16 years and over.

138 Preparation of extracts from these mushrooms (*Psilocybe semilanceata*) is illegal, however.

139 E.g. Working Party of the Royal College of Psychiatrists & the Royal College of Physicians (2000); Drug Enforcement Administration (2011).

140 Moran (1970).

of gaming, lotteries and betting. Scientific reports of shopping, exercise, and sexual behaviour as forms of dependence do suggest that patterns of behaviour which do not involve ingestion or administration of drugs into the body can display the features of dependence described above.[141] A popular literature is concerned with a much wider range of behaviours including, for example, religious behaviour.[142] Caution should perhaps be urged, lest 'addiction' or 'dependence' simply become labels for people whose behaviour is different from our own. However, limitation of the concept of addiction only to the use of drugs and substances external to the human body would equally appear to miss the point. Addiction is something which, directly or indirectly, concerns us all.

An example

George[143] was a churchwarden, and a faithful member of the congregation of his local parish church. He was also a local GP, nearing retirement. Several members of the Church Council had commented that he seemed to smell strongly of alcohol at Church Council meetings, but one member of the congregation had received a visit from him at home one morning, in his capacity as a medical practitioner, and had thought that he smelled of alcohol then, too. She also commented that he had a marked tremor when attempting to examine her.

Although only George's wife was aware of this, his own doctor had told George to cut down his drinking. He said it was damaging his liver. George flatly denied that he drank too much, and told his doctor that he would treat himself in future and that he didn't need advice like that. George's wife didn't dare mention the subject, because George always reacted angrily, but she noticed that he no longer spent time with the family, or reading, both of which he had

---

141 Glatt and Cook (1987); De Coverley Veale (1987); Goodman (1998).
142 Booth (1989).
143 This is a false name, and the case is based on no particular individual, but it illustrates the kinds of things that are very commonly encountered in clinical practice when working with people who are alcohol dependent.

always loved, because he was always going to 'meet some friends'. She was pretty sure that he actually went to the pub, because he always smelled strongly of alcohol when he got home. However, she only ever saw him drinking a couple of glasses of wine with his evening meal.

George illustrates a number of features of alcohol dependence. Salience is especially evident here, as it would appear that George's drinking has assumed priority over his professional, marital and other social obligations, as well as his health. He has also almost certainly been driving when over the legal limit. It would appear that he drinks in the morning, to relieve withdrawal symptoms, but that this is only partially successful at reducing the tremor which he experiences as a part of withdrawal. Although it is not a diagnostic feature of the dependence syndrome, George also illustrates the common problem of denial. Even though everyone else can see that there is a problem, and that his life appears to be self-destructive, he strongly denies it.

Summary of the problem

To summarise briefly, addiction is thus, at the extreme, a pattern of behaviour which is clearly out of the ordinary. It causes significant harm, is associated with distinctive biological, psychological and social disturbances, and is characterised by an apparently self-destructive pattern of behaviour which continues either in the face of denial that there is any problem, or despite the best efforts of the dependent individual to stop. However, addiction is not something which is confined to illicit drugs, or even to socially acceptable but potentially harmful drugs like alcohol. Neither is it confined to only a few people, but rather it touches – even if only indirectly – on the behaviour of us all.

Can it be treated?

Secular (medical, social and psychological) approaches to the treatment of addiction take a variety of forms. At the simplest level, they might include a brief intervention aimed at recognising harm, or potential harm, and encouraging a corresponding change in behaviour to reduce that harm, or risk of harm. At the most intensive level, they might involve residential treatment over a period of months, aimed at breaking the addictive pattern of thought and behaviour and establishing a stable abstinence from all actual or potential objects of addiction. In between these extremes, there are a variety of out-patient and day-patient programmes, or counselling facilities, which address the addictive behaviour itself, and/or the perceived underlying causes of that behaviour.

Brief interventions

Brief interventions have been found to be extremely effective, and especially cost-effective, in the field of alcohol misuse. For someone suffering the early stages of harm as a result of their drinking, an intervention of this kind – usually comprising a short meeting with a nurse, counsellor or doctor – is all that is usually required. However, this should be distinguished from educational measures as a means of prevention of alcohol- and drug-related problems. Generally speaking, educational measures aimed at the whole population (for example, in school) have not been found to prevent alcohol-related harm and, in the case of drugs education, have occasionally increased rather than reduced illicit drug use.

Help for the established addict

For someone with more established or advanced problems, something more than brief advice is likely to be required. A variety of approaches might be employed, but the philosophy of harm reduction is now almost universal. According to this approach, no moral judgement of the rights or wrongs of drug use (or whichever addictive behaviour is the cause of concern) is offered *per se*. The focus of therapy is rather on reducing the harm that the individual and others might experience as a result of that behaviour. This is achieved in a pragmatic and hierarchical fashion. Thus, for example, the advice might be not to use illicit drugs at all but, if the drug user does decide to go on using them, then they are advised not to inject them. Again, the harm reduction philosophy recognises that, when advised not to inject drugs, some drug users will ignore this advice, and so such users are advised to use clean needles and a sterile injection technique. In some cases, drug users are maintained for the short to long term on prescribed doses of an appropriate drug (e.g. methadone) with the aim of eliminating more dangerous illicit drug use.

Interventions to address psychological patterns of behaviour usually involve some kind of counselling or psychotherapy. However, there may be minor or even life-threatening medical complications to address at the outset of treatment – such as abscesses at injection sites, or other infections, liver disease or other organ damage. Such problems will require assessment by a doctor or nurse, even if ongoing counselling is to be provided by someone else.

When dealing with dependence, medical input will also be required in order to determine the most appropriate management of the withdrawal syndrome. This can be merely a case of offering reassurance and psychological support, or it can require in-patient admission, but can usually be managed in the out-patient clinic. Among the most serious complications of any drug-withdrawal syndrome is the condition of 'delirium tremens' in the case of alcohol withdrawal (see above). However, fits (or 'seizures') can complicate various drug-withdrawal states (notably those from alcohol and various kinds of tranquillisers). Proper medical advice is therefore essential and prescription of medication may be required. In the case of alcohol withdrawal, this will usually include a minor tranquilliser and thiamine supplements (to prevent thiamine-related brain damage). In the case of opioid drugs (including many of the stronger painkillers and illicit heroin), a substitute of the same drug group is usually prescribed and then reduced in dose and withdrawn gradually. However, there are also non-opioid medications available which specifically suppress opioid withdrawal symptoms.

Usually, the management of drug withdrawal is a fairly simple medical matter (although, as has been said, not without its complications if neglected or managed badly). The real challenge of treatment lies in the social and psychological measures employed to break the pattern of dependent use. The goal of such treatment may either be to achieve 'controlled' or 'social' use, or to achieve complete abstinence, and discussion of this should usually be a matter for negotiation and agreement at an early treatment session. As has already been mentioned, severe dependence will usually indicate that a goal of complete abstinence is most appropriately indicated, and this may be the only treatment goal with any likelihood of success. However, it can be better on occasions to engage someone in treatment with a goal of dose reduction, or moderation, if they are not willing to countenance abstinence, rather than to lose them from treatment altogether. A supplementary agreement can usually be reached, to the effect that the goal may have to change from moderation to abstinence if moderation proves impossible to achieve.

Among the common psychological approaches employed in treatment are motivational enhancement and relapse prevention. The former recognises that motivation to change addictive patterns of behaviour may vary, and that the addict may be at varying stages of having decided to change or having acted upon a decision to change. The aim is to establish which stage an addict has reached and to work on building motivation for change. Relapse prevention recognises that addictive behaviour tends to relapse and aims at identifying the circumstances in which this is most likely to happen (so-called 'high-risk situations') and develop strategies for coping with such situations. A distinction is also made between a minor failure to adhere to treatment targets, usually referred to as a 'lapse', which may be a learning experience, and a major failure or relapse.

Religious responses

Various responses to the treatment of addiction have been offered from within different religious traditions: e.g. Christian, Islamic, Buddhist and Native American.[144] Among Christian responses, there have been those from a more evangelical tradition, but also those from a more liberal perspective. The former tend to be aimed primarily at a drug-free lifestyle and might be termed 'redemptive' in their theology. Sin and addiction are more or less closely identified in such an understanding. The latter type of response is more likely to be open to a relapse-prevention approach and to recognising the need to meet with people 'where they are', perhaps with little expectation of change in the early stages. This might be referred to more as an 'incarnational'

---

144   Cook, 2009, Marshall, Humphreys and Ball, 2010, p.230

theological approach.[145] Methods employed vary widely, and it would be misleading to offer over-generalisations. Some programmes offer an almost entirely secular programme and their Christian ethos provides largely the rationale and motivation for their work. Others focus almost entirely upon Christian discipleship objectives and draw little or nothing from medical and psychological approaches. Most Christian programmes probably fall somewhere in between these extremes. However, prayer, Bible study, worship and Christian counselling tend to feature, especially in programmes of the more redemptive theological type.

Spiritual responses

Spirituality is also increasingly recognised as being important even within secular addiction treatment programmes. In particular, this is true within the 'spiritual but not religious' mutual-help approach of Alcoholics Anonymous (AA) and its sister organisations (e.g. Narcotics Anonymous [NA]; Cocaine Anonymous [CA]; Al-Anon, for the families of alcoholics; Families Anonymous [FA], for the families of drug addicts), and the professionally led programmes which adopt their '12-Step' philosophy. This approach has been very influential in North America, and now accounts for a significant part of the provision of non-statutory facilities in the UK. Furthermore, AA and NA groups are available all over the UK and around the world. It therefore deserves some further description here.

AA began in Akron, Ohio, USA, in 1935. From the outset, it was a mutual-help organisation that recognised the help that alcoholics could give to each other in their recovery. It was influenced by medical and religious thinking of the time, including ideas drawn from the Oxford Group, an evangelical Christian movement. However, in its efforts to be accessible to people from all faith traditions and none, it came to emphasise the content of its programme as spiritual but not religious, and might now be considered to offer a form of secular spirituality.[146]

---

145 This emphasises the participation of Christ in human form in a fallen world with all its evil and imperfection. According to this model, Christ always precedes us when we seek out those who are in need. This model emphasises the identification of Christ with those who are in need, and sees the drug user more as victim than as sinner. The contrast between these theological positions as expressed in pastoral care is described in more detail by Christopher Moody, 1992.

146 Kurtz, 1996

The philosophy of its programme is encompassed in its 12 Steps – which summarise the experiences of the founding members, and so are expressed in the first person:

1. We admitted we were powerless over alcohol – that our lives had become unmanageable.

2. Came to believe that a Power greater than ourselves could restore us to sanity.

3. Made a decision to turn our will and our lives over to the care of God *as we understood Him*.

4. Made a searching and fearless moral inventory of ourselves.

5. Admitted to God, to ourselves and to another human being the exact nature of our wrongs.

6. Were entirely ready to have God remove all these defects of character.

7. Humbly asked Him to remove our shortcomings.

8. Made a list of all persons we had harmed, and became willing to make amends to them all.

9. Made direct amends to such people wherever possible, except when to do so would injure them or others.

10. Continued to take personal inventory, and when we were wrong, promptly admitted it.

11. Sought through prayer and meditation to improve our conscious contact with God *as we understood Him* praying only for knowledge of His will for us and the power to carry that out.

12. Having had a spiritual awakening as the result of these steps we tried to carry this message to alcoholics and to practice these principles in all our affairs.[147]

The steps include a number of important theological ideas, notably: that help is needed from a 'Higher Power', subsequently referred to

---

147   Alcoholics Anonymous (1977).

explicitly as God; that recognition of personal moral failings and a desire to be changed are important to recovery; and that an ongoing personal spirituality of prayer, meditation and helping others with similar problems must become a rule of life. The emphasis is upon a personal experience of divine grace, but theological terms such as 'grace' are studiously avoided, as are doctrinal statements. The programme must start with recognition of personal powerlessness and an awareness of God as the individual alcoholic is able to understand God. In fact, for the atheist or agnostic, it is not even necessary to believe in God at all – only to recognise that they must turn to a power greater than themselves, whatever they may understand that to be.

Subsequently, various sister organisations formed which met the needs of those addicted to other drugs and behaviours, and the families of those addicted. Each has adopted its own 12-Step programme, modelled on the original wording devised by the members of AA. AA itself has grown to become an international network of over 115 thousand groups, and over 2 million members, operating in 175 countries worldwide.[148]

There is no doubt that AA has helped many Christians, as well as people from other faith traditions. It has itself drawn heavily from the Christian tradition, and so its principles do not conflict with traditional Christian doctrine. However, for some Christians, the lack of affirmation of Christian doctrine is itself a problem, and so various groups have attempted either to revise the 12 Steps, or else to use them within a specifically Christian environment.[149]

How to intervene if you are concerned

What is the appropriate response to encountering someone in your own family, place of worship, or place of work, whom you think might be addicted? This is a difficult question to answer briefly in a chapter such as this, but hopefully reading this chapter of this book could be a good place to start. On the one hand, it is obviously not helpful to 'turn a blind eye', or to pretend that nothing is wrong. On the other hand, wading in with confident accusations is unlikely to be constructive.

---

148 http://www.aa.org
149 See, for example: http://www.overcomersoutreach.org

Between these two extremes, there is the place of knowing enough to know that expert help might be needed, and that tentative and sensitive steps need to be taken at first if a good final outcome is to be achieved. So ... being generally informed is good, and it is that general information that this chapter seeks to impart. But knowing where to get expert help is probably even more important. Where can that be found?

Provision of statutory services for people with drug- and alcohol-related problems and other kinds of addictive disorders is very geographically variable. A good General Practitioner (GP) should be well informed about where help can be obtained, and many GP practices will have direct links with specialist agencies. Usually, there is provision of specialist treatment within the health service, often there is provision by charities, and many treatment programmes are provided privately. In addition to all of these professionally led sources of help, AA and other 12-Step groups offer mutual help and are widely available. Telephone numbers can be found in local directories, and on the internet.[150] Very often, if contacted in advance, members will be willing to come and make contact with a potential new recruit who is coming to a meeting for the first time.

So, apart from being generally informed, and finding out about local services, what are the 'tentative and sensitive' steps that a lay person might take in order to help someone whom they think might be addicted? If non-threatening questions can be raised about drinking, drug use, or other behaviour that is a cause of concern, without simply antagonising the person concerned, then a conversation of that sort might be a good place to start. This is unlikely to be helpful if the subject has already become a battleground, and defensive positions of denial and mistrust are deeply entrenched. In such circumstances, it might be good to go and speak to a specialist counsellor or drug worker, or other professional person, to get advice on how best to help. In other circumstances, however, the trick is to find a non-threatening, supportive and constructive way of introducing the conversation. This might be easier if there is already a tangible focus of concern – such as a doctor's recommendation to drink less, or a warning about drinking at work. In any case, it is always important to

---

150   See, for example: http://www.alcoholics-anonymous.org.uk/ or http://www.ukna.org/

stick to objective facts and personal concerns, not to speculate, jump to conclusions or blame others.

George revisited

Gossip was beginning to spread around the parish, with quite a few people saying that it would be wrong to say anything to George, or else that they were sure there wasn't a problem. Others commented that, in any case, he was soon due to retire. Despite this, Andrew, the other churchwarden in the parish, decided to challenge him one evening before a Church Council meeting. Although he took George to one side, several other people were within earshot. George responded angrily, saying that all Andrew could smell was the mouthwash that he (George) used. Shouting that he'd never been so insulted, he marched out of the Church Council meeting, threatening never to come back again if Andrew was still there.

We don't know exactly what Andrew said to George – but it clearly didn't have a very constructive outcome. Most importantly, George is now not speaking to Andrew, so Andrew has lost the chance to have any further input. If Andrew had spoken first to George's wife, he'd have known that this was not the time and place, and not the right way, to go about trying to get George to see the need for help. However, George's wife is at her wit's end, and doesn't know what to do. Sadly, no one in the parish has noticed this, and she suffers alone. Despite this, the story could still have a happy ending:

George's vicar, seeing what had happened, visited George and his wife at their home the following evening. He stressed that he was simply concerned, and wanted to help. With a third party present, George's wife was able to express her fears, but she didn't go beyond what she knew. She simply said that, even though she never saw him drinking more than a couple of glasses of wine, she knew that something was wrong. She had lost the George she knew and loved. They both cried, and George found himself able, for the first time, to admit that perhaps he did need to seek help.

Theological Reflection and a Christian Response

Various 'models' of (or ways of understanding) addiction have been proposed in scientific writing on the subject. Among these, the so-called 'disease' model has been one of the most controversial and influential. According to this model, addiction is a disease in the same way as many other mental and physical conditions. There is debate and speculation about exactly what the nature of that disease is, but evidence has come to light in support of a genetic basis for alcohol and drug dependence, as well as a variety of biological, psychological and social disturbances that may be identified in the dependent state.

Among many benefits of the disease model is that of reduced stigma. The addict has not chosen to be as they are – they are in need of help, not condemnation. They are victims of the disease; it is not their fault. For many, this has been a huge advance from the so-called 'moral model' which is said to have preceded the more medical perspectives that have developed over the course of the last two centuries. According to the moral model, people are addicted simply through their own fault. They are bad – or at least weak – people who are reaping the consequences of their own behaviour.

The moral model is not popular in clinical or research circles interested in addiction today. It is seen as discredited, and is criticised as being little more than blind prejudice. However, it does place responsibility upon the addict for their plight, and the disease model is roundly criticised in some quarters for removing that responsibility. In fact, both criticisms are somewhat unfair. Those who campaigned against 'intemperance' in the nineteenth century were often very sympathetic to the plight of the addict, whom they saw as a victim of society's unwillingness to seriously address intemperance as much as of their own behaviour, and often worked hard to help those who suffered from 'inebriety'. On the other hand, proponents of the disease model have always emphasised the importance of personal responsibility for recovery on the part of the addict. According to this philosophy, no one is responsible for being an addict, but every addict is responsible for engaging with a programme of recovery.

There are, in fact, many other models of addiction. Among psychological models, perhaps that of addiction as a learned behaviour is the most widely influential. Addicts learn to use drugs because drug use is strongly psychologically reinforced – both by the mood-altering effects of the drug itself, and by social support. Yet others have criticised the concept of addiction altogether, suggesting that it is either a myth, or simply a way of socially labelling deviant behaviour. In different ways all of these approaches tend to normalise the behaviour of the addict.

What are the theological models of addiction? This question could be answered from the perspective of different faith traditions. Thus, for example, we might wish to consider the injunctions of the Quran against drinking alcohol and gambling on the basis of their adverse spiritual effects:

> Satan's plan is (but)
> To excite enmity and hatred
> Between you, with intoxicants
> And gambling, and hinder you
> From the remembrance
> Of Allah, and from prayer:
> Will ye not then abstain?[151]

Or we might wish to consider the importance that Buddhism attributes to the connection between suffering and attachment to things in this world which, in any case, are impermanent.[152] Undoubtedly, there is wisdom in such models, and that wisdom might both inform Christian theological reflection and provide a good starting point for pastoral work with people from other faiths. Indeed, identification of the implicit or explicit theological models that are held by someone who suffers from an addictive disorder might be a very good place from which to start trying to understand how to help them. However, the focus of the

---

151   Sūrah 5:91; Ali, 2000
152   Groves and Farmer (1994); Mason-John and Groves (2013).

present work is on Christian theological reflection and pastoral care, and the present author writes from a Christian perspective, so further consideration of theological models here will therefore be undertaken primarily from that perspective.

Within the Christian tradition, various theological models of addiction might be identified. Thus, for example, addiction might be identified as sin, or at least as a direct consequence of sin. According to this model – which looks very much like the moral model in theological clothing – people are responsible for the ways in which they use and misuse drugs – including alcohol – and any suggestion that addiction is a disease is simply unbiblical.[153] We might refer to this as the 'addiction as sin' model.

Another Christian theological model might be to emphasise that addiction is reflective of life lived in the selfish pursuit of life apart from God. This model recognises that people behave sinfully in response to their own pain, that we are vulnerable to addiction, and that in fact addiction is reflective of the human condition – the way that we *all* are.[154] For shorthand, we might call this the 'sin as addiction' model. It has also been pointed out that in Christian scripture sin is likened to disease, and that this is therefore not as different as it might initially appear, in theological terms, from the disease model.[155] However, it deals with a disease that, in different ways, affects us all. In one sense or another, we are all addicted.

Of course, there are various ways in which these models might be modified or combined. Sin and addiction might be understood as overlapping but distinct domains. On this basis, while they frequently occur together, each may be found without evidence of the other. Addiction may occur as a result of diverse factors, not all of which are necessarily sinful, but some of which may be.[156] We might also imagine a theological model of health and disease within which addiction is understood as disease but not as sin.

If we are looking for a constructive theological model, it should address the theological and scientific realities of the condition. These should

---

153 Playfair (1991).
154 See, for example, Lenters (1985).
155 McCormick (1989).
156 Mercadante (1996); Plantinga (1996).

include the bio-psycho-social, and spiritual, nature of the dependence syndrome on the one hand, and should be consonant with Christian scripture and tradition on the other. It should also be 'reasonable'. That is, given the theological and scientific realities, it should make sense – it should be intelligible. Elsewhere, I have attempted to construct such a model, drawing particularly upon reflections on two Christian texts – one drawn from Scripture (specifically from Romans chapter 7) and one drawn from Christian tradition (specifically from Augustine's *Confessions*).[157]

Both St Paul and St Augustine talk of an internal struggle or division which affects their ability to choose that which is good. We see this, for example, in these verses from St Paul:

> I do not do the good I want, but the evil I do not want is what I do. Now if I do what I do not want, it is no longer I that do it, but sin that dwells within me.
>
> So I find it to be a law that when I want to do what is good, evil lies close at hand. For I delight in the law of God in my inmost self, but I see in my members another law at war with the law of my mind, making me captive to the law of sin that dwells in my members. Wretched man that I am! Who will rescue me from this body of death? Thanks be to God through Jesus Christ our Lord!
>
> So then, with my mind I am a slave to the law of God, but with my flesh I am a slave to the law of sin.[158]

Paul speaks here in a vividly self-reflective manner about his ability to recognise within himself a tendency (which he calls sin) to do that which he does not want to do. He sees this as contrary to reason, as enslaving, imprisoning and life denying. These qualities are themselves evocative of the nature of addiction, but the subjective quality of the inner struggle is especially evocative of the compulsion that is one of the core elements of the dependence syndrome. To what extent are we justified in identifying the two struggles as being the same kind of

---

157 Cook (2006).
158 Romans 7:19-25.

thing? To what extent can we deny the similarities and insist upon their essential difference?

Christian scripture and tradition, as exemplified in the writings of St Paul and St Augustine, reveal a capacity for self-reflectiveness which is at the heart of what it is to be human. The struggles that this capacity reveals within us must include those which we might want to label 'addictive', although this is not to say that addiction and sin are one and the same thing. However, it does suggest that addiction is a pathology which is particularly human – in that it arises when we find that we wish ourselves to be other than we are, or to behave in ways other than those in which we actually do behave. To deny that there is any similarity between the phenomenon of addiction and the human struggle with sin would appear to be rather implausible. However, this is not to say that we are all addicted (to sin) or that all sin is addiction.

Addiction affects people in all dimensions of human experience – biological, psychological, social and spiritual. Thus, divisions similar or analogous to those of which Paul and Augustine speak can be identified at a physiological level in the process of drug withdrawal, at a psychological level in divided motivation, at a social level in the divisions between those who promote or reinforce drug use and those who are its victims and, finally, in the division that addiction causes between human beings and God. To say that such concerns can be reduced entirely to scientific ones is atheistic, but to imagine that they are purely theological is arguably a denial of the Incarnation. A theological reflection upon the nature of addiction thus takes us to the heart of the Christian gospel.

What should a Christian response be? As we have seen, both Christians and members of other faith traditions have developed programmes of addiction treatment or rehabilitation within the framework of their own beliefs, and in response to their differently perceived senses of calling to respond to the needs of those who suffer. However, this is only one level of response. At a wider level, Christians (and others) need to be involved in addressing the economic and social problems that nurture not only addiction, but the broader patterns of behaviour of which drinking is a part. For example, Christian attitudes to drinking and drug taking need to be examined. Outright rejection is likely to be as unhelpful as blind acceptance, but a critical concern needs to be well informed, and sensitively conveyed. This sensitivity will also be needed at the narrower level of response: that of dealing with our own behaviour, and that of those whom we know and encounter. On the one hand, a healthy self-examination may be required, and on the other a compassionate and sensitive willingness to raise questions and seek expert help. However, it is rarely helpful to wade in with an ill-thought-out confrontation. 'You're an alcoholic!' is more likely to elicit denial and hostility than agreement and willingness to accept help.

Do's & Don'ts

- DO be informed.

- DO seek specialist help.

- DO think about how your church can be involved in helping people who struggle with addiction.

- DO have an alcohol and drugs policy for church employees and church premises.

- DO go to an open meeting of AA or NA to find out more about what goes on and how they work.[159]

- DON'T assume that Christian young people have not been offered drugs or that they have never tried them.

- DON'T go beyond your expertise.

- DON'T collude or enable continuing addictive behaviour (e.g. giving money which might be used to buy alcohol/drugs, or protecting people from the consequence of addiction in such a way that they don't need to think about stopping or getting help).

- DON'T take away a person's responsibility for their own recovery from addiction.

- DON'T forget the family and friends of the addicted person – they need help too!

---

159   AA and NA have open and closed meetings. The latter are for members only. Visitors are usually very welcome at the former. Telephone numbers are usually available in the local telephone directory, and also on the internet.

Bibliography and further reading

Alcoholics Anonymous. (1977). *Twelve Steps and Twelve Traditions.* New York: Alcoholics Anonymous World Services.

Ali, A. Y. (2000). *The Holy Qur'an: Translation and Commentary.* Birmingham: IPCI – Islamic Vision.

Babor, T., Caetano, R., Casswell, S., Edwards, G., Giesbrecht, N., Graham, K., Grube, J., Hill, L., Holder, H., Homel, R., Livingston, M., Österberg, E., Rehm, J., Room, R. and Rossow, I. (2010). *Alcohol: No Ordinary Commodity.* Oxford: Oxford University Press.

Booth, L. (1989). *Breaking the Chains: Understanding Religious Addiction and Religious Abuse.* Long Beach: Emmaus.

British Medical Association. (1995). *Alcohol: Guidelines on Sensible Drinking.* London: British Medical Association.

Cook, C.C.H. (2006). *Alcohol, Addiction and Christian Ethics.* Cambridge: Cambridge University Press.

Cook, C.C.H. (2009). Substance Misuse. In Cook, C., Powell, A. and Sims, A. (eds). *Spirituality and Psychiatry*, pp. 139–68. London: Royal College of Psychiatrists Press.

Cook, C.C.H., Goddard, D. and Westall, R. (1997). Knowledge and Experience of Drug Use Amongst Church Affiliated Young People. *Drug and Alcohol Dependence* 46: 9–17.

Department of Health, Home Office, Department for Education & Skills and Department for Culture, Media & Sport. (2007). *Safe. Sensible. Social. The Next Steps in the National Alcohol Strategy.* London: Department of Health.

Drug Enforcement Administration. (2011). *Drugs of Abuse.* Washington DC: US Department of Justice.

Edwards, G. and Gross, M. (1976). Alcohol Dependence: Provisional Description of a Clinical Syndrome. *British Medical Journal* 1: 1058–61.

Groves, P. and Farmer, R. (1994). Buddhism and Addictions. *Addiction Research* 2: 183–94.

Health & Social Care Information Centre. (2013). *Statistics on Alcohol: England 2013.* London: Health & Social Care Information Centre.

HM Government. (2012). *The Government's Alcohol Strategy*. London: The Stationery Office.

Kurtz, E. (1996). Twelve Step Programs. In Van Ness, P.H. (ed.). *Spirituality and the Secular Quest*, pp. 277–302. London: SCM.

Lenters, W. (1985). *The Freedom We Crave*. Grand Rapids: Eerdmans.

Marshall, E. J., Humphreys, K. and Ball, D. M. (2010). *The Treatment of Drinking Problems: A Guide to the Helping Professions*. Cambridge: Cambridge University Press.

Mason-John, V. and Groves, P. (2013). *Eight Step Recovery: Using the Buddha's Teachings to Overcome Addiction*. Cambridge: Windhorse.

McCormick, P. (1989). *Sin as Addiction*. New York: Paulist Press.

Mercadante, L.A. (1996). *Victims and Sinners*. Louisville: Westminster John Knox Press.

Moody, C. (1992). *Eccentric Ministry*. London: Darton, Longman and Todd.

Orford, J. (2001). Addiction as Excessive Appetite. *Addiction* 96: 15–31.

Plantinga, C. (1996). *Not the Way It's Supposed to Be: A Breviary of Sin*. Grand Rapids: Eerdmans.

Playfair, W.L. (1991). *The Useful Lie*. Wheaton: Crossway.

Royal College of Physicians, Royal College of Psychiatrists & Royal College of General Practitioners. (1995). *Alcohol and the Heart in Perspective: Sensible Limits Reaffirmed*. London: Royal Colleges of Physicians, Psychiatrists, and General Practitioners.

UK Chief Medical Officers. (2016). *UK Chief Medical Officers' Low Risk Drinking Guidelines*. London: Department of Health.

West, R. (2001). Theories of Addiction. *Addiction* 96: 3–13.

Working Party of the Royal College of Psychiatrists & the Royal College of Physicians. (2000). *Drugs: Dilemmas and Choices*. London: Gaskell.

World Health Organization. (1992). *The ICD-10 Classification of Mental and Behavioural Disorders*. Geneva: World Health Organization.

CHAPTER FOUR

Pornography and Sexual Addiction

Mark Brouwer and Mark Laaser

It might seem strange on the surface to imagine that sex could become an addiction. It's a natural, biological activity; not a chemical that one ingests into one's system. But just as alcohol and drugs can become addictive, so can activities such as sex, when used to excess, or when used as a means of escaping pain or boredom. This chapter will focus on how sex can become destructive, and map out the road to recovery from addiction.

> Krista's husband, David, was a young and successful attorney. Their new married life was in many ways happy, but also filled with stress and unexpected challenges. Krista felt that David was often withdrawn, and even though he wanted sex very often, he frequently seemed disengaged when they were sexual. She wondered if she was somehow disappointing him, but comforted herself with the thought that he was simply struggling with the pressures of a new career.
>
> She was shocked when, shortly after their third anniversary, he confessed that he had gone to massage parlours several times that year. Over the course of the next several weeks, she learned more. He had received oral sex on his past two visits to the massage parlours. He had been much more sexually active before their marriage than she had previously known. And the pornography use that she thought was just a phase in his single life was still a common occurrence. He had been viewing pornography on their home computer and masturbating several times a week for virtually all of their married life.
>
> These disclosures swept Krista into waves of confusion, anger and hurt. She and David were committed Christians,

and very involved in their church. David had never talked
to anyone about his sexual struggles, and neither of them
knew where to turn. Although Krista knew very little
about addiction, she wondered, 'Is David a sex addict?' If
so, what could she do to help him? Did she even want to?

Krista and David are not alone in facing this kind of struggle. As
sexual mores change in our society, and as pornography and the sexual
activity it portrays become more ubiquitous, millions of people find
themselves becoming compulsive in their sexual behaviour. They
find themselves engaging in unhealthy and destructive habits,
unable to stop.

It is very difficult to find reliable statistics regarding the number
of pornography sites, the amount of traffic and level of usage of
pornography on the internet. A BBC researcher cautioned against use
of statistics that are sensationalist, and provided a discussion on the
complexities of finding reliable data.[160] Nevertheless, there is anecdotal
and personal survey data that points to the prevalence and growth of
pornography, which is an important indicator of the growing epidemic
of sexual addiction.[161] After ten years of research, Dr Patrick Carnes
estimated that about 8% of the total population of men and 3% of
women in the United States are sexually addicted. In the UK, the BBC
reported a more conservative estimate of 3 to 5% of the population.
However, this estimate is based on the number of people who seek
treatment, which is much lower than those who are actually addicted.

People with a religious background are not immune to problems with
the internet. Paul Olaf Chelsen undertook a study among 2,245 male
undergraduate students at Evangelical Christian Colleges and found
that 79.3% of the students had accessed internet pornography at some
point in the previous year and that 61.1% had accessed pornography
at least some amount of time each week. [162] There have also been
studies which show that ministers of religion, priests and members of
congregations have difficulties with internet pornography in the same
way as other males in the population.

---

160 http://www.bbc.com/news/technology-23030090. Accessed 14 December 2016.
161 See appendix to this chapter.
162 http://ecommons.luc.edu/cgi/viewcontent.cgi?article=1149&context=luc_diss Accessed 14 December 2016.

The sexual behaviours of addicts vary widely. These behaviours vary in social acceptability and harm done to others. Here is a list of the various types of sexual 'acting out', separated into three categories:

Basic or building block behaviours

- Fantasy

- Masturbation

- Pornography – magazines, videos, internet, TV, books, movies, music

- Affairs – this includes long- or short-term sexual relationships, 'one-night stands', and/or intimate emotional involvement that is non-sexual.

Level two behaviours

- Prostitution – on the street, over the phone, and massage parlours, escort services, on the internet

- Anonymous sex – the name of the sexual partner is not known

- Voyeurism – observing unsuspecting people who are undressed, naked and/or having sex

- Exhibitionism – sexual arousal from exposing oneself to an observer

- Indecent liberties or frotteurism – touching someone for sexual arousal without their permission or knowledge

- Phone sex/cybersex

- Bestiality – sexual touching or relations with animals

- Sadomasochism – sexual arousal from pain exchange.

Offending behaviour

- Incest – sexual relations with relatives

- Molestation – unwanted sexual contact with someone (could include unwanted sexual touch or intercourse, and is often used to refer to sexual activity with minors)

- Rape – unwanted/forced sexual relations
- Authority rape – using the power of role, status, age or authority to gain sexual access.

The crack cocaine of sex addiction

By far the most common behaviour associated with sexual addiction is internet pornography, which is often referred to as the 'crack cocaine' of sex addiction. Shortly after it was introduced into the marketplace some years ago, crack cocaine changed the rules of drug addiction and treatment. It was cheap, widely available and extremely addictive. People who did not fit the typical profile of a drug addict wound up becoming addicted to crack. The cycle time between someone's first sample of the drug and their addiction to it shortened with the onslaught of crack.

The same is true with internet pornography. Several years ago, sex researcher, Dr Al Cooper, predicted that, because the internet is so affordable, accessible and anonymous, it would radically expand the use of pornography and facilitate new kinds of sexual acting out, and usher in a sexual revolution greater than that experienced in the 1960s. He was right. People who might not otherwise find themselves sexually addicted find themselves drawn in by the power of internet pornography. And people get lured into pornography and other sexual activity through the internet very quickly.[163]

For example, one pastor's wife we worked with was given a computer for Christmas one year. She was new to computers, but since her children had grown and recently left home, she had time on her hands and caught on quickly. She discovered chat rooms in January, and quickly became a heavy user. Soon she was engaging in sexual chats (cybersex). By February she had developed several online sexual relationships, and by March had met several men for in-person sexual encounters. Such rapid escalation of addictive sexual behaviour is extreme, but by no means isolated. And it is fuelled by the affordability, accessibility and anonymity of the internet.

---

163 See http://yourbrainonporn.com. This website shares anecdotes of people who have succumbed to the lure of internet pornography. It also supports people in recovery.

How prevalent is internet pornography use?

Survey data and internet use statistics show changing patterns in the past two decades, but high rates of pornography usage have continued. In fact, not only has porn use increased on a par with the growth of the internet, it has grown faster than the internet and now comprises a larger percentage of internet traffic than it did years ago. The previous edition of this book cited data from internet service providers (ISPs) showing that 20% of web traffic was porn-related. More recent data reveals that this number has grown to 30%.[164] It is notoriously difficult to provide accurate statistics about internet pornography use, partly because different researchers use different measures of use and access in their reports. Mark Ward, the technology correspondent of the BBC, estimated in 2013 that internet traffic that was sex-related (including health matters) amounted to 14%.[165] A more conservative estimate is offered by the Ministry of Truth website which concluded that adult websites 'account for no more than 2–3% of global internet traffic'.[166] Large numbers run the danger of being sensationalist, and the more conservative estimates that exist can be seen as attempts to debunk such claims. Perhaps the conclusion of Dr Ogi Ogas, who co-authored the 2010 research study *A Billion Wicked Thoughts*, is worth bearing in mind: 'Fourteen per cent of searches and 4% websites devoted to sex are really very significant numbers, when you stop to ponder on it.'[167]

Whether pornography accounts for 3% or 30% of internet traffic, the important point to note is that it is instantly available and has become problematic in the lives of many people. (Some statistics about pornography usage in various countries, some stemming from personal surveys, and others from web usage statistics, are available in an appendix to this chapter.)

Sex addiction centred around pornography and masturbation can be challenging because people tend to minimise its destructiveness and may not identify it as problematic. As the statistics about pornography cited earlier suggest, many people are growing dependent on this sexual

---

164 http://www.extremetech.com/computing/123929-just-how-big-are-porn-sites

165 Ward, Mark. (6 July 2013). *More or Less: Behind the statistics*, https://www.bbc.com/news/technology-23030090.

166 http://www.ministryoftruth.me.uk/2013/06/24/how-big-is-online-porn/. Accessed 14 December 2016.

167 http://www.bbc.com/news/technology-23030090. Accessed 14 December 2016.

behaviour, even though they may not realise its power over them. Since they haven't tried to stop the behaviours, they don't realise how much of a hold it has over them. It's much like the situation where college students become binge drinkers and don't realise they are becoming addicted to alcohol. They don't sense their growing dependence on alcohol because heavy drinking is common and accepted among their peers. It doesn't feel problematic. But when challenged to cut down their consumption, they discover alcohol's power over them. What about pornography? What happens when people who think it's OK to view pornography are challenged to stop using it?

The writer of a humour website called 'A Pointless Waste of Time' conducted an informal study of 100 online pornography users – basically people he knew who looked at porn – and challenged them to go without pornography for two weeks. These were people who didn't view their pornography use as problematic, but they decided to take him up on the challenge. Of the 100 pornography users, 6 dropped out of the study, 52 were unable to go even a week without pornography, and 24 couldn't last for three days. In the end, only 28 of the subjects were able to go through the two-week period without pornography.[168]

The author of the study noted that, even though the subjects did not view themselves as addicts, they tended to describe their experience with the study in 'addict's terms'. He writes:

> The participants were not strangers to me and were largely people I know in an online sense. And while I had heard lots of jokes over time about them being alcoholics or hopelessly fat or hopelessly poor, I had never, ever heard any of them talk about being porn addicts.
>
> Until we did the study.
>
> From the first hours on, lots of these guys were suddenly talking about 'withdrawal' and talking about how tomorrow was going to be a 'tough day' with time alone and high-speed access. They were using the language recovering addicts use, which I admit both surprised me and creeped me out a little.

---

168   http://www.cracked.com/article_15725_the-10-steps-to-porn-addiction-where-are-you.html. Accessed 14 December 2016.

When does sex become an addiction?

When does someone become a sex addict? Where is the line that separates a normal, healthy sex drive from sexual addiction? It might be helpful to think of sexuality in terms of a spectrum of behaviour, and to think in three categories. 1) The first category is normal, healthy sexual behaviour. 2) The second category is sexual behaviour that is unhealthy, inappropriate and destructive. 3) The third category is behaviour that is compulsive or addictive. It is possible for someone to engage in unhealthy, destructive sexual behaviour, but not be addicted. A person might occasionally yield to the temptation of pornography, for example, but still not be an addict. The line gets drawn when that person finds him or herself unable to stop, or when they repeatedly go back to the same behaviour, despite negative consequences. Patrick Carnes puts it very simply: 'Addiction is a relationship – a pathological relationship in which sexual obsession replaces people ... The final core belief of the addict emerges clearly: *Sex is my most important need.*'[169]

The medical and counselling community has established several universal criteria for determining whether a substance or behaviour is an addiction:

1. **Use of the substance or behaviour has become unmanageable.** This means that the addict has tried to stop, over and over again, but can't. There is a history of failed attempts. The word 'powerlessness' has also been used to describe this pattern. Sometimes addicts refer to themselves as 'out of control'. Even when an addict creates destructive consequences for him or herself with sexual behaviour, it's not enough to get them to stop. Sexual addicts may be able to stop their behaviours for periods of time; but, until they find healing, will always return to them. Over time, a pattern of repeated failure will be evident.

2. **The addiction gets worse over time.** This means that more and more of the substance or behaviour will be needed over time to achieve the same effect. The chemistry of the brain adjusts to whatever an addict puts into it. Over time

---

169   Carnes, Patrick. (1992). *Out of the shadows: understanding sexual addiction.* Hazelden: Minnesota, p. 72.

the brain demands more to achieve the same effect. For alcoholics, the brain adjusts to alcohol and requires more. Thinking about sex and engaging in sexual behaviour require that the brain produce the brain chemistry to achieve sexual response. New research is finding that the sexual chemistry of the brain can also become tolerant, which means more and more stimulation is necessary to have the same brain chemistry effects – the feelings of arousal, excitement and pleasure. This escalation can take two forms.[170]

The most basic is that the addict does more and more of the same kind of behaviour. An addict might start out masturbating once a month and progress to once a day – or more – in the course of their addiction. 'Fapping', or masturbating while watching internet porn, can have problematic consequences, especially when the individual is involved in 'edging', i.e., maintaining arousal as long as possible before ejaculation. This overstimulation causes its own problems, as it takes more and more of the stimulation to release the dopamine that leads to elevated feelings of happiness. This leads to desensitisation, and a craving for more of this behaviour to achieve the desired effects.[171]

For other addicts, progression means that they will need new kinds of acting out experiences to achieve the same high. So they will look for new or more risky forms of sexually acting out. Almost every addict can point to certain behaviours that they at one time said they would never do, and later find themselves doing. Maybe they would look at pornography in print or online, but not watch a video. Then they start watching videos.

It's important to note that, while this pattern of escalation helps explain how some addicts degenerate into offending behaviours, it is rare for this to happen.

---

170 See Wilson, Gary. (2014). *Your Brain on Porn*. London: Commonwealth Publishing. This book summarises recent research data on the effects of internet pornography use on the brain and its consequences.

171 Ibid., p. 66.

Only a very small percentage of sex addicts become sex offenders. But for addicts, the pattern of escalation over time is universal and inevitable.

3. **Because of the brain chemistry involved, addicts use the thoughts and behaviours that produce the neurochemical highs to either raise or lower their moods.** This is what is meant by saying that addicts 'medicate' their feelings. If an addict is depressed, lonely or bored, he or she can think of exciting sexual encounters – either remembered or imagined – and the arousal part of the sexual response produces chemicals that raise his or her mood. If an addict is stressed, anxious or fearful, he or she will tend to think of the relationship or romance quality of a sexual encounter. These associated brain chemicals create a feeling of well-being and contentment that lowers his or her mood. Most addicts are capable of both kinds of thoughts, and can therefore both raise and lower their moods, depending on their feelings at the moment.

4. **Finally, addicts act out despite negative consequences.** Addicts don't pay attention to negative consequences and are in what is commonly called 'denial'. They usually minimise or rationalise their acting out, despite the consequences. Until an addict decides to surrender control of the fears that prevent him or her from getting help, he or she will continue to act out. As the addict experiences more and more negative consequences for his or her behaviour, feelings of depression and self-hatred will grow. Unless they are somehow helped to find hope and guidance for change, these negative feelings could create the fuel for further sexual acting out.

How people recover from sex addiction

Sex addiction is a multifaceted problem that requires multifaceted solutions. One helpful way of thinking about the variety of issues related to successful recovery from sex addiction is to think in terms of dealing with past, present and future issues.

a. Coming to terms with the past

Addicts are often mystified about why they fail to keep their resolve to abandon destructive behaviours. Addictions are more powerful than mere habits, which can be formed and changed at will. Sex addicts have become dependent on sexual behaviour as a way of dealing with the stress, grief and pain they faced in their past. Most sex addicts found sexual behaviours early in life to be a solution to medicate pain that was overwhelming to them. Very often these addicts find themselves being triggered into these same feelings of shame, loss and stress as adults, and find themselves reaching for the same solutions. As the saying goes, 'old wounds, old solutions'. Until they learn to deal with these past feelings and hurts in ways that are healthy, they will continue to struggle with addiction.

Coming to terms with the ways we've been hurt. Wounds from abuse suffered as children will affect addicts for the remainder of their lives, unless they understand and come to terms with them. Recovery from sexual addiction can only begin when a person comes to a conscious awareness of what happened to them in childhood.

In this connection, people may wonder if sex addicts aren't just trying to blame their families or their abusers for their behaviours. The fact is that unrecovered sex addicts do indeed blame lots of other people, including family members. But focusing on past abuse as a way of shifting responsibility for present behaviour is unhealthy and detrimental to recovery. Recovering sex addicts seek to understand their abuse in order to heal from it.

Understanding abuse allows people to recognise what happened to them and see how they cope with it through their addictions. It helps them to understand how painful the abuse was, how frightened they were, how alone they felt and how angry they are. Acknowledging these feelings and finding healthy ways to express and cope with them can heal them.

There are two kinds of abuse: invasion and abandonment. **Invasive abuse** is what occurs when interactions that shouldn't take place happen in families, or in other significant relationships. These destructive interactions may damage people in several ways:

- emotionally – yelling, screaming, put-downs, name-calling
- physically – hitting, slapping, pushing, shoving, spanking in rage
- sexually – touching or penetrating genital area, teasing about body, sexual humour
- spiritually – judgemental and angry messages about God, self-righteousness, overly negative messages about sex.

When these kinds of boundaries are crossed, victims of the abuse feel afraid, alone, and ashamed. Invasive abuse is extremely stressful and traumatic for children to endure, and sets them up to look for relief and consolation in unhealthy ways.

The other kind of abuse is **abandonment**, which is often harder for people to identify from their own past. It is one thing to remember certain traumatic experiences, and identify them as unhealthy. It's quite another to identify normal, healthy, positive things that *should* have happened, but never did. Abandonment occurs when children do not get the love, attention and nurturing they need to thrive. When children are not listened to, when they receive few (if any) displays of affection, when they are left alone for extended periods of time, when they receive inadequate food, shelter or clothing, when they are not taught appropriate physical self-care, or given information about intimacy or sexuality . . . they may grow up confused and damaged.

When children are abused emotionally, sexually, physically or spiritually, they are too small and helpless to defend themselves against these injuries. What are children to think about themselves when they are being invaded or abandoned? They come to a very logical conclusion: 'If this is happening to me, I must be bad, because bad people are punished.' Or, 'If no one loves me, it must be because I am bad. Good people are loved.'

Sex addicts believe that sexual activity is the only way to meet their needs for love and nurturing. For many of them, sex was the only way they received attention and physical touch. They learned to make the connection between love, nurture, touch, and sex. Sex became their most important need because it was the only association they had between having needs and having them met.

What to do if you can't identify abuse from your childhood

Some of the people we work with struggle to identify with the patterns of trauma listed above. They might not remember instances of abuse, or they might be reluctant to characterise what happened to them as traumatic or detrimental. If you find yourself struggling to identify hurts from the past as a significant issue, keep the following in mind:

(a) The source of trauma from our past that can drive addictive behaviour *might not be our family of origin*. Many of us have been influenced by popular psychology to focus all our attention on what happened in our families, and especially on whether our parents mistreated us. But sometimes the trauma in our lives came from other sources: friends we had growing up, other relatives, teachers or caregivers, other children in our neighbourhood. For example, a man might remember his family life as healthy and nurturing, but then recognise the trauma of being bullied or shamed by other children as he was growing up. These sources of trauma can set us up to search for relief in addictive behaviour just as powerfully as family trauma.

(b) People need frequent reminders about the destructive power of *abandonment* trauma . . . not just the trauma of invasive abuse. Parents and caregivers may not have hurt us with physical or sexual abuse, but if they neglected our needs, this would have been very damaging. The energy that drives sexual addiction is often created by neglect. Abandonment trauma often creates an insatiable craving for affirmation, attention and connection; which then gets tied to sexual arousal, fantasy and acting out.

(c) Don't obsess over trying to identify trauma if you struggle to do so. The information in this section is given to help clarify and confirm what you have probably already identified as problematic or painful about your past. If nothing resonates with you about 'past hurts', keep reading and pursue recovery by focusing on issues related to your present environment and future vision. It's possible that, as you do this work, memories might surface, or new perspectives about your past might emerge. You can deal with them as they come up, trusting that they will come up when you are ready to face them.

Healing versus mourning.

To recover, the sex addict must *come to terms* with his or her own past. To suggest that 'healing' of the past is necessary may create an unrealistic standard or expectation. What does it mean to be 'healed' of past wounds? For many, it means that the feeling of sadness or hurt will go away. Or that relationships will be restored.

Many addicts come to us looking for the magic bullet – some way of magically finding healing from the pain of their past. Often the assumption is that they will remain stuck in their addiction until they have some kind of powerful breakthrough, where they confront parents or other people who mistreated them in the past. Usually those confrontational conversations are unsatisfying, and sometimes can even set a person's recovery back.

Instead we counsel people to simply **grieve** the losses and hurts they experienced. Addicts must learn to feel the painful feelings of anger and loss and deal with them appropriately, rather than try to cover them up or run away from them. In the Beatitudes, Jesus promises 'comfort for those who mourn'. Addicts must learn to mourn, so that they can be comforted. What they have learned to do is to cover up feelings of sadness by distracting themselves with sexual behaviours instead of letting themselves mourn.

b. Creating an environment in the present that provides accountability and support for recovery

Our 'personal environment' includes the relationships we have with friends and family, the habits we develop, the hobbies we take up, the homes and neighbourhoods we live in, the work we do, the music we listen to, the books and magazines we read, the television and movies that we watch . . . in short, all the things that surround us and make up our daily lives. Some aspects of our environment are beyond our control, but many are not. We can change them, if we really want to. The goal in recovery is to create an environment that supports a life of emotional health and sexual well-being.

Many people underestimate the power of their personal environment to shape behaviour. They try to change their lives by exerting will power, rather than by changing their environment. As a result, they try to live in ways that run counter to the environment they live in and expend Herculean efforts to no avail. Instead, they need to create an environment around them that supports and reinforces their values, and encourages actions that lead to their goals. Creation of a supportive environment includes the following:

1. Find a safe community of recovering addicts. This is the most frequently prescribed strategy for recovery, and for good reason. It is vitally important for the recovering sex addict to be in community with other people who understand his or her struggle, and support them in it. In all our work with addicts in recovery, we have yet to find a person who established long-term recovery who was not part of some kind of support group. Even an individual 'accountability partner' is not enough. A person in recovery will need a multiplicity of people who will help him or her in this journey. By being a part of a group, recovering addicts are exposed to a variety of challenges and solutions, successes and failures, ideas and insights.

There is a variety of support groups available for people struggling with sex addiction. There are several 12-Step groups specifically focused around sex addiction, and many church groups as well. We encourage addicts to focus on groups that understand and focus on sex addiction in particular. Sex addiction is unique. It carries its own brand of shame, and is frequently misunderstood not only by the population in general, but also by other addicts. Recovering sex addicts need a place where they can be honest, and where other addicts can be honest with them.

Another reason support groups are so important is that most sex addicts are starved of friendship. Sex addiction is an isolating syndrome. Addicts live 'in their heads', distracted by thoughts of sexual fantasy, plans for acting out, or shame for having acted out. They objectify and fantasise about the people around them, rather than relating authentically with them. Furthermore, sex addicts are isolated because they have created walls of deception to hide their behaviour. They live in fear and shame, convinced that 'if people really knew the truth about me they wouldn't love me'.

The only way to overcome this isolation is to develop safe relationships where addicts can be honest about their stories, and find acceptance and love. And this can be found in support groups with like-minded sex addicts in recovery.

2. Get rid of stash and triggers. For the same reason that an alcoholic should not spend time in a bar, the sex addict needs to monitor the people and images around him or her, and limit the things that will trigger sexual thoughts and fantasies. Certain video channels may need to be blocked, and internet filter or accountability software put in place. The recovering sex addict may decide not to go to certain movies, or visit certain sections of town, beaches, etc. The temptations found in these places are just too powerful.

One area of particular importance is to go through the home and office to make sure that any stash of sexual material is taken away. This obviously includes pornography, but may also include secret email accounts, post office boxes, or mobile phones.

One pastor we worked with was addicted to pornography, and his addiction came to light in a very public and painful way. He worked hard to rebuild his life, his marriage and his ministry. He went to therapy and attended support groups. But in the midst of all the good work he was doing, he kept a DVD of pornographic images hidden in his basement. After two years of sobriety, and a public restoration to ministry, he went through a difficult struggle in his marriage. During this vulnerable time, he went to the basement one afternoon, retrieved the long-hidden DVD, and renewed his involvement with pornography. Not long after, he was discovered viewing pornography by his church staff, and lost his marriage and ministry position.

3. Be hyper-vigilant about emotional health. People in recovery from sex addiction need to learn ways of dealing with the emotional ups and downs of life without acting out sexually. In the past, they have turned to fantasy and sexual activity as a way to manage painful feelings. So when painful feelings arise, addicts must realise that their sobriety is at risk. They have learned to deny or minimise the negative feelings they have, and instead used fantasy and sexual activity as a way to manage these emotions. The process of recovery involves gaining a new sensitivity to the feelings that come up, and developing strategies to deal with them.

In all our groups with addicts, we begin by having each member identify and tell the group what he or she is feeling. It's surprising how hard this exercise is for many people. They don't know what they are feeling, because they have grown accustomed to pushing their feelings aside. The journey of recovery involves developing a new attentiveness to one's emotional state, and implementing healthy coping strategies for painful emotions such as sadness, anger and fear.

4. Work towards reconciliation and health in marriage. Most addicts who are married have significant issues to work through with their partners, and much healing to be done. Sex addiction is especially destructive for marriages. Its very expression violates the commitment to sexual fidelity, and creates tremendous hurt and alienation. Acting out behaviours are almost always accompanied by some form of dishonesty – and often an extensive web of lies – so trust has also been broken and needs to be rebuilt.

Sex addicts need help developing intimate relationships. Their addiction and the lies and guilt it fosters have created a distance and superficiality in their marriage. Most addicts don't know how to process their anger towards their spouse in a healthy way. Because they are used to feeling guilt and shame about their actions, they can't find ways of accepting and expressing their own needs and hurts. When they felt anger in the past, they often acted out sexually instead of dealing with the disappointment or hurt that caused the feeling. Now they need to learn to do this.

But it's more complicated than that. Sex addicts need to learn how to be honest about their feelings and needs *with the spouse that they have hurt deeply*. Their spouse – because of the pain caused by the acting out behaviours – is likely to be struggling to demonstrate acceptance and compassion to them. Many addicts struggle to deal with the mixture of feelings they have towards their spouse . . . often love, compassion, and remorse combined with disappointment and anger. If nothing else, addicts need the support of their recovery group and other trusted friends to help them go through the transition from disclosure of their addiction to openness and healing with their spouse. This will take time.

One more thing needs to be said about marriage. While it is true that working towards restoration of the marriage is an important part of recovery, it must remain a secondary priority. The top priority for the addict is his or her own recovery. Many addicts come to treatment because of fears of losing their relationship, and much of their 'recovery' is dominated by concerns about how to get back in their spouse's good graces. This is evidence of a lack of commitment by the addict to well-being for its own sake. They must want healing for themselves, regardless of what this healing will mean for their marriage. If addicts aren't committed to their own recovery, and simply want to please their spouse, two things are likely to happen. 1) If they start the journey of recovery, and things go well with their marriage, they may stop the process too early. Once the pressure from their spouse eases, they will quit doing the internal work, and stop attending support groups. 2) If they start the journey of recovery, and things don't go well in their marriage, they may get discouraged and drop out. Addicts need to commit to work on their own recovery, regardless of what their spouse does.

c. Establishing a vision for a healthy future

One of the important issues in recovery from addiction is to know what to fill one's life with when confronted by the void created by ending the behaviour. As the saying goes, *'It's hard to say no until you know what yes is.'* It's hard for an addict to give up sexual behaviours that have brought comfort and excitement to life without having hope that other healthy things can meet those needs.

A vision is a picture of the future that draws us forward. For sex addicts, one of the many losses associated with their addiction is a loss of vision. Many addicts are so filled with shame that they have lost hope for a positive future. Their addiction has probably created chaos in their lives. They may have lost jobs because of their addiction, or at least struggled with diminished productivity. As addiction escalates, it eats up more and more of an addict's time. Consequently, many addicts lose touch with the hobbies and pastimes that brought a healthy balance to life in the past. Life feels increasingly grim, and a positive future increasingly remote.

A vision for a healthy future is essential for recovery, but it takes time to develop. In this sense, vision is like a Polaroid picture. When a Polaroid picture is taken, it immediately slides out of the camera, but the 'picture' is just a black box. After a few seconds shapes begin to emerge, but they are still vague. As time passes, the dark shapes become brighter and clearer, and more detail comes into focus. Eventually the picture sharpens into a colourful landscape or portrait. This is how vision usually works – it rarely flashes into our minds with sharp clarity. It emerges, coming into focus over time.

This is especially true for people in recovery. In early recovery, addicts' lives are often still filled with the chaos created by their addiction, and their minds are clouded by denial, rationalisation and hopelessness. The future orientation of early recovery must centre around a vision of a life free from the power of addictive sexual behaviour. Many addicts have lived so long with their addiction, and struggled with attempts to stop their behaviours for so long that they have lost hope. They wonder if living sexually sober lives is even possible for them. Spending time with other people who have gone through the struggle and come through on the other side is helpful at this stage. Seeing other addicts who have established long-term sobriety establishes the beginnings of a vision for an addict, as they start to think: 'If he/she can do this, maybe I can too.'

It's also important for addicts to spend time thinking of healthy ways to experience renewal. Often addicts have lost touch with healthy ways of getting their needs met. Jeff was a sex addict we worked with who had lost touch over the years with anything that brought him joy. Married with four children, his life revolved around family responsibilities and a demanding career. At one point in a group session he noted wryly, 'There is nothing in my life that I do for fun anymore. It's all about work: work at the office and work projects at home. The only thing I do for myself is look at pornography.' For Jeff, part of the recovery journey involved re-establishing a long-neglected hobby of woodworking. Finding ways of directing his creative energy towards positive pursuits, combined with space for solitude in his life, were an important part of the balanced life needed for recovery.

As time goes on, and the addict finds the emotional and spiritual clarity that comes from extended sobriety, his or her vision becomes more clear. Time that had been spent in fantasy and acting out can now be invested in ways that tap into the addict's innate gifts and passions. Our sex drive is, at its most basic level, a creative and passionate urge. Recovery from sex addiction does not involve suppressing this drive, but rather channelling its energy towards other pursuits which can become outlets for one's creativity and passion. In their addiction, many addicts lost touch with the things they were passionate about, and invested more and more of their passion and creativity in acting out behaviours. The process of recovery involves putting that same amount of energy, passion and creativity into healthy pursuits.

Theological perspective

For recovery from addiction, there are three important spiritual questions that must be resolved:

1. Do you want to get well?

In John chapter 5, Jesus heals a man who has been paralysed for 38 years. For all that time he had been lying by the pool of Bethesda, which was said to have healing properties. Jesus knew about this man, and his question to him might seem surprising. We might expect Jesus to ask how he had got that way, or how he felt, or what Jesus could do to help. Jesus' question doesn't seem to be very compassionate: 'Do you want to get well?' Why ask such a question?

Jesus understands human nature deeply, and the paralysed man's answer gives us a clue about why Jesus had asked. The man says, 'Sir, I have no one to help me, and when I go down, someone gets in my way.' Rather than answering in the affirmative, the man explained why others had found healing, but he hadn't. In some way, it seems that the man had adopted the identity of being paralysed. Jesus knew that, for the man to be healed, he had to want to change.

In addiction, part of the addict wants to be free and part doesn't. To use the language of the apostle James, addicts are 'double-minded' (James 1:8). Many addicts question how they could give up their sexual behaviours – for years these behaviours have been the way that they coped, survived and got their needs met. Even though addicts may have a deep religious faith, part of them resists trusting God and surrendering their sexual lives to God.

The strategies for healing are not complicated. The key, however, is whether or not addicts really want to change. If they don't, no strategy, however simple, will work. Anyone who wants healing must get past the hurts and anger of the past in order to say yes to God. Addicts must learn that there are alternative ways to find the love and nurture they need. This requires a lifetime of discovery, but it all starts with willingness.

Alcoholics Anonymous (AA) learned over 50 years ago that it is easier to help alcoholics when they 'hit bottom' – when their lives are so shattered and broken that denial, delusion and excuses are wiped away. One of our favourite AA expressions is 'My own best thinking is what got me here.' When addicts have no place else to turn, and when they have totally lost it, then they are willing to turn to God.

2. What are you thirsty for?

Several years ago, one of us (Mark Laaser) counselled a famous actor in southern California. He claimed to have been sexual with over 3,000 women, including a number of famous actresses and models. His sexual exploits had also included extensive involvement with prostitutes, whose services had cost him over $3 million. He was a depressed, drug addicted, and hopeless man. As he reflected on his experiences, he said, 'All that sex was never enough. I always wanted more.' He was obviously a sex addict. Mark suggested that he was really thirsty for God and that sex does not quench spiritual thirst.

John 4:6-26 tells of a Samaritan woman who had been married five times and was currently living with another man. She had come to a well to draw water at noon to avoid the 'respectable' women of her town, who came early in the morning. There she found Jesus. She was lonely, frightened and ashamed. She was looking for love and nurture and had failed to find it in a series of relationships with men. Jesus knew all of this. The woman offered to help Jesus draw water from the well, but he said to her, 'Anyone who drinks of the water from this well will thirst again.' Jesus offered the woman at the well 'living water', the water of salvation. This water, Jesus promised, would truly satisfy.

Only in a relationship with God can we quench our deep spiritual and emotional thirst. The desires for intimacy, acceptance and ecstasy that we associate with our yearning for sex are closely tied to – and often confused with – our spiritual yearning for communion with God. As G. K. Chesterton pointed out years ago: 'Anyone who knocks at the door of a brothel is looking for God.' In order to heal, addicts must see how their strivings to satisfy their thirst for intimacy with sexual activities have been a failure. They must discover and embrace that for which they truly thirst.

3. Are you willing to die to yourself?

The apostle Paul tells us that we should lead lives of love, just as Jesus loved the Church and gave himself up for her as a living sacrifice (Ephesians 5:1, 2). Paul says we should be 'imitators of Christ', for we can never be truly like him. Christ died for us – he was willing to pay the ultimate price for our sins. As imitators of Christ, we are also challenged to be willing to pay such a price, to die to ourselves.

This is especially important in our context, because the energy and focus of sex addiction reside in self-absorption. Because of the suffering addicts endured in their formative years, they came to believe that they could not trust anyone else to meet their needs. If needs were going to be met, they had to meet them by themselves. This coping strategy – while understandable – establishes a destructive pattern of isolation and self-centredness. Spouses, children and friends are often hurt by the self-absorption of the addict.

Few people are ever called on to physically die for someone else. But if they want to heal, addicts must be willing to die to their desires, which are focused solely on the unhealthy needs of the individual. They must be willing to endure the suffering that will take place as a result of doing the internal work of recovery. They must face the vulnerability of honest relationships. They must be willing to experience the sense of deprivation that is an inevitable part of recovery, as certain acting out behaviours are now laid to rest. It is important for addicts to make the connection between these recovery behaviours and 'laying down one's life' for others.

What to look for

With these thoughts in mind about how treatment takes place, how can one tell if someone they know is having trouble with sex addiction? While sexual addicts will work to conceal their behaviour, they usually exhibit some observable symptoms. People who live, work or are friends with a sex addict might notice some of these.

1. Preoccupation with sexual behaviours.

Sex addicts will first of all be preoccupied with their own sexual fantasies. This preoccupation leads them to search for sexual expression of their fantasies. They will devote more and more time to the preoccupation until they reach the point where sexual thoughts and activities are the central organising principle of their lives.

There are many ways to observe this symptom. Is pornography of any type present? Does the person watch sexually explicit videos? Does the person notice or point out sexually oriented places like bookstores, massage parlours or strip clubs? Do they do double-takes of attractive people? Does their conversation seem to centre on sexual activity?

Sex addicts may use sexual humour a great deal in their conversations. They may engage in frequent sexual teasing or telling sexual jokes, which in most contexts is considered a form of sexual harassment. Sex addicts sexualise most situations and see some sexual humour in almost anything. Sexual jokes can be used to recruit new sexual partners. Sex addicts can gauge the reaction of the person hearing their sexual joke, and if that reaction is favourable, the level of sexual engagement might be taken one step further.

2. Acting distant or withdrawn.

As the pattern of sexual activity escalates, sex addicts can seem more distant and withdrawn because they are preoccupied with their sexual activity, guilt, shame and/or fear of getting caught. They are unavailable mentally and often physically to the people around them. They may seem distant or distracted. They may seem cold, and they may become angry if badgered about what they are thinking. Ask them what the trouble is, and they deny any problem. More and more, their work, activity, interests and relationships suffer from lack of attention.

3. Depression and mood swings.

Sex addicts may be alternately depressed and excited, even giddy. In the sex addiction cycle, the withdrawn character of preoccupation is followed by the excitement of the ritual or the chase – the high of acting out, and then the despair of shame afterwards. Asking them about these mood changes may elicit elaborate denials and perhaps anger.

Sex addicts try to avoid their feelings and avoid being found out. They create enormous defences. If anyone asks questions that come too close to the truth or simply challenges their story, addicts can become greatly agitated. Their behaviour makes them angry with themselves and angry with others. Past abuse issues that have not been dealt with also create hidden resentments and anger. Triggers that remind them of these past events may set off anger that seems unrelated to the importance of the event. Simple questions, insignificant events or basic statements may incite an angry reaction that will surprise you because the reaction is out of proportion to the event.

4. Resistance to supervision or criticism.

Since they hide a large part of their daily behaviours, sex addicts are not very open to criticism, whether or not it is constructively given. They may live with people who would very much like to correct their behaviours and who continue to turn up the volume of their criticisms in order to be heard. This simply drives addicts deeper into withdrawal, because they do not want their sexual behaviours to be challenged. Because sex addiction often consumes a great deal of time and preoccupies addicts' minds, their work may suffer. They may be gone longer than is necessary for errands or tasks, because they are engaging in fantasy or acting out while they should be doing their work.

5. Inappropriate sexual behaviour and sexual advances.

People who have problems with sexual addiction often tell sexual jokes, they may touch people in ways that don't feel right, and they can give too many hugs. Attractive people are often the focus of their attention, and they can be seen following with their eyes the people to whom they are drawn.

As sex addiction progresses, inappropriate sexual behaviours get worse. Spouses should be aware that sex addicts will become increasingly frustrated with sexual activity in marriage. They may avoid sex altogether because of frustration or as a result of sexual activity outside of marriage. Sex addicts may make increasing demands for sex and certain types of sexual activity, or they may not be interested in sex at all.

An unaware spouse may feel guilty at not being able to fulfil the sexual desires of their partner. He or she may feel angry or repulsed by the demands put on them by their addicted partner. It is difficult for some Christian spouses to confront inappropriate sexual demands in marriage because they may assume it is their duty to be submissive. However, they need to assert their right to have sexual standards and preferences.

Once a partner becomes aware of what is happening, he or she will realise that no amount of sexual activity or attractiveness will be enough to satisfy an active sex addict. Even if the sex in a marriage may seem quite good, he or she might not be aware of the partner's frustrations because the sex addict doesn't have the ability to articulate them.

6. Occupational, social, professional and legal difficulties.

As the sex addiction progresses, increasing amounts of time are spent thinking about or obtaining sex. This means less time for work, social life, family, professional responsibilities or other obligations. Ignoring these activities is evidence that energy is being used elsewhere. They can become involved in behaviours which are increasingly risky and can lead to interpersonal, employment, health, reputational, legal or financial difficulties.

A concerned person should demand to know what is going on. Family members have a right to know because they are being hurt by the addiction. Employers also have responsibilities and other legitimate concerns. If work is ignored, jobs and income will be lost. Friendships or other social relationships will be lost. Unethical conduct can result in the loss of professional licences or the ability to practise a profession.

If illegal behaviour is involved, a sex addict may be arrested and could go to jail. Many sex addicts try to explain away arrests – such as for soliciting prostitution – as isolated events that won't happen again. These arrests are rarely, if ever, isolated. More than likely they are part of a longstanding pattern.

In situations before the addict experiences great losses and consequences, look for signs that the addict is ignoring obligations, duties, jobs and relationships. Even if you discern sexual addiction, you might not be able to help a sex addict. Sadly, it appears that some of them need to experience consequences before they are willing to get help.

7. Intuition.

The last symptom is observable not in the sex addicts, but in those who are in relationship with the sex addict. Be an observer of your own intuition. This means taking your own feelings and perceptions seriously, and not being too hard on yourself for ignoring them in the past. Often spouses, bosses, pastors or friends of sex addicts have a sixth sense that something is wrong. This may take various forms and could simply be a combination of impressions from certain events. Friends and family may feel they are not getting the full or the real story. The explanations of sex addicts for where they were or what they were doing on a certain occasion simply don't make sense.

Trust your instincts and act on them. Looking the other way and hoping things will get better is not a caring reaction, for the sex addict is slowly dying, and things will only get worse.

Do's and Don'ts

1. **DO prepare before confronting a sex addict.** Ask yourself some important questions about your motives and goals for confrontation. a) Are you in a co-dependent relationship with the addict?[172] If you need an addict's approval, you may not have the strength or objectivity to confront him or her on your own. b) Is your own conscience clear in relation to sexual behaviour? If not, be very careful about confronting someone else. c) Will you be able to follow through with any intervention or ultimatums you give as part of this confrontation? Don't attempt a confrontation if you are not strong enough to do what you say you will do. To that end, find out ahead of time where help is available, and how to get it. Collect a list of phone numbers for counsellors, treatment centres, and 12-Step fellowships.

2. **DON'T insist on the label of sex addiction.** There is much confusion and baggage associated with this term that is not important to resolve in the early stages of recovery. In our work with clients, we don't impose this label. What matters is whether people acknowledge they are struggling to establish and/or maintain healthy boundaries in their sexual life. The label one chooses for the experience of powerlessness over sexual behaviour

---

172 A co-dependent relationship is where one person accepts, permits, facilitates or enables unhealthy behaviours in order to gain the support, approval or attention of another person. It is often seen where one person in a relationship has problems with addiction or interpersonal violence.

is less important than one's willingness to ask for help and make the changes necessary to recover.

3. **DO expect denial and minimisation when initially confronting sex addicts.** Since sex addiction is surrounded by so much shame, and since addicts live in fear of being found out, expect the truth to come out haltingly, and in pieces. It is very common for addicts to tell only 'part of the story' when they are initially confronted. Then, as they gather more courage, they become willing to tell more. While this is frustrating, and further damages trust, understand that it is common. Work patiently to get at the truth, asking clarifying questions whenever vague language is used.

4. **DON'T blame the spouse for sexual addiction, especially if you're the spouse.** Many spouses of sex addicts struggle with feeling responsible for their partner's addiction. Often influenced by the blame-shifting rationalisations of the addict, spouses come to believe that, if only they were more attractive or more sexually available, their spouse wouldn't have this problem. Not true! We remind spouses of what we call 'The Three Cs' – 'You didn't **cause** this addiction, you can't **control** it, and you can't **cure** it. It's not about you.' As we've pointed out in this chapter, the sexual desires of addicts run deeper than the biological sex drive – they are looking for intimacy and validation that will heal their woundedness. No amount or variety of sexual experiences will accomplish this. The addiction was present before the spouse came on to the scene, and its presence says nothing about the spouse's lack of desire or desirability.

5. **DO find a place of support for the spouse as well as for the addict.** The spouses of addicts need to find safe friendships – and ideally a safe group – where they can share their struggles and be heard. They need outlets for conversation and support where they can share their anger, so that their addicted spouse does not have to be on the receiving end of all of it. Without these additional places of support for the spouse, either the addict will be overwhelmed by the sadness and anger of the spouse, or the spouse will hold back their genuine feelings, and progress will

be slowed. Spouses also need support for decisions they have to make about how to support the recovery of the addict, and how to deal with their marriage and family if the addict is not staying sober. Spouses need support as much as addicts.

6. **DON'T attempt to rush the process of forgiveness**. Forgiveness is not a simple, one-time event. It is a process that takes time. Many spouses of sex addicts struggle because they feel they should forgive their spouse, but don't feel ready to do so. Or if they do extend forgiveness, they may continue to have feelings of hurt and anger, and not know how to express them. Both addicts and spouses need to understand that the *decision* to forgive is different from the *process* of forgiving. The process of forgiving is much like the process of grieving: feelings of sadness, hurt, and anger will come and go like waves. Instead of being squelched ('I shouldn't be feeling this way'), they need to be accepted and heard. Then, over time, the waves will diminish.

Conclusion

Sexual addiction, while painful and destructive, does not need to be a life sentence. Recovery is possible, as our lives – and the lives of countless others on this journey – attest. Recovery happens when addicts come to terms with their past, adjust their present environment to align with their goal of sexual purity and health, and establish a clear and compelling vision of a recovered life for their future.

Suggested reading

Carnes, P., Delmonico, D., Griffin, E. and Moriarty, J. (2004). *In the Shadows of the Net*. Center City, MN: Hazelden. This is a workbook that provides teaching and guidance about the specific issue of online sexual compulsive addiction, including exercises to work through for your own recovery.

Laaser, Deb. (2008). *Shattered Vows*. Grand Rapids, MI: Zondervan. This book provides wisdom and guidance for spouses of people caught in the grip of sexual sin.

Laaser, Mark. (2004). *Healing the Wounds of Sexual Addiction*. Grand Rapids, MI: Zondervan. This book provides a great overview of sexual addiction, and insights into the process of recovery from a Christian perspective.

US Catholic Bishops. (2015). *Create in me a clean heart: A pastoral response to pornography.* http://www.usccb.org/issues-and-action/human-life-and-dignity/pornography/upload/Create-in-Me-a-Clean-Heart-Statement-on-Pornography.pdf

Wilson, Gary. *Your Brain on Porn*. (2014). London: Commonwealth Publishing. This book presents up-to-date research and illustrates the harmful effects of exposure to online pornography.

Websites

www.faithfulandtrueministries.com – the home page for Dr Mark Laaser, which offers resources for understanding sexual addiction, and information about workshops, training events, and intensive counselling experiences to help people find recovery.

www.markbrouwer.com – this weblog contains a host of important information about sex addiction, with many links to articles and research material about addiction, recovery, and healthy leadership.

Appendix

Some statistics on usage of internet pornography

In the USA:

64% of American men view porn at least monthly, and the percentage of Christian men is nearly the same as the culture at large.

79% of men aged 18–30 view porn at least monthly.

67% of men aged 31–49 view porn at least monthly.

55% of married men view porn at least monthly.

(*Digital Journal*, 14 August 2014 – http://www.digitaljournal.com/pr/2123093)

In the UK:

70% of UK teens say porn is seen as normal by their peers at school.

46% of teens said sexting is a part of everyday life for teenagers.

Two thirds of girls and nearly 50% of boys said growing up would be easier if porn was harder to access.

(*Daily Mail*, 19 August 2014 – http://www.dailymail.co.uk/news/article-2729389/Online-porn-easy-access-say-80-18-year-olds-Survey-warns-explicit-material-wrecking-adolescence-young-people.html?ITO=1490&ns_mchannel=rss&ns_campaign=1490)

75% of Christian men view porn at least monthly.

41% of Christian men admit to being addicted to pornography.

30% of church leaders view porn regularly.

(*The Way*, 20 January 2015 – http://www.theway.co.uk/news-9821-over-41-of-men-in-church-are-addicted-to-porn)

In Ireland:

83% of men and 56% of women have viewed porn.

25% of these watch it weekly.
36% who are not in a relationship view porn weekly.

(*Irish News*, 17 January 2015 – http://www.independent.ie/irish-news/most-of-us-watch-porn-even-if-we-do-find-it-disturbing-30914713.html)

In Australia:

70% of Australian men view porn online (according to research from University of Sydney, but other surveys show the number as high as 90%).

80% of 15- to 17-year-olds have had multiple exposures to hard-core porn.

(*Newcastle Herald*, 12 September 2014 – http://www.theherald.com.au/story/2553854/bare-truths-about-porn/?cs=303)

In South Africa:

67% of men view porn several times a week.

News24.com, 19 March 2015 – http://www.news24.com/PressReleases/Are-South-African-men-spornosexual-News24-Mens-Nation-survey-reveals-all-20150319).

In Trinidad:

79% of men watch porn.

52% of women watch porn.

Trinidad has one of the highest per capita rates of searches for porn on Google.

CHAPTER FIVE

Gambling Addiction

James Walsh

Introduction

The intention of this chapter is to give essential information to people in positions of management, leadership or pastoral care concerning the nature of compulsive gambling and its impact on gamblers and their families, what treatment options are available, and how one's Christian faith may guide a response to the proliferation of gambling venues and an appropriate response to the gambler. Most frequently, it is the family, friends and employers of compulsive gamblers who seek help first, as the gambler's relationships deteriorate as a result of the erratic and often illegal behaviours necessary to perpetuate the gambling. Mental health professionals and clergy are usually the first line of defence for individuals suffering from the emotional, financial and spiritual consequences of problem gambling. Gamblers and their families are generally deeply distressed when first seeking help for the devastating effects of compulsive gambling; having knowledge about this problem and being able to provide assurance that there is hope is essential to initiating the healing process. I hope to be able to convey this information through case studies and a review of current literature that describes the possible causes and treatment of compulsive gambling, and also provide a Christian perspective on bringing compassionate care to addicted gamblers and their families.

What is gambling?

According to the Oxford English Dictionary,[173] gambling is an act whereby the participant pursues a monetary gain without using his or her skills. In its more common usage, gambling also includes activities that require skill, such as betting on a sporting game in which one is actually

---

173 As cited in National Research Council. (1999). *Pathological gambling: A critical review*. Washington, D.C.: National Academy Press.

a participant, but in all cases the word 'gambling' is only applicable to the extent that the gambler cannot control the final outcome. That is, in order for an activity to be considered gambling, there must be risk. Gambling exists in a variety of forms including placing wagers on card games, sporting events, horse and dog races, a variety of table games typically found in casinos, slot machines, lotteries, and, most recently, each of these games and others that can be easily accessed, legally or otherwise, on the internet. Indeed, with nearly universal access to the internet, individuals of any age or in any location can now gamble in near anonymity with few restrictions at any time of day or night.

With the passage of the Gambling Act 2005, the United Kingdom entered a new phase in its legal relationship to gambling. There are three stated intentions to this Act: (a) to prevent gambling from being a source of crime or disorder; (b) to ensure that gambling is conducted in a fair and open way; and (c) to protect children and other vulnerable persons from being harmed or exploited by gambling.[174] In setting legal parameters for gambling, however, the Act allows for expansion of available gambling venues and has normalised gambling as an acceptable leisure pastime. The expansion and normalisation of gambling has resulted in a measurable increase in problems related to out-of-control gambling, often referred to as 'compulsive gambling'[175] by members of the self-help 12-Step group Gamblers Anonymous, and as 'Gambling Disorder' in the *Diagnostic and Statistical Manual of Mental Disorders, Fifth Edition* (DSM-5).

Case Studies

In my experience of working with addicted gamblers and their families, I've learned that when you've met one gambler, you've only met one gambler! While all gamblers have much in common, gambling disorder is an illness that affects people in a variety of ways. In order to illustrate the universality and individuality of gambling-related problems, I will present two case studies that are typical of the issues associated with compulsive gambling.

---

174 Office of Public Sector Information. (2007). Gambling Act 2005. [Online]. Available: http://www.opsi.gov.uk/

175 See literature from Gamblers Anonymous, which can be found at http://www.gamblersanonymous.org.uk/

Tom J.

Tom J. began to gamble in high school. He was introduced to gambling by his father, who was his youth football coach and, in a way, his best friend. Tom and his dad spent most of their free time together playing sport, talking sport, watching sport (live and on television) and betting on sport. Tom's dad wagered with a local bookmaker ('bookie') almost daily, usually small wagers but that wasn't what was most important. What mattered most to Tom and his father was winning. Knowing that you had beaten the bookie, beaten the odds and beaten the system felt as good as scoring a goal or winning a match. And doing it together gave Tom a terrific feeling, a connection with his dad that made him feel like a peer, another important person in his father's life. And Tom's dad felt similarly. He often thought about the legacy of love of sport that he was passing on to his only son.

Tom earned many honours as a football player, and his team even won regional championships. By the time he graduated from high school he had many scholarship offers and the eternal pride of a boasting father. But he had also developed a 'partying lifestyle' that included alcohol, marijuana, plenty of women willingly engaged in the 'hook-up'[176] culture of his community, and a lot of time working out bets on all types of professional sporting events with his friends and acquaintances.

After failing college, the next ten years of Tom's life were a steady spiral into substance addiction. As his dependence on alcohol and marijuana increased, his gambling abated as he did not have sufficient money for gambling. He became a transient person: moving from place to place, couch to couch, job to job, city to city. In time he began using cocaine to arouse excitement and opiate painkillers to relax. He became depressed, and as his depression worsened his

---

176 A **hook-up culture** is one that accepts and encourages casual sexual encounters, including one-night stands and other related activity, which focus on physical pleasure without necessarily including emotional bonding or long-term commitment.

substance use stabilised to opiates alone, and eventually to heroin. By the time Tom was 30 years old he was hopelessly addicted, outcast by his family, severely depressed, and on the point of suicide.

Fortunately, Tom was able to make contact with a counsellor who directed him to a residential treatment programme, followed by intensive out-patient services. As Tom recovered from substance addiction, he came to believe that he could not safely use any stimulating substances, and became a regular at local Alcoholics Anonymous and Narcotics Anonymous meetings. It was at these meetings that Tom was reintroduced to gambling, but cautioned by the elders in 'the rooms' to avoid gambling, as it, too, could become an addiction. He heeded their advice by avoiding traditional gambling games and venues, but could not resist the temptation to be involved in the action of sport, however vicariously. He discovered 'Fantasy Premier League', and a new addiction was born.

Fantasy sports betting was classified as gambling by the Gambling Act 2005. In fantasy sports, the gambler drafts imaginary teams of real players of a professional sport, intending to maximise points as measured by daily assessments of each real player's actual game statistics. Fantasy sports gamblers compete against other gamblers pooled together, usually by a corporation licensed to conduct online gambling ventures, such as 'Fantasy Premier League'. A 2008 study conducted by the Fantasy Sports Trade Association (FSTA) and Ipsos Public Affairs estimated that there are between 5.5 and 7.5 million people engaging in fantasy sports playing in the United Kingdom. In the UK, the most popular fantasy sports are football (soccer) and cricket, with the majority interest found in fantasy soccer. The current leading fantasy sports provider in the UK is the English Premier League, which estimated about 3 million users for their recent season. Roughly 5% of the UK population plays fantasy sports.[177]

---

177   https://ipsos-na.com/news-polls/pressrelease.aspx?id=6540

There is more definitive data on the growth of fantasy sports gambling from the United States and Canada. According to the FSTA, the number of people engaging in fantasy sports in the United States and Canada in 2014 was roughly 41 million, representing 14% of the US population and 19% of the Canadian population. These percentages were a marked increase from 2012, when the estimates were 13% and 14%, respectively. This represented an increase of over five million players in the USA and Canada. When viewed by gender, it is clear that the majority of fantasy sports gamblers are male, generally between the ages of 12 and 34, and for older gamblers mostly college-educated.[178]

Given the demographics cited above, it is not surprising that Tom would become involved in fantasy sports betting. Tom retained his enthusiasm for sport throughout his long struggle with substance addiction, and for the sports enthusiast, fantasy sports enable the gambler to once again experience vicariously the highs and lows of competition and winning. Tom had maintained employment consistently throughout his substance addiction, and with the financial burden of buying drugs removed he suddenly found himself with extra funds and a new interest in fantasy sports that he believed was non-addictive. Tom fell prey to gambling addiction, and unfortunately began to bet daily, becoming preoccupied with his team's statistics, spending up to nine hours some days poring over various sources of sports information. As he lost more money, and his stress level rose, he found himself unable to regulate his emotions and relapsed into heroin use. At the time of writing, Tom has gone back into substance treatment and become substance-free once again, and is now attending meetings of Gamblers Anonymous regularly.

Tom's rapid descent into gambling addiction is not unusual. In 1999, the National Gambling Impact Study Commission Report in the United States[179] found that, when a new gambling venue is opened, there is a 50-mile radius surrounding the local community which typically experiences a doubling of the rates of addicted gambling within the first year of the opening. It appears that simply making gambling available results in the proliferation of gambling problems among vulnerable individuals, even if the availability is online rather

---

178 https://ipsos-na.com/news-polls/pressrelease.aspx?id=6540
179 The US Congress commissioned 'The National Gambling Impact Study Commission Report' in 1999. It can be found at http://govinfo.library.unt.edu/ngisc/reports/fullrpt.html

than a bricks and mortar location. The people who appear to be most susceptible to gambling problems are those at risk for depression and who find themselves with high-stress problems in their lives, including a history of substance dependence. Indeed, as described in the National Gambling Impact Study Commission Report, the psychological literature indicates that nearly 100% of gambling-addicted people also suffer from depression and suicidal thinking or attempts. While it is not true that most depressed people gamble problematically, it is certain that there is a strong association between problematic gambling and depression. It is difficult to determine causality, but depressed people are well advised to avoid gambling ventures, and gambling-addicted people nearly always require treatment for depression.

Another interesting aspect of problem gambling is that individuals from ethnic groups where gambling behaviour is considered culturally normative are at greater risk for gambling problems.[180] Tom is not from an ethnic group at greater risk, though being substance-dependent is also a risk factor. But the depressed and substance-dependent gambler is only a part of the story. As we will see from the story of Kevin W., growing up in a culture where gambling is normative, combined with the stressors of career and family life, can lead to a disastrous problem.

Kevin W.

> Kevin W. grew up in a middle-income Jewish home in a borough of New York City. Kevin's childhood was by any standard a good one, with attentive parents, a loving 'Bubbe'[181] nearby, daily attendance in fine public schools and weekly observances of Shabbat at home, and attendance at Hebrew School at the synagogue. Kevin recalls his bar mitzvah with pride and awe, and can laugh about his doting mother, who always considered him her 'golden child'. Kevin attended a fine university, and made his parents and his Bubbe very proud when he graduated a few years later from law school. He married his college sweetheart, joined a local law firm, had a baby boy and

---

180   See the excellent article by Raylu & Oei entitled 'Role of culture in gambling and problem gambling' in the journal *Clinical Psychology Review* 23(8): 1087–114.

181   Most Jewish grandmothers are lovingly referred to as Bubbe!

girl in quick succession, and was truly living the American Dream. For many years all was right in Kevin's world.

In his mid-thirties, Kevin and another lawyer, a close friend, started their own law firm and quickly found success in debt collection litigation. This sort of legal practice required long hours spent figuring out the details of funds paid and unpaid, with frequent appearances in court to argue before a judge. Though lucrative, this practice is high stress for an attorney, due to the nature of the court fights it involves and the long hours it takes to build these cases. At the age of 40, Kevin found himself chronically tired and burned out, and in need of relief. Though his marriage was 'a good one' and his legal practice was lucrative, he found that he and his wife had little time for each other, given the demands of her professional career (not as a lawyer, but also in a demanding career), the demands of their children, and the demands of his clients to collect more and more of their debtors' revenue. Kevin needed relief, and found it at a nearby casino playing the slot machines.

Though Kevin had never gambled much after high school, he remembered the prevalence of gamblers in his Jewish neighbourhood growing up. Prior to the explosion of legalised gambling in the United States in the 1980s, gambling-addicted people seeking treatment in the United States were grossly overrepresented by Italian and Jewish men.[182] For Kevin, gambling was normal, with no references in the Hebrew scriptures that prohibited it (though the Talmud takes a dim view).[183] So when he found himself in need of relaxation, believing he just needed some 'alone time to have some fun', it seemed natural to spend an hour or so after work at the casino. At first his wife knew about his gambling, and approved of it, as her Jewish childhood had also normalised gambling. In time, Kevin found himself

182 Ciarrocchi, J.W. and Richardson, R. (1989). *Profile of Compulsive Gamblers in Treatment: Update and Comparisons. Journal of Gambling Behavior* 5(1): 53–65.

183 https://www.chabad.org/library/article_cdo/aid/604309/jewish/What-is-the-Jewish-view-on-gambling.htm

staying longer than expected when he played, because he found he could not accept losing, as it made him feel even more stressed out than when he arrived. Eventually he began to chase his losses, trying to win back the money he lost. As his losses mounted, gambling became the source of stress, yet the feeling of winning, especially when he was so far behind, was so appealing that he found himself unable to stop. Kevin was spiralling down into gambling addiction, and his lack of awareness would have profound consequences.

One evening while gambling at the casino, Kevin simply ran out of money and knew that, if he began to take money from his joint bank account with his wife, she would learn how badly it was going for him. Kevin had easy online access to the escrow accounts at his law firm where client funds were held until they were scheduled to be dispersed. Believing in the 'gambler's fallacy' – that is, that past random events affect future random events – Kevin told himself that he was only borrowing from the escrow accounts, that he was 'due' to win (the gambler's fallacy), and would quickly replace what he had 'borrowed' and use the remainder as his 'stash', his secret fund for future gambling. As his gambling losses continued, and his desperation mounted, he graduated to playing for higher and higher stakes, eventually burning through over half a million dollars of client funds. Knowing that his exposure was imminent, Kevin decided the only solution was to take his own life. Fortunately for Kevin, his partner and friend at the law firm discovered the misappropriation of funds and contacted Kevin and his wife before he killed himself. After a short in-patient stay at a local psychiatric facility, Kevin was discharged, entered into out-patient gambling treatment, joined a Gamblers Anonymous group, and began the process of repaying his debt to the escrow funds. But as a result of his actions, Kevin was disbarred, and can no longer practise as an attorney.

Kevin's route to becoming a gambling-addicted person is not unusual. Tom, the gambler in the previous vignette, shows evidence of being the so-called 'Pathway Three' gambler.[184] The Pathway Three gambler is considered to be antisocial and impulsive, usually with several maladaptive behaviours, especially substance abuse. Pathway Three gamblers are especially prone to gamble heavily when under pressure and feeling negative emotions. Given his long history of substance abuse and impulsive behaviours, it was almost predictable that Tom would migrate to a gambling problem once he discovered fantasy sports, especially after his positive exposure to gambling as a child. Pathway Three gamblers generally have the poorest outcomes in treatment, and are seen by treatment providers and other gamblers as 'hard core' in their gambling habits.

Kevin, on the other hand, is a classic 'Pathway One' gambler. These individuals tend to fluctuate between periods of regular, heavy and excessive gambling and periods, sometimes quite long, of gambling abstinence. They typically had gambling normalised by exposure to the gambling of family members or other people in their childhood milieu. Though Kevin had gambled in his youth, he did not gamble again until he was aged 40, which is typical of the Pathway One gambler. Though these gamblers have the lowest incidence of extreme problems, if they become emotionally vulnerable, as Kevin was when he began gambling again (and worsened as his losses mounted), they are capable of gambling to catastrophic proportions once they begin chasing their losses.[185] Generally, Pathway One gamblers have good outcomes in treatment, as they are accustomed to taking stock of their gambling and returning to abstinence.

Neither Kevin nor Tom are identifiable as 'Pathway Two' gamblers, who are described as emotionally vulnerable problem gamblers. This category is made up of people with high rates of psychiatric disorder who have family histories of elders with psychiatric disorder and gambling problems. Typically, the Pathway Two gambler gambles to relieve aversive affective states, and finds that gambling provides escape

---

184   See Blaszczynski, A., & Nower, L. (2002). *A Pathways Model of Problem and Pathological Gambling.* Addiction (97), pp. 487-499 for descriptions of Pathway One, Two, and Three gamblers.

185   Chasing in gambling terms is understood as trying to win back the money that was lost.

or a pleasant affective arousal. Outcomes studies of Pathway Two gamblers indicate that they do well in treatment if their underlying psychiatric disorder is adequately treated and if they receive help getting their finances managed and structured, frequently turning to a trusted other to manage their money.

Understanding the problem

Gambling disorder is a multidimensional problem, in that it affects the individual gambler, his/her family and friends, employers and community. In this section I will present a broad overview of the effects of gambling, paying particular attention to the impact of gambling on the families and associates of addicted gamblers.

Historical perspective on gambling

For as long as humans have gambled, there has been apprehension about excessive gambling.[186] Numerous sources have described gambling as a social problem as far back as the early days of the Roman Empire, when gambling was rampant. Indeed, gambling is well documented in both the Hebrew and Christian scriptures, as seen as early as Joshua's conquest of Canaan, when the promised land was divided among seven of the twelve tribes by the casting of lots, and at the foot of the cross, where Jesus' garments were distributed by the same means. Gambling was rampant in ancient Rome, and it is thought that the Emperors Nero and Claudius would meet modern standards for compulsive gambling. Historical texts note that King Richard the Lionheart limited dice playing among the Crusaders. The Russian novelist, Dostoyevsky, described addicted gambling in remarkable accordance with modern diagnostic ideas in his short story, *The Gambler*. During the nineteenth century, gambling, alcohol consumption and drug use were the targets of temperance movements on both sides of the Atlantic, leading to a variety of legislative actions ranging from the limitation of gambling, alcohol and drug availability to outright prohibition. Temperance movements typically adopted a 'moral model', equating gambling, alcohol and drug use with sinfulness. These movements emphasised

---

186   For an excellent review of the cultural history of gambling see *Pathological Gambling: A Critical Review,* published by the National Research Council (Washington, D.C.: National Academy Press) in 1999.

the need for religious conversion in order to recover from the excesses of gambling, alcohol and drugs.

The spiritual and medical models of addictions

In the early part of the twentieth century, the American psychologist, William James, described a model of addiction based on spirituality rather than morality in his book, *The Varieties of Religious Experience.* James' understanding of addiction was based on consumption of alcohol, which he believed stimulated a false spiritual awakening in the drinker. He evoked the nature of this spiritual experience when he stated that alcohol 'is in fact the great exciter of the Yes function in man ...making him for the moment one with truth'.[187]

This spiritual way of understanding addiction led to the formation in 1935 of Alcoholics Anonymous (AA). The founders of AA, Bill W. and Dr Bob, were inspired by James' spiritual view of alcoholism and encoded their strategy for recovery from alcoholism in the Twelve Steps.[188] Addressing the spiritual nature of alcoholism, Bill W. composed the movement's basic textbook, *Alcoholics Anonymous*, in 1939. In his book, Bill stated that the alcoholic is 'willing to grow along spiritual lines. We claim spiritual progress rather than spiritual perfection.'[189]

Nearly simultaneously with the development of this spiritual understanding of addiction, Sigmund Freud promulgated the view that compulsive gambling was part of an addiction triad.[190] Freud's addiction triad comprised alcoholism, drug addiction and gambling. He rejected both the moral and spiritual models of addiction, articulating instead a medical model that became the foundation for the psychological treatment of addicted gamblers. Freud's view of gambling as an addiction and the successful growth of AA across the United States and Europe led to the formation in 1957 of Gamblers Anonymous (GA), the first gambling fellowship. GA adopted the Twelve Steps of AA and modified them to reflect addiction to gambling rather than to

---

187 James, William. (1988). *The Varieties of Religious Experience: A Study in Human Nature.* In William James: *Writings 1902–1910.* Library of America.

188 The Alcoholics Anonymous website (http://www.alcoholics-anonymous.org.uk/) is an excellent source of information concerning the history of AA and the nature of alcoholism and its treatment.

189 *Alcoholics Anonymous: The Big Book by Anonymous.* 4th edition. (2002). Alcoholics Anonymous World Services.

190 See Freud's essay 'Dostoyevsky and Parricide', published in 1928.

alcohol.[191] GA is a spiritually based mutual-help programme and is the primary intervention for gambling disorder in most Western countries.

Psychiatric Diagnosis of Gambling Disorder

The first attempt at a psychiatric categorisation of problem gambling in the United States was made in 1980 by the American Psychiatric Association in its *Diagnostic and Statistical Manual of Mental Disorders, Third Edition* (DSM-III). This first definition of problem gambling (referred to in the DSM-III, DSM-IIIR and the DSM-IV as Pathological Gambling) focused on the consequences of gambling, emphasising progressive loss of control, the damage and disruption to the individual's family, personal or vocational pursuits, and issues dealing with money. More recent editions of the DSM have added criteria similar to those for substance dependence, such as the build-up of tolerance and the presence of withdrawal symptoms.

The current criteria for recognising problem gambling falls roughly into three broad categories. First, there are those symptoms related to how the gambler thinks about gambling. Second are the physical symptoms. The third set of criteria deal with the behavioural signs of problem gambling. There are nine criteria in total. The presence of four or more indicate that the mental health professional may find a diagnosis of gambling disorder (the new designation as found in the DSM-5). It is important to note that six of the criteria are related to observable behaviours.

The first set of criteria relate to how problem gamblers think. Typically, problem gamblers are preoccupied with gambling, as can be seen by the amount of time they spend handicapping bets, planning gambling ventures, reliving past gambling experiences and thinking about ways to get the money needed to gamble. This preoccupation can become so severe that gamblers will neglect basic needs such as eating, drinking, sleep, bathroom needs, and overall hygiene. While it may sound extreme, many counsellors who specialise in treating gambling disorders can tell stories of gamblers who have soiled themselves rather than leave a casino floor, convinced that they were bound to begin

---

191   An excellent overview of the history of GA can be found at its American website: http://www.gamblersanonymous.org/history.html

winning at any moment. More common but no less destructive are the tales of families neglected and opportunities squandered. One client who presented for treatment several years ago had become so preoccupied with playing dice that he offered the title to his sports franchise (an American football team) in order to cover his wager. When he lost the wager, he lost his team.[192]

There are two physical symptoms to look for, which are directly based on the criteria for substance dependence. First, most problem gamblers build up a tolerance, much like substance-dependent individuals, except the tolerance is for risk in terms of the amount of money that is wagered and frequency of gambling ventures, rather than a particular amount of a chemical stimulant. For instance, when Kevin W, the Pathway One gambler mentioned above, began playing the slot machines with regularity, it was his custom to gamble once or twice a week, bringing $100 to the casino and playing $1 at a time. By the time he was planning his suicide, he would not gamble with a stake of less than $1,000, was playing $10 per bet, and was going to the casino several times per week. By his own report, to have played with any lesser amount of money or with any less frequency would have been boring and would not have provided the stimulation he needed in order to find relief from stress. His need to play with more and more money was not solely related to his ever-increasing debt, but was driven equally by his worsening depression and the increased stimulation it was taking to feel better. Similarly, Tom J. was losing nearly £100 per week by the time he came in for treatment, wagering more and more 'in order to keep it interesting'. Like Kevin W., Tom J. needed a greater experience of excitement and anticipation in order to avoid feeling his deepening depression, and only by betting with increasing amounts of money could he generate the levels of excitement he needed.

The second physical symptom is withdrawal, a feeling of restlessness and/or irritability when attempting to cut down or stop gambling. Most addicted gamblers find that their sleep, appetite, concentration and mood are affected when they stop gambling, and that this disruption may continue for several weeks. It is not unusual for the behaviour

---

192   See obituary of Leonard Tose in the *New York Times* at nytimes.com/2003/04/16/sports/leonard-tose-88-is-dead-owned-philadelphia-eagles.html

of problem gamblers to take on a manic quality (little sleep, rapid speech, disorganised streams of thought, excessive risk taking, impaired judgement) for weeks or even months at a time, as all of their energies can become devoted to gambling activities.

Recent research has shown that there is a relationship between the neurotransmitter serotonin, implicated in a variety of psychiatric disorders (e.g. depression and obsessive-compulsive disorder [OCD]), and gambling disorder. Problem gamblers respond well to the same medications used to treat these psychiatric disorders. This research further supports the notion that there are measurable and treatable physical aspects to this disorder. Similar research has found that the brains of problem gamblers have a typical hyper-responsiveness pattern when exposed to gambling stimuli, which is not seen in non-gamblers. Whether these differences in brain physiology and responsiveness precede the advent of gambling problems or are the result of long-term problem gambling behaviours is not well understood, but there is no dispute in the research community that there are biological dimensions to gambling disorder that deserve further inquiry.[193]

In addition to these symptoms, there are seven typical behavioural patterns that are classified as symptomatic of gambling disorder. The first, and most obvious, is that the gambler has repeated unsuccessful efforts to control, cut back or stop gambling. It is not unusual for problem gamblers to make sporadic attempts to return to earlier, non-pathological levels of gambling, usually without success. The second is that gamblers use gambling behaviour as a way to escape from problems (typically, financial problems caused by the gambling itself) or for emotional relief, most frequently from depression. A third behavioural symptom is referred to as 'chasing' behaviour; that is, after losing money, addicted gamblers return, usually on another day but not infrequently later in the same day, to try to get even by winning back the money they have lost. Indeed, asking gamblers whether they 'chase' their losses is probably the easiest way to differentiate between a hobby and a very bad, possibly addictive, habit. Just the gambler's knowledge of what the

---

193   The BBC presented an excellent overview of research in this area. This report may be viewed at their website: http://news.bbc.co.uk/1/hi/health/1013204.stm

term 'chasing' means probably indicates that the gambling has become an addiction.

A recent treatment episode illustrates these three behavioural symptoms. Marion S. was in her late twenties when she went to her pastor for help. She complained that she had been playing the daily lotto game offered by the National Lottery occasionally, but her visits to its website had led her to be intrigued by the variety of games offered (for example, 'Euro Millions', Instant Win games offering up to £100,000, 'Scratchcard' games offering up to £40,000 per year for life) and their ease of play. After playing more than she intended one day, she resolved to play a bit more in order to win back her money ('chasing'). Because she was able to win back her money on the first occasion in which she chased, she found herself easily tempted to exceed her budget for gambling nearly every day ('loss of control'). As her chasing behaviours regularly failed, she began to experience depression and self-loathing, and found that playing at these games online was the only way to relieve her unpleasant state of mind ('escape'). Her descent into gambling disorder was rapid.

While these first three behavioural symptoms focus on the gambler's inner experiences and attempts to cope with their gambling behaviour, the final three criteria focus on the social and legal impact of gambling behaviour. The first of these final three criteria is that the gambler frequently lies to family members, therapists and others to conceal the extent of their gambling involvement. As the gambling behaviour becomes less controllable, this secrecy is necessary for the gambler to continue gambling in order to win back the lost revenue, and frequently covers up the final two of the behavioural symptoms, which comprise loss of job, marriage, educational or career opportunities because of gambling, and obtaining 'bail-outs' – that is, borrowing money from family, friends, commercial lenders and loan sharks in order to relieve a desperate financial situation caused by the gambling.

It is these final three criteria which typically appear when the gambler has lost all control of the behaviour, and are most closely associated with what most addicted people refer to as 'hitting bottom'. At this point, the gambler is finding it more and more difficult to continue gambling, experiencing terrific levels of preoccupation, tolerance[194] and cut-off from financial resources, family, friends, and gambling opportunities. For these reasons, the gambler who meets all or nearly all criteria for this diagnosis becomes a high risk for self-destructive, and often suicidal, behaviour.

A careful review of these criteria makes clear that there are varying degrees of addiction to gambling. For instance, the gambler may not be suffering any of the physical symptoms but may report gambling out of control (playing more money or more frequently than intended), chasing those losses (sometimes during the same gambling session, but other times coming back another day with the express intention of recouping recent losses), keeping knowledge of his/her losses secret from his/her spouse (or someone significant, such as an employer or counsellor), taking time away from work in order to gamble, and asking friends and relatives for small 'bridge loans' to get through a rough stretch (often with a story, such as 'needed' home repairs or an unexpected financial setback). While this individual may not be depressed or suicidal over his/her gambling habits, this person has displayed evidence for meeting five of the diagnostic criteria and is now diagnosable with gambling disorder. It is not unusual for a person in this sort of situation to present to a counsellor, employer or local pastor feeling troubled about gambling but by no means considering him/herself to be 'addicted'. How the helper responds to the troubled gambler is critical. The helper's response is generally guided by what he/she believes about the nature of addiction and how best to treat it, subjects which will be examined later in this chapter.

Gambling-related problems

There are other factors associated with gambling problems that the counsellor or concerned person must take into account when seeking to help a gambling-troubled person, including concerns with suicide, the

---

194 In addiction diagnostics, tolerance is the phenomenon where the person no longer responds to a drug (or a stimulant like gambling behaviour) as s/he did previously, and needs more of the drug or stimulant in order to achieve the same effect. For an alcoholic, this means that more alcohol needs to be consumed in order to achieve the same level of intoxication. For the gambling-addicted person, it means that higher levels of betting are needed to achieve the same level of stimulation.

impact that excessive gambling has on the family of the gambler, the overall financial and social impact of gambling on the gambler (an impact which often extends to the gambler's employment), and the frequency of being addicted at the same time to alcohol or other substances.

First, concerns with suicide. The link between suicide and gambling problems has long been known anecdotally, and was first noted in professional publications in 1983 when it was found that 97% of the 51 men admitted to a gambling treatment programme met criteria for major depressive disorder.[195] Further study in the same in-patient facility found high rates of suicidality in a group of 50 pathological gamblers, all male. Of these, 12% had made a lethal attempt with definite intent to die, 18% had extreme or severe gestures of suicide, 40% had moderate or mild ideations, 10% had slight ideations, and only 20% had no apparent suicidality.[196]

These results were largely replicated in 1991 in a national survey of 500 Gamblers Anonymous members.[197] Though 21% said that they never thought of suicide, 48% said that they had thought about suicide, and 13% had attempted suicide. In 1998, 44 case records of suicide in Australia occurring between 1990 and 1997 in which a state coroner had identified the presence of a gambling problem in the deceased were analysed.[198] The majority of the suicidal gamblers were male, with a mean age of 40 years. Of the sample, 84% were either unemployed or from a low socioeconomic background. Evidence was found that 32% of the cases had previously attempted suicide. Risk factors included comorbid depression, large financial debts, and relationship difficulties. Finally, in 2005, a group at Yale University reviewed records of 986 calls to a gambling helpline and found that 25.6% of those callers acknowledged they were suicidal at the time of the call, and that 21.5% of the suicidal callers had a past suicide attempt.[199]

195   See Ramirez, L.F., McCormick, R.A., Russo, A.M. and Taber, J.I. (1983). Patterns of substance abuse in pathological gamblers undergoing treatment. *Addictive Behavior* 8(4): 425–8.

196   See McCormick, R.A., Russo, A.M., Ramirez, L.F. and Taber, J.I. (1984). Affective disorders among pathological gamblers seeking treatment. *American Journal of Psychiatry* 141(2): 215–18.

197   See Frank, M.L., Lester, D. and Wexler, A. (1991). Suicidal behavior among members of Gamblers Anonymous. *Journal of Gambling Studies* 7(3): 249–54.

198   See Blaszczynski, A. and Farrell, E. (1998). A case series of 44 completed gambling-related suicides. *Journal of Gambling Studies* 14(2): 93–109.

199   See Ledgerwood, D.M., Steinberg, M.A., Wu, R. and Potenza, M.N. (2005). Self-reported gambling-related suicidality among gambling helpline callers. *Psychology of Addictive Behaviors* 19(2): 175–83.

Clearly, attention must be paid to the gambler's state of mind, especially any indication of feeling both helpless and hopeless. Pastoral caregivers must ask the gambler whether s/he has ever thought about suicide, and is feeling suicidal in the moment of presentation. If there is any indication of suicidal thinking or feeling, the pastoral caregiver must be certain that the gambler is seen immediately by a mental health professional who can perform a proper assessment.

After assessing for suicidality, one must pay attention to the impact that gambling has on the family of the gambler. This attentiveness is often achieved easily, as it is not unusual for a spouse or family member of the gambler to be the initiator of seeking help. In addition, there is a growing consensus that interventions that include the spouse and/or family of the gambler improve treatment compliance and outcome.[200] Whether it is the family of the gambler or the gambler him/herself who presents for help, the caregiver must always assess what help the family needs in order to survive the chaos of addiction, particularly the brand of chaos that gambling tends to bring into people's homes.

The social and economic effects of gambling disorder on the family of the gambler are significant. A survey of the spouses of problem gamblers at Gam-Anon, the family component of Gamblers Anonymous,[201] found that most family members had serious emotional problems and had resorted to drinking, smoking, over-eating and impulse spending. Similar studies have found that the spouses of compulsive gamblers suffer from chronic or severe headaches, stomach problems, dizziness and breathing difficulties disproportionately, in addition to experiencing emotional problems such as extreme anger, depression and anxiety. Spouses of problem gamblers are usually humiliated by the debts incurred, feel helpless and fearful of the future, with little hope for restoration of intimacy and relationship. In addition, spouses of problem gamblers feel tremendous isolation, often due to their complicity in 'bail-out' schemes, the lies told by the gambler in order to procure money to pay bills (caused by excessive gambling) or to gamble more. Indeed, it is not unusual for the gambler and/or the spouse to appear for help focused primarily on financial problems, not on the gambling itself.

---

200   For an excellent review of treatment issues in general see J.W. Ciarrocchi's book *Counselling Problem Gamblers: A Self-Regulation Manual for Individual and Family Therapy*, published in 2002 by Academic Press.
201   Information concerning Gam-Anon can be found at their UK website: http://www.gamanon.org.uk/

In a comparison of children who characterised their parents as problem gamblers with those who reported their parents as having no gambling problems, the children of problem gamblers were more likely to smoke, drink, and use drugs. Furthermore, they were more likely to describe their childhood as an unhappy period of their lives. Each of these problems is clearly related to the experience of chronic stress in the family members, stress created by the erratic and, at times, malevolent behaviour of the gambling family member. In a qualitative study of the children of gamblers in Australia, a consistent theme of loss was found among children: loss of parents physically and existentially, loss of relationship with the parents and with extended family, loss of security and trust, and loss of hope for the future.[202] Finally, incidences of domestic violence (DV) within the families of problem gamblers are elevated. A study conducted in American Emergency Rooms indicated that DV rates were elevated by a factor of 10.5x for women whose partner had a gambling problem.[203]

Several studies of gamblers in treatment indicated a great economic cost in addition to the emotional and medical costs inflicted on the family. A 1995 profile of members of Gamblers Anonymous in America found that 28% of addicted gamblers were divorced or separated, due to gambling. Most had borrowed or stolen from funds designated for family needs, and frequently had stolen from their employers. The average gambler had active debts of nearly $100,000 due to gambling, with the average lifetime indebtedness due to gambling exceeding $250,000 per gambler. Roughly one third had lost or quit a job due to gambling and nearly half had stolen from work to pay gambling debts.[204]

The same problem for co-occurring addiction to gambling can be found among samples of substance-abusing people (see Chapter 3: Alcohol and Other Addictions). A study conducted in an in-patient alcohol and drug treatment programme found that 19% of a sample of 458 patients had gambling problems. Another study of the rates of

---

202   See Darbyshire, P., Oster, C. and Carrig, H. (2001). The experience of pervasive loss: Children and young people living in a family where parental gambling is pathological. *Journal of Gambling Studies* 17: 23–45.

203   See Muelleman, R.L., DenOtter, T., Wadman, M.C., Tran, T.P. and Anderson, J. (2002). Problem gambling in the partner of the emergency department patient as a risk factor for intimate partner violence. *Journal of Emergency Medicine* 23(3): 307–12.

204   See Lesieur, H.R. and Anderson, C. (1995). *Results of a survey of Gamblers Anonymous members in Illinois.* Park Ridge, IL: Illinois Council on Problem and Compulsive Gambling (mimeo).

gambling disorders at an out-patient substance abuse clinic confirmed previous research indicating considerably higher rates of problem gambling in substance abusers than in the general population. This study also found that the rate of substance abusers that could be classified as problem gamblers was 10.7%, significantly greater than general population estimates, which at that time were 1% to 4%.[205] In the United States, the National Comorbidity Study conducted in 2008 of people with gambling problems showed that 75% had a problem with alcohol and 38% had a problem with other drugs.[206] This information should lead one to ask if a person with gambling problems is also drinking (or drugging) too much, or if someone with alcohol (or drug) problems has problems with gambling.

Can it be treated?

Origins and treatment of compulsive gambling

There are probably as many opinions about addiction, its origins and its treatment as there are people who are either addicted or affected by the addiction of a family member, friend or loved one. Addictions have been given many labels, including disease, sickness, moral failure, crime, spiritual vacuum, attitude problem, character defect and the like, but the truth is that addiction is a complex phenomenon that resists any easy categorisation. For those who intend to help the problem gambler it is wisest to focus on recognising the signs and symptoms of gambling addiction and the ways it is best treated, and refrain from spending too much time and energy on determining causality. In order to place treatment strategies in the clearest possible context, however, this chapter will provide a brief overview of the theories describing the origins of gambling problems, followed by recommendations for helping compulsive gamblers to find effective treatments.

In coming to an understanding of any theory that describes the origin of a gambling (or any addiction) problem, there are two essential questions one must ask:[207] (a) to what extent is the person considered

---

205 Ciarrocchi, J.C. (1993). Rates of pathological gambling in publicly funded outpatient substance abuse treatment. *Journal of Gambling Studies* 9: 289–94.

206 See Kessler, R.C., Hwang, I., LaBrie, R., Petukhova, M., Sampson, N.A, Winters, K.C. and Shaffer, H.J. (2008). DSM-IV pathological gambling in the National Comorbidity Survey Replication. *Psychological Medicine* 38(9): 1351–60.

207 For a review of the theoretical models of addiction see Brickman, P., Rabinowitz, V.C., Karuza, J., Coates, D., Cohn, E. and Kidder, L. (1982). Models of helping and coping. *American Psychologist* 37: 368–84.

responsible for the initial development of the problem? and (b) to what extent is the person held responsible for changing the behaviour? In responding to these two questions, one finds four general models of addiction beliefs:

1. *The moral model,* in which the person is held responsible for both acquiring and solving the problem.

2. *The medical/disease model,* in which the person is held responsible for neither the development nor the solution to the problem.

3. *The enlightenment (spiritual) model,* in which the person is held responsible for the development of the problem but is incapable of changing without the help of a 'higher power'.

4. *The compensatory model,* in which the person is not held responsible for developing the problem, but is responsible for solving the problem.

Each of these models proposes an approach to treatment of addiction disorders. Perhaps more importantly, each model suggests the attitude one should take towards the addiction and the addicted person. Nearly every person who presents as suffering from an addiction will have formed an opinion concerning the causes of addiction and its treatment, which probably guides their personal response to the problem. It is essential for concerned helpers to be able to recognise not only their own attitudes and beliefs about causes and treatment but also those of the sufferer, as the sufferer's attitudes and beliefs may facilitate recovery as well as impede it. Let's take a closer look at each model.

The moral model

The oldest model of addiction, already alluded to in an earlier section, is the moral model. The moral model is based on the belief that the use of intoxicating substances or indulgence in over-stimulating behaviours, such as gambling, is an immoral choice that the individual makes. In this model, the indulgence in these substances and behaviours is understood as a sign of weak character that requires an act of willpower to regain control in order to return to sober and respectable living. Addicted individuals are further understood as being somewhat lazy, lacking in determination to behave according to societal norms. The solution to the problem is the prohibition of use of the substance or indulgence in the behaviour, and this prohibition is achieved through exhortation (frequently of a religious nature), education, and law enforcement. The foundation of the moral model is the notion that the world is completely just, so that individuals must stand on their own two feet bearing full responsibility for their fate in life.

The moral model certainly has its appeal, in that it makes the treatment of addiction seem simple, but it has little support in any of the research literature. There are two downsides to this model. First, it doesn't seem to help people stop using substances or indulging in addictive behaviours. Second, it seems to actually make the addictive behaviours worse as the addicted individual feels deeply ashamed and isolated as a result of the judgemental tone of the moral model. Addicted individuals are seen as rather weak-willed, pitiful people in this model who should be shunned if they are unable to admit their problems and stop using substances. The shame and isolation heaped upon the addicted individual generally stimulates more of the very behaviours it seeks to diminish, as shame and isolation are factors that are closely associated with the addiction itself. Keeping in mind that it is likely that the addicted individual and his/her loved ones may adhere to the moral model, application of this model by counsellors, employers or family is likely to exacerbate the addictive behaviour. This model is to be avoided.

The medical/disease model

The medical/disease model of treatment marks the beginning of modern treatment approaches, though its point of view certainly stretches back at least as far as the ancient Greek physician, Hippocrates, to whom this quote is attributed:

> Men ought to know that from the brain, and from the brain only, arise our pleasures, joys, laughter and jests, as well as

our pains, sorrows, griefs and fears. It is the same thing that makes us mad or delirious, inspires us with dread and fear, whether by night brings sleeplessness, inopportune mistakes, aimless anxieties, absentmindedness and acts that are contrary to habit. These things that we suffer come from the brain when it is not healthy.[208]

Hippocrates' insight that all feelings arise from the action and effects of the brain is consistent with the belief of medical practitioners through the ages that addiction is a medical disease that requires medical treatment. Prior to the early twentieth century, the medical treatment of addiction consisted mainly 'of a period of "asylum" from responsibilities and from access to alcohol, to take place in a family-like setting, in a milieu of respect, consideration, and social support'.[209] This treatment approach is still widely and successfully used, augmented by the use of psychological and drug therapies, and a growing appreciation of the role of genetic heritage in the origin of an addiction disorder. The medical/ disease model, with its emphasis that addicted people are not at fault for developing the addiction but rather suffer from a progressive, chronic disease, frees them from the debilitating shame they typically feel as a result of their addiction-driven behaviour. In essence, it teaches that the addiction is more about chemistry than about character. However, in addressing primarily the biological aspects of addiction, the medical/ disease model overlooks the role of thinking, behaviours and habits, which is why most, if not all, treatment programmes integrate the treatment tenets of the compensatory model, which puts its primary focus on the psychological and behavioural aspects of addiction.

The enlightenment (spiritual) model

If the moral model was the dominant model of nineteenth-century addiction understanding and treatment, then the enlightenment or spiritual model has been the dominant popular model throughout most of the twentieth and into the twenty-first century through the work of

---

208 Hippocrates. *The Law, Oath of Hippocrates, on the Surgery and on the Sacred Disease.* Translated by Francis Adams. (2009). Dodo Press.

209 Westermeyer, J. (2005). Historical and social context of psychoactive substance use disorders. In Frances, R.J., Miller, S.I. and Mack, A.H. (eds). *Clinical Textbook of Addictive Disorders* (pp. 16–36). New York: The Guilford Press.

12-Step organisations such as Alcoholics Anonymous and Gamblers Anonymous. As described earlier in this chapter, 12-Step organisations ascribe the causes of an addiction to loss of contact with one's 'higher power', most frequently but not exclusively understood as God. In the spiritual model, the individual is fully responsible for losing contact with God as a result of the choice of using mind-altering substances and behaviours. Research into the efficacy of AA has consistently found that alcoholics described a judging, condemning, vindictive deity in contrast with classical religious thought, which understands the deity in terms of forgiveness and love rather than judgement and vengeance. Given this vitriolic image of God, it is no wonder that addicted people frequently feel a spiritual void and sense of alienation from their 'higher power'. The religion of alcoholics (and addicted people) is not the religion of most other religious people. AA (and 12-Step programmes in general) restore the classical understanding of the deity, enabling the alcoholic (or addicted person) to restore right relations with God.[210]

While the spiritual model does assign responsibility for the addiction to the addicted person's choice to abuse substances and behaviours, it also teaches that the addicted person is not responsible for recovery from the addiction. Rather, the spiritual model teaches that, through the intervention of God, facilitated but not caused by the openness of the addicted person to that intervention, the desire to use illicit substances and behaviours will be removed. An examination of the literature of each of the 12-Step organisations will find numerous examples of this sort of divine intervention leading to sobriety and full recovery. Every counsellor can attest to having heard many anecdotes from addicted people testifying to the power of finding God as the only way s/he was able to arrest his/her gambling addiction. Most mental health professionals are quite familiar with the testimony of 12-Step members concerning their perception of God's role in restoring them to sanity.

Twelve-Step programmes are quite pragmatic in that they recognise that addiction has strong biological and psychological components.

---

210   For a thorough discussion of AA spirituality see Gorsuch, R.L. (1993). Assessing spiritual variables in Alcoholics Anonymous research. In McCready, B.S. and Miller, W.R. (eds). *Research in Alcoholics Anonymous: Opportunities and Alternatives* (pp. 301–18). New Brunswick, NJ: Rutgers Center of Alcohol Studies.

As a result, one finds that the tenets of the disease model and of the compensatory model, to which I turn next, are promoted in 12-Step groups.

The compensatory model

The compensatory model of addiction asserts that the individual is not responsible for the development of an addiction because of the complex interaction between biological and learning factors beyond the individual's control. 'Central to the Compensatory Model is the notion that addiction can best be understood as learned adaptive or functional behaviour in the context of personal and environmental factors – i.e. that drug use or other addictive activity is motivated by the individual's attempt to adapt to stress (including stress associated with the consequences of drug use) rather than simple exposure to addictive substances.'[211] The case studies of Tom J. and Kevin W. presented earlier clearly demonstrated how their gambling behaviours helped them to compensate for the consequences of stress and depression and, in time, of the addiction itself.

This conceptualisation of addiction as a complex interplay between personal factors (i.e. temperament, learned behaviours, biological/ genetic vulnerabilities, family of origin problems) and environmental stressors (relationship issues, job and educational problems, poverty, racism, cultural biases, peer pressure) enables helpers to individualise their understanding of the addicted person's problems and to develop specific solutions that take into account the wide variety of treatment options available. This particular approach, when combined with the understanding offered from the world of medicine, relieves addicted persons of the devastating shame that mires them in their disordered behaviours while giving hope, through its vast array of treatment approaches, that there is a way out of the dreadful suffering of addiction. This approach is also frequently combined with the 12-Step model with its stress on spirituality, generally for the benefit of those individuals for whom religious and spiritual practices have played a beneficial role in their lives. The spiritual model's emphasis on developing awareness of the

---

211   Marlatt, G.A., Baer, J.S., Donovan, D.M. and Kivlahan, D.R. (1988). Addictive behaviours: Etiology and treatment. *American Review of Psychology* 39: 223–52.

need to understand the effects of the addiction is completely consistent with the compensatory model's emphasis on the responsibility of the addicted person to find solutions.

What treatment is available?

A comprehensive review of the treatment outcomes literature is beyond the scope or intention of this chapter. However, readers should be aware of what works and what does not, so that they can avoid worsening an individual's gambling problems and discern appropriate interventions and referral recommendations.

There has been a great deal of research on the relationship between involvement in 12-Step programmes and abstinence from addictive behaviour. The literature generally supports that people who actively participate in 12-Step programmes and incorporate their beliefs and practices do well, except for individuals with severe psychiatric disorder, who do significantly better in structured treatment programmes.[212] Generally speaking, counsellors and those concerned with the gambler's well-being are well advised to be aware of local meetings of Gamblers Anonymous[213] and to facilitate participation in those meetings by people troubled by gambling problems.

Most formal treatment programmes incorporate a blend of treatment approaches, including aspects of the medical/disease model, spiritual model, and compensatory model. These eclectic programmes are referred to as 'multimodal model programmes'. Multimodal programmes, which are often referred to as 'the Minnesota Model',[214] include in-patient and out-patient treatment that employs the use of recovering gamblers as peer counsellors, an emphasis on group work including Gamblers Anonymous 12-Step meetings, and work with the spouse and/or family of the gambler. In addition, these programmes emphasise that relapse into gambling disorder requires skilful stress management, acknowledgement of the risks of exposure to gambling friends and venues, and a daily commitment to acceptance that all forms of gambling must be avoided by the compulsive gambler.

---

212 See Project MATCH Research Group. (1997). Matching alcoholism treatments to client heterogeneity: Project MATCH posttreatment drinking outcomes. *Journal of Studies on Alcohol* 58: 7–29.

213 List of meetings can always be found on the Gamblers Anonymous website: http://www.gamblersanonymous.org.uk/

214 For an excellent description of the Minnesota Model and its treatment approach see this website: http://www.hazelden.org/web/public/minnesotamodel.page.

Generally, multimodal treatment programmes are effective, with most research showing roughly 50–60% of people in treatment meeting their treatment goals in one-year follow-up studies. It should be noted that these multimodal treatment programmes utilise specific forms of psychotherapy based on cognitive and behavioural models of treatment, which focus on current thinking and behaviours rather than trying to probe for deeper insight into childhood problems. Also, there is a growing body of literature demonstrating the effectiveness of antidepressants in gambling treatment, particularly the use of the selective serotonin reuptake inhibitors (SSRI) class of antidepressants (e.g. Prozac, Luvox and similar medications) and medications typically used to manage bipolar disorders (e.g. lithium). Programmes based on the multimodal model typically include a psychiatric component that focuses on discerning the need for medication for the gambler, particularly if the gambler is suffering from a co-occurring mental illness.

Over the past two decades, mindfulness-based treatments have entered into the mainstream of mental health and addiction treatment, with much support from empirically measured outcome studies.[215] Mindfulness is understood as 'the awareness that emerges through paying attention on purpose, in the present moment, and non-judgementally to the unfolding of experience moment to moment'.[216] Mindfulness training was first applied to pain management in the programme developed by Jon Kabat-Zinn at the University of Massachusetts Medical School, Mindfulness-Based Stress Reduction (MBSR). Another prominent application of mindfulness that emerged in the 1980s was its use as part of a treatment programme for people who are chronically suicidal, called Dialectical Behaviour Therapy.[217] Since then there have been several mindfulness-based treatments developed, including Mindfulness-Based Relapse Prevention (MBRP), which integrates mindfulness training with relapse-prevention therapy for substance-addicted people.[218] MBRP has been demonstrated to be

---

215 See Baer. R.A. (2006). *Mindfulness-Based Treatment Approaches: Clinician's Guide to Evidence Base and Applications*. Elsevier: New York.

216 See Kabat-Zinn, J. (2003). Mindfulness-Based Interventions in Context: Past, Present, and Future. *Clinical Psychology: Science and Practice* 10: 144–56.

217 See Koerner, K. and Linehan, M.M. (2002). *Dialectical Behavior Therapy for Borderline Personality Disorder*. Guildford Press: New York.

218 See Witkiewitz, K., Marlatt, G.A. and Walker, D. (2005). Mindfulness-Based Relapse Prevention for Alcohol and Substance Use Disorders. *Journal of Cognitive Psychotherapy* 19(3).

an effective treatment for substance-addicted people, and has led to much study of the relationship between 'dispositional mindfulness', which understands mindfulness as a personality trait, and the likelihood of having a gambling problem. Consistent with research about MBRP, people with high dispositional mindfulness have been shown to be much less likely to gamble, and to have strong emotional regulation skills.[219] Though there has not been development of any mindfulness-based treatment for gambling disorder, the author can state anecdotally that including gambling-addicted people in mindfulness training groups has led to their self-report of significant improvement in managing gambling craving and restoring intimate relationships.[220]

How can you help compulsive gamblers and their families?

In my experience as a clinician working with problem gamblers and their families, I have often noted how rarely it is the gambler him/herself who presents for treatment. When gamblers do present for treatment, frequently their chief complaints concern their money problems and their poor relationships with spouses, family members or employers, or problems with the legal system. The resistance and, at times, outright denial experienced by problem gamblers is generally an attempt to redirect attention away from the gambler him/herself and towards 'fixing' the problems (i.e. financial and relational) caused by the gambling. The savvy potential helper must resist becoming enmeshed in the gambler's preoccupation with escaping a temporary crisis. Non-professional helpers especially should find competent gambling counsellors and mental health professionals to begin the process of helping gamblers arrest their gambling behaviours and reconstruct their chaotic living situations. Family members, frequently deeply troubled themselves, should also seek out professional guidance as they begin to address the myriad problems caused by problem gambling.

When the individual with gambling problems presents for professional help it is incumbent on the counsellor to first provide for his/her safety, given the high rates of suicidal thinking, attempts and completion found in this population. The best way to assess for suicide risk is to simply

---

219 See Reid, R.C., DiTirro, C. and Fong, T.W. (2014). Mindfulness in Patients with Gambling Disorders. *Journal of Social Work Practice in the Addictions* 14(4): 327–37.

220 The author teaches MBSR as part of his private practice as a pastoral counsellor.

ask the individual whether suicide is being considered. It is important to determine whether the individual has ever attempted suicide in the past, intends committing suicide in the present, and has access to the means to commit suicide. If the answer to any of these questions is 'yes', then it is best to ensure that the suicidal gambler is evaluated by the nearest in-patient medical facility for admission, whether this facility is a psychiatric or general hospital.

If the gambler is not suicidal then the helping strategy for the mental health professional should include all of the basic elements of competent counselling: listening, assessing and recommending. First, it is rare for problem gamblers to experience compassionate, empathic, non-judgemental listening from anyone in their families or among their non-gambling friends or employers. Generally speaking, problem gamblers have 'burned their bridges' through lying about their gambling, irresponsibility in relationships and obligations including family life and work, possible involvement in illegal activities, over-involvement and preoccupation with gambling, and, most especially, by the bail-outs they have obtained from various people, usually through deceptive means. Kevin W., one of the case studies presented earlier in this chapter, deceived his wife and several family members for five years. His level of deceptiveness, including clever lies and financial manipulations, was experienced by his wife as an infidelity in their marriage and by his adult children, especially his son who had followed in his footsteps as an attorney, as an irreversible fall from grace. At the time of writing, Kevin W. has worked hard to re-establish trust with his wife and family, but there is an understandable wariness in them as they fear the consequences of further betrayal.

By the time they are confronted by reality or come in for help voluntarily, problem gamblers find they are alone, isolated and out of options. Most typically, they see the solution to their problem as getting the money they need to pay off debts and/or provide a stake for the next gambling venture, the one they feel certain will get them out of the financial hole they have fallen into. Anyone who chooses to help the gambler must exercise caution to refrain from engaging in strategies to fix the financial fiasco, which will be the preoccupation of the gambler. Their preoccupation with their financial problems will sound convincing, and frequently diverts the helper from the real problem: the out-of-control gambling. 'Fixing' the financial fiasco is always a losing strategy for the concerned helper.

The helper must instead focus on the person of the gambler. This can best be done by acknowledgement of the level of distress the gambler is experiencing and communicating this understanding, along with the intention to help the gambler find a way to stop gambling. The gambler and, not infrequently, the helper can get caught up in creating inventive ways of 'fixing' the gambler, but the only way to facilitate change is through compassionate, empathic, objective counselling. This may seem unsatisfying to the gambler and, perhaps, to the helper, but establishment of a trusting relationship in which the gambler feels accepted opens other options to the gambler as he/she seeks to make positive change. Once a trusting relationship has been established, it is also very helpful for the gambler to experience an assessment of the extent of his/her gambling problems, something which a competent professional (or the compulsive gambler him/herself) can easily accomplish by using the Gamblers Anonymous '20 Questions', which can be found at their website (http://www.gamblersanonymous.org. uk/#Questions). Professional treatment should also include assessment for depression and co-occurring addiction disorders. Several instruments useful for assessment of gambling disorders, depression and addictions are included in an appendix to this chapter.

Upon assessing for the nature and extent of gambling and related problems, the caregiver can and should make recommendations for treatment. If the problem gambler is suicidal, then referral to an in-patient facility is an absolute necessity. If the problem gambler is not suicidal and is ready for some form of treatment, then the caregiver can make the gambler aware of local meetings of Gamblers Anonymous and local treatment providers familiar with addiction treatment in general and gambling treatment in particular. A full list of Gamblers Anonymous meetings throughout the United Kingdom can be found at the UK website of Gamblers Anonymous noted above. In addition, the UK Gambling Commission, which was created subsequent to the Gambling Act 2005, provides a directory of national telephone helpline services, online help services, financial advisory services, and psychiatric treatment through its website: http://www.gamblingcommission.gov. uk/. The GambleAware website at http://www.gambleaware.co.uk/

also provides much guidance and a directory of gambling treatment providers throughout the UK.

Finally, I would also like to offer a few thoughts on the use of prayer with those suffering from a gambling addiction. Recovery from gambling disorder is a lifetime process frequently complicated by the presence of another psychiatric illness, and nearly always complicated by fractured relationships and catastrophic financial damage. Prayer is not and never should be a first line of defence; attention must be paid to the overall suffering of the individual. But there is research that demonstrates that prayer helps to restore personal well-being to problem gamblers, and the restoration of personal well-being is the foundation for establishing gambling abstinence. If the compulsive gambler is to stop the gambling behaviour, it will only be accomplished by the restoration of a sense of satisfaction with life, a restoration that has been shown to be helped by an active and fulfilling prayer life.[221]

A Christian Response

In working for many years with problem gamblers, I have come to realise how difficult it can be at times to maintain the compassionate objectivity that good therapeutic intervention mandates. Though interventional talk therapy is essential to stimulate and facilitate the change process, it cannot occur successfully in the absence of the compassionate yet objective therapeutic relationship described by the founder of person-centred therapy, Carl Rogers, who asserted that the foundation of personal growth rests on the pillars of genuineness, acceptance and empathic understanding. Rogers believed strongly that these three conditions, when present in the therapeutic relationship, constituted the necessary and sufficient conditions for change. There is strong support for Rogers' principles.

The most salient variable in the change process is therapist presence. Towards the end of his life, Rogers added the condition of therapist presence to his list of three conditions for therapeutic change. He stated that there were moments in the therapeutic process when he was able

221 See Walsh, J.M., et al. (2007). Spiritual transcendence and religious practices in recovery from pathological gambling: Reducing pain or enhancing quality of life? *Research in the Social Scientific Study of Religion* 18: 155–75.

to 'relax and be close to the transcendental core of me', when his 'inner spirit ... reached out and touched the inner spirit of the other'.[222]

It can be a challenge to establish and maintain therapeutic presence when the suffering person presents with problems that appear on the surface to be the result of greed, hatred and ignorance. Addicted gamblers, like most addicted people, become quite self-centred as the craving for the gambling game overwhelms any sense of righteous decision making and application of moral values. I have worked many times as a clinical supervisor for counsellors of problem gamblers, counsellors struggling with remaining non-judgemental and compassionate. Indeed, I can relate to that struggle through my own experiences.

It is fundamental to the helping process that pastoral agents and concerned individuals remain non-judgemental in their worldview while working with anyone who is suffering. This is easy to do when the sufferer is clearly the victim of another person or circumstance that cannot be controlled. It is a far greater challenge when the suffering seems or is self-inflicted. But there are two key facts that the caregiver can never forget: (1) there is only one thing that Jesus asks us to do concerning our neighbours – to love them unconditionally as we love ourselves; and (2) all of the behaviours of the addicted gambler, no matter how self-centred and pleasure-driven they may appear, are evidence of the gambler's suffering.

Jesus' admonition to love our neighbour as ourselves demands a selfless giving, understood in the early Christian world as *agape*, that is reminiscent of the fellowship of the 12-Step programmes and of the quality of relational presence described by Rogers. To extend compassion is to be fully present and to offer theological hope in the simple act of listening with an open heart. There is no greater gift for the Christian to give and, it turns out, this gift of listening is therapeutically efficacious. The concerned individual is well advised to listen, assess (with the aim to maintain safety) and recommend, and to do so from the wellspring of compassion that our Lord gifted to each of us.

Is it enough, however, to offer oneself as a compassionate pastoral caregiver? Though Jesus' preferential option for the poor may be

---

222 See Rogers, C.R. (1986). A client-centered/person-centered approach to therapy. In Kutash, I. and Wolf, A. (eds). *Psychotherapist's Casebook* (pp. 197–208). San Francisco: Jossey-Bass.

expressed in many fashions, is there not a more public response as an advocate for those who suffer that is demanded of each of us? Addicted gamblers generally present as people with self-inflicted wounds, making it easy to lose sight of the role that government and society play in the instigation of their addiction. With the increase in legal availability of gambling and the parallel decrease in social and moral barriers one can see how society has turned a blind eye to the suffering of those addicted to gambling. Yet society enjoys the economic benefits that gambling provides for each of us through the taxes our government is able to collect.

When government and the society that it governs sanction and proliferate a profitable venture that leads directly to addiction, one is led to conclude that its secondary product, gambling disorder, has become a form of institutionalised suffering. While it is necessary to focus on the needs of the individual and that person's family, one is also called to prophetic advocacy on behalf of the victims of gambling at all levels of our society: individually, locally to our communities, nationally to our governments. In his encyclical *Sollicitudo rei socialis*, John Paul II wrote that it is the role of Christians 'to animate temporal realities with Christian commitment, by which they show that they are witnesses and agents of peace and justice'.[223] This call to be a witness and an agent of peace and justice is, in essence, a call to prophetic vision. Prophetic language is essentially the language of protest. 'Those who suffer unjustly have a right to complain and protest.'[224] As members of our communities and our churches, our service to those who suffer demands that we engage actively in a societal-level struggle against the exploitation of the vulnerable. This demand seems all the more salient now that the gambling industry has shifted to calling their product 'gaming', a word generally associated with the computer games played by, among others, children. This subtle change strongly suggests that the gambling industry is targeting children as future customers, a strategy borne out by the proliferation of online fantasy sports betting, a product clearly aimed at a very young demographic. Though this task appears daunting and, perhaps, overwhelming, it is essential that we

---

223   John Paul II. (1987). *Sollicitudo rei socialis*. Mahwah, NJ: Paulist Press.
224   Gutierrez, G. (1987). *On Job, God-talk and the suffering of the innocent*. Maryknoll, NY: Orbis Books.

combine our contemplation with praxis, so that our relationship with God might be informed by our clothing of the naked and feeding of the poor, and our advocacy on behalf of the victims of gambling by the comfort and wisdom of an all-knowing, merciful God. We must inform our fellow members of society about the suffering of those broken by gambling, as a prophetic warning to them to reflect deeply on the effect of gambling expansion on our values and on our people. To do less would be to express a preferential option for the wealthy.

Do's and Don'ts

- DON'T get trapped by shaming moralistic responses to the addicted gambler.

- DO point out the shame the addicted gambler feels, and offer alternatives to continued gambling.

- DON'T get enmeshed in the addicted gambler's preoccupation with the financial chaos caused by the gambling.

- DO focus on the emotional and medical consequences suffered by the family of the addicted gambler. Offer them help and support.

- DO facilitate the addicted gambler's contact with the Gamblers Anonymous community and competent treatment professionals.

- DO realise that gambling is one of the world's oldest professions, and that there are firmly held beliefs and attitudes about it throughout all cultures.

- DO recognise that addicted gamblers suffer morally, spiritually and medically as a result of their behaviours.

- DON'T assume that addicted gamblers are capable of making sound judgements concerning their problem, as the gambling behaviour itself causes impairment to the gambler's biological and psychological self.

- DO recognise that addicted gamblers descend in stages into their gambling problems, usually beginning with chasing behaviours and loss of control, and progressing to increasing tolerance, withdrawal symptoms, and increasingly antisocial behaviours.

- DO pay close attention to the welfare of the family members of addicted gamblers, as their emotional, medical and financial welfare may worsen precipitously as the gambler progresses into full-fledged addiction.

- DO learn about the nature of gambling problems and how to recognise addicted gambling by visiting the various websites listed in this chapter.

Conclusion

In this chapter I have attempted to present the issues that affect the compulsive gambler and his/her family. As gambling becomes more available within a community and online, it is inevitable that people will gamble more frequently and that some people will fall into addicted gambling. While family members of the addicted gambler will bear the brunt of the emotional and financial devastation associated with this illness, there is a ripple effect throughout the community as well, which is typically experienced by employers, law enforcement, and community organisations. Indeed, the National Gambling Impact Study Commission Report in the United States, cited earlier, reported that communities in which gambling venues have been introduced usually experience an increase in a variety of financial crimes, bankruptcies, divorces and suicides. Though gambling expansion provides numerous economic benefits for national, regional and local governments and economies, there is a social price that communities must pay.

The one message I most fervently hope comes through in this chapter is that there is hope for the addicted gambler and his/her family. Addiction treatment works. It is difficult work, requiring commitment to long-term treatment and absolute abstinence from gambling, but therapeutic care can help the addicted gambler to arrest the behaviour and begin recovering from the disorder. Though it is essential to guide the addicted gambler into treatment, it is equally important to assist the family of the addicted gambler, as the stress-related illnesses they experience can be as debilitating as the gambling itself.

I would like to end on one final note. The portrayals presented in the case studies section were based on real individuals. Both are doing quite well as of the date of composition of this chapter. Tom J. has maintained gambling and substance abstinence for over a year, and has been reconciled with his wife and young daughter. Kevin W. has become a leader in the local Gamblers Anonymous community, and has begun to speak publicly to community groups about his descent into gambling addiction. He has not gambled for nearly a year, and his wife has regularly attended couples counselling in order to restore intimacy in their marriage. Kevin W. can now laugh gently when reminded of his complete preoccupation with gambling, reminding himself that he 'lost his mind' and is grateful to live simply and gracefully, even if quite frugally compared to his past lifestyle. 'Every day that I live with the intention to love my wife and family is a huge win,' he says with a smile.

Recommended reading

Berman, L. and Siegel, M.E. (2008). *Behind the 8-Ball: A Recovery Guide for the Families of Gamblers.* iUniverse.

Ciarrocchi, J.W. (2002). *Counseling Problem Gamblers and Their Families: A Self Regulation Manual for Individual and Family Therapy.* Academic Press.

Heinemann, M. (1999). *Losing Your Shirt: Recovery for Compulsive Gamblers and Their Families.* Hazelden Press.

Websites:

http://www.gamblingcommission.gov.uk/
http://www.gambleaware.co.uk/
http://www.gamblersanonymous.org.uk/

Appendix

Gamblers Anonymous '20 Questions'

1. Did you ever lose time from work or school due to gambling?
2. Has gambling ever made your home life unhappy?
3. Did gambling affect your reputation?
4. Have you ever felt remorse after gambling?
5. Did you ever gamble to get money with which to pay debts or otherwise solve financial difficulties?
6. Did gambling cause a decrease in your ambition or efficiency?
7. After losing did you feel you must return as soon as possible and win back your losses?
8. After a win did you have a strong urge to return and win more?
9. Did you often gamble until your last dollar was gone?
10. Did you ever borrow to finance your gambling?
11. Have you ever sold anything to finance gambling?
12. Were you reluctant to use 'gambling money' for normal expenditures?
13. Did gambling make you careless of the welfare of yourself or your family?
14. Did you ever gamble longer than you had planned?
15. Have you ever gambled to escape worry or trouble?
16. Have you ever committed, or considered committing, an illegal act to finance gambling?
17. Did gambling cause you to have difficulty in sleeping?
18. Do arguments, disappointments or frustrations create within you an urge to gamble?
19. Did you ever have an urge to celebrate any good fortune by a few hours of gambling?
20. Have you ever considered self destruction or suicide as a result of your gambling?

Most compulsive gamblers will answer yes to at least seven of these questions.

CAGE: A Screen for Alcohol Problems

1. Have you ever felt you should <u>C</u>ut down on your drinking? ('C')

2. Have people <u>A</u>nnoyed you by criticising your drinking? ('A')

3. Have you ever felt bad or <u>G</u>uilty about your drinking? ('G')

4. Have you ever had a drink first thing in the morning to steady your nerves or to get rid of a hangover? (Eye opener: 'E')

The CAGE can identify alcohol problems over the lifetime. Two positive responses are considered a positive test.

DAST (Drug Abuse Screening Test)

1. Have you used drugs other than those required for medical reasons?   Yes/No

2. Do you abuse more than one drug at a time?   Yes/No

3. Are you always able to stop using drugs when you want to?   Yes/No

4. Have you had 'blackouts' or 'flashbacks' as a result of drug use?   Yes/No

5. Do you ever feel bad or guilty because of your use of drugs?   Yes/No

6. Does your spouse or a parent ever complain about your involvement with drugs?   Yes/No

7. Have you neglected your family because of your use of drugs?   Yes/No

8. Have you engaged in illegal activities in order to obtain drugs?   Yes/No

9. Have you ever experienced withdrawal symptoms (felt sick) when you stopped taking drugs?   Yes/No

10. Have you had medical problems as a result of your drug use (e.g. memory loss, hepatitis)?   Yes/No

Answering 'Yes' to five or more of these questions indicates a possible problem with drugs.

CHAPTER SIX

Dealing With Difficult Behaviours

Jocelyn Bryan

Difficult people are those whose communication style and behaviour patterns serve to manipulate the behaviour and attitudes of others, causing them to feel inferior, threatened, intimidated or frustrated. They have a negative impact on organisations, lowering morale, creating confusion, reducing satisfaction, and impeding the efficiency and effectiveness of a team. People often leave a team or organisation because of the impact of such a person.

When I first worked in management it became apparent very quickly that the major challenges were not necessarily meeting targets and delivering client satisfaction, but managing the difficult people within the two teams for which I had overall responsibility. The most difficult of these was a team leader who was arrogant and aggressive. He always believed he was right and would not listen to others. He lacked sensitivity and self-awareness. When confronted with the effect of his behaviour on the effectiveness of the team, he became very aggressive and threatening. Another difficult person within the team was a friendly, sociable man who was always willing to take on any job you asked of him. Nothing was too much trouble and he was never resistant to anything. However, it became obvious that he was often unable to fulfil all the commitments he made. This was especially difficult when he was promising clients a service which he could not deliver. He had good intentions, but was unable to say 'no' to anyone. This was a source of frustration among both his colleagues and the clients for whom he had responsibility.

We have all encountered difficult people in various contexts and we are all at times 'difficult'. Being difficult is not a clinical condition but it can be on the borderline of personality disorder. Difficult people chronically use problematic behaviour and communication styles which have a negative effect on others and on the effectiveness of any team or organisation they are part of.

Churches can provide a fertile environment which nurtures and even encourages some of these difficult behaviours. Church leaders and the church community commonly affirm behaviours which are characterised by control, suppression, conflict avoidance and denial of anger.[225] This chapter explores some of these habitual behaviour patterns and suggests ways in which they might be modified and how others may cope with them. It also offers the opportunity for us to hold a mirror up to ourselves so that we might be more self-aware and attentive to the times when we become a difficult person. The psychology of anger is presented as a major explanatory tool in the understanding of these behavioural responses. If anger is not recognised or managed in constructive ways both personally and within a family or community, then it inevitably results in psychological and behavioural problems for individuals and the community. There are many examples of this in church life:

- The minister who willingly takes responsibility for everything that happens in the parish and who is always wanting to please and be accommodating to everyone. Within four years in the parish he/she suffers from burnout or has developed a problem with alcohol or another addictive behaviour, such as looking at internet pornography.

- The church where everyone describes each other as 'lovely' and 'nice' and no one dare express any frustration or anger because the gospel states that we should 'love one another' and 'turn the other cheek' – therefore being angry is understood as being unloving. This niceness can suppress all negative feelings and build up anger and resentment. It betrays an inability to trust others with one's actual feelings and suggests a fear of the consequences of sharing anything which might be construed as negative or critical.

- The minister who projects an image of piety and follows every letter of the law and whose preaching might be described as conservative and uncompromising.

---

225 Wicks, R.J. (2004). A Threat to Christian Communities: Angry People Acting Passive Aggressively. *Human Development* 25(3): 8–16.

The way in which the emotions of anger and aggression are handled in Christian communities is a matter of concern. It can lead to the difficult behaviours which this chapter focuses on. In the final section, there is an exploration of how we engage with anger theologically and how we can respond to these difficult behaviours.

Introducing Jim, Sue and Mary

Jim

> Jim has been passed over for a number of new opportunities in the organisation he works for. He carries the label of being a 'difficult person'. He works in a team but his colleagues do not experience him as a team player. Jim is often negative and critical in meetings, but this is expressed in an indirect way – for example, in sarcastic humour. He makes aside comments, niggles and has a tendency to list reasons why change would be impractical or difficult. His attitude is negative but this is expressed indirectly. He is unwilling to volunteer to help other members of the team in new projects but will do so if asked. In such cases he appears to accept the responsibility willingly but he is inwardly resistant and often misses the deadlines agreed and lets down others in the team. He is afraid of conflict and avoids any confrontations.

Sue

> Sue is very involved with her church. She is a church steward and pastoral visitor, organises church bookings and is secretary of the Pastoral Committee. She works full-time and has two children. Sue is friendly, responsive and always willing to do whatever anyone asks of her. She rarely disagrees with anyone and never confronts anyone, whatever their point of view or behaviour. She is very uncomfortable with conflict and often, when there is a disagreement in church over who holds responsibility for a particular task, Sue will step in and take on the responsibility rather than let the situation lead to conflict.

She is sociable and outgoing; most people would say they liked her. She therefore seems unlikely to be a difficult person to deal with. But she frequently makes unrealistic commitments and then lets people down. She makes promises in good faith but then is unable to keep them. The minutes of meetings are never circulated before the meeting and have to be tabled. As a result, members do not have time to give them sufficient attention. There is frequent confusion over who has booked the church premises for what, because Sue has promised it to two different groups at the same time, hoping she can please both parties and then not resolving the difficult situation she has created. Bookings are not recorded promptly or are sometimes inaccurate so people feel frustrated and let down by her. She often can't attend the meetings she is required to be at, but doesn't let the church minister know until the last minute. She avoids sharing negative or difficult information, which leads to misunderstandings and a misrepresentation of the way things really are.

Mary

Mary also carries the label of being a 'difficult person'. She is described as forceful and often aggressive. Mary is impatient, and when her plans are met with resistance or encounter obstacles, her impatience spills over and she becomes indignant and angry. She has a strong sense of what others ought to do and expresses this forcibly and with confidence. It is rare for Mary to acknowledge anyone else's skills or abilities verbally, or in the manner in which she behaves. Mary is experienced as hostile, condescending and sarcastic by her colleagues. She is prone to shouting at them and they find her behaviour and communication style intimidating. Mary is particularly difficult to manage as she is unable to receive feedback and shows little awareness of the impact of her attitude and behaviour on colleagues.

It is difficult to maintain positive relationships with these characters. Together, they represent the most challenging types of difficult people. There are obvious contrasts between them and hence they present very different challenges to those who are their colleagues or those who manage them. Jim and Sue show many of the characteristics of what has come to be labelled passive aggression. Jim disguises hostility by seeming to be nice. He might say he agrees with something but in reality he doesn't and this manifests itself in a lack of commitment and not following things through. He says what he thinks people want to hear and then expresses his actual thoughts and feelings in indirect comments. His words and behaviour are not consistent. He is difficult to deal with because he appears agreeable and compliant, yet his behaviour is problematic.

Sue is super-agreeable, which is often associated with passive aggressive behaviour. She desperately needs to be liked and accepted. She is super-agreeable as a means of seeking and achieving approval; hence she does not express her actual thoughts, especially if they are contradictory. This means that she is not always honest. Like Jim, her words and actions are sometimes inconsistent. She over-commits herself because she fears saying 'no' will result in disapproval or negative feelings towards her and she always has a plausible excuse for her shortcomings. Many of her actions are rooted in her fear of conflict and disapproval. She frustrates those who work with her and is easily threatened when confronted with any criticism. Sue suffers from frequent headaches and has other symptoms related to stress. She believes it is 'unchristian' to express anger and that her role in the church community is to be 'nice' to everyone. Sue also fears expressing anger because this may result in others not liking her.

Mary, by comparison, behaves in ways which have been characterised as hostile aggressive. Mary expresses her aggression and frustration openly and is hostile to those who disagree with her, challenge her or obstruct her in achieving her goals. This can express itself physically and verbally. She has to win. She is intimidating and powerful.

The common psychological feature of all three characters' behaviour is that they manage or mismanage their feelings of anger and aggression in such a way that their relationships with others are damaged or dysfunctional.

R. M. Bramson describes difficult people as a ubiquitous phenomenon which has gone unnoticed and unexamined.[226] It is evident that dealing with difficult people, whether they be colleagues, parishioners, clients or managers, is a frequent source of stress. Difficult people also present a problem to a team or organisation and can have a fundamental effect on the team or organisation's well-being and effectiveness. Bramson, as a management consultant, provides descriptions of the characteristics of 'difficult people' and how to cope with them. He describes a number of patterns of difficult behaviour which are categorised as the complainers, know-it-all experts, silent responsives, super-agreeables, indecisives and hostile aggressives. He proposes that all these various behaviour patterns are motivated by a desire to gain control over other people.

In response to this analysis, the coping strategies he outlines focus on ways which enable the 'power balance' in the relationships with these people to be redressed and also minimise the impact of their behaviour on the immediate situation. A key factor in these strategies is acting with purpose and preparing possible responses to the difficult behaviour patterns. Evidently, it is necessary to ensure that the difficult person does not maintain control in the relationship by using behaviour patterns which enable them to exploit others and exercise a destructive use of power. The effectiveness of coping strategies and successfully changing behaviour patterns depend largely on understanding the motivation for the difficult behaviour and factors which influence it.

Outline of approach

It is important to recognise what characterises difficult behaviour patterns and how they impact on other people and on an organisation. These characteristics will be described in detail before the behaviour patterns are analysed. I will base my analysis on current psychological theories and use these to inform our understanding of the motives and factors which affect difficult people.

I have chosen Jim, Sue and Mary to serve as key examples. The main reason for this choice is the common psychological ground between them; namely, anger and aggression. They also all have self-esteem

---

226   Bramson, R.M. (1981). *Coping with Difficult People*. New York: Dell.

issues and represent the three types of difficult people which people often report as being the most difficult to deal with. [227]

Difficult people are only experienced as difficult in the context of a relationship. It is the way they communicate with others and react to the situation they find themselves in which elicits the behaviour pattern that people find difficult to cope with. Their behaviour is interpreted and experienced as aggressive, negative, condescending, irrational, critical, abusive and frustrating. In other words, it is the way difficult people communicate and present themselves to others which is problematic. This is often accompanied by a lack of awareness regarding the impact of their behaviour on others and by poor sensitivity and empathy. For this reason, any coping strategy must focus on how to manage the relationship and communicate with the difficult person in a way that allows thoughts and feelings to be dealt with, with respect and sensitivity. It requires good communication and listening skills.

There are many writers in managerial literature who make no attempt at this type of analysis, merely offering a description of the behaviour and suggestions for coping strategies. In contrast, I want to suggest that, by seeking to understand the difficult person's motives and the factors which influence these behaviour patterns, we can handle difficult relationships with greater insight and sensitivity, and increase the likelihood of achieving sustainable positive outcomes.

Characteristics of Difficult People

The identification of 'difficult people types' is well documented.[228] Here, Jim, Sue and Mary's behaviour patterns are summarised.

Jim: Passive aggressive

Key Characteristics

- Desire for approval and general agreeableness

- Negative attitude and comments

---

227 Anecdotal evidence B. Geary.
228 Bramson, R.M. (1981). *Coping with difficult people*. New York: Dell; Brinkman, R. and Kirschner, R. (1994). *Dealing with people you can't stand*. New York, NY: McGrew-Hill; Keating, C. (1984). *Dealing with difficult people: How you can come out on top of personality conflicts*. New York, NY: Paulist Press.

- Subtle defiance

- Ambivalence towards most things

- Frequent use of misunderstandings and excessive demands, as excuses for their inefficiency

- Criticism of others outside their presence

- Avoidance of conflict

- Sulking and refusal to discuss contentious issues

- Resistance to suggestions of others

- Lateness and forgetfulness

- Complaining

- Not expressing anger or hostility

- Manipulativeness

- Procrastination over decisions

Passive aggression describes a pattern of behaviour which carries a pervasive negative attitude. It is described as passive because there is normally little direct expression of resistance in interpersonal situations. So the person complies with others in their demands or needs but is passively resistant to them and becomes increasingly hostile and aggressive as a consequence of this. The pattern of behaviour is understood as a defensive response, leading to the avoidance of something the person fears. Often, this is fear of authority, competition, dependency, intimacy or conflict. A common expression of passive aggression is complying with the wishes of another and even committing to work to achieve these with enthusiasm, then failing to carry out the necessary task or action on time, or in a way which is unhelpful and puts the desired outcome in jeopardy.

In the past decade, passive aggression has been recognised as a common syndrome. Examples of behaviours which fall into this category are: agreeing to meet a friend for dinner at 7.15pm and arriving at 8pm, consistently failing to meet deadlines at work, being angry with someone and refusing to talk to them about it, always having a list of excuses for any shortcomings, agreeing to changes in procedures then gradually reinstating old ways of doing things. In daily life, in ministry and in occupational settings, passive aggression presents itself frequently. But by its very nature it can be difficult to identify and deal with. It is a behaviour pattern which disguises underlying emotions.

Sperry notes that passive aggressive employees are relatively common in organisations but far less common in leaders.[229] Interestingly, he goes on to comment that this is not the case in not-for-profit organisations such as religious communities, diocesan offices and public sector institutions, where passive aggression is a characteristic of leaders and employees and is associated with low morale and productivity.

Sue: Super-agreeable

Sue characterises a form of passive aggressive behaviour

- Agrees with other's point of view
- Cheerful and socially outgoing
- Eager to volunteer
- Does not like to say 'No'
- Over-commits
- Does not see things through
- Dislikes conflict and the expression of anger or discussion of anything unpleasant
- Makes promises in good faith
- Avoids confrontation whenever possible
- Fails to meet deadlines or is late
- Affirms others and makes them feel liked
- Never expresses anger
- Is negative about others when they are not present
- Minimises problems

---

229   Sperry, L. (1990). Passive Aggression in Organisations. *Human Development* 11(2): 41–2.

Super-agreeable people are difficult to deal with because of their agreeableness. It has been suggested that the super-agreeable manipulates the presentation of reality to gain approval.[230] The fear of conflict and disapproval is a significant factor in their behaviour patterns and this is undoubtedly linked to issues of self-esteem and the need for affirmation and acceptance by others. The expression of anger is often interpreted as a sign of weakness and lack of self-control and hence it becomes associated with fear of rejection and the lowering of self-esteem. This is especially apparent in church settings in which cultures are created where anger is often denied (and disapproved of) and conflict avoided. It is also the case that many churches are experiencing a decline in membership and there are more and more demands made on the existing members of the church community. Hence there is considerable pressure on individuals to be agreeable and take on additional responsibilities. This, coupled with the desire for approval as a Christian who lives out their discipleship in acts of service and puts others before themselves, makes super-agreeableness a problem in many churches. There are some obvious examples of how, within church communities, passive aggression and super-agreeableness combine to result in a stagnant community where the psychological and spiritual well-being of both the people and the community is at risk.

- The 'nice' church which is so fearful of conflict that it resists making any changes becomes stagnant and members drift away.

- The parish priest who 'loves' everyone, agrees with everyone, and is afraid to say 'no'. He is overworked, increasingly stressed, and fails to meet his deadlines.

- The church treasurer who grumbles about the amount of money being wasted throughout the church to anyone who is willing to listen but never raises it as an issue in the finance committee meeting or makes suggestions to improve funding.

---

230   Bramson, R.M. (1981). *Coping with difficult people* (p. 90). New York: Dell.

Mary: Hostile aggressive

Characteristics

- Impatient
- Abrupt and intimidating in interaction with others
- Needs to prove to herself and others that she is right
- Presents as self-confident
- Has an aggressive and abrasive manner
- Lacks care for and trust in others
- Lacks capacity to receive and accept feedback
- Has poor listening skills
- Lacks empathy
- Arrogant with a strong sense of how others should think and act
- Lack of control of anger and frustration expressed verbally and sometimes physically

Hostile aggression is associated with a variety of characteristics as the list above illustrates. However, it is important to recognise that hostility and aggression are different, but that both are negative responses and inflict hurt, either physical or emotional, on another person. A person can be hostile but not aggressive, for example, by ignoring someone or being unresponsive to another. Emotional hurt can be inflicted intentionally without aggression being present. It is also the case that aggression can be an expression of caring for someone, or one might respond with aggression through indignation on behalf of a friend or relative. In the context of relationships, aggression and hostility are frequently expressed in response to conflict or a perceived threat and consequently have a high emotional intensity. It is evident from the characteristics listed above that aggression in hostile aggressive behaviour is a means of asserting power and establishing increased self-esteem. It seeks to intimidate the other person into submission, or undermine or ridicule them, or provoke them into a state of irrational anger. If an aggressive person holds a position of power within an organisation then they can be extremely difficult to deal with.

Jim, Sue and Mary's behaviour patterns reveal difficulties in their management of conflict, anger and aggression. When anger is not recognised or worked with constructively, it results in personal and social difficulties. Aggressive behaviour is often an expression of anger and frustration, and manifests itself verbally and non-verbally in relationships. It is a response mediated through the sympathetic nervous system and 'the fight or flight' reaction stimulated by adrenalin. Hence, in the case of the behavioural characteristics such as those listed above, we are dealing with a universal innate human response which is being managed or mismanaged in the particular social setting and which is usually influenced by the personal goals of the individual.

Understanding aggression

These insights enable us to understand the nature of aggression and not only our own aggressive tendencies but those of others. They also help us to develop strategies which enable us to manage relationships which are characterised by anger and aggression.

What factors influence aggressive behaviour and how does our expression of anger and aggression develop?

In Jim's case, his aggression and frustration are suppressed and then expressed in his negativity, sullenness and resentment, and lack of commitment. Sue believes that if she shows her anger she will be rejected and it will damage the affirming relationships she desires, and so she disguises her anger and seeks alternative channels to express it. On the other hand, Mary's hostile aggressive behaviour is an expression of her mismanagement of her aggressive feelings in her social context, and this leads to abrasive, angry, threatening and, in extreme instances, violent physical behaviour. In each case, the mismanagement of aggression leads to relationships which are difficult and damage the social unit they operate in.

Motivation for aggressive behaviour

Anderson and Bushman see all aggression as including the intent to harm.[231] However, they distinguish between hostile and instrumental

---

231 Anderson, C.A. and Bushman, B.J. (2002). Human Aggression. *Annual Review of Psychology* 53: 27–51.

aggression. Hostile aggression is defined as impulsive, driven by anger and motivated by the goal of harming the other. It is conceived as being in response to a perceived provocation and is sometimes called *reactive* aggression. In contrast, *instrumental* aggression is seen as a premeditated means of obtaining a goal other than harming the other person. It is defined as proactive. A person may be verbally aggressive towards someone in order to bully them into supporting one of their proposals, but not to harm them as such.

Current theories of aggression

There are a number of different theories of aggression which help us to understand how aggressive behaviour develops and what influences it. These are outlined briefly below.

Social learning

Undoubtedly, some people are more aggressive than others, but what determines this depends on how they have learned to express aggression and anger through their upbringing, observing others, and the beliefs and expectations regarding social behaviour which they have been taught and exposed to. This draws on social learning theory which explains how we develop our understanding of the expectations of the social world we inhabit, and behave accordingly. We observe and experience aggression in our early lives and, through these experiences and observations, we learn when and how to express aggression in our social world. The key influences in this learning process are the observed aggressive behaviour patterns in families and other significant social settings, such as school.[232]

Script theory

Heusmann suggests that we store our experience and awareness of patterns of aggressive behaviour in what he calls 'aggressive scripts'.[233] A script is defined as a well-established concept held in our memory which is essentially a set of connected actions linked to goals and

---

232 Ibid.
233 Heusmann, L.R. (1998). The role of social information processing and cognitive schema in the acquisition and maintenance of habitual aggression. In Green, R.G. and Donnerstein, E. (eds). *Aggression: Theories, Research and Implications for Policy*. New York: Academic.

likely outcomes. It contains causal links so that the relationship of 'If . . . then . . .' is programmed into the script. We hold scripts for numerous behaviour patterns, ranging from catching a bus or eating in a restaurant, to dealing with a distressed child. When behaviour patterns are well rehearsed or frequently repeated, they are activated or accessed more easily. They also have a large number of links and associations connected to them in memory. This increases the chances of these behaviour patterns being activated across a number of situations. In this way the behaviour becomes generalised through the association network which it accumulates in the memory system.

This theory is particularly helpful in accounting for how a child, who has frequently witnessed aggression in their parents' marriage as a means of establishing power and influence, acquires a script incorporating this pattern of behaviour which is then readily activated across many situations in their subsequent interpersonal and social relationships. So when the child can't get his or her own way in the playground, the script is activated and the child behaves aggressively towards his or her peer group. The cue for activating the script for aggressive behaviour is the child being obstructed in achieving his or her goal. Likewise, the child is more likely to throw a tantrum which includes physical violence towards his or her parents and teachers if the child has frequently seen and experienced such outbursts as resulting in obtaining power and influence. Hence, a behaviour pattern of aggressive behaviour is evoked when the person feels threatened or wants to exert power and influence over someone or over a particular situation.

Social interaction theory
Another theory which has significant explanatory power in this field is social interaction theory. This explains aggressive behaviour as a form of social influence behaviour. It suggests that aggression is used to produce changes in the behaviour of another person. This is particularly helpful in understanding our example of Mary, as it begins to shed light on the motivation behind her aggressive behaviour. Aggression is seen as a coercive behaviour which is used to obtain something of value – e.g. support for a proposal, money, help or goods, or to exact retribution and right a perceived wrong, or to build up a self-image or social identity of, for instance, power, influence or competence. In this

theory, aggressive behaviour is a set of premeditated actions directed towards achieving a desired outcome. Hence, there is a reasoned goal motivating the aggression which could be anything from inflicting punishment on someone as negative reinforcement for a perceived provocation, to bolstering one's social image of being a tough person who is determined to achieve a particular end-result.

Recent findings suggest that aggression is often elicited by threats to high self-esteem, in particular in cases of unwarranted inflated self-esteem.[234] The theory explains many aggressive behaviour patterns in teams and communities where aggressive behaviour is used as a means to enhance one's self-image and self-esteem.

An extension of this theory is related to parenting style. This has been used to explain the development of passive aggressive behaviour patterns which the individual uses to cope with either threatening and restrictive or inconsistent parenting. In the case of inconsistent parenting, many of the characteristics of passive aggressive behaviour – e.g. indecisiveness and contradictory behaviour – were modelled by parents. The child does not then develop either the cognitive understanding or emotional maturity to assess what is expected of them socially or emotionally. This contradictory parenting style results in a lack of assertiveness and poor self-esteem in the child, which continues into adulthood. The child becomes fearful of commitments, unable to confidently predict the responses of others, uncertain of their abilities and afraid of expressing emotions overtly. In parenting styles where the child's needs and desires are frustrated, the child may not risk losing attention or fear possible rejection from expressing anger directly. Hence, the frustration and anger are expressed indirectly in negativity and resistance while at the same time maintaining compliance for fear of rejection.

Other factors to consider

- **Personality traits**: some people are predisposed to higher levels of aggression.

- **Sex:** males have a higher tendency to aggressive behaviour linked to their levels of testosterone. Males are more likely

---

234 Bushman, B.J. and Baumeister, R.F. (1998). Threatened egotism, narcissism, self-esteem and direct and displaced aggression: Does self-love or self-hate lead to violence? *Journal of Personality and Social Psychology* 58: 156–63.

to express aggression directly, while females prefer indirect aggression. This may well be linked to gender differences in social learning, with parents and schools modelling and reinforcing different behaviour patterns of aggressive behaviour according to gender.

- **Beliefs:** if a person believes that aggressive behaviour can lead to the outcome they desire they are more likely to be aggressive in a given situation. However, if a person's faith tradition views aggression as negative and a sign of weakness or moral failure, they are less likely to express their aggression directly.

- **Provocation**: probably the most significant single cause. This may include insults, criticism, thwarted plans. Baron, studying workplace aggression, found perceived injustice as positively related to aggression in this context.[235]

- **Frustration**: when someone can't attain or obtain what they want, they become frustrated. Sometimes this leads to aggressive behaviour towards the person who has been identified as responsible for the lack of goal attainment, but it is also the case that the target of the aggression may not be this person and the aggression is displaced and directed towards another person or organisation. In both Jim and Mary, frustration is a key situational factor in the behaviour patterns shown.

Jim's aggression

In the case of Jim, a passive aggressive person, we can see how these factors combine to lead to some of the characteristics of his behaviour. Jim is frustrated in his work and feels undervalued and overlooked. He has an overwhelming need to be liked, and avoids and resists any conflict. He is frustrated and angry about his position. His self-esteem is being lowered by his current situation. However, he believes that, if he shows others in his organisation that he is angry about the number of

---

235 Baron, R.A. (2002). Social and personal determinants of workplace aggression: Evidence for the impact of perceived injustice and the Type A behaviour pattern. *Aggressive Behaviour* 25: 281–96, quoted in Anderson, C.A. and Bushman, B.J. (2002). Human Aggression. *Annual Review of Psychology* 53: 27–51

opportunities for which he has been overlooked, he will risk damaging his chances for the future and face rejection or condemnation. Jim believes that showing aggression has a negative effect on relationships and seeks to exert social influence in other ways. Hence, he expresses his anger and frustration indirectly by being inefficient, negative and critical of others behind their backs and resistant to any new ideas. As is often the case with passive aggression, he may be unaware that these are expressions of his anger or of the damaging effect he is having on the organisation and his relationships within it.

Sue's aggression

The identification of how Sue manages her anger and aggression is more difficult, because it is avoided. Like Jim, she avoids conflict and sees anger as a negative emotion. From social interaction theory, Sue's behaviour can be understood as the repression of aggression helping her to achieve her desired outcome of maintaining affirming relationships and being accepted. Her motivation for repressing any feelings of anger is that she believes this would put her relationships at risk and, in her understanding of social norms, she believes that displays of anger are unacceptable and show lack of self-control and weakness. Hence, she is fearful of the consequences of expressing anger and the effect it will have on her relationships. From social learning theory, Sue's parents' attitude towards the expression of feelings and her church background will also be influencing her behaviour. However, it is likely that Sue will be expressing aggression in ways she is unaware of. Some of her inefficiency may well be unintentional, but she excuses herself by listing the demands she is facing rather than learning to say 'no'. The same can be seen with her increasing tendency to be forgetful. Alongside this, she might well become increasingly resentful about her workload for the church for which she receives little reward and no thanks! In addition, her symptoms of stress may well be related to the repression of her anger.

Mary's aggression

Mary is a hostile aggressive. We see some of the factors described above working out in her in a different behaviour pattern. Mary is motivated by proving herself and having power and influence in the team. It is important that she achieves her objectives and this is an important factor in her self-esteem. When others resist her ideas or plans, she becomes irritated and frustrated. Her self-esteem is threatened. To bolster her self-esteem, she uses aggression to threaten others and achieve power over them in order to achieve her goals. She is forceful and self-confident. She does not listen to others and firmly believes she is right. Some of her anger she understands to be 'righteous anger'. In Mary's case, this is a learned behaviour pattern which has a reasoned goal. When Mary is thwarted or frustrated, her aggressive script is activated and she adopts the behaviour pattern which she has acquired through observation and experience.

Self-esteem

Another important psychological factor in each of our characters is their self-esteem.

Self-esteem is defined as an overall affective evaluation of one's own worth.[236] It is evident in each of our characters that their difficult behaviour patterns are related to their self-esteem. Branden, in his book on how to raise your self-esteem, suggests that low self-esteem causes people to be less ambitious, less creative in their work and less likely to treat others respectfully.[237] Furthermore, they are less likely to assume responsibility, and will look for others to blame.[238]

Research using adolescents and college students found that low self-esteem was associated with a tendency to reject or be overly sensitive to criticism, an avoidance of making decisions and a resentment at being told what to do.[239] Hostile aggressive behaviour is frequently elicited when criticism is voiced. The confrontational response and bullying behaviour of hostile aggressives acts as a façade to hide the wound that criticism causes to an already low self-esteem. Their behaviour pattern may also include sarcasm, boasting, arrogance and overestimating their

---

236 Balscovich, J. and Tamaka, J. (2001). Measures of Self Esteem. In Robinson, J.P., Shaver, P.R. and Wrightsman, L.S. (eds), *Measures of personality and social attitudes*. San Diego, CA: Academic Press, quoted in Rayens, B.L. (2001). Predicting Difficult Employees: The Relationship between Vocational Interests, Self Esteem and Problem Communication Styles. *Applied H.R.M. Research* 6(1): 33–66.

237 Branden, N. (1988). *How to raise your self esteem*. New York: Bantam Books.

238 Hamachek, D.E. (1987). *Encounters with Self*. New York, NY: Holt, Rinehart and Winston.

239 Rosenberg, M. (1965). *Society and adolescent self image*. Princeton, NJ: Princeton University Press.

abilities to appear superior. All of these are strategies to establish a sense of power or inflate their self-esteem.[240]

In the case of passive aggressives, low self-esteem is expressed as a fear of being rejected or behaving inappropriately, so they procrastinate when making decisions, they offer very little input in meetings, they may be negative and will not volunteer for any new responsibilities because of the risk of being disliked or rejected.

Super-agreeables classically fear rejection and have an overwhelming need to be accepted and affirmed. Their self-esteem is fragile, and anything they perceive as potentially threatening to their relationships and their acceptance is resisted. They fear the consequences of saying 'no', disagreeing with others and expressing their anger.

While low self-esteem can manifest itself in difficult behaviour patterns, it is also the case that inflated self-esteem is associated with problematic behaviour, especially in communication and relationships. When someone with inflated self-esteem feels that their authority or competence is being threatened, they respond with an aggressive communication style. Individuals with inflated self-esteem make unrealistically positive claims about themselves.[241] Consequently, they set themselves unrealistic goals which can lead to failure. When failure threatens their egos, they compensate for their deflated self-esteem by using sarcasm and negative communication styles to intimidate others and make them appear inferior, thereby restoring their own feelings of superiority.

Further reflections on passive aggressive behaviour

The role of self-reflection and self-awareness

When someone is acting out any difficult behaviour, we recognise it as such because of the reaction we experience in ourselves. Passive aggression is by its very name 'passive' and is consequently hidden from the person acting out in this way. So not only is it important that we recognise the characteristics of passive aggressive behaviour in others but we also need to be self-reflective and open to the possibility that we too might

---

240 Rayens, B.L. (2001). Predicting Difficult Employees: The Relationship between Vocational Interests, Self Esteem and Problem Communication Styles. *Applied H.R.M. Research* 6(1): 33–66.

241 Baumeister, R.F., Heatherton, T.F. and Tice, D.M. (1994). *Losing control: How and why people fail at self-regulation.* San Diego, CA: Academic Press.

be acting passive aggressively. It is also the case that if we are aware of this behaviour in ourselves we are more likely to be able to deal with it constructively in others. This is an important and necessary task for nurturing life-giving discipleship in the life and mission of the Church.

Robert Wicks points out that when we act passive aggressively we are psychologically trying to disguise our negative feelings.[242] This is usually because we believe this to be the appropriate behaviour or the right thing for our situation. For example, we might not produce a report on time for the minister but we believe that we are doing the best we can to support the church and, what's more, we have taken on more responsibility than most, but if we were challenged about not meeting the minister's deadline we would feel hurt and angry and not able to share this. This kind of response requires honest self-reflection to uncover why we might be behaving in this way. What is the underlying motivation for taking on so much responsibility in the church? What is the motivation – if there is one – for being late with the report?

In prayer or a period of quiet time, the Christian practice of the examen offers an opportunity for honesty and openness before God concerning our deepest fears, goals and motivations.

Wicks suggests a number of questions that are helpful in this process:

- What did I get angry at today?

- With whom did I get angry?

- In addition to the apparent reason for my anger, what other reasons might be responsible for the strength of feeling I experienced?

- How did I deal with my anger? Did I deny it? Did I use Christian language to cover it up? – e.g. 'It's not about him as a person; I love him, but the way he behaves sometimes is just inappropriate.'

- Did I review my feelings of anger and deal with them constructively so that I could initiate an open discussion about our differences?

---

242 Wicks, R.J. (2004). A Threat to Christian Communities: Angry People Acting Passive Aggressively. *Human Development* 25(3): 8–16.

- Did I surprise or scare people, or try to keep them on my side by being passive and giving in?

- Did I connect my anger to its source, or did I project it on to someone else or even make myself believe I wasn't angry?[243]

Wicks recommends a review of possible passive aggressive tendencies as also helpful in bringing our own aggression and anger to our attention. Applying the following questions might also facilitate a more empathetic approach to dealing with these difficult behaviours:

- Did I act in ways that were obstructive?

- Did I dawdle or procrastinate?

- Was I stubborn or forgetful?

- Was I surprised by someone else's anger at something I did or said?

Can it be treated?

Many of the people we have considered in this chapter do not have diagnosable personality disorders or suffer from mental illnesses (although this may sometimes be the case). While many people can benefit from therapy, it is not always necessary, nor will everyone be open to it. There are, however, interventions that can be helpful.

Super-agreeables often need to learn how to be more assertive. They find it hard to say 'no', and can create difficulties for themselves that can lead to frustration, resentment and feelings of not being appreciated. They can also benefit from group therapy where their avoidance of conflict and negative emotions will be challenged in a supportive setting. This can provide the corrective emotional experience that will give them greater resilience in interpersonal situations. Adjusting to new behaviours may lead to a period of clumsy interactions. However, after a period of time, the super-agreeable, by learning their own limitations and respecting the boundaries of others, can become an asset to the church or organisation. Many church groups now provide training in

---

243   Ibid., p. 12.

conflict management and assertiveness to help clergy, volunteers or workers to deal with uncomfortable emotions, especially anger. There are also training agencies that provide similar training for therapists, psychologists, social workers, and people in other work settings.

Passive aggressives can be more difficult to help, as so much of their energy is invested in avoidance and denial. Much of their behaviour disguises their feelings of anger and so their anger is often not recognised. Obstructive behaviours, forgetfulness, procrastination and inefficiency impede progress and elicit frustration in others. However, the explanation that they are 'doing their best' can lead to others feeling guilty about their response to a passive aggressive person. The first important step to helping someone who is acting in this way is to recognise the underlying anger and its source.

Workshops on communications and assertiveness can be effective, although this may need to be supplemented by therapy that focuses on emotional expressiveness, as passive-aggressives have difficulty owning and articulating their own feelings. Group therapy can also be helpful for them. Irvin Yalom, who has worked extensively with psychotherapy groups, writes:

> Members of dynamic therapy groups, which have ground rules encouraging open feedback, may obtain considerable information about maladaptive social behaviour. A patient may, for example, learn about a disconcerting tendency to avoid looking at the person with whom he or she is conversing; about others' impressions of his or her haughty, regal attitude, or about a variety of other social habits that, unbeknownst to the patient, have been undermining social relationships. For individuals lacking intimate relationships, the group often represents the first opportunity for accurate interpersonal feedback.[244]

Passive aggressive persons often require feedback in a safe setting in order to identify, understand and begin to change their behaviour. Individual therapy can also be helpful, but group therapy is probably more valuable and effective for people who behave in this way.

---

244   Yalom, I.D. (1995). *The theory and practice of group psychotherapy* (p. 16). New York: Basic Books.

Aggressive individuals often resist any kind of help. However, they too can benefit from workshops on assertiveness and aggressiveness where they can see how their behaviour is affecting other people, and experiment with new behaviours that enable them to get their needs met without trampling on the needs or feelings of others. They can also benefit from cognitive behavioural therapy that helps them to reflect on their life goals and their values, and whether or not their behaviour is helping them to achieve what is important for themselves or the organisations they belong to. The comments made about group psychotherapy for passive aggressive individuals also relate to aggressive people. They can benefit from receiving feedback in a safe setting. Other group members can be helped to give direct feedback which is often difficult – and difficult for the aggressive individual to hear – in social or work settings.

A Christian Response

In this chapter, I have suggested that the management of anger and aggression is a significant factor in the three types of difficult patterns of behaviour described. Anger is a powerful emotion which is often expressed in aggressive behaviour patterns. Within the Christian tradition, anger and aggression are responded to negatively. However, it was only in the nineteenth century that the psychological category of emotions was established. Prior to this time, these psychological states were understood as passions and affections of the soul.

Passions were seen as signs of and punishment for the original sin of Adam and Eve. They were interpreted as manifestations of the disobedience to the will and were in tension with the affections of the soul which were viewed as the more refined, spiritual and aesthetic desires which drew the person towards beauty, truth and goodness.[245] Hence anger was understood as an emotion to be tamed, avoided, repressed or controlled. It was associated with sin, disobedience and failure. The challenge for the Christian Church over the past century has been to develop a response to emotions which is consistent with our understanding of the nature of God, of relationships, and our human nature created in the image of God in the light of our ever-increasing knowledge of human psychology.

---

245 Watts, F. (2002). *Psychology for Christian Ministry*, (p. 67). London: Routledge.

Throughout the history of psychology as an academic discipline, the complexity of our emotional landscape has challenged understanding and theory. Many conflicting and complex theories of emotions have been proposed and these too have contributed to the confusion in the Church and the continued dominance of the historical negative interpretation of emotions such as anger, depression and anxiety.

The biblical narrative also presents a picture of contrasting and contradictory responses to the expression of anger. The New Testament gospel of good news reveals the God of love, mercy and grace, whose sacrificial love for us led Jesus to the cross in loving obedience to his Heavenly Father. But alongside this we have to place the anger of God portrayed in a dreadful destructiveness in the Old Testament.

There are over 400 references to God's anger in the Old Testament. Responses to this aspect of God's nature probe at the heart of our understanding of the very nature of God and how God interacts with his creation. One approach sees his anger as a reflection of his holiness and part of his relationship with humankind. Another is to emphasise the passionate nature of God where 'love is experienced not only as peaceful creativeness but as violent breakthrough'.[246] Jurgen Moltmann, a German theologian, develops this in his understanding of the suffering God, suggesting that 'love is the source and the basis of the possibility of the wrath of God . . . As injured love, the wrath of God is not something which is inflicted, but a divine suffering of evil'.[247] Although this is appealing in the sense that it maintains the love of God as the central core of his being while at the same time not denying God's anger, it falls short of explaining the divine destructiveness and terror which we find in some of the Old Testament texts.[248]

There remains a degree of mystery and unease in God's anger. Part of the challenge of our spiritual journey is not only to engage with and respond to God's grace in our lives but also to explore within our dynamic relationship with God how to live with the mystery of his being and active presence in creation.

---

246 Haughton, R. (1981). *The Passionate God*. London: Darton, Longman & Todd, quoted in Campbell, A.V. (1986). *The Gospel of Anger* (p. 8). London: SPCK.
247 Moltmann, J. (1974). *The Crucified God* (p. 272). SCM.
248 Campbell, A.V. (1986). *The Gospel of Anger*. London: SPCK.

The condemnation of expressed anger is echoed throughout the New Testament. Jesus in the Sermon on the Mount says: 'if you are angry with a brother or sister, you will be liable to judgement'.[249] Likewise, Paul in the Letter to the Ephesians writes: 'Lead a life worthy of the calling to which you have been called, with all humility and gentleness, with patience, bearing with one another in love, making every effort to maintain the unity of the Spirit in the bond of peace.'[250] And later in this chapter he writes: 'Be angry but do not sin; do not let the sun go down on your anger.'[251] In this letter, the link between how we behave and our spirituality is clearly recognised. The Christians in Ephesus are instructed in this chapter to deal with anger appropriately. Paul quotes Psalm 4:26 saying that anger should not lead them to sinful behaviour. In other words, they need to manage their anger and deal with it before they sleep at night because, if not, they are vulnerable to the devil. The way we deal with our anger can give us an insight into the kind of spirituality we are living, and also helps to shed light on the way we are living holiness in practice in our lives. We are called to Christian living which demands expressing our anger in ways which reflect the life and love of God. But the tendency to deplore human anger as sinful continues in Christian communities and this has a negative effect on both church communities and the spiritual growth of individual Christians.

Yet, there are obvious examples of Jesus expressing anger. The memorable scene in the temple after his triumphal entry into Jerusalem, when Jesus overturned the tables of the money changers, is arguably when his anger was most dramatically expressed.[252] Here we have a significant example of Jesus exhibiting a necessary expression of anger in response to the misuse of God's house, but its significance goes beyond this as it illustrates that anger can be justified in the face of abuse and injustice.

The acknowledgement of anger leading to a positive outcome goes back to early Christianity. Lactantius in his *Wrath of God* makes the helpful distinction between righteous and sinful anger[253] but, as Watts

---

249   Matthew 5:22
250   Ephesians 4:1-3
251   Ephesians 4:26
252   Matthew 21:12, 13
253   Lactantius. The Wrath of God. In *The Fathers of the Church, vol. 54*, ed. R.J. Defarri. Washington, D.C: Catholic University of America, quoted in Watts, F. (1997). *Zygon* 32(2): 255.

notes, the acceptability of displays of anger was probably dependent on the person's status in society.[254] However, the distinction between different types of anger and whether it can be constructive or destructive depending on the circumstances, is found in much of the psychological literature.[255] There are many situations when anger can lead to positive developments in human relationships as well as to the reversal of acts of injustice and exploitation. This demands a more positive and functional approach to anger. Righteous anger – anger expressed in response to situations of injustice, exploitation and victimisation on behalf of others or in personal situations when something significant is threatened – can be a catalyst for positive development in relationships and eventual outcomes.

The more people care about something or someone, the more likely they are to feel angry when situations lead to disappointment or frustration. Campbell develops this and suggests that the closeness between anger and love can be approached creatively by considering how a loving anger might overcome both apathy and enmity.[256] Anger is also ignited when a person's sense of vulnerability or inadequacy is touched. By reflecting on the circumstances in which anger is elicited, self-knowledge is increased and the emotion managed more appropriately. Any Christian response should therefore incorporate in its framework the adaptive nature of anger and its positive outcomes, as well as the negative effects of its expression.

One of the most fruitful ways to proceed through this maze of contradictory understandings is by building on the distinction between the emotion or feeling of anger and its expression. Condemnation of the aggressive or passive aggressive expression of anger which leads to physical or emotional hurt is a very different matter from condemnation of the emotion itself. This is a point recognised earlier in the discussion of Ephesians chapter 4.

Anger is part of our daily lives and it has an effect on our health and well-being. Luther warns that, without anger, we might reach a state of oblivion where nothing changes and where in the end love itself loses

---

254 Watts, F. (1997). *Zygon* 32(2): 255

255 Bowlby, J. (1980). *Attachment and Loss, vol. 3. Loss, Sadness and Depression.* London: Hogarth Press; Fromm, E. (1973). *The Anatomy of Human Destructiveness.* New York: Holt Rinehart and Winston.

256 Campbell, A.V. (1986). *The Gospel of Anger* (p. 95). London: SPCK.

all power. The way we deal with anger is connected with spirituality.[257] Spirituality is not something to be kept in our hearts but touches all of life, including the words we speak and the way we relate to and interact with others. Many difficult pastoral situations arise through the use or abuse of anger. The confusion and uncertainty it gives rise to, both theologically and personally, cause many Christians to feel lost and lacking in confidence when dealing with it. Frequently, the expression of anger is ignored or avoided. This view is supported by Fox, who observes that the avoidance of anger in Christian communities may remove justified anger from the centre of Christian prayer life.[258] This leads to love of neighbour being confused with 'being nice'. Such 'niceness' can result in a number of negative effects in the ministry of pastoral care, ranging from negative feelings being repressed to the accumulation of resentment and a pattern of denial in relationships which engenders a culture of conflict suppression.[259] Likewise, Campbell argues that, while anger can be denied, it cannot be eliminated from human life.[260] He suggests that the more we refuse to face it, the more it will undermine the possibilities of true Christian love through a cloying 'niceness' or ill-concealed resentment.

How can we respond to anger and the difficult behaviour patterns that arise from it in a way which is hopeful and positive and incorporates our understanding of the gospel and Christian living? An approach of personal re-education and management can lead to changes within the Christian community's approach to anger and passive aggression. This involves discovering the cause of personal anger, working with this constructively, avoiding both angry outbursts and any indirect expressions of the emotion. It also seeks to reduce the anxiety concerning the effect of expressing disagreement in relationships and looks to develop an approach which includes respect for self and others. This requires trust, honesty and, to some extent, taking the risk of vulnerability with others. Recognising our anger, owning it, trying to understand it and communicating it constructively are envisaged as key stages in this process. Wicks claims that, once Christians and

---

257 Ferder, F. (2000). *Words made Flesh* (p. 68). Ave Maria Press.
258 Fox, M. (1979). *On becoming a Musical Mystical Bear*. Philadelphia: Paulist Press.
259 Augsburger, D. (1979). *Anger and Assertiveness in Pastoral Care*. Philadelphia: Fortress Press.
260 Campbell, A.V. (1986). *The Gospel of Anger* (p. 94). London: SPCK.

religious communities stop seeing anger as being either good or bad, and recognise it as a sign of personal vitality, they will be able to distinguish between experiencing the emotion and expressing it.[261] This is essential to managing anger constructively and eliminating the avoidance, passivity, denial and suppression which has led to difficult behaviour patterns in many individuals.

In leadership, the inability to express personal anger or cope with the experience of anger in others can be a major factor in the avoidance of dealing with difficult people. In Christian leadership, it is often the case that shame is associated with personal feelings of anger and also with the discovery that the leader may elicit anger in others. As this chapter has illustrated, such responses can be the source of difficult behaviour patterns in leadership and organisations.

Dealing with difficult people is a necessary task in enabling the Body of Christ to flourish and to fulfil its mission. For some Christians, defining another human being as difficult is to be judgemental and to show a lack of compassion and respect which is out of keeping with the commandment to love our neighbours as ourselves. However, it is undoubtedly the case that there are patterns of behaviour which are difficult to deal with and have a detrimental effect on relationships and the effective functioning of organisations. The mismanagement of anger is arguably one of the underlying causes of some of these common difficult behaviour patterns. By managing our own anger and the anger of others in constructive ways, the vitality encapsulated in this emotion can be directed positively towards building up the Body of Christ for its service in the Church and the world. This depends on good methods of communication, empathetic listening and a more positive approach to our emotional life.

Dealing with Difficult People

How do we manage these difficult people in ways which enable them to modify their behaviour patterns and improve the quality and effectiveness of their relationships?

---

261 Wicks, R.J. (2004). A Threat to Christian Communities: Angry People Acting Passive Aggressively. *Human Development* 25(3): 8–16.

General points:

DO'S

- **Identification of the difficult behaviour pattern.** Identify what are the behaviours that are presenting the problem and analyse these in more detail. What, when and how often? Is there a pattern?

- **Ask questions; keep them simple.** What makes you feel angry about what is happening in the project at present? I am aware that you have taken on this new project, but you already appear to be fully stretched with your other commitments. Would it be better to ask someone else to take on this project? Asking questions of others in the team or organisation is also helpful.

- **Name the problem** and listen to the response of the person concerned with empathy, asking gentle probing questions to uncover what the person is thinking and feeling.

- **Identify possible solutions.** Identify a number of options to address the issue positively.

- **Follow through the chosen plan and monitor regularly.**

The passive aggressive:

DO'S

- Passive aggression arises out of the mismanagement of anger and aggression. It is repressed and hidden. To recognise it, it is helpful **to be attentive to unexpected feelings of anger in ourselves and others**. Passive aggression is covert, and the person behaving in this way may not be sufficiently self-aware to realise the effect of their behaviour on others. They are trying to avoid being seen as aggressive even though they feel negative and angry about something.

- **Empathise and probe gently.** What makes the passive aggressive angry? Within the relationship encourage the discussion of feelings in a non-judgemental way. Build up trust in the relationship.

- **Attend to inconsistencies between their actions and words.** Give them feedback and probe what this might suggest about their feelings.

- **Affirm assertive behaviour**. They are frustrated and annoyed and they cannot express this in an appropriate manner. Affirming their assertiveness encourages them to express their emotions and thoughts and reduces their fear of being judged negatively for doing so.

- **Manage your own expectations of their efficiency and inability to complete tasks.** Work with them to set realistic achievable goals which can be reviewed regularly. This will increase their self-esteem through the achievement of goals and reduce your feelings of frustration with the passive aggressive.

DON'TS

- Agree with their complaints and negative comments but listen to them.

- Be afraid at times to interrupt, especially if you are having difficulty controlling the structure of the conversation.

The super-agreeable:

DO'S

- **Reassurance of personal acceptance and respect for their honest opinions will encourage trust and openness within the relationship.** The super-agreeable person has low self-esteem and is fearful of conflict and disapproval. The more accepted and affirmed the super-agreeable feels, the more likely they are to be honest about their feelings and limitations.

- **Affirm assertive behaviour.** Conflict avoidance is a controlling factor in their behaviour pattern; the affirmation of assertiveness and saying 'no' to requests will enable them to manage their commitments more realistically.

- **Be clear with them on priorities and help them plan their commitments.**

DON'TS

- **Allow them to make unrealistic commitments**

- **Allow tension and disagreement to escalate.** When tension increases, they are more likely to agree to things they cannot achieve.[262]

The hostile aggressive:

DO'S

- **Give them some time to 'calm down'.**

- **Listen and try to ascertain what the cause of conflict/ frustration is, and how they are feeling about it. It is also necessary to be able to express your own feelings.** Good listening skills and the ability to express yourself well are important in resolving a problem involving hostile aggressive behaviour.

- **Draw attention to the way you are being treated without becoming hostile.**

- **Share how you feel, but do not attack the person.**

- **Watch the non-verbal expression of anger and control.** If they are not seated, encourage them to sit down.

- **Maintain eye contact.**

- **Be empathetic and try to establish the facts.**

- **Stand up to the hostile aggressive without fighting!**[263]

DON'TS

- Attack the person.

- Worry about always being polite – you may need to interrupt.

- Argue with what they say or try to demean them.

---

262 Berglas, Stephen. (Fall 2016). Chronic time abuse. In *The Harvard Business Review*, How to work with toxic colleagues, pp. 77–9.
263 Bramson, R.M. (1981). *Coping with Difficult People* (p. 25). New York: Dell.

Conclusion

Difficult behaviours are encountered throughout all organisations. In this chapter, I have examined three types which are commonly cited as the most testing to manage, especially in a Christian context: passive aggressive, hostile aggressive and super-agreeables. These all share difficulties with handling anger, conflict and aggression. I have suggested that the psychological understanding of anger and aggression provides useful insight into analysing these difficult behaviour patterns and developing coping strategies to work constructively with the emotional response which is elicited.

There is confusion and avoidance surrounding anger and its expression in the Christian tradition. This has led to Christian communities failing to deal with difficult people and sometimes to a cloying niceness and lack of growth. This has been explored in the discussion of a Christian response. Many theological questions arise from this, but I have sought to keep this chapter focused on our response. The question of God's anger, to name but one, has received grossly inadequate attention. What is abundantly clear is that, when anger is elicited, it will be expressed. How it is expressed can determine whether the outcome results in a difficult behaviour pattern or not. The consequences of the management of this potent emotion can damage relationships and the effectiveness of an organisation. The way in which anger is expressed by an individual has been shown to be influenced by a number of interacting factors, including parenting style and self-esteem. Dealing with anger requires recognising our own anger, the positive function of anger and how it can be used constructively in relationships and organisations.

Recommended further reading

Bramson, R.M. (1981). *Coping with Difficult People.* New York: Dell.

Campbell, A.V. (1986). *The Gospel of Anger.* London: SPCK.

Keating, C. (1984). *Dealing with Difficult People: How you can come out on top of personality conflicts.* New York: Paulist Press.

CHAPTER SEVEN

Adult Bullying

Brendan Geary and William Macgregor

Stephanie was an administrative officer in a Community Health Centre. Just after joining the centre she was invited to a party by Michael, one of the doctors and the office manager, which led to a period of dating. Stephanie, however, found Michael possessive and controlling. She suggested that they stop seeing each other as a couple. Michael was not pleased, but appeared to accept her suggestion. After that, he was cool towards her and began to find fault with her work. He criticised her at meetings of the practice, but did not find support as the other doctors were pleased with her work. As office manager, he decided to reorganise the administrative assistants' responsibilities and areas of work. He significantly lightened Stephanie's workload and increased the workload of the others. It was obvious to Stephanie that he was using his position to manipulate the situation to make it look as if she was not necessary and could be made redundant.

The word 'bullying' almost immediately brings the playground to mind, and the way that some children are badly treated by others. In recent years, however, there has been a growing awareness that the behaviours we associated with children who ridiculed, attacked, ostracised or threatened others was also part of the culture of many organisations in the adult world. The fallout from the publicity surrounding allegations of sexual abuse by Harvey Weinstein,[264] with the exposure of abuse and exploitation by politicians, celebrities and people in positions of power, has resulted in a higher profile being given to this issue. In February 2018, Oxfam, a highly regarded international aid agency, was at the

---

264   http://www.bbc.com/news/entertainment-arts-41594672. Retrieved 19 February 2018.

centre of allegations of sexually inappropriate behaviour (including the use of prostitutes by Oxfam staff in Haiti[265]), and allegations of a culture of bullying within Oxfam and other international aid organisations. As with other organisations, like the Catholic and Anglican Churches and football clubs, there appears to be evidence that inappropriate and criminal behaviour was covered up to protect the good name of the organisation and powerful individuals.[266] The purpose of this chapter is to look at the disturbing and distressing world of bullying in adulthood.

A search of the professional literature on adult bullying will show little written before the 1970s. Since then there has been an almost exponential growth in research, particularly in the Scandinavian countries, and more research, books, reports, websites, TV and radio programmes devoted to this topic. It is clear now that bullying is pervasive and, as many authors have pointed out, exists wherever human beings have opportunities to use power, and can exploit, manipulate, threaten or inflict pain and unreasonable demands on others.[267]

The issue of bullying in the workplace was given considerable publicity with the award of £817,000 to Helen Green, an administrator at Deutsche Bank in the City of London, as a result of suffering treatment from four female and one male colleague which led to a nervous breakdown. She described their behaviour as 'offensive, abusive, denigrating, bullying, humiliating, patronising, infantile and insulting'.[268] The high award, which was controversial, was partly to compensate for loss of future earnings. This, however, is only one in a series of cases that have changed the legal landscape regarding the issue of workplace bullying.

Further evidence of the change in society's sensitivity to this issue appeared in an edition of the Daily Telegraph in 2007 which carried an article on bullying in the workplace[269] and one that related to bullying in the Church.[270] These two reports demonstrate that in both business and church contexts it is sadly not unusual to find examples

---

265 https://www.thetimes.co.uk/article/top-oxfam-staff-paid-haiti-quake-survivors-for-sexmhm6mpmgw
266 https://www.theguardian.com/commentisfree/2018/feb/12/aid-worker-oxfam-scandal-haiti-abuse-bullying-culture. Retrieved 19 February 2018.
267 https://en.wikipedia.org/wiki/Workplace_bullying. Retrieved 19 February 2018.
268 https://www.workplacebullying.org/uk-green2/
269 *The Daily Telegraph.* (5 September 2007), p. 11.
270 Ibid., p. 3.

of behaviour that could be characterised as bullying. More recently, the death by suicide of Elliott Johnson, a young Conservative party activist, and allegations of bullying in the Conservative party, led to an investigation and the resignation of Grant Shapps, the Party Chairman. Mr Johnson's father, Ray, alleged that his son was caught up in a campaign of victimisation.[271] As can be seen from the above examples, there are reports of bullying in a range of professions, including politics. Sadly, this behaviour also affects the 'caring' professions, like medicine and nursing,[272] international aid organisations[273] and counselling organisations.[274] There have also been allegations of intimidation and harassment by Russian agents against embassy employees and journalists in Moscow, leading to a complaint from John Kerry, at that time US Secretary of State, to President Vladimir Putin.[275]

This chapter will provide a definition of bullying and a description of bullying behaviour and its consequences. There will then be a discussion of the characteristics of perpetrators and victims, as well as a section on bystanders who witness this behaviour. In trying to understand bullying, there will be a discussion of characteristics of workplace cultures that appear to facilitate bullying behaviours, before going on to look at the law on bullying and harassment in Great Britain. The chapter will conclude with suggestions for intervention and treatment, and a discussion of a Christian response to this phenomenon.

What is bullying?

> It is axiomatic that wherever there is power it is likely to be abused, and wherever there is vulnerability there is likely to be exploitation.[276]

Before going further, it is important to provide a description of the phenomenon that is the focus of this chapter. Bullying has been defined as 'the aggressive behaviour arising from the deliberate attempt to

---

271 http://www.independent.co.uk/news/uk/politics/elliott-johnson-death-tory-activist-who-accused-party-of-bullying-killed-himself-coroner-rules-a7058096.html. Retrieved 9 September 2016.

272 https://www.theguardian.com/society/2016/oct/26/nhs-staff-bullying-culture-guardian-survey

273 http://www.bbc.com/news/uk-43107985. Retrieved 19 February 2018.

274 Kierski, W. and Johns-Green, J. (2014). When the bully is a fellow therapist. *Therapy today* 25(4): 20–3.

275 Parfitt, T. and Deng, B. (29 June 2016). Kremlin rewrites rules on scaring diplomats. *The Times*, p. 36.

276 Randall, P. (1997). *Adult Bullying: Perpetrators and Victims*. Routledge, p. 49.

cause physical or psychological distress to others'.[277] There are three important components to this definition. First, it involves aggressive *behaviour*. Bullying involves behaviours that can be identified, observed and, in an empirical sense, measured. It is not sufficient for someone to claim that another person does not like them or is 'out to get them' in some unspecified sense.

Bullying involves actions that can be located on a scale of frequency and intensity. For example, a manager might inform an employee about poor work performance as part of a job appraisal. This ought to be done in private, in a respectful manner, with appropriate professional vocabulary which describes work behaviours in relation to expected outcomes or agreed procedures. On the other hand, the manager might speak to the employee in public, using sarcasm, and in a loud, hectoring voice. This could result in public humiliation, belittlement and intimidation.

Secondly, bullying is deliberate. This takes us into the murky waters of evaluating the intention of another person. We will return to this when considering the legal issues around harassment and bullying. To some extent, an accusation of bullying relies on the subjective experience of the victim. At the same time, if an action is done repeatedly, whether or not it is witnessed by others, it is reasonable to assume some measure of deliberate choice on the part of the perpetrator. It appears that bullying can be both premeditated[278] and opportunistic. A great deal of bullying appears to happen when an opportunity presents itself – e.g. a sarcastic comment, or belittling someone because of alleged poor work. The victim is often in a weak position to defend him or herself due to power imbalances and the culture of the organisation. It is, however, an intentional act, over which the perpetrator has control. Bullying is persistent over time and does not refer to one-off acts.[279]

The use and abuse of power is a central focus of the study of human relationships. Political science concerns itself with ways in which human societies distribute, monitor and control the use of power. In any group of people there will be a pecking order, and variations in the amount of influence that different people possess. Power can be used

---

277 Ibid., p. 12.
278 Clarkson, P. (2008). *Beating the bullies*. London: John Blake, chapter 19.
279 Carter, M., Thompson, N., Crampton, P., Morrow, G., Burford, B., Gray, C. and Billing, J. (2013). Workplace bullying in the UK NHS: A questionnaire and interview study on prevalence, impact and barriers to reporting. *BMJ, open.*, 3(6). e002628.

positively to help groups achieve their aims, and to enable others to use their abilities in pursuit of a group task and personal goals. It can also be used negatively, to manipulate, dominate or coerce others, in order to achieve the goals of one individual or group, with no care for the well-being of others who might be involved.[280] This can be seen, for example, in countries where one ethnic or linguistic group is favoured at the expense of others. Bullying involves the deliberate misuse of power in a way that has a specific, negative impact on another person (or group).

The third important component of the definition is the physical or psychological distress which is caused to another person. It can be reasonably argued that leadership and management require injecting a certain amount of stress into a group, parish, organisation or diocese to generate some energy in order to motivate people to achieve important goals. Research on stress suggests that there is a kind of pressure which generates some adrenalin, increases motivation, and raises levels of performance. This is called *eu*stress, and is distinguished from *dis*tress, which is the kind of pressure that leads to anxiety, decreased motivation, performance deficits, and a range of mental health and psychosomatic illnesses. Bullying leads to distress. No matter how charismatic the leader, if his/her actions lead to physical or psychological distress then this may be bullying behaviour, even if it is dressed up as aggressive management.

Bullying is mainly a psychological phenomenon and it may be hard to distinguish between 'workplace banter' and bullying. It tends to begin subtly, then develop into systematic 'criticism' or 'negative remarks'. It is often done in private and can be harder to prove as there may be no witnesses. Harassment can be psychological but can also be physical – e.g. sexual harassment. It can be easily recognised as harassment due to the overt nature of the behaviour and the specific nature of the language used in legal definitions. It has a clear focus – e.g. ethnicity, gender, sexual orientation. There is more awareness generally regarding harassment and it is a more serious allegation and can result in criminal action.

---

280   See Arbuckle, G.A. (2003). *Confronting the demon: A Gospel response to adult bullying*. Collegeville, MN: Liturgical Press, p. 20.

It may be helpful to consider some of the following data regarding adult bullying:

- It has been suggested that the cost of bullying to organisations in the UK could be as high as £13.75 billion.[281]

- Of the 255,000 doctors, nurses and back-office staff who responded to a questionnaire in 2015, just under 25% reported that they had experienced bullying or harassment.[282]

- According to the WBI U.S. Workplace Bullying Survey (June 2017) 19% of Americans experience bullying and another 19% witness it. The report suggests that 61% of Americans are aware of abusive conduct in the workplace.[283]

- Up to 18.9 million working days are lost as a result of bullying.[284]

- The National Workplace Bullying Advice Line received 5,156 enquiries and 4,598 cases of bullying between January 1996 and May 2001.[285]

- A recent review of European prevalence studies found that between 9% and 15% of employees may experience occasional bullying, with 3% to 5 % experiencing serious bullying.[286]

- In a US survey in 2014, 72% of respondents said that they were aware of bullying in the workplace.[287]

It is clear from these statistics that we are dealing with a subject of major importance to public health and the economy. A significant number of people have been or are victims of bullying, have witnessed others being

---

281 Giga, S.I., Hoel, H. and Lewis, D. (2008). *The costs of workplace bullying.* University of Manchester Institute of Science and Technology.
282 http://www.dailymail.co.uk/news/article-3152886/NHS-bullying-threat-patients-Health-ministers-warning-toxic-culture-survey-finds-quarter-doctors-nurses-staff-fallen-victim.html. Retrieved 9 September 2016.
283 https://www.workplacebullying.org/category/science/
284 http://www.workplacebullying.org/halifaxeveningcourier/. Retrieved 9 September 2016.
285 Peyton, P.R. (2003). *Dignity at Work.* Routledge.
286 Carter, M., Thompson, N., Crampton, P., Morrow, G., Burford, B., Gray, C. and Billing, J. (2013). Workplace bullying in the UK NHS: A questionnaire and interview study on prevalence, impact and barriers to reporting. *BMJ, open.,* 3(6). e002628.
287 http://workplacebullying.org/multi/pdf/WBI-2014-US-Survey.pdf. Retrieved 9 September 2016.

bullied, or are perpetrators of behaviours which should have no place in churches or the workplace. This has now been recognised and people have the protection of law, as has been shown above.

Examples of bullying behaviour

Jonathan

> Jonathan was a member of a legal cooperative in a South London Borough. The cooperative was committed to equal opportunities practice, and actively worked with low-income families, people from ethnic minorities, immigrants, and young people who had become caught up in the criminal justice system. Jonathan, however, was intolerant of anyone who did not show the same commitment to the ideals of the organisation as he (and a select group of friends) did. He frequently berated people at meetings who appeared to be backsliding on the cooperative's values and philosophy. He had alienated the trustees (many of whom worked for prominent City firms) who raised funds for the cooperative's pro bono work. He was also impatient, sarcastic, and belittling of new colleagues who were struggling to adjust to the new work culture and ethic. He was particularly critical of male colleagues whom he would accuse of sexism, racism, patriarchal bias, or abuse of power. Individuals gradually left, with a number breaking away to form their own legal practice.

Joan

> Joan was a parish assistant in an inner-city parish. She was employed after completing a degree in theology, by Fr Frank, a priest whom she had met at some workshops and conferences. Many demands were made on Frank's time by the parish and diocese, and with the decrease in vocations to the priesthood, he saw employing Joan as a way to share the workload and promote lay partnership in ministry. Things went well for three years and then

Fr Frank was transferred to another parish. He was replaced by Fr Joseph who, though younger, was not enthusiastic about having a lay assistant. He reminded Joan continually of the cost of her salary to the parish, and quickly began to be critical of her work. Nothing she did seemed to be acceptable. He would humiliate her at meetings, and, on one occasion, when she was playing the organ at Mass, shouted at her from the altar because music was prohibited at that part of the Mass in this liturgical season. Joan struggled on as she felt a sense of loyalty to the parishioners. However, her self-esteem plummeted, she began to forget commitments, was awkward when speaking from the pulpit or making presentations to parishioners, and found herself apologising continually for mistakes and shortcomings. She took time off work due to stress, and after two months received a letter saying that she was no longer employed at the parish. She had no contract, and felt she would have no redress if she took the case to a tribunal. In any event, she was too afraid and psychologically battered to face going over all that had happened. She eventually returned to live with her parents, entered counselling, and took almost a year before beginning to think about putting her life back together and beginning a new career.

These stories highlight a number of features about adult bullying. In the first place, it involves behaviour by a person who has either *position* power, like Fr Joseph, which is conferred as a result of a role or elected position, or *referent* power. Referent power is power which is given to someone by other people. This would be the situation with Jonathan who was technically an equal in the cooperative, but who was given power by the other members of the group. This also happens in prisons and in neighbourhoods where some families can terrorise other people. Power imbalances are the breeding ground for bullying behaviour, particularly where there are individuals who are vulnerable because of personality or economic or social factors.

Bullying is systematic – i.e. it is repeated over time, is deliberate and designed to cause hurt or embarrassment, or to increase the power and control of the bully in ways that are oppressive or demeaning. It leads to decreased self-esteem, loss of confidence, poor morale in the workplace and unpleasant or hostile atmospheres. The intention of the perpetrator is to bring about pain, distress or belittlement to the victim. Bullying behaviour can involve physical violence, and there is plenty of evidence of violence against employees.[288] However, in most cases the following range of behaviours is involved:

- Aggressive shouting

- Public humiliation

- Work overload

- Unjustifiable or inconsistent discipline

- Constant use of insults

- Unpredictable changes in work routine or holidays

- Exclusion from social events

- Gossip/rumour-mongering

- Intimidation through home contact, text or email messages

- Sexual/racial harassment[289]

- Marginalisation (being sent to Coventry)

- Intimidation

- Discrediting someone's professionalism, directly or through insinuation

- Ridiculing people's arguments at meetings (using scorn)

- Poking fun at people's accent, ethnic features, pronunciation, weight, body shape or disfigurement, or mannerisms.

The development of the internet and text messaging has provided more opportunities for bullying to take place. There has been considerable publicity given to cyberbullying among school children, but it can also

---

288   see Randall, P. (1997). *Adult Bullying: Perpetrators and Victims*. Routledge, pp. 48–9.
289   https://www.gov.uk/workplace-bullying-and-harassment. Retrieved 23 January 2017.

happen in the adult world. Helen Green, who was mentioned at the beginning of this chapter, reported that her name was removed from the firm's global intranet directory and from circulation lists.[290] A group of students at Kent University created a Facebook site which posted offensive and cruel comments about a librarian who was unpopular because he implemented the policy on the need for quiet in the library. Emails can also be used to harass and threaten someone. As has been seen with children,[291] text messages can also invade a person's home and privacy, leading to a feeling of never being able to escape the cruelty of the oppressor(s).

It appears that most workplace bullying is covert rather than overt. It tends to be cumulative, corrosive of well-being and self-esteem, and carried out over the long term. People can become the butt of jokes, or the focus of the ire of a manager, colleague or group of employees. Scandinavian authors write about the phenomenon of 'mobbing', which involves a group of people who systematically bully another individual.[292] Mobbing can easily happen where a group takes pleasure in ridiculing another person. One author gives an example of a gay man who became the victim of a work crew. What may appear as harmless fun can quickly become part of a work culture where certain behaviours or kinds of humour are tolerated, even though they cause considerable distress to the victim. It is extremely difficult for someone to stand up to this without being ridiculed for being soft or overly sensitive. The consequences, though, can be very destructive. In some cases this kind of behaviour has led to mental breakdowns or suicide.

While most research in Britain has focused on bullying by individuals, Charlotte Rayner suggests from research she conducted with over 1,000 part-time students at Staffordshire University that, in fact, most people (81%) are bullied by groups. This can also be seen in offices and workplaces where individuals side with the bullies or patterns of bullying behaviour to curry favour or protect themselves from being victims. It may appear as harmless fun, but it is unlikely

---

290 Clarkson, P. (2008). *Beating the bullies*. London: John Blake, p. 15
291 Clarkson, P. (2008). *Beating the bullies*. London: John Blake. (Various chapters demonstrate this.)
292 Leymann, H. (1996). Mobbing and psychological terror at workplaces. *European Journal of Work and Organisational Psychology* 5: 119–26; Salmivalli, C., Lagerspetz, K., Björkqvist, K., Österman, K. and Kaukiainen, A. (1996). Bullying as a group process: Participant roles and their relations to social status within the group, *Aggressive Behaviour* 22: 1–15.

that the participants would relish finding themselves on the receiving end of their own behaviour. Rayner also suggests that bullying by groups lasts longer, and is more difficult to resolve.[293] An accountant who had worked in a number of firms as trainee, accountant and manager made the observation that it is fairly easy to deal with a 'shouter', someone who tries to get what they want by being loud and aggressive, but subtle group bullying is more insidious and more difficult to challenge and change.

Two special cases: sexual harassment and racism

While bullying has only recently achieved prominence in people's consciousness, the subjects of sexual and racial harassment have long been given attention in law, if not always in employment and social practice.

Racism

What we are describing here is discrimination, or harassment and bullying based on a person's ethnicity. Bullying and discrimination often happen on the basis of perceived difference, and skin colour or ethnic features are very obvious ways of noting difference. This also happens on the grounds of religion, as happened, for example with Jewish people over the centuries, or in Northern Ireland or the West of Scotland, where Catholics were often disadvantaged because of their faith.

Discrimination is a way of keeping power; economic, political or social, in the hands of one group. This can be particularly strong at times of economic difficulty. (It has been shown, for example, that lynching of black people in the United States tended to increase when white workers felt under threat in terms of employment or economic hardship.) Lyn Quine, in a study of workplace bullying in junior doctors, reported that 37% of junior doctors identified themselves as having been bullied in the previous year, but that Black and Asian doctors were far more likely to be bullied than white doctors.[294] A separate study showed that black and ethnic minority NHS staff reported higher levels of bullying than

---

293   Rayner, C. (1997). The incidence of workplace bullying. *Journal of Community and Applied Psychology* 7: 199–208.

294   https://www.ncbi.nlm.nih.gov/pmc/articles/PMC101400/

white staff.[295] Of significance for the next section of this chapter is that Lyn Quine's study showed that female junior doctors were more likely to be bullied than male junior doctors.[296] There have been reports of increases in hate crimes and racial attacks due to fears about the rise in immigration in the UK, and terrorist attacks involving people from Muslim groups.[297]

Discrimination, harassment and bullying thrive where prejudice and ignorance go unchallenged. Groups which are disadvantaged can find themselves victims of abusive, unfair and violent behaviour which is often a result of misplaced aggression, or jealousy at the achievements and good fortune of others.

Sexual harassment

One of the significant historic achievements of the twentieth century in developed countries was the granting of political power to women through the right to vote, and the admission of women to politics, the professions, universities, the armed forces and so on. While there has been rapid advance, it is recognised that women still fall behind men in terms of proportion of promoted positions, high status jobs, equal pay and political influence. Alongside this 'glass ceiling' there is also the reality of sexual harassment.

Sadly, this is still a feature in places of war, where women (and men or boys)[298] are raped or humiliated sexually in various ways. There is also a growing awareness of the numbers of women (and girls) forced into prostitution. However, there is also sexual harassment in the workplace, which can involve flirting, sexual humour and the use of calendars that present women as sexual objects. It can also involve unwelcome attention, coercion for sexual favours, or withdrawal of promotion prospects if sexual favours are not granted. The subject of sexual harassment received international prominence as a result of

---

295   Meikle, James. (2 June 2016). Black NHS more likely to be bullied than white colleagues. *The Guardian.* https://www.theguardian.com/world/2016/jun/02/black-nhs-staff-more-likely-bullied-than-white-colleagues. Retrieved 16 December 2016.

296   Quine, L. (2002). *Workplace bullying in junior doctors: questionnaire survey.* Retrieved 18 October 2007 at http://www.bmj.com/cgi/content/full/324/7342/878

297   http://www.independent.co.uk/news/uk/crime/brexit-hate-crime-racism-stats-spike-police-england-wales-eu-referendum-a7126706.html. Retrieved 9 September 2016.

298   https://www.theguardian.com/world/2017/nov/03/revealed-male-used-systematically-in-libya-as-instrument-of-war. Retrieved 19 February 2018.

the allegations against the film producer, Harvey Weinstein, in October, 2017. According to an article on Wikipedia, 83 women have accused him of harassment or assault and 13 have accused him of rape. On 29 October, a male actor accused Kevin Spacey of having made a sexual advance toward him when he was 14 years of age. Subsequently, more allegations of inappropriate behaviour by Spacey towards young male actors were made, especially during the time that he was artistic director at the Old Vic theatre in London. These allegations led to the series of allegations and revelations that became public on the @MeToo hashtag, which led to further allegations against media personalities, politicians, businessmen and others. Some have referred to this movement as a tipping point in the efforts to support women and men who are victims of sexual harassment. One person commented on the British politics programme, Question Time, that a friend told her that she had never been on the receiving end of an unwanted advance or behaviour by someone who had less power than her in the organisation. There have been cases where people who have harassed others have been exposed in the past, but none have had the same impact as the fallout from the Harvey Weinstein revelations. Weinstein has lost his job and has had honorary degrees and awards removed from him. Others caught up in these revelations have resigned from political positions, including Michael Fallon, the British Minister of Defence. Time Magazine nominated the people who broke silence and shared their stories on @MeToo as the Time Person of the Year, and the heightened awareness of issues related to sexual harassment formed the backdrop to the Golden Globes awards, which took place on 7 January 2018. As noted in the introduction, there have also been allegations of sexual exploitation and abuse against International Aid Workers.[299]

This is not exclusively a female phenomenon as men have also suffered as a result of the unwelcome attention of female managers. Michael Douglas used this as the basis for the film, *Disclosure*.[300]

One of the difficulties in this area is that men and women tend to perceive the issue of sexual harassment differently. It should be borne in mind that men are often in a dominant position in organisations, and humour may be experienced as a way of maintaining power imbalances.

---

299 https://www.theguardian.com/world/2018/feb/10/oxfam-faces-allegations-staff-paid-prostitutes-in-chad. Retrieved 19 February 2018.
300 Levinson, B. (Director). (1994). *Disclosure* (Motion Picture). Warner Bros International.

The important point, however, is that if a woman finds a behaviour offensive and demeaning then an employer who believes in creating a healthy and respectful work environment should make it clear that such behaviour is not acceptable.

Another significant area where bullying is all too often present is in the treatment of homosexuals (this also affects other sexual minorities such as transgender individuals). Homophobia, which can be defined as 'an unreasonable fear of or antipathy towards homosexuals and homosexuality',[301] is best understood as a prejudice against homosexual people. Research suggests that homophobia is more common among people who have strong feelings about traditional gender roles, who are strongly religious, consider sexual orientation to be a matter of personal choice (rather than genetic influence) and are less well educated. It is also more common in men than women. While homosexuals constitute around 4% to 5% of the population, around 30% of young people who commit suicide are homosexual. Research from the United States suggests that 80% of gay, lesbian and bisexual young people have experienced verbal insults, around 35% have been chased or followed, 25% have been sexually assaulted and around 8% have been assaulted with a weapon.[302] 'Gay bashing' has led to murder both in the United States and in Britain (the murders of Matthew Sheppard in the United States and Jody Dobrowski[303] in England both achieved national prominence and, partly as a result of the levels of violence used in the attacks, generated revulsion in the media). Recent changes in public attitude, as expressed in granting the right to marriage to gay people, has revealed a significant advance in the rights of gay and lesbian citizens in many Western countries.[304]

The effects of bullying

In her book, *Dignity at Work*, Pauline Rennie Peyton refers to a Health and Safety Executive claim that 30% to 50% of all stress-related

---

301 Miracle, T.S., Miracle, A. W. and Baumeister, R.F. (2003). *Human sexuality: Meeting your basic needs.* New Jersey: Prentice Hall.

302 Ibid.

303 https://en.wikipedia.org/wiki/Significant_acts_of_violence_against_LGBT_people

304 http://www.pewforum.org/2015/06/26/gay-marriage-around-the-world-2013/. Retrieved 9 September 2016.

illnesses in the workplace are a consequence of workplace bullying.[305] Victims of bullying have reported a range of symptoms, including loss of confidence, stress, a generalised sense of not being able to cope with life, and lowered self-esteem. Some have reported thoughts of suicide and, as noted at the beginning of this chapter, some victims resort to suicide as a result of bullying behaviour.

Gary Namie, Research Director for the Workplace Bullying Institute (WBI) conducted an Instant Poll with 516 people, in 2012, regarding the effects of workplace bullying on mental and physical health.[306] This research has limitations due to the size of the poll, and the fact that these findings cannot easily be generalised, however, the results reflect what is known about the effects of workplace bullying from other reports and sources. Unfortunately, Namie did not ask respondents their gender, however, a previous WBI online survey (2003) noted that 80% of the respondents were female.

Namie reported that the top 15 health problems identified in the survey, in order of highest to lowest frequency, were as follows: anticipation of next negative event, overwhelming anxiety, difficulties with sleep, loss of concentration or memory, uncontrollable mood swings, states of agitation or anger, pervasive sadness, heart palpitations, insomnia, high blood pressure, obsession over personal circumstances, intrusive thoughts, loss of affect, depression, migraine headaches.

Namie noted that anxiety was reported by 80% of the respondents, and that half had been diagnosed with clinical depression. The report shows that 71% had sought help from a doctor, and 63% had contacted a counsellor or mental health professional regarding their symptoms; 22% began to use medication for mental health problems for the first time (e.g. anti-depressants) or required increased dosages; 29% mentioned suicidal thoughts, and 14% had thoughts of violence directed towards others.

This report is helpful as it offers a perspective on the most common effects of bullying. Others have noted the impact on self-esteem and self-confidence of the victims. Being bullied is a profoundly shaming experience. People are suddenly put in a position of exposure, and

---

305   Peyton, P.R. (2003). *Dignity at Work*. Routledge.
306   http://www.workplacebullying.org/multi/pdf/WBI-2012-IP-D.pdf

become vulnerable. There is a cultural expectation that once people leave school they should be able to 'stand on their own two feet' and look after themselves. 'Life isn't fair, and you just have to get used to it' is often the unstated position taken by bullies or some bystanders. People often fail to realise that the systematic, unrelenting nature of bullying significantly undermines the capacity of victims to be more assertive or to defend themselves. A favourite tactic of bullies (and, indeed, torturers) is unpredictability.

Martin Seligman, an American psychologist, noticed that, when shocks were administered to dogs in an unpredictable way – i.e. where they had no control, not even being able to prepare for the effects of the shock – they ceased trying to escape even when it became possible. As Seligman noted, 'Nothing they did mattered.' He labelled this phenomenon 'learned helplessness'. [307] This parallels what we know about approaches to torture which seek to break down the resistance and defences of victims. A similar phenomenon can be seen in bullies, who use their power to demoralise and weaken their victims, often on the basis of whim, rather than as a direct consequence of particular actions.

Some victims of bullying develop the symptoms of post-traumatic stress disorder (PTSD). This is a diagnostic category which is used for people who meet the following criteria:[308]

The person has been exposed to a traumatic event in which both the following are present:

1. the person experienced, witnessed or was confronted with an event or events that involve actual or threatened death or serious injury; or a threat to the physical integrity of self or others.

2. the person's response involved intense fear, helplessness or horror.

People who are diagnosed with PTSD re-experience the trauma in various ways, including distressing recollections, nightmares or flashbacks. They also go out of their way to avoid anything that will remind them or result in having contact with the source of the trauma.

---

307   Seligman, M.E.P. (1990). *Learned optimism* (p. 20). New York: Pocket Books.
308   APA. (1994). *Diagnostic and Statistical Manual of Mental Disorders IV.*

Other symptoms include psychosomatic illnesses similar to those noted by Ellis above, cognitive dysfunction (memory and attention deficits), avoidance of others, either flatness of affect (appearing neither depressed nor interested in life) or extreme mood swings. These will impact all aspects of the person's life. PTSD victims also tend to be hyper-vigilant, anticipating danger and attack at all times.

Victims of bullying, instead of using their energy to achieve important goals, tend to be more focused on avoiding situations where they will encounter the bully. Avoidant striving, as this is called, is a less effective way to manage one's life than achievement striving. Emmons[309] shows that people with a large number of avoidant strivings experience more distress than people who are motivated by positive life goals. Avoidant goals set up the person for failure, as he or she is never rewarded by achievement. One constantly uses up one's energy by being vigilant to escape opportunities for contact with the bully. Examples of avoidant strivings for victims of bullying could be:

- Avoid offending the bully by maintaining a safe distance.

- Avoid eye contact with him or her.

- Avoid disagreements or opportunities for discussion.

- Avoid social situations where he or she will be present.

- Avoid tasks where one might fail or be criticised.

- Avoid conversations that relate to work or performance.

Stress-related illnesses have a significant negative effect on the lives of individuals and on the economy. As we have seen, there are links with a number of illnesses, including some cancers. People who are under severe stress are also more accident prone, which, of course, tends to offer more opportunities for criticism to the bullies. According to The Mental Health Foundation, there is evidence which suggests that 12.7% of all absences from work are due to mental health problems.[310] While not all alcohol, suicide, heart disease or mental health problems are due

---

309   Emmons, R.A. (1999). *The psychology of ultimate concerns.* New York: Guilford.
310   https://www.mentalhealth.org.uk/statistics/mental-health-statistics-mental-health-work

to stress or bullying, there is a direct effect of bullying on mental health and this has an impact on productivity and well-being.

Employers are also beginning to become aware of the costs of bullying on productivity. The price is paid in resentment, lowered morale and its impact on motivation, and a reduced sense of loyalty. This is particularly important in charitable organisations[311] or voluntary organisations like churches. A considerable amount of income is lost due to absenteeism, and replacing workers who leave. If an employee contacts a union representative or uses legal means, then time and money will be spent in hearings and trials. It is often the economic cost that leads to a change in work culture rather than concern for the well-being of employees.[312] While bullying may bring short-term benefits to bullies, and sometimes managers, the long-term costs are increasingly considered unacceptable.

How does bullying develop?

A key question regarding bullying is how people become bullies, given that the word has such a pejorative connotation. There are two main approaches to this question. The first approach looks at the personalities of bullies and victims, and the second looks at the cultures or systems which enable, facilitate or encourage bullying.

The bullies

It is important to bear in mind that all of us are capable of bullying behaviour; we may have memories of participating in the bullying, mocking or humiliation of someone else while at school. However, most of us learn how to curb our tongue and adjust our behaviour when tempted to act in this way. Research on children has shown that children are most vulnerable in the early teenage years, but by the late teens most young people find bullying behaviour distasteful and do not want to be involved.[313] There is also research which suggests that childhood bullies develop into adult bullies, and that they are at risk for a range of negative outcomes, including antisocial behaviours and

---

311 40% of charity workers are bullied, reveals study. (26 December 2007). *The Herald*, p. 7.

312 Randall, P. (1997). *Adult Bullying: Perpetrators and Victims*. Routledge.

313 Pepler, D.J., Craig, W.M., Connolly, J.A., Yhuile, A., McMaster, L. and Jiang, D. (2006). A developmental perspective on bullying. *Aggressive Behaviour* 32: 376–84.

involvement in crime. A study of 500 children suggested that children who were aggressive at eight years of age were more likely to be involved in criminality and violence when they were thirty.[314]

The study of childhood development has shown the importance of early attachments in healthy development. In the first years of life, infants have a range of needs, and are not able to communicate verbally. It is crucial that children experience care and soothing when they experience distress for whatever reason. It is also important that caregivers enable children to learn how to regulate their own strong feelings. The early experiences of soothing and warmth can be built on, once children are able to speak. They learn that internal emotional stress or experiences of frustration, emotional arousal or conflict can be resolved using language and negotiation, rather than resorting to coercive strategies to release tension.

Children also learn from what they see and experience. If parents model aggression, inconsistency and rejection, then that is what the child will learn. Parents, and later teachers, have the important task of socialisation: explaining and maintaining rules and boundaries, encouraging the development of empathy, disapproving and punishing appropriately any solutions which infringe the rights and well-being of others. Children who come from aggressive backgrounds learn aggressive tactics. Likewise, children who see their parents treating others in a disrespectful or exploitative way will learn that this is an acceptable (and effective) approach to achieving their own goals.

Bullies also often have a core sense of self that says 'I am bad', which can lead to poor self-esteem. Parental styles that are authoritative rather than authoritarian or *laissez-faire*,[315] where children can express anger and other feelings but learn how to verbalise their feelings rather than act them out or repress them, tend to lead to children who are socially mature and morally responsible.[316] On the other hand, harsh discipline and parental neglect or rejection can help to sow the seeds of aggression and poor self-image which ripen into bullying and poor self-control in adulthood.

---

314   Eron, L.D., Husemann, L.R., Dubow, E., Romanoff, R. and Yarmel, P.W. (1987). Aggression and its correlates over 20 years. In Crowell, D.H., Evans, I.M. and O'Donnell, C.R. (eds) *Childhood Aggression and Violence: Sources of Influence, Prevention and Control* (pp. 249–62). New York: Plenum.

315   Santrock, J.W. (1999). *Life Span Development*. McGraw-Hill.

316   Randall, P. (2001). *Bullying in adulthood*. Routledge.

There are a number of other factors that can contribute towards the development of an aggressive, bullying personality. These include issues related to poor mental health in the parents, especially the child's mother. The presence of parental conflict, economic difficulties, addictions and other stressors all have their part to play. The presence of one of these stressors may not cause insurmountable problems; however, it is difficult for a child to overcome the effects of multiple deprivations. It is important to make clear that this is not a class issue; bullies can be found at all levels of society.

Bullying personality

Bullies often carry a great deal of 'baggage' from their childhoods. This can result in being envious of others, feelings of loneliness and inadequacy, a fragile self-image, limitations in expressing emotions, and a need to be in control as the world is perceived as dangerous and hostile. They are often loud, taking up more 'emotional space' than their colleagues, and can have an overpowering manner. Unlike mature adults who find the distress of others embarrassing (which is a component of empathy) bullies can continue to inflict pain when a person is clearly at the point of humiliation. They tend to be selfish, self-promoting and indifferent to the needs of others. They are noted liars; they may forget agreements, hide important papers, withhold or provide false information. They also lead the victim to believe that he or she is in the wrong.[317] They tend to have favourites but, as Arbuckle points out, they can create unhealthy relationships where someone becomes dependent on them. The recipients can feel obliged to behave in submissive ways. The choice of favourite can also change rapidly, with a previous favourite becoming the next victim.[318]

Some bullies fit the description of antisocial or narcissistic personality disorders, or have identifiable features of these two disorders. People (mostly men) with antisocial personality disorder lack empathy, tend to be impulsive, can have superficial charm, but are callous and irritable. They are easily aroused to anger and can be unpredictable in their behaviour and relationships. Adolescent units and prisons contain a

---

317 Peyton, P.R. (2003). *Dignity at Work*. Routledge.
318 Arbuckle, G.A. (2003). *Confronting the demon: A Gospel response to adult bullying*. Collegeville, MN: Liturgical Press.

high percentage of these individuals as they tend to be contemptuous of social norms, and their need for excitement leads them into criminal behaviour and substance abuse. Churches are not immune to these people. There have been cases of embezzlement, and, of course, there is the behaviour of some clerical child molesters. There are also some church personnel whose behaviour seems far from the values of the gospel, and leaves many hurt individuals – fellow clergy and parishioners – in its wake. These people surround themselves with sycophants, and use religion for their own purposes. They are, of course, spiritually shallow, often going through the motions rather than being open to personal conversion.[319]

Narcissistic people have an inflated sense of their own importance, and use people to gratify their own needs. Like people with antisocial personality disorder they can be exploitative, but tend not to be aggressive or recklessly impulsive. They tend to over-promote themselves, and then blame others for their failures. They are intolerant of criticism, and cannot accept responsibility for failures or mistakes. Such individuals may bully others to reduce their frustration when they are not promoted or appreciated in the way they feel they deserve.[320]

Differences between men and women

One of the clearest differences between men and women is in the area of aggression. Simply put, men appear to be more violent and prone to use force to solve problems and get their own way than women.[321] There are significantly more men than women in prison. Almost 90% of sex offenders are men. The play of boys and girls is also different, with more rough and tumble play among boys and more relational and conversation-based play among girls. This difference also appears to manifest itself in bullying behaviour. Adolescent girls tend to use indirect methods of aggression, such as backbiting, gossip, social exclusion and belittling, while boys appear to use more direct methods, such as physical hitting, pushing, shoving and taking revenge in games. [322]

---

319 Sperry, L. (1998). The psychopathic minister. *Human Development* 19(2): 34–7.
320 Randall, P. (2001). *Bullying in adulthood*. Routledge
321 Baron-Cohen, S. (2005). *The Essential Difference*. Penguin.
322 Björkqvist, K., Lagerspetz, K.M.J. and Kaukiainen, A. (1992). Do girls manipulate and boys fight? *Aggressive Behaviour* 18: 117–27.

In adulthood, both men and women make use of covert aggression, but men tend to focus on performance, and use aggression that has a 'pseudo rational' basis in the context of work – i.e. the focus of the bullying will appear to relate to an aspect of poor work performance. Women, on the other hand, are more likely to use social manipulation, or find ways to criticise personal features or belittle the person. The tendency of women to use social manipulation and covert forms of bullying may make it more difficult for a manager to confront the problem, as tensions may be explained away or may masquerade as personality differences. While bullying of women by women may not be given as much prominence as bullying sexual harassment by men, it can be no less destructive or harmful to the well-being of the victim or to the morale in an office, parish or workforce.

Victims

Bullies often choose people who are vulnerable as their victims. People who are different – for example, homosexual men and women, or people from religious or ethnic minorities, are often chosen as the victims of bullying. Victims are often highly conscientious, law abiding, and afraid to take risks or assert themselves. They tend to have low self-esteem, be submissive and sensitive, and more prone to experience anxiety and depressed moods.

Those who have studied the personalities and developmental histories of victims have noted that children who were bullied often become victims in adulthood. It has been shown that children with parents who are under- or over-controlling in their parenting style can grow up feeling anxious and insecure, lacking in social awareness, with poor ability to be assertive in the face of aggression. One author used the phrase 'submission reaction pattern' to describe their default coping strategy.[323] They often have problems in interpersonal relationships, are lonely and in need of friends. Sadly, they often elicit little sympathy from their peers, and teachers (and later supervisors and managers) may do little to intervene to help them when they are bullied. It is not unusual to hear people say, 'He asked for it.'

---

323   Olweus, D. (1993). *Bullying at school: What we know and what we can do.* Oxford: Blackwell.

The bystanders

Many people have seen their colleagues being bullied. A Finnish study on aggression among university employees, for example, reported that 32% of the respondents had witnessed bullying,[324] and research in an NHS Community Trust suggested that 42% of employees had witnessed one or more types of bullying.[325] Witnesses to bullying are often afraid to act in case they become the next victim, or simply may not want to become involved. Witnesses can also be affected by stress and insecurity, and it appears that one in five may leave their place of employment.[326]

Organisational factors

Bullying has been looked at as the outcome of a relationship between bullies, victims and the organisation they are part of. Each organisation has its own culture which embodies a set of values, with behaviours that are acceptable and others that are unacceptable. Bullying can be tolerated or sometimes flourish in certain cultures. A culture can be defined as:

> A pattern of shared meanings and values, embodied in a network of symbols, myths and rituals, created by a particular group as it struggles to adjust to life's challenges, educating its members about what is considered to be the orderly and correct way to feel, think and behave.[327]

Some cultures, such as politics, management and football, appear to encourage or value people who can dominate and abuse others. Some football managers have been admired for their bullying attitudes to the players. In the world of entertainment, the TV show, *The Apprentice*, appears to enshrine bullying as a management tactic in testing prospective entrepreneurs.[328] Patriarchal systems encourage oppressive

324 Björkqvist, K., Österman, K. and Hjelt-Back, M. (1994). Aggression among university employees *Aggressive Behaviour* 20: 173–84.
325 Randall, P. (2001). *Bullying in adulthood*. Routledge.
326 Higginbottom, K. (3 November 2007). Innocent bystanders? *The Guardian*, Work section: 1–2.
327 Arbuckle, G.A. (2003). *Confronting the demon: A Gospel response to adult bullying*. Collegeville, MN: Liturgical Press, p. 67.
328 Jones, F. (2006). More questions than answers. *The Psychologist* 19(10): 640.

behaviour towards women, and some cultures are permissive of racism and sexual harassment. Church cultures also have features that can facilitate bullying behaviour.

The quality of the work environment is an important factor in understanding bullying. Lack of effective leadership, poor opportunities to exercise personal control over work, and role conflict all contribute to a culture where bullying can emerge.[329] Bullying is also more likely to occur where there is an extremely competitive environment, especially if people fear for their job security. This can also be compounded by authoritarian management styles, and the uncertainty caused by organisational change or excessive workloads. Work cultures that place a lot of emphasis on targets may also contribute to cultures of bullying. Melanie Reid writes:

> The right targets force the system to respond . . . but in so many areas we have reached the point when the pressure becomes pressure for its own sake; when it amounts to institutional bullying and causes mental ill health and leaves the workforce sour and miserable. Unremitting targets ultimately result in exhaustion and jiggery-pokery, not greater efficiency.[330]

While bullying can be done by peers, and sometimes by people in lower positions than the victim (see Dirk Bogarde in the film, *The Servant*,[331] where a servant bullies and controls the rich young man he is paid to look after), it is most often the case that a manager, boss or supervisor is the bully.

The Church as a culture where bullying can develop

There have been a number of reports of church leaders being accused or found guilty of bullying, including the Archbishop of Granada, in Spain, who was fined €3,750 after being convicted of bullying by a

---

329 Rayner, C. and Hoel, H. (1997). A summary review of literature relating to workplace bullying. *Journal of Community and Applied Psychology* 7: 181–91.
330 Reid, M. (4 February 2007). *The Times*, p. 19.
331 Losey, J. (Director). *The Servant* (Motion Picture). Springbok Films.

former canon of the city's cathedral.[332] There have also been instances in the Church of England, with a vicar being found guilty of bullying by a church tribunal,[333] and of an Oxford college being accused of bullying by a former member of the lecturing staff.[334] The Churches, which exist to promote the values of the Kingdom of God, are, sadly, places where bullies can be found.

The website www.balmnet.co.uk exists as 'A resource for damaged ministers'. It makes available stories of ministers who have felt bullied by their congregations (or significant groups in congregations), by superiors or colleagues. Members of religious communities, curates, deacons, parish assistants and lay workers can all become victims of bullying in church contexts. In some ways, the Christian teaching of offering forgiveness, turning the other cheek and loving your enemies can be distorted or misapplied in situations of exploitation or abuse. One person described a church worker as *pastoral aggressive* in her ability to use Christian principles, guilt and moral manipulation to bully others into doing what she wanted.

Ministers are often encouraged to pray for those who cause them harm, to see this as a test of their faith or commitment or to extend understanding to the perpetrator. Church cultures are often uncomfortable with anger and the expression of strong feelings, so bullies can thrive as many churchgoing people would rather rationalise, deny or repress conflict than confront it honestly. Often in circumstances of conflict between an incumbent and a curate or worker, the worker or curate is moved and the incumbent is allowed to continue as before. The characteristics of bullies, victims and organisational cultures described above all apply to church contexts. The lack of clear roles, poor leadership and unclear lines of accountability can contribute to stress at times when a priest, minister or other superior is changed. Recent unpublished research on Roman Catholic deacons shows that the arrival of a new priest can result in considerable distress and anxiety on the part of deacons who are almost completely dependent on the good will and attitude of the priest. Deacons also indicated a desire for

---

332   Bullying archbishop convicted. (15 December 2007). *The Tablet*, p. 31.
333   Gledhill, R. (24 January 2008). Vicar branded a liar and a bully and should be sacked, tribunal rules. *The Times*, p. 37.
334   Yeoman, F. (8 January 2008). Christian broadcaster sues church college. *The Times*, p. 19.

role clarity. This makes sense as they would then be less susceptible to the whims and priorities of changing parish priests.[335]

Bullying, harassment and the law

Before going on to explore what can be done, it is important to look at the law regarding bullying and harassment. All people have the right to go to work and be free from discrimination, harassment and any other form of interference with their legal right to seek employment and be safe and secure in the work place. Yet it is clear given the weight of case law in this area that discrimination, harassment and bullying do occur and, sadly, often. The law protects both the employee and the employer from this kind of action and has enacted several statutes to provide legal mechanisms for the resolving of such situations.

The law is at pains to distinguish between bullying and harassment in the workplace, not least because harassment implies a greater degree of trauma than bullying. At present, there is no legal definition of bullying either supplied by statute or common law (Act of Parliament or precedent). This creates a problem in one sense as, given the law does not provide a definition of the term, bringing action against the alleged bullies has to be done on a subjective and case by case basis, with the court, or more likely the Employment Tribunal, having to be convinced that behaviour amounting to bullying has taken place.

Bullying in the workplace

Bullying in the workplace still continues. However, since the enactment of the Equalities Act 2010, employees are now offered greater protection.[336] This Act makes employers liable for damages for the actions of employees towards one another. All companies and large organisations now have grievance and disciplinary procedures in place that govern the interaction of managers and staff.[337] Once activated, these procedures place an onus on the employer to ensure that complaints are taken seriously and that an investigation of them

---

335   Geary, B. (2007). Unpublished research data on 247 Roman Catholic Deacons in England and Wales, and Scotland. Ushaw College, Durham.

336   https://www.gov.uk/workplace-bullying-and-harassment

337   Required by sec 199 Trades Union and Labour Relations (Consolidation) Act 1992 (TULRCA).

is carried out. Failure to do so would make the employer liable for damages to the employee at any subsequent tribunal hearing.[338]

While the Equalities Act provides safeguards for the employee, the UK Coalition Government muddied the waters in 2012 by introducing tribunal fees into the system. This has been a controversial move as the number of cases taken to tribunal has plummeted since the introduction of fees. There is still no legal definition of bullying, although the Protection from Harassment Act 1997 does define harassment in section 8 as:

> a course of conduct which amounts to harassment of another and –
>
> (a) is intended to amount to harassment of that person; or
>
> (b) occurs in circumstances where it would appear to a reasonable person that it would amount to harassment of that person.

A table of current legislation is shown below.

Cyberbullying

Cyberbullying is more problematic and has received more attention from the mass media in the last few years, especially when it has led to the death of an individual. Cyberbullying is the modern equivalent of the 'poison pen letter'. While it can be agreed that bullying in any form will cause some harm to the recipient, it is the definition of what constitutes the act of cyberbullying that seems to give most legislatures trouble.

The Canadian lawyer and broadcaster, Sam Middlemiss, provides the following useful definition: *'Cyberbullying involves the use of information and communication technologies to support deliberate, repeated and hostile behaviour by an individual or group that is intended to harm others.'*[339]

While the law now deals with harassment as a type of abuse, it has been slow to catch up with the development of the internet as a medium for the transmission of aggression and threats. Members of

---

338 See ACAS guidance for procedures to be followed http://www.acas.org.uk/index.aspx?articleid=1461
339 http://cyberbullying.org/

the general public meanwhile have been quick to use this new medium of expression to vent their spleen at their victims in an environment which has been likened to the old Wild West,[340] where it can appear that they are beyond the reach of the law. While bullying *per se* is not a specific criminal offence anywhere in the UK, it is important to remember that some types of harassing or threatening behaviour – or communications – could be a crime – for example, under the Protection from Harassment Act 1997, the Malicious Communications Act 1988, the Communications Act 2003, and the Public Order Act 1986.[341] In relation to Scotland, there may also be recourse to Section 38 or 39 of the Criminal Justice and Licensing (Scotland) Act 2010.

As can be seen from the list of legislation below, the Acts that are being used to control this type of behaviour were written some considerable time ago; indeed, many were written before the internet was even thought of or for situations that are entirely different from online behaviour – e.g. the Public Order acts.[342] The result of this approach is a mishmash of pre-internet broadcast and telephone network controls that are out of date. What is required now is a review of current legislation and new protections for online users that prohibit bullying and harassment and control and regulate adult material. Given the number of needless deaths caused by online bullying, it is time that Parliament took notice of this aspect of social behaviour and provided some much-needed safeguards.

Legislation

The following legislation may be applicable to instances of cyberbullying and harassment.

Public Order Act 1986	Sections 8–11 apply to Scotland
Communications Act 2003	Section 127
Malicious Communications Act 1988	Section 1

---

340 Jacob Rowbottom. (2012). *To rant, and converse: protecting low level digital speech*; Cambridge Law Journal.
341 Sections 8-11 relate to Scotland only and reflect the unique position of Scots Law.
342 Jacob Rowbottom. (2012). *To rant, and converse: protecting low level digital speech*; Cambridge Law Journal.

Protection from Harassment Act 1997	Section 2A
Offensive Behaviour at Football Matches and Threatening Communications (Scotland) Act 2010	Section 6 and subsequent
Criminal Justice and Licensing (Scotland) Act 2010	Section 38 or 39
Defamation Act 1996	(in Scotland)
Defamation Act 2013	(in England and Wales)

The Acts detailed above are available in full from www.hmso.gov.uk.

The main issue in cases of bullying is whether procedure has been followed. As in all areas of law, procedural impropriety leads to appeals and the overturning of verdicts or judgements and can be a *prima facie* reason for a case coming before the court. Employers are required to lay down legal provisions for the protection of their employees against bullying and harassment. Complaint and grievance procedures should be made clear in case that protection should fail.

Constructive dismissal is where, due either to an act or omission of the employer, a member of staff feels it necessary to resign. For example, if a head teacher of a school was being blanked and ignored by the chair of governors and other members of the governing body to the point where he/she could not do his/her job and subsequently resigned, he or she could sue for constructive dismissal. The governors have acted in bad faith, causing the resignation of the head. That is illegal.

Points to note:

1. If a person makes an allegation of bullying, the employer is legally obliged to investigate and, if necessary, impose sanctions on the bully.

2. Failure to do so by the employer is a breach of a statutory duty.

3. In some cases, both the employer *and* the employee who is the bully are liable. Under the principle of vicarious liability, the

employer takes the legal consequences of any action brought against employees while acting in the course of their duty as employees. However, in order to remedy the loss arising from the action brought against the company, they may dismiss the offending member of staff. In addition, the claimant suing the employer may also seek separate – even criminal – action against the bully.

4. Procedures are vitally important for protection not only of the employee but also of the *employer*. Lack of grievance procedures is not only unadvisable, it is illegal.

Most people's first point of contact with these issues is through ACAS, which has an extremely helpful and accessible website (www.acas.org.uk) with a free e-learning programme to guide people through the relevant issues on harassment and bullying. There are often issues concerning redress. ACAS is able to offer free legal advice in this area. Very often cases relate to some form of sexual harassment and relevant statutory provision will be found in the Equality Act 2010. Before contacting solicitors, it is worth checking first with ACAS.

Responses and interventions

Organisations and churches should have clear anti-bullying and anti-harassment policies. However, having the policies is not enough. It is necessary to provide training for managers and employees, to ensure clear procedures for reporting any abusive behaviour. It is also important to train managers in early recognition of bullying behaviours. It is often the case the bullying behaviour is tolerated or even valued within the culture of the organisation. Managers and clergy need to actively create an environment which fosters open communication, respect for employees, clients or members of congregations, and dignity, security and trust in those in authority. Involvement in Employee Assistance Programmes (EAPs) can also help to provide support for those who suffer as a result of bullying.

As well as having good policies, it must be clear that policies will be implemented when necessary, and that anyone found to be bullying or harassing an employee will be dealt with appropriately. Having said that, there must be even-handedness, and victims may also be required to change aspects of their behaviour. It is essential that victims or managers keep written records detailing any incidents and the attendant circumstances. In larger organisations it is important to make use of the personnel department and trade union representatives. Small organisations often have no trade union representatives, and if there is an unpleasant work culture bullying can continue unchecked. Employees are reluctant to invoke formal mechanisms, as seeking redress can have serious implications for future career prospects and working relationships.

There is evidence to suggest that morale is higher in organisations that have specific anti-bullying policies. A report from the University of Portsmouth Business School (2006) suggests that effective action on bullying leads to lower absence rates, fewer incidents of abuse, with resultant investigations and possibly legal action, and a committed workforce which values diversity and inclusivity.[343]

Intervention

Can bullying be treated? Randall provides a number of case histories but is rather lukewarm about the benefits of counselling for bullies.[344] Peyton suggests that it depends on the type of bully. She suggests that bullies who are afraid and vulnerable themselves, who have low self-esteem and who feel that they are being persecuted, can be helped with coaching and training. This also applies to those whose behaviour is based on copying behaviour that has been modelled by other managers. Again, retraining and coaching can be helpful for these people. The bullies who are self-righteous, with antisocial personality features, are less likely to benefit from counselling, coaching or retraining, as they will tend to see victims as the source of the problem rather than themselves. Counselling and assertiveness training can, of course, be helpful and sometimes necessary for victims. Peyton has excellent advice and information for counsellors and managers,[345] and the website of the Andrea Adams Consultancy (http://www.andreaadamsconsultancy. com/) is also well worth visiting for advice for victims and managers.

---

343 https://www.ulster.ac.uk/__data/assets/pdf_file/0017/227033/bullying_in_the_workplace_2.pdf
344 Randall, P. (1997). *Adult Bullying: Perpetrators and Victims*. Routledge.
345 Peyton, P.R. (2003). *Dignity at Work*. Routledge.

Susan Johnson, in an article on workplace bullying prevention, notes that managers can contribute to the prevention of bullying through their presence, the promotion of normalising behaviours, including modelling appropriate behaviours and highlighting codes of conduct and organisational values, and controlling unacceptable behaviour by catching it early, intervening and enforcing behavioural standards. She also noted that most managers preferred to use soft disciplinary techniques, such as pointing out inappropriate behaviours, rather than using disciplinary procedures. The consequence of this approach is that bullying can continue to flourish and members of staff can suffer.[346]

Lastly, Professor Cary Cooper of Lancaster University recommends that those who witness bullying should not turn away but should inform the Human Resources department or a supervisor. They can also help the bullied by expressing concern and support. They should also not be afraid to act, as the whole organisation suffers when bullying is allowed to continue unchecked.[347]

A Christian Response

The Psalms, which were the foundation of Jesus' prayer, regularly invoke God on the side of the poor and oppressed. In Psalm 142, for example, we read:

> Rescue me from persecutors
> stronger than I am.
> Free me from this imprisonment,
> And I will thank your name once more.[348]

The story of Susanna in the book of Daniel (Daniel 13) is a clear example of bullying and sexual harassment. Two judges, who were elders in the community, attempted to have a woman who resisted their sexual demands put to death. The case is brought before Daniel who discovers the dishonesty of the two judges.

---

346 Johnson, S. (2015). Workplace bullying prevention: A critical discourse analysis. *Journal of Advanced Nursing* 71(10): 2384–92.

347 Cooper, C. (2007). In Higginbottom, K. (3 November 2007). Innocent bystanders? *The Guardian*, Work section, p. 2.

348 *Jerusalem Bible*. (1966). DLT.

Jesus began his ministry by quoting from the prophet Isaiah:

The spirit of the Lord has been given to me,
for he has anointed me.
He has sent me to bring the good news to the poor,
to proclaim liberty to captives
and to the blind new sight,
to set the downtrodden free.

Luke 4:18 (Jerusalem Bible)

Jesus ministered to people from all sections of society, but clearly had care for those who were marginalised, rejected or bullied. The woman taken in adultery, for example, was being bullied by the men who dragged her in front of Jesus (John 8:1-11), and Zacchaeus (Luke 19:1-10), although in a position of power because of his role as a tax collector, was marginalised and considered a sinner. However, Jesus chose to dine at his house.

Christians, when faced with violence of any kind, find themselves challenged to support the weak and vulnerable, but not to reject the perpetrator. Jesus' injunctions to 'forgive seventy times seven', and to 'love your enemies, including those who persecute you', have enabled Christians to extend empathy to perpetrators of violence and have provided a basis for rehabilitation of offenders. On the other hand, Jesus also advises his followers: 'If your brother does something wrong, reprove him' (Luke 17:4). Avoidance of conflict and denial of the existence of difficulties are not Christian virtues.

Gerard Arbuckle offers five principles for preventing bullying, which are worth repeating here:

1. Recognise that bullying is an evil and an assault on the dignity of the human person.

2. Acknowledge that everyone is capable of bullying because we are all prone to sin.

3. Understand that God has a preferential love for the victim and so must the followers of Christ.

4. Foster the values and structures of openness in organisations and clearly state that bullying is to have no place in them.

5. Identify and challenge prejudices within oneself, one's workplace and one's community, because prejudices lie at the root of bullying.[349]

Perhaps the most important injunction for Christians is to 'do unto others as you would have them do unto you'. If we place ourselves in the position of victims, what would we want from others? As Gerald Arbuckle writes, God is on the side of the victim and the oppressed. A Christian response requires support for the victims, positive interventions to prevent bullying, and active approaches to management to create, disseminate and implement anti-bullying policies in workplaces and churches.

Cardinal Cardijn,[350] who founded the Young Christian Workers' movement, encouraged the use of a simple formula: See – judge – act.[351] Christians are asked to look carefully at what is happening in their community, church or place of work. This involves an ability to stand back and notice how people are being treated and affected by the behaviour of others. The second stage involves making an evaluation of what is seen. Is this respectful of people? Is it furthering the goals of the organisation? Are the values of the organisation being put into practice or ignored or undermined in some way? Is this consistent with my own values and beliefs?

The third stage involves action.[352] This is undoubtedly the hardest part when it comes to witnessing bullying or harassment. Laws protecting whistle-blowers, for example, would not exist unless there were serious costs to reporting criminal or abusive behaviour. At the same time, it is not difficult to see the cost of looking the other way or passively supporting behaviour which we would not condone. The Church of England, in its report concerning care of vulnerable adults, offers the following reflection:

> Jesus constantly showed himself to be compassionately on the side of the outcast, the marginalized and the stranger,

---

349 Arbuckle, G.A. (2003). *Confronting the demon: A Gospel response to adult bullying*. Collegeville, MN: Liturgical Press, pp. 97–111.
350 https://en.wikipedia.org/wiki/Joseph_Cardijn
351 https://www.ycw.org.au/index.php
352 Graham, E., Walton, H. and Ward, F. (2005). *Theological reflection: Methods*, chapter 6. Praxis. SCM.

reaching across social barriers with the inclusive love of God ... The risen Christ's commission to his followers ('As the Father has sent me, so I send you' [John 20:21]) requires the Christian Church to exercise that same concern for those whom some in society treat as the outsider and the stranger, to reach across barriers of exclusion and demonstrate a love which shows itself in compassionate pastoral care and in the quest for justice in all our relationships.[353]

However, the authors were also aware of the costs of intervening and reporting, and include a recommendation that 'Colleagues should not be penalized for following this guidance or for taking action regarding others and this guidance.'[354] The decision to act requires good judgement and an awareness of possible consequences. As has been seen in the Churches and in the professional world of childcare, clerical and other cultures can exert a powerful influence over people to keep silent and conceal malpractice and abuse. While it is easy to encourage intervention, only the person in his or her circumstances can weigh the various benefits and costs and decide what is right in his or her situation.

Conclusion

This chapter began with the story of Stephanie, who was bullied by one of her bosses. Stephanie spoke to the other administrative assistants and told them that she would not be helping them with their workloads, as had been their normal practice, as it would lead to the perception that she was underworked. The senior partner was made aware of the situation and called a practice meeting to say that the current arrangements were not working and a reorganisation of workloads was necessary. Stephanie kept her job, but Michael was never confronted. Low-level hostile aggression, with sniping and subtle belittling, continued. It would have been gratifying to suggest that he was confronted and his behaviour changed, but sadly that is not the typical outcome of these situations at present.

---

353 *Promoting a Safer Church.* (2006). Policies for safeguarding adults in the Church of England. 1.4, p. 3. Available at https://www.churchofengland.org/sites/default/files/2017-11/promotingasafechurch.pdf

354 Ibid. 2.4., p. 15, Available at https://www.churchofengland.org/sites/default/files/2017-11/promotingasafechurch.pdf

This chapter has attempted to present information about the incidence and effects of bullying in workplaces and churches. Characteristics of bullies, victims, bystanders and organisational cultures have been explored. Legal issues have been clarified with up-to-date information with respect to the law on bullying and harassment. Recommendations for intervention have been offered and a Christian response has been suggested for those who work in organisations and churches.

Do's and Don'ts

- DO have anti-bullying policies in place.

- DO ensure that policies are implemented where necessary and appropriate.

- DO provide training for employees and managers.

- DO make use of Employer Assistance Programmes.

- DO not pretend that bullying cannot exist in your organisation or church. Caring professions are just as susceptible to bullying as are industrial and commercial organisations.

- DO create a work culture that values honesty, open communication, respect, trust and the dignity of all.

- DO maintain an ethos of professionalism, with appropriate professional courtesies and manners.

- DO provide support for victims, and counselling and/or training for bullies.

- DO not walk away from incidents of bullying, but report to those who are responsible.

- DO keep written notes of incidents and circumstances.

- DO be informed regarding the law and procedures in your organisation.

- DO avoid racist and sexist language and humour that offends colleagues.

Recommended reading

Arbuckle, G.A. (2003). *Confronting the demon: A Gospel response to adult bullying.* Collegeville, MN: Liturgical Press.

Peyton, P.R. (2003). *Dignity at Work.* Routledge.

Randall, P. (1997). *Adult Bullying: Perpetrators and Victims.* Routledge.

The following websites are also helpful:

- www.balmnet.co.uk – bullied and abused lives in ministry.
- http://www.acas.org.uk/ – information and free advice.
- www.hmso.gov.uk – Acts of Parliament.

CHAPTER EIGHT

The Digital Age

Bex Lewis

The twenty-first century is commonly described as the digital or information age. In 2008, a Christian event was advertised as follows:

> There is a revolution sweeping across the globe, driven by the massive growth of the internet and internet related technologies. Known as the Digital Revolution it is on par with other great global shifts such as the Agrarian Revolution and the Industrial Revolution. And it is completely changing the landscape of how we communicate, how we influence, how we relate. This isn't simply about coming to grips with a new technology to assist us in our work, but requires of us a fundamental shift in our processes, our structures and approaches. If we don't respond then as Eric Hoffer states, we will find ourselves, 'beautifully equipped to deal with a world that no longer exists.'[355]

In 2015, in the Richard Dimbleby lecture, Martha Lane-Fox, formerly the UK government's Digital Inclusion Champion, said, in a much shared quote, 'The internet is the organising principle of our age, touching all our lives, every day. As the late activist, Aaron Swartz, put it, *"It's not OK not to understand the internet anymore"*.' At present we may use sites such as Facebook and Twitter for social purposes, but must acknowledge that they are subject to economic rather than philanthropic pressures. Lane-Fox was calling for a more engaged process, in which relationships could be transformed rather than for simple monetary exchange.[356] Aside from 'digital pockets', the Church has been slow to pick up on the opportunities for digital transformation.

---

355 The Anglican Cathedral of Second Life. (2008). 'The Digital Revolution and the Church'. Retrieved from: https://slangcath.wordpress.com/2008/12/03/the-digital-revolution-and-the-church/

356 Lane-Fox, M. (2015), 'Dot Everyone: The Richard Dimbleby Lecture 2015'. https://www.bbc.co.uk/mediacentre/speeches/2015/martha-lane-fox-dot-everyone

In 2013, Batts' research showed us that, while many churches are finally starting to get that the online landscape is important, they still need convincing that something more radical is needed than a new website, and are typically seen as being progressive when there are opportunities for (digital) interaction within a service, rather than seeing the digital as part of the bigger picture for the Church as a whole, including pastoral situations.[357]

Has everything changed?

There is no doubt that there have been profound changes in recent decades, although with a combination of continuous negative media stories and a feeling that 'everything has changed', there is a sense of panic surrounding the impact of digital technologies upon our contemporary culture. Krinsky defines this:

> A moral panic may be defined as an episode, often triggered by alarming media stories and reinforced by reactive laws and public policy, of exaggerated or misdirected public concern, anxiety, fear, or anger over a perceived threat to social order.[358]

We need to remember that, so far as the news is concerned, bad news is really the only kind of news, so we get a warped view of what technology is doing to us as a society, and particularly in relation to topics such as abuse, addiction and difficult behaviour. Media Studies lecturer, Marcus Leaning, refers to the huge amount of early research that concentrated on online identity, which was heavily focused on the loss of face-to-face clues, and on deceit. These academic attitudes have filtered down into everyday thinking and continue to feature in the press, and help us understand why online identity remains such a huge concern to society.[359] If we were to rely upon newspaper headlines in relation to people online, particularly children, we would

---

357 Batts, S. (2013). 'Informing, inviting or ignoring? Understanding how English Christian churches use the internet'. Unpublished PhD thesis, http://phdinprogress.wordpress.com

358 Krinsky, C. (2013). *The Ashgate Research Companion to Moral Panics*. Retrieved from: http://www.ashgate.com/pdf/SamplePages/Ashgate-Research-Companion-to-Moral-Panics-Intro.pdf, p. 1.

359 Leaning, M. (2009). *The Internet, Power and Society: Rethinking the Power of the Internet to Change Lives*. Chandos, p. 1.

see only disaster: children are addicted to screens, being abducted via Facebook, giving away all their information, sexting, running up bills, becoming couch potatoes, watching porn, meeting strangers, and bullying and trolling at every opportunity – although of course this is happening to other people and their children! This is an exaggeration, but then so is the news, which by its nature is focused on the new and the unusual and has left many people with a feeling that there's very little they can do. As a result, users may end up compromising their safety by going online without an understanding of steps that can be taken to protect themselves, or may be left feeling that the safest option is to go offline altogether.

With digital technology, however, we need to cultivate an attitude of respect, rather than of risk-avoidance. The digital is a part of our everyday lives, and it's not going to go away. There are huge opportunities available for those who have learned how to be critical, constructive and confident inhabitants of the digital environment. A total of 42% of the world's population is online, increasing to around 80% in developed nations. Ofcom has demonstrated that, within the UK, 88% of adults are now online, while among 16–34-year-olds that increases to 98%, and those aged 65+ are the fastest growing area of take-up with digital technology, especially via tablet devices or smartphones.[360] The most obvious elements of digital culture are social media – sites such as Facebook, Twitter, Instagram, YouTube and Snapchat, but emails, texting and tools such as Skype still have an important role to play, particularly in more sensitive situations where private discussion is preferable to public broadcast as a means of communication.

Seize the opportunities

There are many positive opportunities online for pastoral situations, especially if churches or pastoral workers have taken the time to familiarise themselves with the digital. Professor the Reverend David Wilkinson frequently says: 'God is extravagant in communication – he is not a silent God who has to be tempted into communicating with people: "In the beginning was the word, and the word was God …".'[361]

---

360 Ofcom. (2018). 'Adults' Media Use and Attitudes Report 2018. Retrieved from: https://www.ofcom. org.uk/__data/assets/pdf_file/0020/58223/2014_adults_report.pdf

361 Lewis, B. (2010). 'The God who communicates: David Wilkinson, #medialit'. Retrieved from: http:// drbexl.co.uk/2010/06/21/the-god-who-communicates-david-wilkinson-medialit/

God wants to share his word with us. Social media, if we concentrate on the word 'social' rather than 'media', is at its heart about relationships and communication. The natural style of church fits with the creative and participatory culture of the social media world, although that requires letting go of the broadcast hierarchical structure that some have adopted. We look to see what digital technologies allow us to do differently, and capitalise upon that. We are no longer limited to our geographical or 'Sunday' lives. Digital allows churches to practise whole-life community, actively engaging with what is going on in the world, to listen and to respond to what is going on in our local, national and international communities in ways that are meaningful to those who are listening to us. Pastoral care reaches outside of the church walls, and technology can allow us to do more of that.

Within this pastoral context, when we are dealing with challenging topics of abuse, addiction and difficult behaviour, it can be harder to highlight the 'good', but typically every negative use of technology is accompanied by a new positive use. One of the dangers of seeing the digital as 'revolutionary' is that we focus on the technology, and forget that it is still human beings using the technology. Undoubtedly, digital technology offers us new ways of doing things, both good and bad, but we are still dealing with basic human needs for love and connection. Often what we see as negative technologically is down to the person using it. Although the technology may have given them more power to spread messages faster and more widely, it's ultimately like giving someone a brick – they can choose to build a house with it, or throw it through a window.

Often, when people speak about the digital, they talk about it as a 'virtual' space. It is more helpful to think in terms of online and offline, rather than 'virtual' and 'real'. Online life is part of 'real' life, and life is not risk-free. We cannot lock ourselves away, and the more that we understand the digital environment, the more confident people can be in using it. In the same way that in learning to swim or ride a bike, we are supported by auxiliary devices, or when we take children to the park, use care in which areas we visit and who our children speak to, understanding the digital environment empowers us to use it responsibly. We need to judge it on its own merits, rather than measuring it against other forms of communication. Professor Sonia Livingstone says:

Even though in practice, face-to-face communication can, of course, be angry, negligent, resistant, deceitful and inflexible, somehow it remains the ideal against which mediated communication is judged as flawed.[362]

This chapter considers digital culture from the perspective both of those in pastoral support positions, and the particular opportunities and issues facing those whom they are supporting. Issues addressed include cyberbullying, sexting, revenge porn, abuse, addiction to games, porn or digital, and issues of connection and disconnection with those exhibiting difficult behaviour – but the chapter also looks at opportunities, including the ability to connect with others in similar situations unrelated to geography.

Human beings are still human beings!

Within digital culture, there's a geographical loosening: distances are no longer a barrier to friendship, people move on more, and there's a real sense of transience for many. Information moves faster and by a multiplicity of means, but human beings are still human beings, although mediated by new forms of technology, so remembering the rules for good relationships that have always existed are key. Knowing what you stand for, and ensuring precision of communication, as American writer, James Thurber, says in the *New York Times*, 'is important, more important than ever, in our era of hair-trigger balances, when a false, or misunderstood, word may create as much disaster as a sudden thoughtless act'.[363] In digital culture people tend to engage with increasing numbers of 'friends', especially those who are already extroverted, those who are introverted may find it more energy-efficient to limit the numbers of connections, while those with unusual interests can find those with similar interests more easily online. Online forums or groups can be found for almost any topic, including some of the more dangerous topics, such as pro-anorexia, self-harming or pro-suicide forums. These can allow people to discuss their fears, but

---

362 Livingstone, S. (2009). *Children and the Internet: Great Expectations and Challenging Realities*, p. 26.
363 Dale Carnegie Associates. (2011). How to Win Friends and Influence People in the Digital Age. *New York Times*. Retrieved from: https://www.nytimes.com/2011/10/04/books/excerpt-how-to-win-friends-and-influence-people-in-the-digital-age-by-dale-carnegie.html

more typically encourage people in ways to be 'more successful' in their endeavours. A number of pastoral workers have taken time to hang out in such forums, seeking opportunities to step in where appropriate, while others have sought to ensure that legitimate information is easily accessible online. It is important to note that there are support sites which aren't pro-dangerous behaviour, that are moderated to ensure they are solely for support, and raising awareness of these is important. Topping noted that sites such as Tumblr, used extensively by young people, have introduced warnings that pop up when users search for terms related to self-harm, directing them towards sites offering support and calling on users to report blogs with 'inappropriate content' so they can be taken down.[364]

Media features have promoted the idea that the internet is changing our brains, typically for the worse: shorter attention spans and more data in our brains. Oxytocin levels are raised in the blood by social media engagement – which increases feelings of trust and security, and reduces anxiety. In much media coverage there's a sense of moral panic. From Smith, we hear that attention spans have dropped from 13 seconds to 8 seconds in 15 years, that the average Facebook user is on the site for 81 hours per year, that office workers are checking their emails 30 to 40 times an hour, that we switch devices 21 times every hour, and that simultaneous use of devices has grown by 500% in three years.[365] This is then impairing our ability to read and write, fuelling narcissism, and diminishing the abilities of our memories. In the Pew survey 'Imagining the Internet', however, specialists emphasised how every activity we engage with will affect our brain functioning or our thinking, but that doesn't make an activity inherently bad. Communications consultant, Stowe Boyd, said:

> The reason that kids are adapting so quickly to social tools online is because they align directly with human social connection, much of which takes place below our awareness. Social tools are being adopted because they

---

364 Topping, A. (2014). Self-harm sites and cyberbullying: the threat to children from web's dark side. *The Guardian*. Retrieved from: http://www.theguardian.com/society/2014/mar/10/self-harm-sites-cyberbullying-suicide-web

365 Smith, J. (2015). How Social Media Is Rewiring Your Brain [Infographic]. *ChurchMag*. Retrieved from: https://churchm.ag/how-social-media-effects-your-brain/

match the shape of our minds, but yes, they also stretch
our minds based on use and mastery, just like martial arts,
playing the piano, and badminton.[366]

We hear of 'Facebook depression', but typically social networking can
make people feel more positive. It is the most vulnerable, as it is
offline, to whom we need to offer additional support, as they are the
most likely to experience negative experiences online, as they would
offline. We need to seek to understand those who exploit the vulnerable,
or those who target, for example, feminist activists (who draw a lot of
negative attention online) rather than putting the weight of expectation
upon the vulnerable.

What does the digital enable?

Users can have a sense of being invisible, which can lead to irresponsible
(and even illegal) behaviour, but can also provide the anonymity
necessary to encourage someone to engage with online support sites.
It is important to note, however, that with a little work, almost anyone
can be found and identified based upon the data trail left behind,
unless situated in the Darknet. The Darknet is a space popular among
journalists and bloggers, especially those living in countries where
censorship and political imprisonment are commonplace, although it
also attracts the more criminal elements of the world.[367] Most people
have an online identity, whether or not they have actively contributed
online: it's worth checking your name on Google and seeing what
results are returned. If sharing information online, it's worth thinking
about whether you are happy for your parents, children you engage
with, your worst enemy, or the front pages of the newspapers to see it,
and whether you are prepared for kickbacks if the content you've shared
is controversial. Privacy and anonymity of data online are big debates,
but surveys have indicated that what people say they are concerned
about isn't matched by the online behaviour. Card claims that there are

---

366 Anderson, J.Q. and Rainie, L. 'Imagining the Internet: Millennials will benefit and suffer due to their
hyperconnected lives'. Pew Research Center. Retrieved from: http://www.pewinternet.org/~/
media//Files/Reports/2012/PIP_Future_of_Internet_2012_Young_brains_PDF.pdf
367 Walsh, D. (2015). A Beginner's Guide to Exploring the Darknet. *Hubpages*. Retrieved from/: http://
electronician.hubpages.com/hub/A-Beginners-Guide-to-Exploring-the-Darknet

options available to limit the openness of data, but many people aren't using them, although it is simple to do.[368] Simply search for 'privacy settings' on Google or the platform in use. Once information is posted online, it can be hard to get content removed because of the global nature of the web, and often asking for removal brings more attention to them than would otherwise have been the case.

Campaigns related to topics such as domestic abuse, body image, mental health and LGBT issues, which require attention and awareness, get a better hearing and more exposure online. There is much inaccurate and alarmist information online, so churches and other trusted organisations can play their part in providing good information, or directing those affected and their supporters to pre-existing content online, or opportunities to connect to organisations such as *Diverse Church*,[369] which supports LGBT Christians. Alongside this online provision, churches and their weekly groups are in a good position to raise these issues within sermons or peer support groups, encouraging awareness of signs to look out for, confidence in steps to take, knowledge of support, and a listening ear for cries for help, while ensuring that practical provision is also clearly highlighted. Youth groups could use resources such as OiiMySize to encourage conversation about what is appropriate between boys and girls.[370] A search for terms such as 'domestic abuse' on YouTube offers a lot of stories of hope from those who have escaped and survived, although, as with any form of media, weeding out the poor quality content is key.

Livingstone highlights the fact that, although there is a risk of encountering negative incidents online, those with pre-existing psychological difficulties are more likely to experience intense or longer-lasting harm. Those who are resilient offline are more likely to adapt well online, whereas those vulnerable offline are also more vulnerable online, and need extra support.[371] Group spaces in which conversations about what is 'normative' are powerful, sharing stories

368   Card, J. (2015). Anonymity is the internet's next big battleground. *The Guardian.* Retrieved from: http://www.theguardian.com/media-network/2015/jun/22/anonymity-internet-battleground-data-advertisers-marketers

369   Diverse Church, http://diversechurch.website/

370   Oii My Size, http://www.oiimysize.com/

371   Livingstone, S., Haddon, L. and Gorzig, A. (2012). *Children, Risk and Safety on the Internet: Research and Policy Challenges in Comparative Perspective.* Polity Press, p. 208.

of case studies, actions that have helped, considering how individuals can be helped, and the wider group encouraged to take responsibility. A number of vicars and chaplains are taking opportunities to offer ongoing pastoral care via Twitter or Facebook private messages, but emphasise that one needs to know when face-to-face contact is needed and appropriate. Clearly, there is a need for planning, strategies and risk assessments organisationally and individually, and a consideration of the tools available, such as Facebook 'secret' groups where users can discuss sensitive topics – particularly in establishing a sense of trust with other members of the group, and in managing times of transition when ministerial workers move on from specific roles.

Abuse

This section attempts to look at the ways in which the perpetration of abuse (and the impact it has) has been affected by digital technology, largely focusing upon domestic and child abuse, then returning to online abuse, including trolling and cyberbullying, in the section on difficult behaviour. Domestic abuse can be defined as a pattern of coercive or controlling behaviour enacted by one person towards another. An abuser may bully, manipulate, exhaust, isolate, degrade, confuse, physically hurt or sexually abuse their partner. The abuse may involve preventing their partner working or seeing family and friends, minimising and denying their behaviour, making their partner feel they are going mad, having affairs, spying on their partner or using finances to control their partner. An abuser is motivated by a desire to have power over and control of their partner; this is rooted in believing they own their partner and are entitled to do whatever they want. Although the UK definition of abuse involves people over 16 years, young people old enough to have intimate relationships can perpetrate or be subjected to abuse.

As highlighted earlier, few of these issues are specifically created by technology, but technology does add extra dimensions. One aspect to be aware of is disinhibition, which occurs when the technology appears to offer a buffer from traditional consequences, because the face of the 'victim' has been lost behind a screen, or the abuser is disguised behind a false identity. People will say and do things online that they would not otherwise say or do, because they have lost the visual clues of the feedback cycle. Disinhibition can have positive consequences, providing those who are shy or unable to speak up in person with a space to ask questions that would otherwise be too difficult to ask, especially via online forums such as those available on Mumsnet or via Women's Aid,[372] where users are advised to be careful with the information shared, assuming that it is public.

Motivations: power and control

While considering the new technologies, we must bear in mind that the motivations of abuse – power and control, ownership and entitlement – and overall strategies for abuse are as old as time. An abuser's intention is to frighten, upset or embarrass the victim, and technology gives a faster, cheaper, easier and longer reach, leading to the term cyber-stalking. Grantham notes that, overall, the ability to control and dominate someone via cyber-stalking is achieved by constant presence.[373] Unsurprisingly, as digital is a part of everyday life, in 98% of cases, abusers will use technology to further abuse the victim, including GPS or other software used to track from a distance in real time.[374] There are five main ways an abuser may use technology:

Monitoring content: After gaining access to the victim's digital content, either openly through demands/manipulation or secretly, the abuser will monitor all digital content, preventing their partner accessing help, contacting friends/family or using content to accuse their partner of having an affair. An abuser may also use Spyware to listen into their partner's phone calls remotely or insist their partner uses Skype/Facetime as a remote CCTV for the abuser to hear and see all of their conversations. Natalie Collins, a specialist in preventing and ending abuse, has described a case she is aware of where a young man effectively used Skype as a personal CCTV service by insisting

---

372   Women's Aid, Survivors' Forum. https://survivorsforum.womensaid.org.uk/
373   Grantham, P. (2010). 'Stalking and Harassment in a Digital Age'. Retrieved from: http://www.olemiss.edu/depts/ncjrl/pdf/Law%20Enforcement%20Materials/Stalking%20%20Harassment.pdf
374   Rawlinson, C. (2015). Cyber-stalking increasing, 'easy' ways to abuse women: domestic violence report. *ABC News*. Retrieved from: http://www.abc.net.au/news/2015-06-22/cyber-stalking-on-the-rise-domestic-violence-report-says/6563186

that his girlfriend keep it permanently switched on. Once content has been monitored, the abuser may insist their partner take specific action, such as deleting contacts, unfriending people on Facebook, or sending unkind messages to people. An abuser may also prevent their partner having access to digital content, by breaking or hiding devices, changing passwords or deleting messages/missed call logs.

Monitoring location: Through GPS software on their partner's digital devices (phone, car, tablet, watch, etc.) an abuser will monitor their partner's location. An abuser may insist on their partner proving her location by sending photographs to the abuser or using video calling facilities on a device (e.g. Skype or Facetime). This also prevents their partner seeking help, connecting with family and friends and leaves them with no way of escaping.

Bombardment: During the relationship or once it has ended, an abuser may bombard their partner (or ex) with calls, texts, emails and/or via social media messages. This may wear the victim down and leave them feeling exhausted. The abuser may encourage other people to do this too (friends, family members or online contacts).

Misuse of information and content: Throughout the relationship and once it has ended, digital content can be used as a weapon. An abuser may coerce or encourage their partner to pose for naked or sexual photos, then threaten to (or actually) post the images online (the legal term for this is 'revenge porn'). They may sign in to the victim's social media accounts and pose as the victim, sending messages that either confuse or alienate the victim's friends. Natalie Collins notes it is the norm among young people for all passwords and pincodes to be shared as soon as the relationship begins. She says there is a culture of mistrust until full access to a partner's digital content is shared. The abuser may use financial details to run up debts or may even implicate the victim in criminal activity online.

Online sexual abuse: An abuser may use online sex sites to meet other people for sexual activity. They may coerce or force their partner to sign up to group sex sites or disclose details of the victim's sexual history. They may use sexual rating sites to rate the victim's sexual performance.

New dangers

As with 'traditional' child maltreatment, sexual or emotional abuse, the internet offers further opportunities to reach out to children, but with the added risk that children may not see those that they connect with online as the 'stranger danger' they have been warned about, especially if they believe the person at the other end to be a child, or if that person has been introduced electronically by a friend. As ever, sexual offenders often target children with particular characteristics, including

> children in the care of the state; children who have experienced prior maltreatment; emotionally immature children with learning or social difficulties and problems with peer friendships; love or attention deprived children; children with strong respect for adult status; children from single parent families; children who will co-operate for a desired reward (such as money, computer games); and, children with low self esteem.[375]

Natalie Collins explains that a perpetrator of child sexual exploitation may buy a smartphone for a young person, paying the bill or offering pay-as-you-go vouchers in exchange for sexual or other coerced activity, or as a way of building a relationship with the young person, which can then be exploited. The smartphone also serves as a way of controlling the young person, taking inappropriate images that can then easily be shared, or exposing them to unsuitable images. Legitimate chat sites and apps such as Skype are used for live-streaming child sex acts, using hard-to-trace virtual currencies such as Bitcoin.[376] Collins created The DAY Programme, a youth domestic abuse education programme, and trains practitioners across the UK to use the material with young people.[377] She explains that the internet makes it easier to share resources, either openly, or as part of a password-protected package.

---

375 Stanley, J. (2001). 'Child abuse and the internet'. Australian Institute of Family Studies. Retrieved from: https://aifs.gov.au/cfca/publications/child-abuse-and-internet

376 AFP. (2015). Online child abuse moving to Skype, Bitcoin: Europol. *The Economic Times*. Retrieved from: https://www.rappler.com/world/global-affairs/84961-online-child-abuse-report

377 Collins, N. (n.d.) The Day Programme. http://www.dayprogramme.org

New hopes

Deaf Hope is a site that offers specific help to the deaf community, and includes a quick escape key for users.[378] Users should note that most web browsers do keep a record of sites visited, so it's worth checking out options for private browsing, clearing the browser history, or using search sites such as DuckDuckGo,[379] which allow anonymous surfing. Of course, such anonymous surfing can be used to the benefit of both the abuser and the victim. In other cases, such as that of Linah Keza, a UK woman murdered by her ex-partner, living away from the rest of her family, her partner removing the tools of communication was an effective means of maintaining control over her.[380] One of the biggest problems for women in particular is that they are often not believed when reporting cyber harassment, and perpetrators are able to make victims feel 'crazy'. This has a huge impact upon their mental health, especially if they are unable to see where attacks are coming from (for example, when someone has infiltrated their computer or personal devices) and are unsure when it is going to stop.[381] Alongside this, police officers are often ill-equipped to understand digital abuse, leading them to offer advice like 'well, switch the location software off then'.

Digital culture

So, what are the *particular* characteristics of digital culture? We need to re-educate people that digital material is both more ephemeral and more enduring than previous communication methods. Although difficult to remove, it is easy to change, replicate and share, which can make it difficult to distinguish between originals and their replicas. What the community chooses to highlight may not be what the author intended, and material can be distributed speedily, but this also means that rejoinders can be made more quickly. Digital offers a 24/7 global culture, with an increasing amount of interaction undertaken on the

---

378   Deafhope. Together we can end violence. http://www.deaf-hope.org/

379   DuckDuckGo, Search Engine: https://duckduckgo.com/

380   Walker, V. (2014). My friend, the murder statistic: Domestic violence victims might seem like just a number – until it's someone you know. *The Independent*. Retrieved from: http://www.independent.co.uk/life-style/health-and-families/features/my-friend-the-murder-statistic-domestic-violence-victims-might-seem-like-just-a-number--until-its-someone-you-know-9541853.html

381   Rawlinson, C. (2015). Cyber-stalking increasing, 'easy' ways to abuse women: domestic violence report. *ABC News*. Retrieved from: http://www.abc.net.au/news/2015-06-22/cyber-stalking-on-the-rise-domestic-violence-report-says/6563186

move through mobile technology. The digital is not some kind of 'Wild West', where laws don't apply. It may be largely self-regulated, but its inhabitants are expected to abide by the laws of the country within which they live.

Many would refer to the younger generation as 'digital natives', a generation apart who have never known a world without technology. Knowing how to use technology, however, doesn't mean that we understand how it works, any more than driving a car means that we're mechanics. The term 'digital native' was created by Marc Prensky in 2001,[382] but if we buy into the idea that children are essentially different from 'the rest of us', we are not seeing the fundamental humanity at the root of our technological use. Traits such as collaboration, innovation, transparency and openness are often ascribed to the younger generation, and they may indeed be found there, but research demonstrates that they can also be observed across all generations. The 2012 EU Kids Online study found that only about 20% of the 25,000 children they interviewed fitted this stereotype.[383] Factors other than technology can easily account for the differences. A more helpful idea was developed by a team at Oxford University led by Dave White in 2011: that of the 'digital resident' and the 'digital visitor', defined more by attitude than by age. 'Visitors' use the internet as a tool: go in to complete a task, and leave. 'Residents' regard themselves as members of communities that exist online, rather than having access to an online toolbox.[384]

Watch what you share

Users need to be particularly careful about the information that is shared, whether by themselves or by their friends, and all users need to look out for clever tricks, such as 'viral' missing person posts, whether for partners, or for children. Some are a hoax, others are for people in hiding or under police protection, and others are for children who have been adopted because of the risk of significant harm. If you are even thinking of sharing, check with police or Interpol records, but

---

382 Prensky, M. (2001). 'Digital Natives, Digital Immigrants'. Retrieved from: http://www.marcprensky. com/writing/Prensky%20-%20Digital%20Natives,%20Digital%20Immigrants%20-%20Part1.pdf

383 EU Kids Online II (2009–2011). (2012). London School of Economics, http://www.lse.ac.uk/media-and-communications/research/research-projects/eu-kids-online/about/eu-kids-online-ii

384 White, D.S. and Le Cornu, A. (2011). Visitors and Residents: A Typology for Online Engagement. *First Monday* 16(9). Retrieved from: http://firstmonday.org/ojs/index.php/fm/article/view/3171/3049

in any case, notify the police, so that they have the opportunity to offer safeguarding protection if required.[385] Refuge centres have to be extra vigilant about staff and residents' use of their own technology, as abusers are using GPS tracking on devices, or those of the victim's children, to track down victims.[386] The more positive sides of sharing online include the ability to keep logs of abusive materials and to obtain professional counselling online, which allows full control of what is being shared, offenders' access to victims can be restricted (with expert help), and victims can be kept involved in any legal processes and connected with appropriate organisations. As we saw with Linah Keza, the more that those being subjected to abuse can maintain healthy external relationships, the more likely they are to be able to escape from an abusive partner.

Online, it is entirely possible for material to become 'viral', spreading fast among friends and connections online. Returning to Natalie Collins, we highlight a couple of campaigns that seem to have offered 'quick wins' around the topic of abuse on the back of 'viral' items online, but can be seen to be problematic. In 2015, 'the dress' became a phenomenon online, when half the people seeing the picture saw a white and gold dress, and half saw a black and blue dress. This inspired an advertising company to produce a campaign, depicting an obvious victim of domestic abuse, asking why it is so hard to see black and blue (bruises); the ad company then partnered with the Salvation Army South Africa to deliver the campaign. Collins notes that advertising agencies, rather than those with an understanding of the issues, make such campaigns.[387] In this particular campaign, the offender is invisible and the woman is posed as a sexualised object. When the majority of abuse is invisible (psychological, emotional, sexual, financial), with the advert only showing bruising, this could prevent victims identifying with the advert, creating another barrier to seeking help. Collins

---

385 Chapman, K. (2015). Be careful about 'missing person' posts. *Google+*. Retrieved from: https://plus.google.com/+KimberlyChapman/posts/gn8ZrgGnMXK; Barefoot Social Work. (2015). 'The Dangers of Social Media for "Missing" Children'. Retrieved from: http://barefootsocialwork.weebly.com/blog/the-dangers-of-social-media-for-missing-children

386 Gorrey, M. (2015). Technology used to stalk and harass domestic violence victims in the ACT. *The Canberra Times*. Retrieved from: http://www.canberratimes.com.au/act-news/technology-used-to-stalk-and-harass-domestic-violence-victims-in-the-act-20150318-1m22rx.html

387 Collins, N. (2015). Salvation Army 'The Dress' advert: It's raised awareness, but of what exactly? *Christian Today*. Retrieved from: http://www.christiantoday.com/article/salvation.army.the.dress.advert.its.raised.awareness.but.of.what.exactly/49542.htm

questioned whether the agencies behind the campaigns were prepared to deal with any consequences of a campaign produced very quickly after the original viral campaign. Another campaign, 'Slap Her', asks young Italian boys to slap a silent young girl, which they refused to do 'because I'm a man'. Rebecca Hains, a media-literacy academic, found it problematic that the video was made as 'clickbait' (designed to make the viewer feel good, and therefore want to share the content) to increase 'likes' for a Facebook page, rather than seeking to reduce violence against women. With the girl never asked her opinion on any of the activity that is happening to her, this is seen as perpetuating the status quo, and without the opportunity to follow up other resources at the end has no value outside of commerce.[388]

Promoting cultural change

A number of campaigns seek to promote cultural change rather than crisis response. Everyday Victim Blaming seeks to change the narrative in the media, which tends to portray women and children as being at fault for the abuse men perpetrate against them and needing to empower themselves, rather than showing men as being responsible for their choices to abuse:

> This campaign is about changing the culture and language around violence against women and children. We aim to challenge the view that men cannot help being violent and abusive towards women and children. We want to challenge the view that women should attempt to 'avoid' abuse in order to not become a victim of it.[389]

Those using the site are not asked to register their data but only to provide a name, which doesn't have to be a 'real name'. Comments submitted to the site retain only the email and IP address of the computer used, and are held on a secure server. In a more gender-neutral fashion,

---

388 Hains, R. (2015). 'Slap her': Fanpage.it video objectifies girls, exploits boys, and trivializes domestic violence. *RebeccaHains.com*. Retrieved from: http://rebeccahains.com/2015/01/06/slap-her-fanpage-it-video-objectifies-girls-exploits-boys-and-trivializes-domestic-violence/

389 Everyday Victim Blaming. (2015). 'Responses to Media', https://everydayvictimblaming.com/media-complaints/

See the Triumph seeks to share empowering messages that people can overcome their abuse and create positive, non-violent lives, describing strategies that have worked for other survivors and promoting a positive view of survivors as courageous and resourceful.[390] Project Unbreakable, in 2011, was a photography project that aimed to give a voice to survivors of sexual assault, domestic violence and child abuse.[391] Each person is pictured holding a hand-written sign indicating their feelings, or things they wish they had said or done – with faces hidden if desired. The founder was not a survivor herself, which caused issues with some, but she believed that she was using her skills to raise awareness. She noted that she was not qualified to give advice, but referred visitors to places that could help, and has left the site archive up, although unable to actively maintain it now.

Addiction

From 2006, the term 'internet addiction' started to appear, with reference to repetitive, compulsive and uncontrollable use of technology. It was defined as an official disorder in 2012, with symptoms similar to other addictions,[392] although the origins of the problem need to be investigated more widely than the technology itself. In recent years, the term nomophobia has been created, defined as the fear of being out of mobile phone contact, although many would argue that it is not a phobia, and that in the majority of cases it is only regular anxiety, because the phone now functions as diary, camera, information source and address book, among other things. Those who are experiencing clinically problematic symptoms wake up multiple times to check for texts, emails or social media updates, feel extremely anxious when phones need to be silenced or turned off, and, in focusing so intently on their phones, tend to struggle with work, school or other relationships.[393] Others may be using their phones obsessively to pursue gambling, shopping, video gaming, pornography or other unhealthy habits, but

---

390 Murray, C. and Crowe, A. (n.d.). See the Triumph, http://www.seethetriumph.org
391 Brown, G. (2011). Project Unbreakable, http://projectunbreakable.tumblr.com
392 Walton, A.G. (2012). Internet Addiction: The New Mental Health Disorder? *Forbes Magazine*, http://www.forbes.com/sites/alicegwalton/2012/10/02/the-new-mental-health-disorder-internet-addiction/#4205d5625230
393 Weiss, R. (2015). Understanding Nomophobia: Just Something Else to Worry About. *Psychology Today*. Retrieved from: https://www.psychologytoday.com/blog/love-and-sex-in-the-digital-age/201505/understanding-nomophobia-just-something-else-worry-about

in these cases it is not the phone to which the user is addicted so much as the behaviour that it enables.

Is digital technology truly addictive?

An article in *Christian Today* feared that the internet is turning us into addicts, hyper-connected in a way that we have never been before.[394] Studies have shown that brains receive dopamine highs as we interact with others, and the 'always-on' nature of technology means that the brain receives a constant hit, similar to that given by nicotine or cocaine. The article claims that this affects our sense of self, as we keep checking back in to see if we have more 'likes', and distracts us from the 'real' highs and lows of life. We have heard of four-year-olds addicted to iPads, requiring expensive detoxification therapy, and Chinese children sent to military boot-camps for addiction therapy, but the 2012 EU Kids Online project discovered that nearly half of the children questioned were happy to describe themselves as addicted (if no specific definition was offered), as in many ways the term is seen as a 'badge of honour'.[395] It was also found that only about 10% demonstrated true signs of addiction.[396] It can be an unhelpful term to use, for children and adults, in the same way that we wouldn't describe most of those who drink alcohol as alcoholics, even if they drink to excess on occasion. Those who *do* tend to struggle with digital technologies are those who are likely to struggle no matter what – their addictive personality is more likely to be at the root of the problem, rather than the technology itself.[397] With the ubiquity of digital, in the same way as police crime figures are noted as containing more references to Facebook and Twitter – because more people are using them – increasing addiction to technology, or the material that it gives access to, is hardly surprising.

Antony Mayfield, a digital consultant, notes that we like to believe that we're in thrall to our devices – 'Oh, I must take this call' – but

---

394 Saunders, M. (2015). Your dopamine addiction is hurting your soul. *Christian Today*. Retrieved from: http://www.christiantoday.com/article/your.dopamine.addiction.is.hurting.your.soul/56723.htm

395 EU Kids Online II (2009–2011). (2012). London School of Economics, http://www.lse.ac.uk/media@lse/research/EUKidsOnline/EU%20Kids%20II%20(2009-11)/home.aspx

396 Quoted in Lewis, B. (2014). *Raising Children in a Digital Age: Enjoying the Best, Avoiding the Worst*. Lion Hudson, p. 166.

397 Weiss, R. (2015). Understanding Nomophobia: Just Something Else to Worry About. *Psychology Today*. Retrieved from: https://www.psychologytoday.com/blog/love-and-sex-in-the-digital-age/201505/understanding-nomophobia-just-something-else-worry-about

the machines don't care what we do.[398] Signs of true addiction will be the same as for any other addiction: increasing activity to get the original 'high', withdrawal symptoms when disconnected, increasing conflict or disconnection with those in the social circle, the likelihood of relapse, and evidence of the 'sunk cost' fallacy – not wanting to abandon something after so much time has been sunk into it. It is interesting to note that we'll frequently talk about internet addiction, but this accusation is not made at those whose noses are buried in a 'good book' or a newspaper. There's something about the digital that attracts particular criticism, and we need to consider whether it is valid condemnation, or whether any of our habits or lifestyles, when viewed as a whole, require more consideration. In contemporary society, the outside world can feel unsafe, particularly for children, and therefore we spend more time inside our homes, where it becomes natural to pick up our mobile devices and engage with our online connections. We regularly hear in the news that melatonin production is being affected by the lights on our electronic devices. It's worth keeping up to date with the debates on the latest health discussions relating to technology, and to experiment with, for example, leaving your phone out of the room, and see if life changes for the better.

Time to unplug?

While the majority of digital users would see what they are engaged in as valuable, in building relationships and in developing themselves, a large number would also love to be able to unplug. The importance of developing boundaries cannot be overstated in a 24/7 digital culture, and some will undertake month-long digital disconnections, or a 'digital Sabbath' each week, to seek to understand their relationship with technology. Lewis highlighted how a number of users have tested extreme detoxes,[399] including six months in the case of Susan Maushart, writing for the *Daily Mail*, in which she included her entire family, and a year for Paul Millar, a technology journalist. Millar found that, after an initial ultra-productive period, he found other ways to develop bad habits that 'wasted time'. Both felt that afterwards they

---

398   Mayfield, A. (2010). *Me and My Web Shadow*. A & C Black, p. 14.
399   Lewis, B. (2014). *Raising Children in a Digital Age: Enjoying the Best, Avoiding the Worst*. Lion Hudson, p. 101.

were able to make more informed technology choices. Good habits to develop include a healthy set-up for the space where devices are used most often, ensuring that frequent rests are taken from the screen, and ensuring that opportunities are sought to use technology away from a fixed point, including undertaking activities such as geocaching, which beautifully mixes the GPS-navigational power of a smartphone with a physically based treasure-hunt.[400]

The pull of games

A *Guardian* survey in 2014 established that nearly 70% of the UK population has played games in some form, that 52% of those gaming are women, with an increasing number connecting to games via their mobile phones, with adults playing an average of six hours a week. Unusually, game playing is a very focused activity, unlike much of online interaction.[401] It is clear that game developers have taken the time to learn about human psychology. Unlike early games which were limited by the capacity of a software cassette, online games are developed that will cause users to 'play just one more level'. With no ultimate goal to the game, there's no specific end to them, with add-ons and opportunities for in-world chat: games are designed to reward those who put in the hours online. People who become involved in playing these games can find that large sums of money quickly disappear. Many games are initially free, but in-game purchases need to be paid for, and small sums can quickly add up to significant amounts of money. We also note that the more outrage a game provokes in the papers, including MMORPGs (Massively Multiplayer Online Role-Playing Games) such as *World of Warcraft,* the more it sells. With gaming, therefore, there's a mix of underlying compulsive behaviour and clever game development and marketing to contend with. More positively, some have put forward the theory that increased computer gaming has contributed to falling crime rates and reduced numbers of teenage pregnancies.[402]

---

400   https://www.geocaching.com/play
401   Stuart, K. (2015). UK gamers: more women play games than men, report finds. *The Guardian,* http://www.theguardian.com/technology/2014/sep/17/women-video-games-iab
402   Kain, E. (2011). Virtually Crime Free: How Video Games May Help Prevent Crime. *Forbes.* Retrieved from: http://www.forbes.com/sites/erikkain/2011/08/10/virtually-crime-free-how-video-games-may-help-prevent-crime

The pull of pornography

A study by the London School of Economics highlighted how the ubiquity of pornography, both men's and women's, has warped people's ideas of body image, sex and sexuality – all becoming 'increasingly unrealistic'.[403] Increasingly younger children are exhibiting more extreme sexualised behaviours.[404] Childline, in launching the app 'Fight Against the Porn Zombies' to help children, highlighted how over 1,000 children had contacted them between 2013 and 2014 about porn, about the fact that they enjoyed it, felt worried or pressurised by it, and worried that they are addicted.[405] The numbers are high – young people searching for adult material of a sexual nature has been common for years; in many ways it's a 'rite of passage'. The core difference is that until recently it took some effort to acquire printed pornographic material, whereas huge amounts circulate freely online, much of it more hard-core and violent in nature than before. A study by digital analysts, Juniper Research, concluded that adult smartphone users would each watch an average of 348 porn videos on their devices in 2015.[406] A key issue identified is the lack of 'reality' of what is seen online, and that this is changing expectations about what people (particularly women) will do. In 2010, a Home Office report warned that the 'drip-drip' exposure to sexual imagery – including pornography, 'lads' mags', and sexual imagery in advertising – was warping young people's perceptions of themselves; 'encouraging boys to become fixated on being macho and dominant, and girls to present themselves as sexually available and permissive'.[407] Too much emphasis in porn on 'the perfect body' is leaving people unhappy when their own bodies don't match up.

To any concerned with any of these possible addictions, whether digital, gaming or porn, we would emphasise the importance of conversation and a consideration of the bigger picture. These particular

403 Santhanam, A. (2013). The harm of digital pornography in real lives. *Polis*. The London School of Economics and Political Science. Retrieved from: http://blogs.lse.ac.uk/polis/2013/11/22/the-harm-of-digital-pornography-in-real-lives

404 Reist, M.T., http://melindatankardreist.com

405 F.A.P.Z – Fight Against Porn Zombies. (n.d.). Childline, http://www.childline.org.uk/Explore/OnlineSafety/Pages/fapz-fight-against-porn-zombies.aspx

406 Telegraph Men. (2015). Smartphone porn use set to rise dramatically by 2020. *The Daily Telegraph*. Retrieved from: http://www.telegraph.co.uk/men/the-filter/11712836/Smartphone-porn-use-set-to-rise-dramatically-by-2020.html

407 Barford, V. and Iqbal, N. (2012). 'Should children be taught that porn is not real?' *BBC News Magazine*. Retrieved from: http://www.bbc.co.uk/news/magazine-20042508

addictions don't occur in a social vacuum; the fact that pornography and violent games are considered forms of entertainment is problematic and needs to be addressed by wider conversations regarding cultural change. Internet filtering is often presented as a solution, particularly to pornography, but this doesn't deal with the root problem, and there are many workaround solutions to filtering. Accountability options can be more productive, while Johann Hari's TED talk encourages us to look at how we can reconnect people with society, so that people feel less driven to addictive practices.[408]

Difficult behaviour

One noticeable difference in the digital era, especially as the social platforms have stabilised, is that it's difficult to leave anyone behind, and relationships occur within a more compressed timeframe, which can be delicate to negotiate. Sites such as Facebook, encouraging users to share the highlights of all their relationships, can make it difficult to disentangle oneself once a break-up has occurred. Space to disconnect to enable healing to occur is not possible, especially with friends in common.[409] Generally, it is socially unacceptable to delete a Facebook friend one knows. Typically, it is done after a fight or break-up: the act of 'defriending' is spiteful and intentionally designed to hurt the other person. This emphasises the reality of our 'online lives', and how they interconnect with the rest of our lives. Behaviour online can be described as 'human nature amplified', so those who exhibit 'difficult behaviour' offline will typically do so online too, sometimes in an even more extreme form, due to the speed, and brevity, of the messages shared.

For those who wish to disconnect from others, the 24/7 nature of the internet can make it hard to escape – time out is often a requirement, with an encouragement not to respond immediately. Online communication can be shorn of the visual and tonal cues that we are used to, although frequent users will argue that we learn new cues, and digital content has

---

408 Hari, J. (2015). 'Everything you think you know about addiction is wrong'. TED Talks. Retrieved from: https://www.ted.com/talks/johann_hari_everything_you_think_you_know_about_addiction_is_wrong

409 Weiss, R. (n.d.). Love and Sex in the Digital Age. *Psychology Today*. Retrieved from: https://www.psychologytoday.com/blog/love-and-sex-in-the-digital-age/201501/breaking-is-hard-do-especially-virtually; Ngak, C. (2013). Breaking up is hard to do in a digital age, study says. *CBS News*. Retrieved from: http://www.cbsnews.com/news/breaking-up-in-the-digital-age-is-difficult-study-says/

become increasingly visual. Many messages, however, can come across as particularly abrupt or negative, or visual content tends to depict the best of people's lives. With the expectation of an immediate response, users have to remember that just because someone has responded doesn't mean that they have to reciprocate – at least not immediately. Users need to take care with the 'trigger finger'. In the heat of the moment, it's much easier to share negative content – to which some would respond 'HALT': if you're hungry, angry, lonely or tired, is pressing 'send' really the most constructive use of your time, whether in personal emails, or more publicly via social networks? As with offline communications, remembering that those we connect with are human, it is surprising how quickly we can disarm someone if we show support, while being careful that we are not taken advantage of.

There is much positive content that can be shared, although it doesn't take much for conversations to turn sour, particularly over the finer points of doctrine! Andrea Weckerle, founder of Civilination says:

> Conflict isn't a bad thing in and of itself, and instead can, under the right conditions, create an opportunity to work through differences in a constructive way. However, when people engage in negative conflict, they're less interested in trying to see if they can come to a mutually beneficial resolution than they are in maintaining power over the other side and trying to prove they are 'right,' regardless of the methods used or the people hurt.[410]

We need to question how we deal with those who simply express unpalatable views online.[411] Trolls attack others in order to get a reaction; if an emotionally loaded reaction is achieved, they will continue. So-called sockpuppets assume fake identities with the intention of misleading others, while cyberbullies seek to attack others, and harassers and defamers undertake illegal attacks. Those participating range from

---

410   Andrews, M. (2013). In Conversation with Author Andrea Weckerle, Civility in the Digital Age. *A New Domain*. Retrieved from: http://anewdomain.net/2013/04/07/in-conversation-with-author-andrea-weckerle-civility-in-the-digital-age

411   Lewis, B. (2014). Should McCann Twitter abuser have been doorstepped on TV, *The Conversation*. Retrieved from: https://theconversation.com/should-mccann-twitter-abuser-have-been-doorstepped-on-tv-32593

the intentional power-hungry aggressive through to the clueless user who simply leaves chaos in their wake. We all have a responsibility to influence our culture but the UK government has recognised the need to step in, and in June 2015 set up the 'Stop Online Abuse' site, providing legal advice and practical tips in responding to derogatory comments online.[412] For those who have become victims of smear campaigns, websites can be legally required to take content down (although content may already have been copied and shared). Sometimes, the only effective way to remove negative content is to fill the online space with positive content related to your name.

Beware the bully

Cyberbullying is a major concern for many, particularly with regard to children, although it is present across all age groups. The core difference between 'traditional' bullying and 'online' bullying is the pervasive nature of the latter – in all locations and at all times of the day and night, leaving a feeling of no escape. Online, it is also much easier for others to get involved fast – for good and for bad – and for an issue to resurface long after the initial incident, potentially prompting another episode of bullying, with accompanying public humiliation. Cyberbullying can take a range of forms, including threatening or hateful texts, email or chat messages, pictures or video clips, including 'happy slapping', silent or abusive phone calls, stealing a phone and using it to harass others, nasty comments posted on websites or social media, creating internet polls such as 'Who's hot', blogging to damage the reputation or privacy of others, including sharing personal data, or forcing users to share messages, threatening 'social isolation' for non-compliance. As with all forms of abuse, the risk factors are typically the same as those offline: those who are most vulnerable will again be the most likely to be affected. Extra factors in identifying those being cyberbullied include particularly secretive computing use and extreme possessiveness of phones, to which nervous looks are directed in expectation of the next message. Good communication is key to help those affected to understand that this is not their fault, that they shouldn't respond but

---

412   Gentleman, A. (2015). Government launches anti-trolling website to help victims of online abuse. *The Guardian,* http://www.theguardian.com/society/2015/jun/27/government-launches-anti-trolling-website-help-victims-online-abuse

should save copies of messages and search websites for how to block users, while wider cultural change is required to help bullies understand the harm they are causing. The role of bystanders is often ignored in discussions about online bullying, but they can play an important role in encouraging others to take action. Don't forget the famous saying attributed to Edmund Burke: 'The only thing necessary for the triumph of evil is that good men do nothing.' When a situation is already difficult, the real-time nature of social media can feed the situation, but it can also be used to ease tension and allow friends of the victim to declare themselves as 'digital allies'. If someone spots a hurtful comment, others can pre-agree to come in and protest against the posting. There are many books addressing this topic in more depth and *The Guardian* has an entire category on the topic.[413]

Managing online pressure

Online pressure comes in many forms, of which sexting is particularly prominent in many minds. A widely used definition of sexting is: 'The act of sending sexually explicit messages or images, primarily between mobile phones.'[414] With easy access to mobile technology, images can speedily spread, with emotional, social and criminal consequences. Those who send these messages probably want desperately to fit in, to 'prove' they are ready for a relationship, and, being impulsive, don't consider the consequences of their behaviour. The development of apps such as Snapchat has given the illusion of control, as the image 'disappears' after a few seconds, but users must understand that copies of it could be made, and are stored on servers on the way through. There is increasing social pressure to provide sexts, but in many ways it is simply the technological development of that old chestnut 'If you loved me, you'd sleep with me', with threats made that relationships will be broken off, or previous photos circulated, if photos are not provided. For those struggling to understand notions of sexual consent, sites such as 'Pause, Play, Stop' can help users through interactive material.[415] The biggest danger point for sexted photos comes when a relationship ends,

---

413   Cyberbullying, *The Guardian*. http://www.theguardian.com/society/cyberbullying
414   https://www.e-safetysupport.com/articles/13/sexting#.V3gbkpMrK9s
415   Somerset and Avon Rape and Sexual Abuse Support. (2015). 'Sexual consent: Do you get it?' http://pauseplaystop.org.uk/

when photos may be shared in revenge. For every photo shared, work on the assumption that there is a good possibility it will not remain private. Once out in the public domain, it can quickly multiply and never be taken back. If you receive a sexting image, you should remove it quickly – police can access a data trail in search of 'proof' as to what you did with the image.

Challenges in the Workplace

The ubiquitous nature of digital has also raised new questions for both employers and employees, requiring a redrawing of boundaries. A 2015 survey highlighted that 87% of people check work email outside of work, and 50% check it on vacation;[416] few countries have gone as far as France in 2016, which introduced a 'right to disconnect' law, enabling employees in larger companies to fully relax in their time off. [417] There is also the question of employees accessing the internet for personal reasons during work time. This could be either on their work machine, in which case the employer is entitled to monitor usage,[418] or on personal mobile devices, either of which could have a profound effect on productivity, especially if someone is spending excessive time internet shopping or dealing with family issues. For any employees engaging in gambling or accessing pornography at work, there may be bigger questions that human resources departments need to deal with, including addiction and financial concerns. There are also questions as to the kind of content that employees are posting online, including publicly expressing grievances.[419] Companies need to develop responsive and flexible policies on the use of digital tools at work, and make these clear to employees. The use of social media could be banned altogether, but this fails to recognise that social media is a legitimate communication tool for some, or that work-life balance is important

---

416 Reaney, P. (2016). 'U.S. Workers Spend 6.3 Hours A Day Checking Email: Survey'. Retrieved from: http://www.huffingtonpost.com/entry/check-work-email-hours-survey_us_55ddd168e4b0a40aa3ace672
417 Ruiz, M. (2016). 'The French Girl's Guide to Not Checking Your Work Email'. Retrieved from: http://www.vogue.com/13440376/france-work-email-banned-on-weekends/
418 Citizens Advice Bureau. (2016). 'Monitoring at work'. Retrieved from: https://www.citizensadvice.org.uk/work/rights-at-work/basic-rights-and-contracts/monitoring-at-work/
419 ACAS. (2016). 'Social media, discipline and grievances'. Retrieved from: http://www.acas.org.uk/index.aspx?articleid=3378

for staff morale, especially when staff are putting in hours over and above what they are paid for. ACAS suggests that it can be helpful to set guidelines on 'reasonable use', in consultation with any unions, to make expectations clear, and in a way that is seen as fair.[420]

So far we have looked at questions that have a legal aspect, but there are also questions of etiquette, and one that concerns many is the use of laptops, tablets or mobile phones during face-to-face meetings. This is also a question that has occupied those within higher education. Taneja, Fiore and Fischer summarised how digital technologies have become 'necessary to do the work at hand' and that laptops have been 'found to improve students' attentiveness and engagement in class', although it is also possible that this can lead to people undertaking off-topic tasks.[421] In 2015, Lewis considered the use of computers within the classroom in an annual media-literacy training course:

> In the early years of MediaLit, some delegates found the continuous presence of laptops within the classroom overwhelming, although the increasing use of mobile devices has made the 'barrier' laptop lids less problematic. Over time, the presence of technology has become more normative, although conversations continued to arise as to what technology was bringing to, or taking away from, the classroom experience. Taneja, Fiore & Fischer (2015) noted that students look to others within their group to understand 'acceptable behaviour'. If social pressures to engage with material unrelated to the course are strong, students are more likely to 'cyber-slack'.[422]

A lot of educationalists and pastors have accepted that, if the content is engaging enough, people will engage. That engagement, however, may include looking up related content online, sharing material, or the digital equivalent of doodling. For those who don't understand

---

420 ACAS. (2016). 'Social media and managing performance'. Retrieved from: http://www.acas.org.uk/index.aspx?articleid=3376

421 Taneja, A., Fiore, V. and Fischer, B. (2015). Cyber-slacking in the classroom: Potential for digital distraction in the new age. *Computers and Education* 82: 141–51.

422 Lewis, B. (2015). 'MediaLit: Engaging Faith and Media in a Digital Age'. Retrieved from: https://www.academia.edu/13281147/MediaLit_Engaging_Faith_and_Media_in_a_Digital_Age

what others are doing, this can appear as disrespectful or distracting, leading to frustration. This may require conversation, being prepared to explain what one is engaging with, or not jumping to conclusions as to what others are doing. People learn and engage in a range of ways, sometimes in ways that can be seen as multitasking, of which we can define two types:

- Constructive: having Instant Messenger, music or search open, which contributes to something the user is working on;

- Distractive: watching TV on demand, videos, or playing games, which pulls users away from the current focus.[423]

It is appropriate to have conversations about expectations for meetings, and, at times, to indicate that the content requires engagement without a digital presence, or reassurance that the meeting's purpose is being respected by participants.

Conclusion

Throughout this chapter we've seen that the internet has offered new opportunities, both negative and positive, for dealing with these difficult topics. Fundamentally, we can see that much of this still comes down to unchanging human nature, but we need to raise our awareness of the digital context within which we work.

Do

- Look for opportunities to talk about digital culture where possible, highlighting that we all have a responsibility for change.

- Remember that underneath the technology we are all human. Technology offers new opportunities, but doesn't necessarily make things inevitable.

- Take care with how much information you share, especially over-sharing that makes you, or those you know, vulnerable.

---

423   Lewis, B. (2014). *Raising Children in a Digital Age: Enjoying the Best, Avoiding the Worst*, p. 170.

Don't

- Freeze in panic. Take a step back, and look at the options available to you.

- Put all the weight of expectation for solving the problem on the victim. There are a number of supporting bodies, official and unofficial.

- Avoid the internet altogether. There are so many positive opportunities online.

Further Reading

Lewis, B. (2014). *Raising Children in a Digital Age: Enjoying the Best, Avoiding the Worst.* Lion Hudson.

Turkle, S. (2013). *Alone Together: Why We Expect More from Technology, and Less from Ourselves.* Basic Books.

Weckerle, A. (2012). *Civility in a Digital Age: How Companies and People Can Triumph Over Haters, Trolls, Bullies and Other Jerks.* Que.

CHAPTER NINE

Autism and Asperger Syndrome

Tracey Hume

Autism is a condition that has been the subject of films and television programmes over the years. Typically, these highlight the challenges of the condition but particularly in relation to the more severe end of the spectrum. Dustin Hoffman's portrayal of savant autistic, Raymond Babbitt, in the film 'Rain Man' is a case in point. While the film was effective in introducing people to the condition, it also had the effect of creating false assumptions – for example, that all autistic people have exceptional memories, are mathematically gifted, and have a tendency to sit in a corner rocking gently while reciting phrases over and over again. This is the case for some, but not all people who are affected by autism. Understandably, people fear that they would not know what to do if faced with this behaviour and, as a result, can shy away from any engagement with these people and their families.

Autism is also often a hidden condition. There are no bandages or crutches to indicate that the person has a disability and therefore any symptoms can come as a surprise. Many people with autism are also high functioning and can appear very knowledgeable and well-spoken, which can lead to assumptions about their social capacities. Such a person could, for example, make a very candid comment about another person's weight, not realising that there are certain social proprieties regarding what should and should not be said in public, that preclude making this kind of comment in a social situation.

There are also different forms of autism, and this can cause confusion. One is not necessarily worse than the others, but they are different presentations of the same condition. It would therefore be helpful to provide an overview of the spectrum of disorders related to this condition, with their similarities and differences, before considering how to engage with the condition. It is estimated that one in every hundred people has an autism spectrum disorder. There are therefore approximately 650,000 people, children and adults, with an autism spectrum disorder in the UK.

What is Autism and Asperger Syndrome?

Autism spectrum disorder is the name given to a group of conditions which share a 'triad of impairments', but which present in slightly different ways. According to Jordan and Jones, 'Autism Spectrum Disorder is the name given to a family of biologically based disorders which comprise a number of different medically diagnosed conditions.'[424]

The following conditions are the ones most commonly associated with this condition, and which are considered part of the autism spectrum:

- Kanner's, or classic autism

- Asperger syndrome

- Semantic pragmatic disorder.

The term 'autism' was first coined by Bleuler in 1908. It comes from the Greek word 'autos', meaning 'self'. This reflects the tendency to solitary withdrawal rather than seeking social interaction, which is a feature of this condition.[425]

Before describing classic autism and Asperger syndrome in a little more detail, it is helpful to understand the triad of impairments which is common to all.

The Triad of Impairments

The triad of impairments was first defined by Wing and Gould in 1979. Prior to this, there were records of symptoms and observations of children exhibiting difficulties with social interaction and language. These were initially identified by Kanner in the 40s and also by Hans Asperger at approximately the same time. Wing and Gould brought together the works of Kanner, Asperger and others, and noted three dominant issues which they termed the triad of impairments, which refer to difficulties with social communication, social interaction and flexibility of thinking. Prior to Kanner and Asperger's works, children presenting with these difficulties were often wrongly diagnosed as having schizophrenia.

---

424   Jordan, Rita and Jones, Glenys. (1999). *Meeting the needs of children with Autism Spectrum Disorders.* London: David Fulton.
425   Jordan, Rita. (1999). *Autistic Spectrum Disorders.* London: David Fulton, p. 22.

Social communication

People on the autism spectrum have difficulties in communicating effectively and in understanding the communication of others. They can find it difficult to know which register to use when addressing people, and will often talk to everyone in the same way, whether they are a teacher, pupil, head of state or grandparent. They often demonstrate a lack of eye contact and find that talking to other people makes them feel rather uncomfortable.

They also have difficulty understanding the subtleties of language. The relevance of change of tone, inflection or emphasis on certain words when listening to someone else is often lost for them. An example of this would be the sentence, 'I didn't say she stole my money.' If you put the accent on the first word, 'I', the hearer could infer that you are suggesting someone else said it. If you put the accent on the word 'she,' the hearer might infer that you are suggesting someone else had done it. And if you put the accent on the word 'money', the hearer could infer that you are suggesting they stole something other than money. Through the process of emphasising different words, we communicate different things. To someone on the autism spectrum, this subtlety is difficult or impossible to spot. When something is written down this becomes even more difficult, as we often have to guess which word the author intends to accentuate or emphasise. Of course, in written texts we all need to try and deduce which meaning was intended, but we are able to use our previous knowledge of the text and characters so far, and knowledge of social conventions, all of which help us to have a 'best guess' at the meaning. With autism, the ability to see this bigger picture, and to infer and break down character traits, is often absent or limited.

In addition to all of the above, people with autism can be very stilted and lack intonation in their speaking. Some sound almost like robots or can be extremely formal. This can be the case, in particular, with Asperger syndrome (AS). Consequently, when reading literature, they can find reading speech confusing as this can involve the use of less formal language in an attempt to convey the inflections, pace and colour of everyday speech.

Social interaction

People with AS often experience difficulties in the important area of social interaction – for example, in recognising and negotiating social cues such as personal space, understanding facial expressions, or knowing when someone is clearly bored with what you are saying. In demonstrating these symptoms, they can often appear to be socially awkward. They might say inappropriate things in situations because they don't understand that what they are saying is inappropriate. From their perspective, they are simply stating the obvious. For example, in a supermarket, a child may turn to their mother and say: 'Why is that woman in front of us so fat?' They can therefore appear rude at times, due to this lack of understanding.

They can have a general lack of understanding of social cues. For example, most young people develop an awareness that, when someone asks you a question, you try and answer it. A young person with an autism spectrum disorder may either not like the question which has been asked and choose to ignore it, or may decide that what the person has asked is irrelevant and will insist on talking about something of significance to them instead, or simply ignore them altogether. Let me give a personal example. My son, when he was seven or eight years old, would ignore friends and family if they waved or said hello to him. He did not understand that he appeared rude. We had to talk about why people say hello or wave, then explain that they are simply being friendly. A couple of weeks after this explanation, my son mentioned that he had noticed that some people don't say hello, they say hi. This common social convention had been completely lost on him. While it was, perhaps, obvious to the rest of us, it was a revelation to him.

Emotional intelligence is often lacking or a challenge for people with this condition. Emotional intelligence is the ability to know and manage your own emotions, recognise emotions in others and manage relationships effectively.[426] For example, my son once commented that he did not understand why his brother had water squirting out of his eyes. He had not made the connection that that meant he was crying, which in turn meant that he was sad or upset.

---

426   Goleman, Daniel. (1996). *Emotional Intelligence – Why it can matter more than IQ*. London: Bloomsbury, p. 43.

People on the autism spectrum can often demonstrate and understand only a small range of emotions themselves, usually extreme ones. They can possibly identify extreme happiness or profound sadness in others but not the subtle degrees of emotion which are found between these extremes.

Flexibility of thinking

Many people on the autism spectrum can be very rigid in their thinking. They may follow self-imposed rules or routines and can often have obsessive, compulsive issues. They may believe that the first way they have done something is the only way to do it. In this way, they can 'fail to transfer or generalise their learning to other situations'.[427] They find coping with unexpected change very challenging and such changes can often result in meltdowns, screaming, fleeing or hiding. Occasionally, they can also lead to self-harming behaviours.

The lack of flexibility of thinking also relates to language. They can have a very literal understanding of language. For example, a child being told to keep their eye on the ball in a PE lesson may be found bending down to literally put their eye on the ball. This can cause problems in conversation where they can misinterpret the intention of the speaker. A difficulty with understanding idioms and other figures of speech can be a bigger problem in reading, as there are no facial clues as to whether the person is being serious or not. The intended meaning can be so easily missed as the person gets bogged down with the literal meaning of a word or phrase. We so often use words which have two meanings and usually the context helps us to determine which meaning the author or speaker intended, but children with autism have a tendency not to see or interpret the context.

Theory of Mind (empathy)

In addition to the above, one overarching difficulty relates to what is known as theory of mind. Theory of mind 'refers to a person's ability to understand that another person has his or her own unique way of thinking and feeling'.[428] In essence, it is the ability to put yourself in

---

427   Attwood, Tony. (1998). *Asperger's Syndrome*. London: Jessica Kingsley, p. 118.
428   Boyd, Jeffrey H. (2008). Have we found the Holy Grail? Theory of Mind as a unifying construct. *Journal Of Religious Health* 47: 366–85.

someone else's shoes. Although it is a little more complex, commonly this is experienced and understood as empathy.

The capacity to work with theory of mind usually develops from the age of four, when children begin to be able to work out what another person is thinking or feeling. Prior to this, they believe that everyone else is thinking exactly the same as themselves.[429] People on the autism spectrum 'have some difficulty conceptualising and appreciating the thoughts and feelings of another person'.[430] This is key in the development of emotional intelligence and also moral development. The ability to imagine how someone else may react or what they might be thinking contributes significantly to how we may choose to behave. If we see that someone is crying after we have hit them, we don't tend to keep on hitting them. Without a capacity for theory of mind, the world revolves around our own feelings and beliefs. Cavanagh (1995) rightly claims that the ability to empathise is 'the cornerstone of morality'.[431]

Classic Autism and Asperger Syndrome – A comparison

Classic autism is often characterised by an early difficulty with language development. Children with autism often have delayed, little or no language, by the age of four. In Asperger syndrome, spoken language often develops quite normally although those with this syndrome are often considered to be very shy and tend to avoid conversational and social situations.

People with both classic autism and Asperger syndrome have a difficulty in processing language. This can often be masked with Asperger syndrome as they can develop a remarkable vocabulary, often far beyond their years, and can learn to read (decode) at an early age, but their understanding of read or spoken language can be quite literal, and their comprehension lacks the ability to infer anything from a text which is not explicitly there.

People with Asperger syndrome are usually of average or above-average intelligence and can have an extraordinarily in-depth knowledge of certain topics, some of them unusual, such as washing machines or

---

429   Ibid.: 370.
430   Attwood. *Asperger's Syndrome*, p. 112.
431   Cavanagh, Michael E. (1995). Rediscovering Compassion. *Journal of Religion and Health* 34(4): 320.

agricultural machinery. Those with autism can have focused interests too, but they are generally focused on collecting things or favourite TV or film characters. It is difficult to say precisely why they develop these keen interests or in-depth knowledge but it is possible that the 'sameness' and control they have with these things becomes reassuring when change is so difficult to cope with. Some are known to retreat to the keen interest when stressed as a way of calming themselves down.

People on the autism spectrum can be a little inconsistent in their responses to stimuli. This can be due to how they are feeling at that moment, what else is going on in their life and how suddenly the stimulus has been presented to them. This can mean that on one occasion a person with Asperger syndrome copes quite well with an activity or regular chore but on another day may be clearly distressed. This can be confusing for well-meaning people who want to help.

Autism and Asperger syndrome can lead to some challenging behaviours which can make the observer feel anxious, intimidated or irritated. Such behaviours can include screaming, repetitive sounds, humming, repetitive actions including hand flapping, walking around, shouting out and asking questions. Within the context of church, work or school or a more formal environment such as a church service, these can appear quite disruptive but are generally outward signs of inward confusion and anxiety. There are many ways, such as the behaviours mentioned above, which can make attendance and involvement a challenge not only for the person involved and their family, but also for those trying to work or engage with them.

An issue for the Church?

Over the last two decades especially, churches have become much more inclusive. In part this is due to legislation such as the Disability Discrimination Act of 1995 and the Equality Act of 2010, which requires public buildings to take disabilities and inclusion seriously, ensuring that 'reasonable adjustments are made' in order that 'a provision, criterion or practice' does not 'put a disabled person at a substantial disadvantage in relation to a relevant matter in comparison with persons who are not disabled'.[432]

---

432   Equality Act 2010: see https://www.legislation.gov.uk/ukpga/2010/15/section/20?view=plain

In some areas, the Church has been ahead of other parts of society regarding sensitivity to the needs of people with impairments or disabilities. Most churches, for example, have had hearing loops installed for over 20 years to support those with hearing impairments. Many church buildings have ramps installed, wherever possible, to enable wheelchairs and pushchairs to access the buildings. Some churches even have braille hymn books for their blind members. This is all good and should be encouraged, but churches often find it easier to address these issues as they are visible, and the hurdles and barriers to participation are more obvious.

Autism is one of many invisible or hidden conditions which can make it difficult to define the potential problems that are experienced by those with the condition, and respond appropriately. An appropriate response from a church in this instance does not involve simply installing a ramp or making sure a person can physically access the building or a service. The adjustments involved are far larger than that and require a change of mindset. If we accept the importance of mutuality and interdependence in our lives, then this will lead to a desire to do all we can to support one another, to learn from one another and identify and use the gifts God has given to all of us. I will consider this value in more detail later in the chapter.

Inclusion is an issue for the whole Church, local and national. The decision regarding whether or not to take this issue seriously should not depend on the presence or otherwise of a person on the autism spectrum as a member of a local parish, congregation or church-related business or activity. The absence of such people may be related to the way the local church functions, which may prove to be a barrier to attendance and involvement. If people on the spectrum are present, it is important to ask whether they are merely being tolerated or if they are being fully included and seen as an equal member of the Body of Christ in this community, with all that this implies.

I have spoken to many families where they have wanted to and have tried to attend their local church but where the reactions to the member of the family with autism or Asperger syndrome by members of the congregation have discouraged and dismayed them, and, in some instances, have put them off for life. Katie's experience provides a good example of this reality.

When I was introduced to Katie and her Mum, Sarah, Katie was 4 years old. Katie has autism as well as a couple of other disabilities. Sarah was a keen church attender and attended regularly with her 7-year-old son. When Katie came along, Sarah looked forward to taking both her children to her local church. However, when she took Katie for the first time, Katie screamed from the moment the first hymn started until Sarah decided to take her home, due to Katie's distress. No one said anything to Sarah but she sensed the tutting from the pews at the noise Katie was making and she decided never to return as it was too stressful. She was already an exhausted and stressed Mum dealing with the challenges presented by everyday life. I met Sarah and we talked about the issues and I realised that the problem was that Katie had no idea when the organ was going to strike up because she was unable to follow the service, due to her reduced language abilities. I developed a visual order of service for Katie which showed her when the hymns would be sung, and explained that that would mean the organ would play. Katie and Sarah went to church the following week to try out the visual order of service. Amazingly, Katie managed the whole service happily. The unknown, which was a source of stress, had been removed. I have to admit to feeling a lump in my throat each time I spotted Katie, her brother, and Sarah walking to church each week after that!

This was a simple solution to a difficult situation for all involved. Understanding how the person thinks and experiences the world can make a huge difference to how you help to pre-empt difficulties and deal with them.

Later in this chapter I will outline some more practical ways in which people on the autism spectrum can be supported and involved in the local church and other work and life situations. Before that, we need to consider the theological reasons why we should take this issue seriously as a Church.

A Christian Response

So how should we respond and why?

If we are to believe that we are all made in the image of God (Imago Dei) and that, as St Paul claims in 1 Corinthians, we are all members of one body, with many parts (1 Corinthians 12:12-27), then we also have to accept that people with autism are also made in the image of God and are a vital part of the body. For me, if people with autism are missing from our churches then the Church is poorer for it. We are missing something important as Church – a vital experience of Christ.

From Genesis 1:26, we know that we are made in the image of God, and as God is in relation with the Son and the Spirit, we are made for relationship and interdependence. Yong suggests that in relation to creation this means 'particular things are valued for what they are, precisely because they are constituted by their unity in dynamic relationship with others'. This is true for the Church too. In 1 Corinthians 12:21 we read, 'The eye cannot say to the hand, "I don't need you!"'.[433] The interdependence is such that we cannot manage without one person. We are not in the Church as individuals but as a body and as community. Cornelia Crocker suggests: 'For as an individual enters the body of Christ, the focus does not remain on that one person but shifts to the community of believers as a whole.'[434] Thomas Reynolds takes this further and claims that this need for interdependence rather than individuality requires a 'genuinely inclusive communion that results from sharing humanity with one another in light of the grace of God'.[435] Our humanity includes our vulnerabilities and weaknesses. In our search for wholeness we discover that we can only be whole when we are interdependent with others, ALL others, not just the others we consider to be capable. If we are selective in our interdependence we are incomplete – Reynolds goes so far as to use the phrases 'unfinished' and 'deficient'.

Yung Suk Kim suggests that a common interpretation of the idea of the Body of Christ is that of unity, but he challenges this and suggests

---

433 New International Version.

434 Crocker, Cornelia Cyss. (2004). *Reading 1 Corinthians in the 21st century*. London: T&T Clark International, p. 101.

435 Reynolds, Thomas E. (2008). *Vulnerable Communion: A Theology of Disability and Hospitality*. Grand Rapids, MI: Brazos Press, p. 18

that St Paul was actually suggesting that the Body of Christ was about diversity, and not about being the same. He says: 'Understanding the "Body of Christ" as a metaphor for those associated with the crucified one allows for identifying that body with many broken human bodies and communities through history and culture.'[436] Society generally has a tendency towards conformity. The Body of Christ can be counter-cultural in its diversity and inclusivity.

It is only when we rediscover this that we can move beyond seeing changes as compliance with legislation or lip-service to well-meaning reports, to full inclusion. The World Council of Churches once stated that 'Churches without persons with disabilities are disabled churches.'[437]

This may raise the question of whether within the Body of Christ there is disability at all? Maybe what we all have to offer the body is dependent on what we bring as ourselves – disabilities and all. Deland[438] suggests that being made in the image of God means that we see things not through one lens but through many. It is only then that we can appreciate the whole. The lens of disability provides a valuable perspective on the Church and the world which, if absent, means our view is missing an important dimension. Disability becomes an important part of what people offer as members, just as autism does. For some this is a controversial view. The suggestion that their disability is a 'gift' from God to the community disturbs them. Instead they may feel that their disability is something that should be healed or cured. My own view is that, through disability, God chooses to reveal another aspect of himself.

Another important aspect of being the Body of Christ is accessibility. If we are motivated to be fully inclusive in our churches, what does this mean? We read in 1 Corinthians 12:26: 'If one part suffers, every part suffers with it; if one part is honoured, every part rejoices with it.' (NIV). To be in community as the Body of Christ, we need to notice and respond to one another's needs and concerns.

---

436 Kim, Yung Suk (2008). *Christ's Body in Corinth, the politics of a metaphor*. Minneapolis: Fortress Press, pp. 3, 11.

437 Moltmann, Jurgen. (2010). In Eisland, Nancy L. et al. (ed.). *Human Disability and the Service of God*. Nashville: Abingdon Press, p. 22.

438 Deland, Jane S. "Images of God through the lens of disability" which appears in the Journal of Religion, Disability and Health, vol 3 1999 issue 2, p. 47.

Salier suggests the question 'Who is here to worship God?'[439] is a good place to start our conversation on this topic. A subsequent question would then be: *how* can we enable each individual to worship God in this place? If these were the questions, we might be in a better place to respond as we would be asking corporate questions rather than focusing on a few individuals who need things done a little differently.

In considering accessibility, Reynolds suggests 'Genuine love is prevented from coming to fruition when physical and social barriers prevent access.'[440] Nancy Eisland claims that 'For many disabled persons the church has been a "city on a hill", physically inaccessible and socially inhospitable.'[441]

For many churches, however, the problem has not been one of deliberately making church and worship inaccessible or ignoring the needs of people with autism or Asperger's, but more simply not knowing the best way forward. I suspect the majority of people do not need to do theological gymnastics to accept that people with autism are as much a part of the Church as you and I. The difficulty they have is how we make our churches autism-friendly and how to ensure that the gifts of people with autism are used to build up the body, in the same way as everyone else.

How can we help people on the Autism Spectrum and their families?

Due to its complex nature, knowing how to help someone on the autism spectrum can feel like a minefield but, in truth, it is usually small gestures which can make the biggest difference. Whatever we do needs to be manageable and effective, to enable those on the autism spectrum not only to access a building or service but also to participate and contribute. Whole books have been written on this topic but for the purposes of this overview I have identified five main ways which can provide effective support in a variety of contexts.

---

439   Salier, Don E. (2010). In Eisland, Nancy L. et al. (ed.). *Human Disability and the Service of God*, p. 30.
440   Reynolds, Thomas E. *Vulnerable Communion*, p. 238.
441   Eisland, Nancy. (1994). *The Disabled God: Toward a Liberatory Theology of Disability*. Nashville: Abingdon Press, p. 20.

Information

Getting to know and understand a person is key to what Jesus was about and is therefore key for those of us who wish to follow him. When anyone comes to a church, school, or workplace for the first time, getting to know each other is the first step in making someone feel valued, and to feel that they are an important part of this group or community. The same should be true for people on the autism spectrum, the only difference being that there are a few more things you need to try and discover about the person in addition to what we would do in standard situations. How this is done will depend on the person themselves and their age.

Children

If you have a family in your church or school who have a child on the autism spectrum, or you are aware that such a family would like to start attending, then early knowledge will make the biggest difference. The more you know, the more you will understand and the easier it will be to help and support.

Earlier in the chapter I told Katie's story. Making a difference for Katie was as simple as listening to her Mum about what Katie's reactions were in the service and when they happened. We very quickly worked out that hearing the organ play set off distress for Katie. Knowing that led to us creating a visual order of service for her so that she knew when the organ would be playing. That simple change meant that Katie could go to church with her family and participate the same as everyone else.

One of the key things to understand about people with autism is that on the whole it is not that they cannot cope with change; it is that they cannot cope with *unexpected change*. So for Katie, knowing the sound would be coming was manageable. It was not knowing that a change was about to take place that was the problem. Just knowing this fact about autism can remove fear from situations for all involved, and greatly reduce behaviours associated with anxiety.

An early conversation with the parent(s) can help you to learn so much about the child and how their condition affects them. Autism presents slightly differently in each person, so it is important to know how the condition presents itself in the particular situation of this child.

If the parents would like their child to attend your Sunday School activities or Messy Church-type activities, then some basic questions such as the following may be of benefit:

> Does the child know any other children in the church? This is useful for pairing up with other children. Familiarity reduces anxiety in these children.
>
> What is your child good at? When we deal with issues of disability we so easily look for the problems and the difficulties, but it is important to balance this with strengths and positivity. Knowing what a child is good at can help ensure some activities incorporate these strengths and can also help the church identify possible ways the child can make a positive contribution to the whole church family. For example, many children and young people on the autism spectrum are very interested in technology, especially computers, and they can have exceptional skills in this area. Knowing this may mean that a young person with autism could help to create PowerPoint presentations for services, etc. Asking the positive question early on gives the parents the reassurance that you are not simply concentrating on the challenges.
>
> What interest does your child have? Knowing this can be really helpful. Children on the autism spectrum often have one or two interests which are almost obsessions. Knowing what they are can provide an entry point for gaining their attention. It also maintains their focus and interest, as well as their ability to cope with a new situation. For example, if a young child was obsessed by Thomas the Tank Engine, then providing them with a small Thomas train, or a colouring picture of Thomas, may help them to come into the church building or Sunday School room with a reduced amount of anxiety, as their interest will compensate for some of the anxiety that they experience as a result of being in an unfamiliar place. Interests can also be used to link in with themes, or simply to be presented as a small visual stimulus or decoration on a worksheet.

Does the child have any difficulties with sound, touch, taste or smell? People on the autism spectrum often have some problems with sensory stimuli. It may be that they struggle with even small amounts of sensory input from one or more of their sensory channels or, conversely, they may require greater stimulation in order to function. You might not think that a church is a terribly sensory place but there are many unfamiliar sounds such as loud instruments, often stone or tiled floors, which mean every sound is amplified. There are large spaces where sounds can often echo, and after a service there is lots of chatter. Flower displays can provide a beautiful visual centrepiece, but if a person with autism has an over-sensitive nose the smell of flowers can make them feel sick or can overload their senses and cause fright or flight reactions. We also have a tendency in churches to want to demonstrate our welcome and friendliness by offering a handshake at the door or a pat on the shoulder. During Communion we 'pass the peace' which usually involves a handshake or a hug. If touch is something you find difficult then being expected to shake the hand of many strangers can be very stressful. Knowing if the child has any issues with sensory input can enable the church to make some suitable adjustments, or alert the parent to occasions which might be coming up which the child may find more challenging than normal.

It is also useful to know how the child usually copes with being separated from its parents. If this is difficult, it may be better to try and organise some activities for the child to do while remaining in church, for example, as opposed to trying to make them go out into Sunday School or the children's liturgy with other children.

It is also useful to ask the parents how anxiety and pleasure manifest themselves in their child. Some children on the spectrum may clap and squeal when excited, or some might hum constantly as a means of trying to reassure themselves. They may do this to drown out what is happening around them if they are feeling distressed. There are as many behaviours as there are children, but knowing how *this* child behaves means you can pre-empt further distress or react quickly. It can also mean you are reassured that the child is actually happy. Some of this information may be suitable to share with the congregation as long as you have permission from the person or parent in order to reduce the chances of people getting frustrated or annoyed at disturbances in the services. Once people understand, they are usually a lot more patient and accommodating.

This is not an exhaustive list of questions but it is a good starting point for information gathering. This can make an enormous difference regarding whether or not a child with autism is able to adjust to the new environment of the church, a new school, or new activity.

Adults

Many of the strategies for children can be adapted for adults and the same areas need to be considered. Adults on the autism spectrum have the same struggles with sensory issues, social interaction, communication and so on as children with these conditions.

In the work place it is often helpful to discover any employees' strengths and play to them. This is especially important when interacting with people who have autism. They will be able to cope and work more efficiently if they are engaged in activities which they are good at and which motivate them.

It can also be helpful to try and ensure that their environment supports their needs. If visual stimuli are a distraction in an office environment, then providing a screen around the person's desk can significantly minimise the impact of this difficulty, and ensure they can work in a relaxed way. The impact of sensory stimuli cannot be overstated in people on the autism spectrum. They can respond to these stimuli in physical ways, including headaches, nausea, and fright and flight reactions. If an employee has a strong sense of smell it may be more helpful, for example, not to place them right by the kitchen or coffee machine.

Many adults on the autism spectrum also find structure and routine helpful. They will often prefer to have a list of jobs to work through or a logical plan to follow. They may even find it helpful to have certain days allocated to certain jobs. If changes need to be made to the usual schedule, or meetings arranged, providing as much advance warning as possible will be helpful and is to be advised. As I mentioned earlier, it is not change *per se* that is the problem for people on the autism spectrum but unexpected change. Consequently, making the effort to alert people to a possible change in advance is vital for their emotional stability.

As with children, adults on the autism spectrum do not always realise that general instructions are for them. If instructions are being given to a whole department or office, it is helpful to ensure that the person on the autism spectrum has these things explicitly mentioned to them to ensure they have understood expectations. A written memo can be helpful as well as a verbal instruction.

People on the autism spectrum can also lose track of time very easily, especially if they are engaged in an activity which they find interesting. My son can spend hours on a computer, but when challenged about this, he thinks that only half an hour has gone by. It has been known in workplaces for people with autism to completely miss their breaks. Ensuring that they take their lunch and breaks may mean setting a specific time for that person to take their lunch and to be told it is time for lunch.

Managing time can also be a challenge. These adults can find it difficult to break larger, more long-term tasks into smaller tasks. It can also be helpful to break a larger piece of work into smaller tasks with clear deadlines. Regular supervision can alleviate this problem to ensure that they are working to a deadline and can meet the smaller targets along the way. This may feel a little controlling and not something you would consider for other employees, but it can be immensely helpful to someone on the autism spectrum.

Conclusion

As I suggested earlier, many people are very cautious around conditions such as autism because the manifestations of the condition can be extreme, but, as is often the case in life, so often small changes can make the biggest difference. Pre-empting issues is the key and this involves relationship. There needs to be an openness which allows insights to be shared and a plan developed which will enable the person, young or old, to function to the best of their ability and make a valuable contribution.

We are all disabled in some way; it is often our environment or situation that disables us. On any ordinary day my fear of deep water is not a problem and therefore my 'disability' is hidden. It is only if I walk past a canal and see someone drowning that my 'disability' may become more apparent. In autism it is often the environment or situation which causes the disability to become apparent. If these things can be pre-empted and managed well, the person on the spectrum will predominantly be seen for their strengths and their ability rather than judged or experienced only through their disability. We need to work together to bring out the best in each other. As a result, our churches, schools and workplaces can be friendly places for people with autism or Asperger's, who have the same desires as the rest of us for acceptance, and for the sense of well-being that results from knowing we are contributing our best in a given situation.

Further Reading

Wicks, R.J. (2004). A Threat to Christian Communities: Angry People Acting Passive Aggressively. *Human Development 25* (3): 8-16.

Harvard Business Review. (August, 2016). How to work with toxic colleagues (HBR OnPoint Magazine).

CHAPTER TEN

Violence in the Workplace

Michael Fitzsimons

Introduction

I was visiting the French shrine of Lourdes in July 2016 when I heard the news of the murder of Fr Jacques Hamel in his church in a small village in Normandy in an attack by so-called Islamic State terrorists.[442] By the next day, security around the pilgrimage sites and the shrine had visibly increased and much of this security remains to date. The resulting media focus raised the real potential and concern about future anti-Christian hate crimes and need for churches to review security measures. In the time since that attack, I know of at least four priests in my own or neighbouring dioceses who have been victims of violent physical attack or threat, not due to hate crime, but rather to attempted thefts and general intimidation. In nearly every church and parish I have served at, in the inner city and in smaller towns, there have been issues of vandalism, young people (and not so young) causing disturbance or minor damage around church premises, and I have needed to respond personally to specific situations of aggression. It would seem that the terrorist attack in France is at one extreme end of a range of real and potential harmful incidents of violence which can be directed towards clergy and other church workers.

Recently, when disposing of the junk 'mail' which regularly clogs up our office fax machine, one of the papers caught my attention; in between the offers of debt collection and hire cars, there was a crime management firm advertising security services. This is not unusual until you consider its headline which targeted organisations seemingly at risk from antisocial behaviour. It listed schools and educational establishments, public transport, empty properties, parks and then, perhaps surprisingly, churches. Having worked in the voluntary sector for a number of years, I was accustomed to thinking about these issues,

---

442 http://www.bbc.co.uk/news/world-europe-36892785

but initially I was relatively surprised that churches were now being seen as prime targets for such services. Then almost immediately I began to reflect on how the current church premises I work from have regularly been subjected to vandalism. Groups of young people often gather in or nearby the churches and church houses in the area where I live and cause disturbances. Indeed, there has been a growth of violence and violent attacks made on clergy and other church workers in recent years. It was not hard to bring to mind numbers of situations known to me personally where clergy had suffered from intimidation, theft and burglary and occasionally violent attacks. Perhaps I shouldn't have been surprised at this fax at all.

The issue of violence and aggression is current in our society and generates much discussion as to its causes and its perceived growth. Acts of violence and aggression directed against caring professionals, including clergy and other pastoral workers, are seemingly more commonplace and often attract significant media attention and wide coverage. This serves both to highlight the issue and potentially increase fear of such attacks which generally, thankfully, are still not commonplace. However, it should encourage us to think critically about the threat of aggression and violence in our workplaces and pastoral activities, and actively consider steps to promote the safety and well-being of employees, clergy, pastoral workers and those who work in the voluntary sector. What can be done to further understand this problem and how can we make an effective response?

What is Violence in the Workplace?

We often make various assumptions about violence and aggression, both in terms of what it actually is and what causes a person to become violent and aggressive. Some of these assumptions can be helpful, but often they do not take the full situation into account. Firstly, let us consider defining violence. We may wish to assume that an act of violence is when someone is physically harmed, but what about intimidation or threat which can be equally debilitating and cause equal fear? We can assume that all violence is intentional but then we must consider whether sometimes the aggressor is out of control due to the influence of alcohol or drugs, or is simply at the end of their tether.

Maybe we would want to say that all violence is unjust or unfair, but how do we define legitimate self-defence?

In reality, violence is a more widespread phenomenon than we might at first imagine. Let us think of the many times when we are asked to offer pastoral care to individuals or groups we would consider to be 'victims' of violence. This may include situations of abuse, domestic violence, neighbour threats and intimidation, violent crime, racial or homophobic harassment, working with asylum seekers or refugees fleeing institutional or political violence, to name just a few. Any definition would need to include direct physical violence and threat of violence but also the wider social, structural and cultural aspects of violence. Engage[443] offers one possible definition:

> Violence is any physical, emotional, verbal, institutional, structural or spiritual behaviour, attitude, policy or condition that diminishes, dominates or destroys ourselves or others.[444]

This definition goes on to recognise that violence is motivated by fear, anger, greed or the desire to control and dominate, but can also at times be motivated by frustration in the face of perceived injustice, or used by people with the conviction that they are attempting to overcome past violence directed towards them, and that there is no other way. It also notes that violence often provokes new and additional violence in a spiral of retaliation.

The reasons why individuals resort, deliberately or otherwise, to aggression, violence, intimidation and threat are myriad and potentially complex. It is possible to identify and summarise up to eight possible groupings of theories about the causes of aggression and violence:[445]

1. Natural or innate theories see aggression as a natural part of every animal and indeed every human being. Humans, as the most dominant species, are the most aggressive of all and are the only group who will fight over an idea or a belief,

---

443 Engage is a study programme and a project of *Pace E Bene* Nonviolence Service, Las Vegas, Nevada.

444 Definition from Engage in Slattery, L., Butigan, K., Pelicaric, V. and Preston-Pile, K. (2005). *Engage, Exploring Nonviolent Living, a study programme for learning, practicing and experimenting with the power of creative nonviolence to transform our lives and our world*. Oakland, CA: Pace e Bene Press.

445 Braithwaite, R. (2001). *Managing Aggression*. London/New York: Routledge/CommunityCare.

and furthermore we are continuing this need to dominate by destroying ourselves in warfare. More positive theories propose that aggression can be used to survive difficult situations and challenges in life.

2. The frustration theory proposes that people become aggressive when their needs are not met and this is a response to the frustration generated. The frustration is relieved, permanently or at least temporarily, once the aggressive act is over.

3. Behavioural theories suggest that aggression is a learned process. Behaviour is controlled by past experiences and the consequences derived from those experiences. If someone has learned that the use of aggression and violence achieves their aims and desires, there is no incentive to change.

4. Ecological theories note that people are affected by the conditions in which they live. Some theories identify that people resort to violence when food, air or space is scarce. Environmental factors such as overcrowding, poor lighting, shabby furniture, enforced use of shared or inadequate facilities can all contribute to aggressive behaviour.

5. Sociological theories identify the causes of aggression and violence as being rooted in culture, roles and stereotypes created by and within society. The potential for conflict and aggression is increased when society distributes its resources based on stereotypical norms (class, gender, ethnicity, educational achievement, accent) and thus they are distributed unequally.

6. Psychodynamic theories place emphasis on the influence of our past and how others, particularly significant relationships, related to us. Being constantly told as children that we were bad or naughty, or regularly and unfavourably compared with siblings or others can have a significant impact on our lives. Not having the skills to give this appropriate expression as children or when tired or frustrated, aggressive behaviour is perceived as rebelliousness. The resultant reaction of parents or teacher reinforces the child's sense of 'badness'. Hence anger is bottled up, sometimes over many years, until it explodes in violent

temper outbursts or can be triggered by someone, often an authority figure, who reminds us of our childhood protagonist.

7. Interactive theory understands violence as a process influenced by others. If we are hostile to another person, this may lead to hostility and aggression in them. Violent acts may then be perpetrated, thus giving our initial aggression validity. This theory sees violence and aggression as a continual vicious circle of hostile acts and responses which deepen the initial hostility and aggression.

8. Finally, chemically induced theories propose that chemicals, be they introduced by use of alcohol or drugs, or certain foods that contain toxins, or produced internally due to physical illness or hormonal imbalance, can give rise to aggressive behaviour.

Added to this are certain behaviour patterns or actions which combine different and various aspects of some or all of the theories identified above. However it is understood, most forms of violence and aggression do require a cause of some sort. If we stop and consider ourselves for a moment and think about what can make us angry, upset or nervous, we can then ask ourselves what happens when this intensifies or escalates to a certain degree or level. Once we reach a particular threshold, most of us can feel aggressive or even potentially violent. If we are being honest, most of us can think of situations where we would at least be tempted to become aggressive, especially if we felt the aggression was justifiable in the context.

It is also possible to learn that if we use violence we can get our own way. This can be from a very early age and we can observe the schoolyard bully learning that if you threaten someone with violence, then they may give you their sweets; if as an adult you walk into an advice project, community centre or church and patiently sit and wait your turn someone will eventually come to you, yet if you walk in and start to shout and bang the tables with your fists you are guaranteed the immediate attention of at least one member of staff – sadly, some people have learned that resorting to violence can get you what you want.

Violence against professionals

Violence against professionals in the community was the focus of research funded by the Economic and Social Research Council in 2001.[446] This study examined the nature and extent of violence and whether it was socially patterned by the professional's age or gender, and secondly how these professionals responded and managed both the threats and actual incidence of violence. The research focused on GPs, probation officers and Anglican clergy. The most common form of aggression reported was verbal abuse. A total of 71% of clergy indicated that they had been verbally abused at least once over the previous two-year period. In the same period, 22% of Anglican clergy indicated that they had been threatened with violence, with those working in inner-city areas reporting a significantly higher incidence compared to those working in rural areas. Female clergy reported slightly fewer threats than males.

Across all the professional groups, 10–12% reported being assaulted, with slightly higher levels of reporting among the clergy. For the most part, these assaults involved being pushed or shoved without injury. Some key differences emerged for the clergy who reported these assaults. While the majority of assaults on GPs and probation officers occurred in their main place of work, most assaults on clergy were in their homes, on the street or local estates rather than in or near church buildings. Whereas the majority of GPs knew their assailant, almost half the clergy reported being assaulted by someone not known to them. All the professional groups reported that being assaulted affected the way they dealt with clients and made them feel less secure. Given that many of the clergy had experienced assault in their home, there is potential for these feelings of insecurity to be higher.

It is interesting to consider what the research tells us regarding the varied responses from different professional groups to such violence and aggression. The fluid and elusive nature of some risks, combined with the complex working relationships between professionals and the people they work with and how they understand such relationships, was significant. The clergy, alongside GPs, were the least likely to use formal risk assessment procedures, utilising these measures much

---

446   https://researchcatalogue.esrc.ac.uk/grants/L133251036/read

more haphazardly and reactively. The increase of women clergy in the past few years may also be a significant factor. Although this research focused on Anglican clergy, there is a growing presence of women working in pastoral care in all of the churches. In fact, the majority of workers in lay-led initiatives tend to be women. The presence of women has challenged conventional working practices such as making late-night home visits alone which perhaps assumed the presence of male clergy. Women in all three professions reported both higher fear of violence and being more likely to take precautions on a regular basis. The reported incidence of threats and assaults was lower for women than for their male colleagues.

A number of commentators within different churches responded to this research by associating aggression and violence with the alleged decline in respect for clergy, and indeed all professional groups in society. Interestingly, in the ESRC research there was a generational shift in this area, with older clergy and GPs explaining the rise in aggression as due to a perceived loss of status. Younger clergy and GPs, on the other hand, were more likely to identify aggression in contextual terms such as the socioeconomic or personal circumstances of the communities and individuals they serve, and possibly stressing a more egalitarian relationship between clergy and people.

This research corresponds with other evidence on violence in the workplace and specific research on threats against clergy. In 2006, focused research on violence experienced by clergy found that 48% of a sample of 90 clergy had suffered at least one violent assault in the preceding 12 months[447] and other evidence suggests that certain occupations are at special risk including nurses, social workers, those providing care and advice, and those who work alone.[448] You are more likely to face direct violence and aggression in the 'care' sector than in retail, banking or even the security sector.

Being aware of the complex nature of violence and aggression and the possible causes of such behaviour enables us to identify the elements over which we have some control. We can then start to formulate effective approaches both to reduce and minimise the risk of having to

---

447   Tolson, Nick. 'The Clergy Lifestyle Theory' at https://www.professionalsecurity.co.uk/news/news-archive/clergy-lifestyle/

448   Chappell, Duncan and Di Martino, V. (2000). *Violence at Work,* 2nd Edition. Geneva: International Labour Office.

face such aggression and even strategies to confront and resist violence when it occurs.

How to Deal with Violence in the Workplace

The first response when considering the risk of encountering violence and aggression in our ministry and work is to reflect on how this risk can be prevented or minimised. There are two aspects to prevention: firstly, examining the physical security of our buildings and homes (particularly as many clergy use their home as a place of work, seeing various people in need there) and, secondly, looking at safer working practices that will reduce the risk of violence or assault. Physical security measures can include considering:

- Security lighting
- Door entry systems
- Perimeter fencing
- CCTV
- Alarms and panic buttons.

Local and community police can often offer advice and support around issues of physical security and can be a useful source of information and support. Police forces can also be a good source of information for those concerned with hate crime.

The use of door entry systems, CCTV or a simple spy hole in a door can be both effective and relatively inexpensive. Where possible, also consider the layout and use of premises. Keep rooms near to the entrance for interviews and counselling and support and, where possible, have more than one entry or door to these rooms. Think about the layout and use of furniture in the room – ensure that you can be seated nearest the door. This also applies to counsellors, nurses or care workers who interview vulnerable adults, some of whom may be violent or under the influence of alcohol or drugs, or be suffering from a personality or organic disorder such as schizophrenia. Furnishings should be warm and welcoming but eradicate any unnecessary risks by the removal of heavy ashtrays or other ornaments that could be thrown or used as a weapon.

Having examined the physical safety of your premises, next consider your work practices and procedures. Are there ways of reducing risk? Firstly, consider that you are much more at risk when you are working alone. This cannot always be avoided when offering one-to-one support or confidential services, but having someone else around in the house, church, office or project will significantly reduce your risk. The person does not have to be working directly with you, but a colleague, receptionist, secretary, sacristan or church volunteer who may be doing other work will both reduce the risk and ensure that there is someone to raise the alarm if necessary. There is strong evidence that simply having another person present can significantly reduce the possibility of violent or aggressive behaviour, even if they are not trained, experienced or even expected to deal with any violent situation or threat.[449]

Often, people in need call unexpectedly or 'out of hours', but do consider whether this should be encouraged and whether it can be avoided. Think carefully about what you are actually able to do. Some organisations that offer 24-hour telephone support, for example, have a policy of not opening the door after a certain time at night. In cases of emergency, the police can be called. If you do allow someone entrance, consider calling a colleague or a parishioner, for example, and tell them that you are allowing someone in and ask them to call you back in 30 minutes. Similar arrangements can be put in place where clergy or care workers are 'on-call' and asked to attend or visit other people's homes. A few practicalities should be borne in mind. Firstly, always carry a mobile telephone and personal attack alarm, even if you know the people you are visiting. Remember, even if you know the person you are visiting, you do not know who else might be present, such as another family member or an ex-partner. Again, consider letting someone else know that you are going out to see someone, and tell them to phone you on your mobile phone at an agreed time, or inform them that you will contact them when you return.

These practices may initially seem excessive or overly cautious, but they are basic common sense and would be expected of many other professionals working in community settings. Just consider the following scenario. One evening you have allowed someone into your home who

---

449 Tolson, Nick. 'The Clergy Lifestyle Theory' at https://www.professionalsecurity.co.uk/news/news-archive/clergy-lifestyle/

has arrived unexpectedly in a distressed state. You call a parishioner and ask them to call you in 15 minutes. When you return to attend to the caller, he has become more agitated and at times aggressive, and you feel uncomfortable and under threat. When the parishioner calls in 15 minutes, it allows you to leave the room to answer the phone. You can then decide if you need extra help, such as someone to call or even the police if appropriate.

All this consideration of risk reduction and prevention of violent attack may seem contrary to the purpose of an organisation, or the mission and ministry of clergy. Surely we want our places of employment, churches, church houses and projects to be places of welcome, highly accessible and open to all people and especially anyone in need of care or support? Focusing specifically on churches, we could be the safest church, presbytery or rectory, with the safest work practices and procedures, and end up being distant, removed, inaccessible and entirely irrelevant to the communities we seek to serve and minister to. Equally, though, we also have a duty of care to ourselves and others who work and serve alongside us. We need to be aware of our limitations and feel able to say no at times when we feel vulnerable or unsafe. Safety and risk reduction, and accessibility and welcome are not diametrically opposed, but rather need to be in constant dialogue.

A word of warning, though – we can become over-reliant on technology and risk reducing work practices without thinking what they will actually achieve. I remember reflecting once with staff in a local prison after an alarm bell had been triggered which immediately resulted in radio contact with staff and a number of officers being present at the scene within seconds and minutes, with other specially trained and equipped staff potentially available quickly – I couldn't help but compare this with the homeless drop-in centre where I was then working. The centre also had an alarm bell which set off a loud and potentially usefully distracting siren, but ultimately still left me and the four or five volunteers present to deal as effectively as possible with any potential incident of violence or aggression. Consideration can be given to the possibility of having panic and personal alarms automatically connected to police or security centres. This will be helpful in some settings, but over-reliance on technology, practical security measures and risk assessment is not enough.

Given that you have considered physical security and balanced that with the desire to be accessible and available, there is still the potential of having to deal with an unknown person, or indeed the known aggressive person who has turned up unexpectedly, or dealing with him or her until help can be summoned. In this section, I will attempt to offer some practical, non-violent, and realistic responses. In effect, I will try to offer ways of directly responding to an incident of violence and aggression directed at an individual. The first task is to attempt to gently defuse the situation, slow things down and hopefully avoid actual violence. In reality, many violent or aggressive incidents occur very rapidly, giving you little time to think through a strategy or response. Here, in effect, I will examine any given violent or potentially violent encounter in 'slow motion', considering the assessment of the situation and those involved, responding, dealing and then managing the incident, and finally attempting to avoid escalating the situation and so bring it to a successful outcome.

When confronted with aggression, threat or actual violence, certain 'automatic' responses can immediately kick in. These can be typified by the fight, flight or freeze responses which are all natural, biological, physiological responses to situations of fear, violence and aggression. Natural angers, fears, frustrations and panic quickly come to the surface when we are faced with such situations. Before we know it, we are thinking and responding: 'how dare he speak to me like that, I'm going to give him a piece of my mind', or 'she has a knife – get out of here', or 'they're coming at me – what should I do?' Each of these responses is natural and understandable and indeed is controlled by the automatic physiological changes that happen in situations of stress. These same physiological factors are occurring in the aggressor, and these control and promote their behaviour and reactions. While these initial responses are all understandable, they may not always be the most appropriate ways of responding to situations of conflict, aggression and violence.

Initially, it is essential to stay calm and to try and relax. This is easier said than done when faced with the actual aggression, but it is achievable, and is essential to buy you time to make an effective assessment of your situation. The following steps will immediately allow you to attempt to calm yourself, and as much as possible to relax and stay in control of your mind and your body:

- Say STOP to yourself
- Breathe in deeply, breathe out slowly
- Drop your shoulders
- Relax your hands
- Do it again!

As has been stated, we often spring into reaction when faced with violence. Just stopping ourselves from immediate reaction is the first step. Allowing ourselves to breathe deeply and slowly is a powerful relaxation agent. This allows time to make an assessment of both the environment and the aggressor. First consider if there is any avenue of escape. No one should feel under any obligation to remain in a situation of violence or potential violence if they can legitimately remove themselves from it. If you can leave a room, do so, thereby locking a person out from accessing you and potentially causing you harm. Remember that no threat to property or resources can be compared to any individual's personal safety and security. A second assessment is needed about whether anyone else is present.

- Who are they and how near are they?
- Are they people you have a responsibility for – service users, parishioners or colleagues which possibly means that you cannot leave without endangering them?
- Are they people who can help or summon assistance such as the police?
- Are they also potential threats?

As has already been stated above, the presence of another person, whoever they might be, is a significant factor in reducing the threat of violence or assault.

The final factor to consider in your physical environment is whether there are any large objects such as desks or church benches that could serve as barriers. If someone is being verbally threatening from the other end of a large desk or table, I will certainly feel slightly better than if I am in a small room with chairs that is isolated from others in the project and there is no effective barrier between myself and the aggressor.

The next assessment needed is of the threatening person themselves:

- Who is this person?
- Do you know him/her?
- What is your relationship?
- How near are they to you?
- What is their emotional state?
- What is being said and how?
- Is there evidence of alcohol or substance use?
- Do they possess any weapons, such as a gun or a knife?

All this information is important for you as you try and remain calm and keep control of the situation. Any of the above information will help us make better informed responses. It is more likely that we will know the aggressive person, as most reported incidents of violence are from people known to the victims. Evidence of alcohol or substance use can indicate that the person is more likely to resort to violence or aggression. But equally, if they are highly intoxicated, it may be easier to make an escape if needed. As well as the possession of actual weapons, also consider the availability of any makeshift weapons such as smashed bottles, cutlery, or lightweight furniture which could be thrown. Be aware that even objects we do not ordinarily consider as potential weapons, such as candlesticks or lamps, could very easily be used against us.

Having made the fullest assessment possible, we now have to try and open communication with the aggressor. The most influential channel of communication will be non-verbal:

- Often it is all we have initially, but it is first and immediate.
- It buys time and can have a powerful calming effect.
- It accounts for approximately 75% of all we communicate!

There is a problem here as fear and violence look similar! Naturally, you will feel fear or indeed aggression – you are in fight or flight mode, which is how we are 'hard-wired' to deal with threats to our person. Indeed, most people would consider it reasonable to be fearful if someone is acting aggressively, especially if they are threatening actual physical harm. Naturally, our bodies will want to communicate this fear or even our own aggression and defensiveness. The problem is that we ought not to show this fear but rather signal non-aggression. In other words, we must teach our bodies to lie! Yes, we may feel fear, but what we will try to display and signal is an attitude and position of non-aggression. Signalling non-aggression is powerful and also puts you in a position of strength, not weakness, while still resisting and confronting the violence. To signal non-violence:

- Create space
- Relax your posture
- Drop and extend your arms
- Open your hands
- Lower your voice
- Slow your movements.

Having signalled non-aggression, we can now attempt to try and calm the situation. In all the following strategies it is worthwhile to note that we cannot solely calm and resolve this aggression and potential violence. This will take two parties, you and the aggressor. Remember all that has been said about non-verbal communication, which is still a primary tactic at this stage. We can, however, now start to encourage talking and use verbal communication ourselves. Offer reassurance where appropriate. While there remains a high potential for violence, at this stage no one has been physically hurt, and therefore the situation is not out of control. It has not gone too far and can still be resolved amicably. So often in my experience it has been possible to reassure an aggressor that things can still be managed and at this stage no sanction will need to be imposed. This was particularly the case while working in homeless projects and hostels when people often felt that they had nothing left to lose and they were sure they would be barred or evicted from the project. People engage in high-risk strategies when there is little to lose and a high-risk gamble appears to be worth taking. If people perceive that a change of attitude or behaviour may result in a better outcome, there is a higher likelihood of reducing the emotional temperature.[450] Hearing that, at this stage, it may be possible for them to remain and explain their need, often leading to a defusing of tension and a reduction in the threat of violence.

It is essential when dealing with any incident of violence or aggression not to rush to resolve it or run ahead before the aggressor is starting to calm and engage with you. It is better to proceed gradually and surely. I can think of numerous situations when dealing with an incident of violence when I have made assumptions about how someone will respond without allowing them time to calm. This inevitably led to inflaming the situation further. A violent incident can often attract attention from many others present which is not always helpful – consider a fight in a school yard which will soon attract a good crowd of children to observe, and even encourage, the fight. As a person starts to calm, consideration can be given to moving to a less public space to avoid an audience. Clearly, we should never isolate ourselves with an aggressor, but perhaps we can ask others present to back off a little or to continue with the ordinary and everyday activities of the project. Finally, at all times continue to anticipate violence and ensure continuing vigilance. People who are aggressive rarely calm down in seconds and minutes and must be given appropriate time to relax and allow their aggression to dissipate.

Once a situation has been calmed, we can move to further stages of relating to the aggressive person and ultimately managing the situation. We might not particularly feel like relating with someone who has threatened us, let alone dealing with them with understanding and warmth, but if we set it in the context of resolving the situation and protecting ourselves from further violence it is a worthwhile thing to do. Try to encourage agreement and verbalise this with 'yes' statements that both of you can agree. Remember it takes both you *and* the aggressor

---

450   Leith, Karen P. and Baumeister, Roy F. (1996). Why do bad moods increase self-defeating behavior? Emotion, risk-taking and self-regulation. *Journal of Personality and Social Psychology* 71: 1250–67.

to successfully resolve the issue without the use of violence and so use 'we' statements to agree that we can resolve the issue peacefully, and that we don't wish to hurt or harm the other person. It is only at this stage that we can move to verbal communication and then continue to try and manage the situation non-violently. Open up channels of communication, thank them and use praise appropriately and sensitively if they start to cooperate. Ask them to sit down and see if there can be any compromise or alternative solution to their problems. Always include the other person in trying to resolve the issue so that they feel included and empowered. As any violent situation seems to be diffused or resolved, one final note of caution is to avoid escalating behaviour. So often violence and aggression can be re-triggered or re-inflamed by the wrong word at the wrong time. Avoid criticising the person, or belittling them, especially in front of others. Try to be aware not to use unhelpful gestures like pointing which can appear authoritarian or controlling.

Finally, no guide to dealing with violence and aggression would be complete without referring to self-defence. Surely we all have the right to use legitimate force to protect ourselves from violent attack? The answer is, correctly, yes, but within the limitations of what is deemed to be both necessary and reasonable. Here a sense of proportionality must come into effect. Thus, in considering what force is necessary, we must take into account what is reasonable. For example, it may be considered both necessary and reasonable to use force which may seriously injure, or even kill someone when faced with the real possibility that your own life is endangered, but it could hardly be justifiable when responding to verbal insults or spitting, however unpleasant these may be. In order to help define 'necessity' and 'reasonable', a number of factors should be considered: the gravity of the crime being prevented; whether it was possible to prevent it using non-violent methods; whether you were willing to try those means first; and, finally, the relative strength of the persons involved.[451] Alternatives considered by some organisations, projects and individuals are implementing training in breakaway techniques or developing the use of control and restraint. This is

---

451 Dawes, M. and Winn, D. (1999). *Managing the monkey: How to defuse the conflicts that can lead to violence in the workplace*. Hailsham, East Sussex: The Therapist, p. 57.

the official Home Office-approved technique for the management of violence in the prison system but has also been adapted to many healthcare settings. While each has their uses, they also have significant limitations. Breakaway techniques can be both complex and varied and, in the heightened atmosphere of a physical attack, a victim could easily become confused in their application.[452] Would you necessarily remember more than a handful of techniques for very specific situations anyway? Control and restraint is only applicable in certain settings and it would be unwise to try and simply replicate it in church or voluntary settings. It is taught by approved trainers over a period of anything from up to two days to a week, with specific follow-up refresher training. Given the disadvantages of its specific training, its potential misuse and even the possibility of escalating violence if applied inappropriately,[453] it is not really a suitable strategy or response by individual workers, clergy, small projects and churches. So, broadly speaking, while it is both desirable and fair to say we all have the right to self-defence and to use physical force to protect ourselves when we are faced with violent, physical attack, this needs to be tempered with the notions of what is both reasonable and necessary, and the inherent difficulties in deciding what falls within the parameters of these terms.

As has been stated above, a key factor in safety or reducing the risk of violent attack is working with another person rather than in isolation. Given this, it is worthwhile to consider how to respond if you witness aggressive behaviour or even a violent attack directed at a colleague. The first principle is always to raise the alarm. Let others know what is happening and either call for the appropriate back-up and support (which may obviously include the police) or ensure someone else is doing this. Only then is it helpful to make any intervention to directly support the person being attacked. This can appear to be callous, but it is better to ensure that help is on its way before – in a worst-case scenario – there are two people trapped by a violent aggressor. Any immediate intervention is best taken from a safe distance. Let the aggressor know that you are present and are witnessing the incident. If direct physical harm is being inflicted, or the victim is being physically

---

452 Ibid., p. 62.
453 Mason, T. and Chandley, M. (1999). *Managing violence and aggression: A manual for nurses and health care workers.* Edinburgh: Churchill Livingstone, p. 157.

restrained, repeatedly tell the aggressor to stop or let the person go. Final consideration can be given to physical interventions such as dragging the aggressor off the victim, disarming him or using restraint. Firstly, it is essential that any such action and intervention is thought out carefully to ensure there will not simply be two victims rather than one. In addition, notions of reasonable force and proportionality, as discussed above, would come into play. If you intervene physically and your colleague is freed to help you in restraining the initial aggressor, consideration must be given to the relative strength of the two parties involved – it has become two against one! Again, what was the severity of the crime being prevented and did you use non-violent means first? It is worthwhile to remember at all times that your mere physical presence is a significant factor in reducing the possibility of violent attack.

These responses outlined above are deliberately non-aggressive, but are NOT passive or weak. They do not rely on practical security measures. They are simple and don't require physical training or regular practise such as are necessary in self-defence or with breakaway techniques. However, it is worthwhile to consider training in the management of violence and aggression. Numerous courses can be offered both to individuals or bought in on a group or project staff team basis which can be tailored to specific situations and settings. When considering attending or buying in training, *do* check that the training organisation and individual trainers understand the sensitivities of churches or specific voluntary projects and indeed their limitations. The web, CVS, local authorities and local training providers and consortia are useful places to start to find appropriate resources.

Can it be treated?

My focus here will be in two parts. Firstly, I will briefly consider what support and response need to be given to a victim of violent attack which is experienced in the course of work or ministry. Secondly, I will examine what can be done to treat or respond to people who are highly aggressive and who routinely use threats and violence. In considering the aggressive and violent person, I by no means wish to reduce the importance of responding to the needs of those who are victims of violence. Their needs are always paramount. However, in the course of my ministry and working life I have encountered many individuals who regularly become aggressive and even violent, but who deeply regret their violence and would dearly love to find alternative ways of dealing with their feelings and learn different patterns of behaviour.

Firstly, let us consider who might need support or need to take action after an incident of aggression and violence and what needs to happen post-incident. The following people or groups all need to be taken into account:

- The victim
- The victim's family
- Colleagues
- Other people who attend the church or use the services offered
- The wider organisation or church.

The primary focus is, of course, the victim. An immediate concern is that they receive any medical or health intervention needed if they have been physically harmed. Secondly, it is essential that the victim is debriefed and has an opportunity to talk through what has happened. It is important to do this in the immediate aftermath of the incident so they can calm themselves, but also that at an appropriate time in the future an opportunity be made available for further reflection, and, if necessary, counselling. Considerable progress has been made in what is known as Critical Incident Stress Management. It appears that, while people benefit from the opportunity to talk through what has happened, intensive counselling at this stage can be counter-productive as it invites people to loosen their natural defences at a time when they need to maintain them. If, after about six months, the person is still affected by the event, that is the time to offer more thorough therapeutic support.[454] It is also worthwhile to remember the victim's family can also be very distressed and upset at the news of the incident. Particular concern and intervention is needed if the incident has taken place in the home where the victim and any other family members live.

---

454 Rothschild, B. (February 2005). Applying the brakes. *Counselling and Psychotherapy Journal* 15(1).

After a serious violent incident it is important to consider informing any other people who may work from the same premises, such as other employees, ministers, administrators, housekeepers and volunteers. Often, such people can also feel vulnerable, even if they were not directly involved in the incident. This is especially the case if the aggressive person has left the premises, not been detained by the police or other authorities and there is the potential of further threat if they return. Consideration should also be given to alerting neighbouring priests, ministers and projects if it is likely the aggressor may turn up at their homes or premises. (This is also the case with 'con artists' who are skilled at manipulating people who work in the caring professions.)

Remember that all those who use a given project or the whole church community will be affected by a violent incident. Many will simply be concerned, while others may be fearful of being vulnerable if they come to the church or the project premises. Church officials in dioceses or other structures and management boards and managers in the voluntary sector also have a responsibility to ensure that appropriate support and any necessary follow-up response is in place after an incident. There should be clear and commonly understood procedures regarding who needs to be informed and what action each person responsible should take. All too often there are no reporting or responding mechanisms in place in church organisations or smaller voluntary projects, which results in incidents of violence not being recorded appropriately or responded to effectively at a managerial or organisational level.

Secondly, there needs to be a brief discussion on the needs of those who are violent – or use violence – and how they can be helped. The reality is that there is little help or treatment available. It is not exactly considered a worthy cause for help and support. However, I do know of people who have been greatly disturbed and upset by their own violent tendencies or their willingness to resort to violence – even extreme violence. These people may be disposed to benefit from help if it were available to them.

As we have seen, there is a wide range of complex and often interacting reasons why people may use violence and aggression and any treatment response would be highly dependent on any individual's specific needs. Additional to this is the focus of the arena in which the person becomes violent – for example, some use violence in the home, others against children or other vulnerable people, and others when under the influence of alcohol and drugs. Specific treatment and interventions may be considered in other chapters of this book. The reality is that a number of people have difficulty with expressing their anger or frustrations. Due to lack of experience of the range of options in dealing with anger, they may resort to violence or other negative ways of expression. We need to ensure that those who are willing to constructively engage with their behaviour are not further disadvantaged and isolated.[455] Working on an individual basis, some people will respond well to befriending and support schemes, particularly where a relationship can develop to explore feelings and emotions, and possible strategies can be suggested to deal with these feelings. Additionally, empowerment and advocacy schemes may be of assistance to individuals to help develop alternative strategies to ensure their needs can be met.

Group-work initiatives, such as anger management, would offer a specific treatment response. However, such initiatives are virtually inaccessible until after you have offended! Therapeutic groups are offered within the criminal justice system by prison and probation services but in one sense they are being offered too late. Group therapy can be particularly effective in these cases, as people explore their beliefs, feelings and behaviour, and learn strategies for managing their anger and learning how to become more empathic towards others. Sadly, there is little financial support for this kind of group in the community. Finally, the other responses are incarceration or imprisonment, hopefully alongside therapeutic help and rehabilitation, and medical or psychiatric intervention. Again, these responses are usually only available after a violent attack or a potentially serious offence has taken place, and are usually only initiated in the most serious of cases.

One of the great sources of sadness for those working with these groups is the difficulty in accessing such treatments and interventions where they actually exist. Most treatment and intervention is only offered within the criminal justice system or more secure aspects of mental health services. Being aware of the few services that might be willing to help and support, and how to refer people to them, could be a critical factor in offering pastoral care to those who struggle with violence.

---

455   Braithwaite, R. (2001). *Managing Aggression*. London / New York: Routledge / CommunityCare, p. 167.

A Christian Response

When my writing of this chapter came up in conversation with other people, including those who work in ministry, many responded that it was interesting and worthwhile. However, people often commented, usually towards the end of the conversation, that while non-violence was a nice theory, in the end there were always situations when you would have to use violence or at least physical force. Now I don't want to criticise those people or even necessarily disagree, but a belief that the use of violence is inevitable saddens me and, more importantly, leaves me with a real sense of disquiet. I can't help but think that we have a new idolatry of violence which deceives us into thinking in destructive and ultimately aggressive terms.

Walter Wink identifies what he has termed 'the myth of redemptive violence'[456] which has been present in religious and literary writings from the earliest times, from early Babylonian myths to contemporary cartoons. Citing the Babylonian creation myth and the modern Popeye cartoons, he shows that violence is seen as a creative force that ultimately liberates us. He argues that this myth is so successful and strong that it hardly seems mythic at all, but rather simply the way things actually are. 'Redemptive violence gives way to violence as an end in itself. It is no longer a religion that uses violence in the pursuit of order and salvation, but one in which violence has become an aphrodisiac, sheer titillation, an addictive high, a substitute for relationships. Violence is no longer the means to a higher good, namely order; violence becomes the end.'[457]

As has been seen in preceding pages, there are various ways we can choose or sometimes simply instinctively respond to aggression and violence. In shorthand, a number of frameworks can be identified to describe how we often react.[458] We can choose to avoid violence, remove ourselves from its presence and isolate ourselves from risk; or we can accept or accommodate it, seeing it as inevitable; or we can respond with counter-violence, as the ends justify the means, or to ensure that

---

456 Walter, W. (November 2007). *Facing the Myth of Redemptive Violence*. Retrieved from: http://www. ekklesia.co.uk/content/cpt/article_060823wink.shtml

457 Ibid.

458 Slattery, L., Butigan, K., Pelicaric, V. and Preston-Pile, K. (2005). *Engage, Exploring Nonviolent Living, a study programme for learning, practicing and experimenting with the power of creative nonviolence to transform our lives and our world*. Oakland, CA: Pace e Bene Press.

through force justice will be achieved. A fourth and more authentic way is to resist the violence through active non-violence.

Christianity has been identified with all these ways of responding, from pacifism to the use of morally justified violence. Sometimes the accusation of passivity has also been levelled at Christians – i.e. that we simply stand by passively, neither resisting nor defending ourselves against violence. In reality, there has also been a long tradition of active resistance through a spirituality of non-violence, but all too often this tradition has been silenced or smothered by the myth of redemptive violence.

Martin Luther King commented on how difficult it was to get his message of non-violent action understood, when so many people had just not heard of its methods. Moreover, they simply did not make sense to them – they were so used to avoiding violence, accommodating violence, or believed that the only other response was violent resistance. 'We had to make it clear that non-violent resistance is not a method of cowardice. It does resist. It is not a method of stagnating passivity and deadening complacency. The non-violent resister is just as opposed to the evil he is standing against as the violent resister but he resists without violence.'[459]

We can turn to the person of Jesus as an ideal role model for non-violent resistance. There are many who would wish to dismiss Jesus as accommodating violence and oppression, advocating that his followers turn the other cheek and not resist evil. Yet you can see posters and T-shirts depicting Jesus in the image of the revolutionary Che Guevara with the phrase 'meek and mild? – as if!' Two opposite sides of the same coin, both of which are equally false. Jesus rejected both absolute pacifism and violence, and rather promoted a new third way of active non-violent resistance. Walter Wink points out the scriptural translation and contextual problems of Matthew 5:38-41.[460] An alternative translation of 'Resist not the evildoer' can be rendered 'Don't react violently against the one who is evil.' He further contests that the platitudes that follow of turning the other cheek, giving your cloak and going the extra mile can all be seen in the context of Jesus' audience in first-century Palestine. These are direct, cultural references which actually inspire

---

459   King, Martin Luther. (1992). *I have a Dream. Writings and Speeches that Changed the World*, ed. by James M. Washington. San Francisco: HarperSanFrancisco, p. 30.

460   Wink, W. (2003). *Jesus and non-violence. A third way.* Minneapolis: Augsburg Fortress, pp. 10–12.

and call the people to take control and to stand as equals to those who would subjugate them, rather than recommending being meek and submissive. This third way of Jesus, the way of non-violent resistance, resonates with his teachings and example. He calls his followers to love their enemies and to bring about the gospel. He encourages them to acknowledge their own faults and violence, and to take up their cross in solidarity with him to effectively challenge and overcome oppression.[461] We can add to this the profound social and communitarian dimension, and the objective of Jesus' teaching to transcend the individual and transform the community – if not the whole world. Indeed, we can see how Jesus would want to direct us, along with Martin Luther King, to a very different destination from that of violence. 'The end of violence or the aftermath of violence is bitterness. The aftermath of non-violence is reconciliation and the creation of a beloved community.'[462]

Do's and Don'ts

- Do consider the risks of violence and aggression

- Do take practical steps and consider your security

- When faced with a violent person, do stay calm

- Do signal non-aggression

- Do try to communicate verbally and negotiate

- Don't let your guard down, even when the situation seems to be resolved

- When feeling vulnerable, do ask for assistance

- Don't assume it will never happen to you, in this area, etc.

- Do access appropriate training.

Conclusion

I started by reflecting that there are no easy answers. How anyone reacts when faced with direct violence and aggression needs to be

---

461 Walter, W. (November 2007). *Facing the Myth of Redemptive Violence*. Retrieved from: www.ekklesia. co.uk/content/cpt/article_060823wink.shtml

462 King, Martin Luther. (1957). *The power of non-violence*. Retrieved from: http://teachingamericanhistory. org/library/index.asp?document=1131

understood and accepted. Christians in daily life should be wary not to set themselves up as saints! We would all like to have more ideal responses or be convinced that we could resist resorting to violence, but we can also recognise in ourselves, if we are honest, that we are subject to anger, frustration and irritability which can be expressed destructively and even violently.

> There is so much focus on the distinction between non-violence and violence, between non-violent people and violent people. But in reality it's not easy to take sides like that. One can never be sure that one is completely on the side of non-violence or that the other person is completely on the side of violence. Non-violence is a direction, not a separating line. It has no boundaries.[463]

We, as Christians, just should not be debating whether we are non-violent, passive, pacifist, or willing to use morally justified violence in certain settings. Rather, we can all agree that we are heading in the direction of non-violence – rejecting violence both as a preferred mechanism to achieve goals and its seductive power as a solution to our problems, in favour of active peacemaking and becoming agents of love and genuine encounter with others.

Further reading

Davies, W. and Frude, N. (2000). *Preventing Face-To-Face Violence: Dealing with Anger and Aggression at Work.* Leicester: The APT Trust.

Slattery, L., Butigan, K., Pelicaric, V. and Preston-Pile, K. (2005). *Engage: Exploring Nonviolent Living, a study programme for learning, practicing and experimenting with the power of creative nonviolence to transform our lives and our world.* Oakland, CA: Pace e Bene Press.

---

463   Thich Nhat Hanh. (2005). In Slattery, L., Butigan, K., Pelicaric, V. and Preston-Pile, K. *Engage, Exploring Nonviolent Living, a study programme for learning, practicing and experimenting with the power of creative nonviolence to transform our lives and our world.* Oakland, CA: Pace e Bene Press.

329

PART II

CHAPTER ELEVEN

Caring for Yourself

Alison Moore

Introduction

Welcome to this chapter, and the subject of 'caring for yourself'. It is written primarily for those who find themselves in a leadership position and faced with a seriously difficult situation. This could be because someone they have responsibility for is involved in one of the situations described in this book or any other situation that is testing and not easily resolvable. It is also relevant to any concerned individual who is caught up in this kind of situation, or indeed anyone who is interested in the areas of leadership and self-care. It is written for Christian contexts, for example churches, and for leaders in other organisations who are Christian.

You might have picked up this chapter out of a precautionary interest, 'in case I ever need it', or you might be checking out how it compares with what you have experienced in the past. But it is possible that you are *at this moment* caught up in a difficult situation, and you are the person I have mainly in mind. You will be under pressure to perform in a properly professional manner, quite possibly more in the public eye than normal, and in unusually stressful conditions. Your capacity to do this will be affected by various factors, as will the length of time it takes for you to come through to the other end of the experience and regain your normal balance and perspective. Some of those factors are internal and personal to you. What sort of personality do you have? What sort of previous experiences, professional and personal, do you bring to this situation? Other factors are external. Is this difficult situation time-limited, though unpleasant, or is it apparently endless and unresolvable? What sort of organisation do you belong to? What kinds of procedure and support are available?

If you haven't the energy to read this chapter, then please give it to a colleague or friend, who can point you to any parts that might be helpful to you.

The first section describes what self-care looks like, and moves on to look at normal short-term responses to shock and longer-term responses to stress. The second section explores ways of approaching sensible self-care. It invites you to take a step back to assess the bigger picture. This applies both to you (how do I 'tick'?) and to the situation as a whole (what sort of an organisation am I working in?). If you are in the middle of a crisis situation right now, this is the part you will probably be tempted to skip. It is counterintuitive to step back once the adrenalin is flowing and events are unfolding by the minute. However, anyone who needs to do a good job under pressure will still take the time to check that their tools are in good order, knowing that this will pay off later. So I suggest it will be worth reading it. The third section gives a brief defence of the rationale for self-care. In spite of the commandment that all Christians agree on to 'love our neighbour *as ourselves*', self-care can still be a contentious area, where people experience considerable discomfort. The final section offers some lists of practical suggestions that might help, gleaned from observation, anecdotes and the experience of people who've been through just such situations.

What does self-care look like?

Should we be leading perfectly balanced lives? In spite of the current popularity of phrases like 'work-life balance', I've rarely encountered anyone who feels they achieve this. Actually, we aren't called to be 'balanced', but to be disciples, made in the image and living the life of our complex vibrant God. Part of this calling is to be thoroughly human. This means that we are subject to our physiological and psychological make-up. Therefore, when exposed to trauma or stress, we experience the normal physiological and psychological consequences of this. When we sometimes describe ourselves as 'in pieces', this does not mean that God doesn't love us, nor that we have been the wrong sort of Christian. It probably means that we've been subjected to a heavy weight of one sort or another. I've sometimes gone to the kitchen cupboard for a particular plate only to find that it's mysteriously cracked. Then I see that it has been at the bottom of a great stack of assorted plates since last year. It was not a faulty plate. It was simply subjected to too much pressure. Like the plate, we can be broken by prolonged stress; unlike the inanimate plate, we have the possibility of regeneration and repair.

What is self-care?

1. Care of self is to do with the whole self.

In other words, self-care applies to our physical, mental, emotional, behavioural and spiritual experiences, which are interrelated. If you doubt this, think about these examples:

- If you feel excited (*emotional*), your heart beats faster (*physical*).

- If you have flu (*physical*), you feel miserable (*emotional*).

- If you think you cannot speak in public (*mental*), you probably won't be able to do it (*behavioural*).

- If you eat too much sugar (*behavioural*), you will crave more (*physical*), and you will think you cannot function without another chocolate bar (*mental*) so you will eat another (*behavioural*) and feel guilty (*mental/emotional/spiritual*).

- If you receive through the Eucharist (or other religious service) a sense of God's love and purpose for you (*spiritual*), your anxiety decreases (*emotional*) and your knotted stomach relaxes (*physical*).

Sensible self-care recognises that these are linked and makes allowances.

2. Care of self is to do with long-term ways of living.

We are physically designed to alternate between stress and rest, tension and relaxation. People who do only one or the other lose touch with their humanity. The purpose of a rubber band is to hold something together by being stretched in tension. However, if it is left permanently in the stretched position, it will stop functioning and need to be thrown away. Rubber bands last longest if they are put back in the drawer in relaxed mode until needed again. Like rubber bands, most people can stretch to function well under stress, and our bodies are designed to do just that. However, when we habitually override the instinct to rest, we reach a point where we can no longer relax, mentally, emotionally, spiritually, behaviourally or physically.[464]

---

464 See Sarah Horsman's helpful work on stress reactions described in *Tend My Flock* by Kate Litchfield (Canterbury Press, 2006). See particularly chapter 4 sections 4.28–31.

3. *Care of self is essential for good leadership and management.*

You may agree with what has been written so far, but still see that the world (including the Christian world) is full of people who seem to succeed without taking any notice of the principles of self-care. So many people do push themselves hard, by choice or circumstance, and make a success of this, that we may well wonder what's wrong with this. What *is* the point of 'self-care'? Remember the rubber band: we too can become useless if we habitually overextend ourselves.

'Becoming useless' might include:

- *physically* – exhaustion, sleeplessness, appetite change, minor or major illness;

- *emotionally* – numbness, incapacity to see or respond to others, or to receive feedback from others, overreactions, inappropriate reactions;

- *mentally* – skewed thought patterns and illogical approaches, inability to assess situations, inability to realise this;

- *behaviourally* – excessive drinking, caffeine intake, extremes of sexual activity, obsession with detail, longer but less productive hours, anger outbursts, irregular eating patterns;

- *spiritually* – avoidance of prayer or only praying for miracles, superficial external religious compliance, skewed sense of responsibility and therefore guilt that blocks receiving compassion, emphasising some Christian themes more than others, ignoring failure as a route to new possibilities, acting out of pride disguised as responsibility.

Looking at this list, it becomes clear why the overstressed leader is not good for his or her organisation or those he or she is responsible for. The likelihood of serious errors of judgement is increased, as well as serious breakdown in relationships, illness or self-harming behaviour.

A certain level of self-knowledge and awareness is simply sensible, particularly in our twenty-first-century Western society where compliance with legal and good practice guidelines is essential.

4. *Care of self will look different in different people.*

Our personalities really do make a difference here: the introvert will sometimes need to withdraw from others in order to function well; the extrovert is more likely to seek people out; some people are energised by activity, others by quiet; some need regular strenuous physical exercise to be able to think straight; some need more sleep than others. We often forget this and feel we must follow someone else's good advice, rather than trust our own instinct about what *we* need; or we become worried about someone's apparently odd behaviour, when in fact they are looking after themselves in their own way.

Normal responses when a difficult situation arises

Normal initial responses to shock [465]

When we are faced with a seriously difficult situation, we are likely to experience at first the sorts of reaction common to any significant loss. If nothing else, we will have lost our normal routine. There are various ways of describing the pattern of reactions after such a loss, but common to them all is the idea of *shock*. Remember that the whole self will be affected. So physical sensations, behaviours, thoughts and feelings are likely to be different from normal. People typically report signs like these:

- *Physical* – feeling sick, tight chest, weight in stomach, losing appetite, adrenalin flow.

- *Behaviours* – sleep disturbed, extra alert and energetic, complete loss of energy, inability to concentrate.

- *Thoughts* – questions ('Why me/us? What should I do?'); going back over conversations, images, situations; denial ('I don't believe this is happening' 'This happens to other people, not me'); clear thinking.

- *Feelings* – depending on the nature of what is happening, initial feelings can include anger, fear, pity, revulsion, excitement; or there might be an absence of emotion.

---

465   There are many good descriptions of responses to sudden loss. Any book on bereavement will cover this, e.g. Worden, J.W. (2001). *Grief counselling and grief therapy* (3ʳᵈ edition). Bruner-Routledge.

Of course, a feature of shock is that any of these can change dramatically and without warning, as vacillation of feelings and thoughts is very normal. In the morning, there is a sense of calm and of handing it over to God; by the afternoon, only a sense of despair that it's all out of control.

Shock reactions are normal and there for good reason. Physiologically we need to survive and it is as if, with a limited amount of energy available, parts of us shut down temporarily so that other parts can function well. For example, sadness is likely to follow a close friend's move to another country; but it can be some months before this is felt, because at the time you were sharing their excitement, joy and anticipation. Many people find that when they are bereaved they cannot do their own grieving because of the normal demands of life – young children, vulnerable parents or simply work. Some of the reactions that were not able to happen at the time will rise to the surface later when there is opportunity. In my counselling work, I've met many who are distressed and astonished to find themselves 'cracking up' or 'in pieces' when they are at last settled, secure and happy, having survived prolonged difficult spells. It's as if something inside us knows when it's time for the difficult or painful thoughts and feelings to be allowed to the surface. It's been described as 'putting them in the freezer' – they don't go away, but thaw much later. Unlike a cook, the person doesn't usually even know that this stuff is in the freezer, and is surprised when it emerges and thaws on the carpet of their new and happier life.

Many people in a leadership position experience the positive aspect of shock reactions – adrenalin leads to clarity, decisiveness and more energy than normal. *'I am energised in a crisis,'* said one manager, and another: *'I operate very clearly and well under stress.'*

However, there is a down side: too much adrenalin can paralyse thinking processes. Worst of all, you can be completely confident that you are functioning clearly, when actually you are unaware that you are *not* seeing the broad picture in a way that you would normally. If others normally see you as a competent leader, they are unlikely to question your decisions now. This can lead to unwise decisions and actions that can create difficulties for later.

'Looking back on that time, I think the staff would say that my judgement was affected sometimes.'

So it is clear that in the early days of a difficult situation there will be an impact on your *role*. People will have added expectations of you as a leader or manager: you will be expected to function competently as normal, and manage the unfolding situation in a wise way, and anticipate and meet the needs of those you are responsible for. You are unlikely to succeed in meeting these expectations, or certainly not for long.

Equally, your relationships, at work and personally, will be affected. As leader/manager, how you perform is going to be the focus of other people's interest, advice and quite possibly criticism. A difficult situation is likely to bring with it certain delicacies which mean that the whole truth cannot be revealed to all the people all the time. So misunderstandings can flourish, and relationships suffer. Sometimes criticism or advice will be offered directly, sometimes not. *'When people gave me their opinion or advice, all I could say was 'thank you for that', although I knew they only knew one side of the story.'*

By being unable either to explain or defend yourself, you can find yourself becoming a different sort of leader from the sort you thought you were. People who had trusted you may trust you no longer.

In church contexts, the divide between work and personal relationships can be much less clear than in other work situations, and church members may well not be conscious of the need for different roles in different circumstances. If the difficult situation is open knowledge, there might be much warm personal support for you. If not, the confusion and hurt of not knowing why the minister 'has no time for me at the moment' can cause problems.

At home, family relationships are inevitably affected. The difficult situation may take a lot of time, and will certainly drain your energy. Relationships at home might be robust enough to accommodate a period when you are preoccupied, but if there are ongoing demands there too (young baby, elderly parents, family bereavement, teenagers …), it can be challenging to keep functioning well, particularly when your energies are already depleted.

Normal mid- to longer-term responses to shock

One manager who faced two unrelated major difficult situations in his firm within a short space of time, described how the cumulative exhaustion from the first incident was still very much around when the second broke. He found himself thinking '*Not again*' but at the same time '*Oh, OK – I know can do this.*'

His recognition that emotional exhaustion was still present months after a difficult situation is over is very realistic. Once a situation has been dealt with and things are pretty much back to normal, or some way has been found to deal with them, the relief can lead to a belief that we are quite back to our normal selves. At this point we don't realise that our perception is distorted, so we are unable to see our own dysfunction. We might continue with excessive leaning on stimulants to get us through, and still experience disturbed sleep patterns.

Also at this stage, the delayed emotional and physical reactions from the initial 'shock' phase can kick in, bringing waves of tiredness. '*I felt "dead"*', was how one man described it.

Even two or three years after a seriously difficult situation, a loss of confidence can still be felt. I listened recently to two competent and self-aware professional women comparing notes. They had each gone through quite separate prolonged difficult situations, in both cases involving sustained personal criticism. One commented, '*I know that I am not as confident as I used to be when I'm speaking in public, though it's gradually coming back.*' The other agreed: '*I'm aware that I'm not putting myself forward in the way that I used to.*'

At this stage, the impact on *role* and *relationships* is going to be just as strong, but possibly less obvious. David's approach to management was goal-oriented. '*When a situation arose, I would sort out how to deal with it and move on.*' Faced with an ongoing situation involving someone who frequently exhibited difficult behaviour, he had to come to terms with the fact that a different role was demanded of him – containing rather than solving.

'*When it started I hoped that once we understood the problem properly, we could solve it. Later it was clear that it was not going to be solved, so my role was to manage and contain the ongoing difficult situation. It was depressing to think that it would probably go on for ever.*'

As manager or leader in an organisation, the ongoing effects will still be with you, but others are likely to forget this. Relationships can change as a result.

Wendy was a highly approachable tea-shop manager, who ran her small team in a friendly and cooperative manner. Her difficult situation emerged when she became suspicious that one of the staff was molesting children. After agonising, she contacted the police whose investigations finally led to a prison sentence. However, the other staff, as well as the customers, had not believed the allegations to be true, with the result that some regular customers stopped coming in and a couple of staff left for other jobs. A year later, Wendy found herself wondering what was wrong because she had ongoing anxiety, and her husband had difficulty persuading her to go out at the weekend with him, because she felt people didn't like her.

Relationships can also be affected where there are long-term complicated confidentiality issues. As leader/manager, you will need to go on keeping your guard and monitoring how you respond to enquiries, comments or criticisms.

What does 'normal' mean for me?

So far, I have described some recognised 'normal' responses to shock and stress. However, our individual reactions will differ depending on our personality and usual way of functioning. My 'normal' is likely to be different from yours. We can be surprised by reactions, our own or other people's because, under stress, some people become *more* like their usual self while others become *less* so. It can be helpful for you and those around you if you are familiar with your own tendencies.[466]

Approaching self-care
Seeing the wood for the trees

Whatever the difficult situation that now faces you as manager/leader, some of the following are likely to be true:

---

466   The Gilmore Fraleigh 'Style Profile' work is easily accessible and makes a useful distinction between typical reactions when life is calm and when it is stormy. See, for example, Gilmore, Susan K. and Fraleigh, Patrick W. (2004). *Style profile for communication at work*. Eugene, OR: Friendly Press.

The difficult situation	. . . the consequence
You have neither chosen nor planned this. Any plans you had for this week/month/period are now up in the air. So . . .	. . . you experience a loss of control.
Your sphere of contact is suddenly bigger. This might be your first experience of dealing with police, social workers and the media as well as church authorities, senior colleagues, your organisation's hierarchy. So . . .	. . . you are on a steep learning curve.
Your 'day job' responsibilities continue. There might be no immediate colleague to share with or delegate to. In organisations with a strong culture of self-sufficiency, like the church, it can be difficult to hand over responsibilities. Also, you will need to respond to others, who will want to talk about what is going on. So . . .	. . . your overall workload increases, while the time available to do it decreases.
Because the difficult situation is by definition unusual and serious, you are likely to be operating at the edge of or just outside your competency zone. So . . .	. . . you need to be extra alert.
As leader, you are expected to pick your way wisely through complexity. So . . .	. . . you need time for reflection when there probably isn't any.
As leader, you are expected to make the *right* decisions, in the *right* way for everyone, at the *right* time. So . . .	. . . you are bound to fail.

Some people thrive on the rollercoaster experience of a crisis, shown in the right-hand column; others don't. Whichever category you come into, if you want to do as good a job as possible, while keeping an eye on your sanity and health, it makes sense to take time to assess, or 'map' both the situation and yourself.

Mapping the situation

1. Assessing the demands of the difficult situation and the resources available

Different people will be caught up in the difficult situation, not necessarily all part of your organisation. It helps to be clear where the lines of responsibility lie between these people, and what the roles are. You might need to have different roles at different times and in different relationships. Some of these will be incompatible.

'I offered pastoral support' (to the church member and her husband, who had been accused of an offence), *'but later they didn't want to talk to me'* (the minister was asked to give evidence in court). Churches are often unclear organisations, with a volunteering culture that can take good practice for granted rather than setting out clear guidelines.

There follow suggestions for structured ways of making sure you are clear about the elements of the difficult situation. It is sensible to look at these with someone else, or to ask someone else to look at your answers. Two heads really are better than one, once a difficult situation is under way. If you can make yourself do some of this, so that you are reasonably confident that you have considered most aspects, it will help you channel your energy where it is needed – for example, by clarifying priorities and deciding what interventions *you* should make.

Try answering these questions:

- *Who* and *what* are being affected by this difficult situation? List these. For example: the victim; the perpetrator; colleagues of either – senior or junior; families; neighbours; church members; yourself; any children; the domestic situation; the project; the rota; the corner shop . . . think beyond the obvious.

- What are the *needs* of each person or project? This can be set out in a new column or in a different colour.

- Whose *responsibility* is it to meet each of these needs? Use a third column or colour.

You should now be able to see two things clearly. Firstly, which needs are not being met. Secondly, where *your* responsibilities lie. Now you can make some decisions. If your name appears in the third column as being responsible for meeting all the needs, your first decisions will be about priorities, support and delegation; if it appears against some but not others, you can focus just where you need to and point people in other directions if they come to you inappropriately.

> 'When tragedy struck a retired Anglican priest and his wife, the local vicar visited and the bishop kept in touch. It was the churchwarden who realised after a few days that the couple's niece was the one who was bearing the brunt of the situation, but no one had been in touch with her.'

Which legal or organisational policies or guidelines, if any, require compliance?

- Child Protection Policy
- Vulnerable Adults
- Health and Safety
- Good Practice guidelines
- Grievance and disciplinary procedures
- Staff handbook
- Any other.

If you are not sure, then consult with any designated advisers in these areas, or your human resources department or equivalent.

'We had a good child protection policy, which I followed, and I consulted with independent advisers recommended by my organisation. My main advice to others is to make sure you have a robust child protection policy.'

What resources are available through your organisation?

These might be designated officers like the Child Protection Officer, someone in the legal or human resources department, specialist advisers in pastoral care or communications, mental health or a particular chaplaincy.

Perhaps you have an in-house peer supervision scheme or mentor who can provide a sounding board. A senior colleague might know of others who have been through something similar.

Your firm might have an arrangement with a counselling agency.

Which outside agencies and experts are involved? What is your role with them? How can you check this out?

'Some of the 'experts' were actually pretty unhelpful, and at the start there was a lot of disorganisation.'

'Whenever the media contacted me, I made sure I took a brief thinking space and rang them back with my response.'

'At times my role was very clear – for example, at the funeral *(this is a minister speaking)*. At other times it was much less so, and I had to work out what I was offering. I checked with the police to make sure my responses wouldn't get in their way. For some of the time my role was providing a place for the other professionals to meet over coffee.'

What are the lines of responsibility and accountability inside your organisation?

Identify the person to whom you are accountable, and/or the person who acts as your line manager or equivalent. Next, identify who is accountable to you and who you are responsible for. In the current difficult situation, can you work out what each of these people should know, and what each should be doing? This will remind you who needs briefing about what, and might help you ask for what you need from senior management.

'I sent the bishop all the relevant papers *(an Anglican priest is talking about a situation that had been going on for many months)* but he hadn't read them before our meeting. He expressed no concern about my well-being, nor did he express his confidence in me or the way I was handling the situation.'

This quote demonstrates how simple it can be to offer support to junior colleagues or staff members, if you remember to do it: express concern about their well-being, and (if you can) express your confidence in them.

2. The Drama Triangle

This schematic way of analysing situations can be very helpful when you are trying to map a difficult situation, particularly when things seem stuck, or you find yourself responding in ways you are not happy with. As its name suggests, the 'drama triangle' looks at the role people *actually* find themselves playing. This will probably be different from the role they *think* they are taking.

Without realising it, people can slip into one of the three positions shown in the drama triangle, '**persecutor**', '**rescuer**' or '**victim**'. They then find that they are thinking and feeling just what the named role suggests. The added difficulty is that the roles can quickly swap round. If you can spot which role you are playing, you are well on the way to being able to do something positive about it.

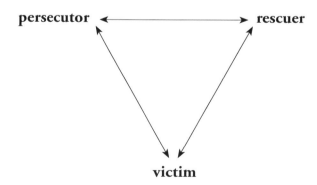

The best way to explain how the triangle can form and the havoc it then causes is with an example where there is an ongoing difficult situation. I have chosen a church context here, but you will see how it could occur in any organisation:

> Alan is a difficult person in the church. He is latching on to Mary, your friendly pastoral assistant, who is starting to feel hounded. Others are worried about her. You need to take some action.

Here the roles are: Alan – **persecutor**; Mary – **victim**; you – **rescuer.**

> You have a quiet word with Alan, who takes offence and complains about you to Mary, who reassures him.

Now you are **persecutor**, Alan is **victim** and Mary is **rescuer**.

> When others in the congregation see that the situation hasn't changed, they berate you and Mary defends you.

Here is a new triangle: you are now **victim**, Mary remains **rescuer** and the congregation becomes **persecutor**.

> You feel depressed and misunderstood and start to think about a change of job.

You have by now behaved, thought, felt or been seen as, in turn, a **rescuer**, a **persecutor** and a **victim**. You've paid a pretty high emotional cost, but the difficult situation remains exactly what it was.

How to change this into a 'winners' triangle'? One of the three players must stop trying to change the others and concentrate on changing their own behaviour. In the drama triangle, the **victim** acts as if she does not have the resources to solve the problem and she feels without thinking; the **rescuer** takes too much responsibility for someone else and ignores his own needs; the **persecutor** is absorbed in his own needs and disregards others.

The 'winners' triangle' shows how each player *can* make a change:

- the **victim** can become **vulnerable** – i.e. recognise his bad feelings, but think sensibly about how to get help to do something about it;

- the **rescuer** can become **caring** – i.e. show concern and offer help, but within her own limits and without taking over;

- the **persecutor** can become **assertive** – i.e. find ways of getting his needs met but without bullying or punishing others.

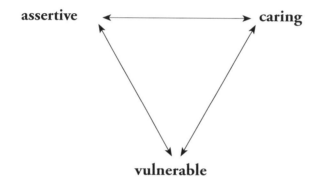

In our scenario, we can re-run the events like this, showing how you can make changes:

> Alan is a difficult person in the congregation; he is latching on (**persecuting**) to Mary, your friendly pastoral assistant, who is starting to feel hounded (**victim**). You need to take some action (**rescue**).

Re-run:

> You spend time with Mary, listening carefully to her predicament but not solving the problem for her; thus she is enabled to think clearly (as well as feel strongly) and she discovers she has some ideas about what to do.

You've become **caring** instead of the **rescuer**; Mary is **vulnerable** but not **victim**.

Or this:

> You have a quiet word with Alan, who takes offence and complains about you to Mary, who reassures him. Now you are **persecutor**, Alan is **victim** and Mary is **rescuer**.

Re-run:

> You go back to Alan, and explain clearly and calmly what your concerns are about his behaviour and why you have spoken with him. You understand that he is angered by your earlier conversation. You wonder what ideas he has about how you both can address the situation.

You've become **assertive** instead of **persecutor**; Alan has the opportunity to solve his own problems, rather than become **victim**.

Or this:

> When others in the congregation see that the situation hasn't changed, they berate you and Mary defends you. Here is a new triangle: you are now **victim**, Mary remains **rescuer** and the congregation becomes **persecutor**.

Re-run:

> You realise you're feeling helpless and phone your peer supervisor to help you think through what's happened. As the conversation progresses, you can see what's been happening, and you recognise how your role has changed. You decide this is not as serious as you first thought, that you are actually competent in ministry, and that you will take your time to decide how or whether to respond to the critics.

You've become **vulnerable** not **victim.**

Mapping yourself

Suggestions for assessing how you function

This is not the moment to go in for prolonged self-awareness exercises. If you are interested in that you are likely to have done this already on other occasions; if you are not, you will be tempted to skip this part. However, this section should be helpful whatever you are like: if you are already familiar with this material, it will give you a quick route to remind yourself of what is currently relevant; if this is new to you, it should give you some pointers that you can use fairly easily to help in the current difficult situation.

There are three areas it is worth mapping here: personality, past experiences and current events in your personal life.

Personality

There are various personality type theories, which give you some sense of how you 'tick'.[467] If you are familiar with one of these, take a moment to revisit its insights, to remind yourself how you function under normal conditions, what sorts of behaviour you are likely to exhibit under duress and what resources you need to draw on to thrive. But you don't need to know the theories to think about what you are like when you are in leadership role. Calm? Organised? Focused? Chaotic? Dominating? If in doubt, just ask a friend or colleague how they would describe you. Then consider what you are like when under stress – the same or different? More organised? Anxious? Deadpan? Like a headless chicken?

Even a small amount of awareness can help you and those around you make sure that you access the right sort of resources in a difficult situation. What is right for you might not be obvious to you or those around you.

> As head teacher, Jill likes to know precisely what is going on in her primary school and has a tendency to micromanage. Under duress, she does this even more. When the difficult situation erupted, her colleagues tried

---

467 Most familiar are Myers-Briggs Type Indicator and the Enneagram. Gilmore Fraleigh, mentioned before, is more concerned with communication styles than personality.

to help by protecting her from routine school issues. However, this only made her more stressed. Jill also likes to think things through first alone rather than talk with others. Her deputy head now recognises that the best way she can support Jill is by keeping her fully briefed on the day-to-day school issues and by asking her when she would like to discuss things.

It is useful to know whether you would normally change behaviour under stress or remain the same. If you are not sure what you do, ask someone who lives with you or has worked with you for a while.

I am normally a focused achiever at work. But I become an indecisive procrastinator under stress. My husband, in contrast, simply becomes even more of a focused achiever when under stress, and works determinedly through what needs to be done.

It's also worth being clear about how others can help you when you are in stress conditions. The 'focused achiever' just quoted went on to explain that, under stress,

what I need from others is affirmation. I want someone to ask me how I am and tell me that I can do it. What he needs is to be left alone, free to ignore everyone, until things are back under control. For some years, when either of us was under stress, I offered him encouragement and he left me alone – exactly the opposite of what was helpful. The resulting mutual incomprehension simply added to the difficulties.

Knowing what your likely behaviour is – and also what you most need from the people around you – can help. If you and those you live or work with can recognise this, expectations are realistic and many crossed wires (and cross exchanges) can be avoided.

Relevant past experiences

Our past experience is bound to be relevant to our current situation in ways that we will be more or less conscious of. If you have gone through difficult situations before, you will bring the learning from that into the present. However, there might well be previous experiences which, although entirely dissimilar from what is happening now, will still affect how you are currently responding.

Experiences of being under pressure

Cast your mind back – there are probably times in your life when you have had to find extra resilience under pressure. When you have remembered one, answer these questions:

- How did I behave during that time? Was this helpful?
- What and/or who helped me get through that time?
- In what ways was I strong in that situation?
- In what ways was I vulnerable?

It is likely that your answers will give you guidance about how to approach the current difficult situation so that you can maintain your sanity and perform as well as possible.

> I was determined not to give in to depression, so I didn't tell anyone. I just made myself get on with each day's work, and read funny novels to take my mind off what was happening.

This person worked through the emotional demands on her own, and this drew from her strengths. So she can probably trust her instincts to do the same this time.

However, someone else said:

> I was determined not to give in to depression, so I didn't tell anyone. But I just felt worse and worse because I was so isolated and lonely and in the end I couldn't get out of bed and had to see the doctor. I felt really stupid.

When a new stressful situation arises, this person needs to recognise her vulnerability and make it a priority to identify trustworthy others with whom she can share.

Other previous experiences

Our present is inevitably affected by our past experiences. You don't need to sign up to psychoanalytic theory to see the truth in this. We are often quite unaware that we are reacting to people or situations in an inconsistent way. The phrase 'learned behaviour' is useful here. This simply describes how, when the *dynamic* is the same or similar to something we have experienced previously, we will *react* in a way similar to our previous behaviour. The familiar phrase 'that pushes my button' describes how each of us has our own sensitive spots that are unrelated to the person we are with.

Sometimes these are superficial: for example, I will react strongly to a tone of voice that sounds like a frightening teacher from my past; you won't even notice. Others are more ingrained.

Andy, a Baptist minister, has a current long-term difficult situation: someone with a borderline personality disorder[468] has joined every church group and attends every meeting, causing anxiety and distress. Andy makes excuses, ignoring evidence of distress and not wanting to talk about it when colleagues try to raise the issue. He is usually assertive and decisive. Andy grew up in a family which dealt with the alcoholism of the uncle who lived with them by trying to ignore it. Excuses were made, evidence was covered up, no one talked about it and everyone lived as if it wasn't happening.

Under stress, Andy's unconsciously 'learned behaviour' predominates.

---

468 People with Borderline Personality disorder have difficulties with emotion regulation. They also have difficulties with boundaries, are prone to addictive and self-defeating behaviours and have a tendency to idealise and then reject significant people in their lives. They fear abandonment, and have often been victims of abuse or disorganised parenting in their childhood. They have a fragile sense of self and can have destabilising or destructive effects in churches or organisations.

Relevant current experiences

Sometimes our personal and professional lives can experience a kind of subterranean crossover, which we experience emotionally rather than rationally.

> Tim Basker is senior partner in a small solicitors' firm which retains the sense of a family-run business. One autumn, three colleagues leave, all for good reasons (move to another area, maternity leave, retirement). Tim's been in the legal business for 25 years, has seen colleagues come and go many times and can't understand why he feels so hollow and depressed. He's even snapping uncharacteristically at everyone. A friend points out that during the summer, Tim's son has emigrated to Canada and his daughter has left home to work in Scotland after finishing her college course.

The hollow sensations have crossed over from home to work.

Take a moment to scan what's going on in your life at the moment. Are you, or members of your family, in a significant transition stage (for example, children leaving home, important anniversaries, retirements, new jobs, marriages, new generations being born, parents dying)? Or perhaps other members of the family or close friends have just been through restructuring at work, or redundancy, or financial difficulties. Perhaps someone you care about has experienced something traumatic. If any of these is part of your 'wallpaper' at the moment, this could impact on how you are experiencing the current difficult situation, with crossover feelings and reactions.

Can it be treated?

The goal of self-care is to manage our lives and work in such a way that 'treatment' does not become necessary. Having said that, it is often sensible to have someone you can talk to, especially in difficult situations. Sometimes a good friend, line manager, supervisor or spiritual director can be helpful when we need to vent, explore options or reflect on how we have handled a problem. Given the stresses and the range of demands made on professionals today, a number of roles have been developed which can be a support for people in management.

Non-managerial supervision

Many healthcare professionals make use of 'non-managerial supervision'. This is a relationship entered into between someone in work or ministry with another professional with (usually) more experience, whose role is to help the supervisee to reflect on their work and to explore areas of conflict, tension, stress or difficulty.[469] It provides a level of professional accountability and support which is not confused with the managerial accountability that is owed to your boss or employee. It is important that the person who is invited to be the supervisor does not have another relationship with the person seeking supervision – e.g. friend, manager, priest – as this will result in a dual relationship, which can cloud judgements and interfere with the primary task of helping the professional development of the person seeking supervision. Freedom is required on both sides so that the supervisee can be transparent in what he or she chooses to share or reveal, the supervisor can be appropriately challenging, and the supervisee can risk being vulnerable. This is a requirement in some professions – e.g. counselling – and is increasingly made use of by people in ministry.

Coaching

Coaching is a relatively new area. Ilona Boniwell writes: 'Coaching aims to produce fast personality changes through the setting and acquisition of goals. It is explicitly concerned with the promotion of well-being and performance.' [470] Working with a coach may help to improve work-life balance, to identify goals for personal and professional development, and explore aspects of personality and behaviour that are preventing goals being achieved.

When treatment is necessary

Unfortunately, many individuals who work in the caring professions, especially those with responsibility for management, can suffer from

---

469 http://www.infed.org/biblio/functions_of_supervision.htm
470 Boniwell, I. (2006). *Positive psychology in a nut-shell.* London: Personal Well Being Centre.

what is known as burnout. Burnout has been identified as a syndrome that involves emotional exhaustion, a loss of a sense of self and reduced personal accomplishment. It tends to develop over time, with a slow erosion of spirit, loss of idealism, possibly cynicism, and lack of a sense of efficacy or agency (a belief that my work is making a difference).[471] Burnout has been seen as a maladaptive response to stress. Once stress becomes overwhelming, one way of coping is to 'switch off'.

Burnout is a serious psychological condition, and Loudon and Francis reported that 14% of the Catholic priests who responded to their survey said that they felt burned out from their parish ministry and a further 16% said they were uncertain. In a study of Australian, New Zealand and English clergy, it was noted that 7% reported feeling filled with sadness they could not explain.[472] This represents a significant number of clergy who are at the very least unhappy, and possibly suffering from some kind of mental health problem. Burnout also affects doctors, nurses, teachers, social workers and other people in the caring professions. When someone reaches the stage of burnout, an intervention from a line manager may be necessary. It is often difficult for people to realise how far they have slipped into the state of burnout, as they may continue to function, but at considerable personal cost, and with reduced effectiveness. Treatment for someone in this situation will probably involve time off from work or ministry, and individual and/or group therapy. Employers may be able to make use of Employee Assistance Programmes, or organisations such as the College of Counsellors in Durham diocese, which was set up to provide counselling support for clergy and their families.

A Christian Response

Christians have mixed reactions to the idea of 'self-care'.

Surely, we say, we are meant to 'take up our cross, lay down our life, turn the other cheek, go the extra mile'? Don't we believe 'it is more blessed to give than to receive'? Isn't 'caring for self' just pandering to selfishness, which is rampant in our individualist, hedonist Western society? The Protestant work ethic still seems to be in our bloodstreams,

---

471 Loudon, S.H. and Francis, L.J. (2003). *The Naked Parish Priest*. London: Continuum.
472 Francis, L.J., Kaldor, P., Robbins, M. and Castle, K. (2005). Happy but exhausted? Work-related psychological health among clergy. *Pastoral Sciences* 24(2): pp.101–20.

ensuring niggling guilt when we remove our noses from the grindstone. Over and over again I've witnessed wise and pastoral people encouraging others to care for self, while patently not applying this to themselves. Even those who really believe in self-care inhabit a world (in and out of the Church) that is so busy, complex and demanding that finding ways to look after themselves seems quite unrealistic.

While acknowledging the truth that self-denial is an important part of Christian discipleship, it is also important to remember how at the centre of the Christian faith is the idea of wholeness of life: life lived in proper perspective, acknowledging that power, wisdom and love are sourced in God, seen in Christ and experienced through the Spirit. Life lived in joy and hope of new beginnings. Life lived with energy, against the odds. Life created in the image of God, and therefore complex and always re-patterning. Life full of surprises, but also carrying responsibility. Life that takes in as well as gives out. Life that reflects as well as acts. The second commandment is, 'Love your neighbour *as yourself.*' This carries a profound psychological insight – that how we treat ourselves is linked with how we are able to treat others. The need to have some rhythm to life is central to the Jewish Christian understanding in the commandment to keep the Sabbath holy, in order to regain energy and perspective and savour life. '*Even the horses need to rest on a Sunday,*' my farming grandfather used to say.

In other words, 'self-care' is NOT the same as 'selfish'.

Practical suggestions

This section is set out as lists, with quotes where people have made suggestions from their own experience. This is to encourage you to glance quickly through the headings and see what catches your attention that might be relevant to you or someone you know. There is some overlap between the sections.

For general health

- **Be realistic about life being different for a while.**

  Cancel unimportant engagements but keep some fun or social engagements.

- **Be realistic about sleep and tiredness.**

  It is normal to have disturbed sleep and easier if you don't try to fight it. The cumulative tiredness is likely to be debilitating.

- **Be realistic about eating patterns and using stimulants.**

  It is not a major sin to use stimulants – '*my evening whisky was probably a little bigger than usual*'; strong coffee keeps you alert; chocolate has a proven 'feel good' effect; energy dips are staved off with cake. However, you might not notice that you are becoming dependent on the quick-fix effects of sugar or the relaxing effects of alcohol.

- **Be realistic about emotions.**

  They might well go higher and lower than is normal for you.

  Sometimes I got very angry, but couldn't put it anywhere. So I would ring a friend who lived far enough away from us to be safe.

  Don't be surprised by your own murderous capacity!

- **Be realistic about prayer.**

  If you can, keep the regular rhythms of your spiritual life. If you can't do this, don't waste energy on guilt. Ask someone else to undertake to pray on your behalf over this period. They don't need to know the details of what's going on, so long as they will carry you while you're carrying the weight of this difficult situation.

For general sanity

- **Remember the big picture.**

  Who are you? A person loved by God. What is the point of your life? To live life, glorify God, love others and savour the world.

  A concentration camp survivor described how he found something that the guards could never take away from him – the sun. This helped him survive and kept him sane.

- **Remember what normally helps to keep you sane.**

  Do this, at least sometimes.

- **Remember to stay in touch with writings, projects and people that are good.**

  This is particularly important if your difficult situation involves violence and evil. '*Whatever is true . . . noble . . . pure . . . lovely . . . admirable . . . etc., think about such things*' (Philippians 4:8).

- **Remember to keep your world bigger than the difficult situation.**[473]

  If you have young children, spend time with them; if you don't, at least spend time with friends' children or any people who have no connection with your circumstances.

- **Remember to be creative.**

  Play football, write a poem, go for a run, play the piano, tidy the office, buy a potted plant, go in the garden, take a short walk at lunch-time, have a haircut or a manicure . . .

- **Remember humour.**

  The power of venting difficult emotions through laughter is well known by those who work in demanding jobs. It can make a difference in short-term difficult situations too.

  Our small voluntary organisation was in chaos – it looked as if it could all close down. When we volunteers met, we told each other the worst stories we'd heard that week, criticised everyone in the organisation shamelessly, indulged in outrageous joking, laughed till we were exhausted. But then, after the meeting, we got on with our jobs with the public, who never knew what was happening.

---

473 Jerusha Hull McCormack describes this in her book, *Grieving – a beginner's guide* (DLT, 2006). Instead of waiting for the grief – or in this case the difficult situation – to diminish in order to have space in life for other things, she suggests deliberately enlarging your world so that the grief or difficult situation does not completely fill it.

- **Remember the power of routine.**

  Keeping going, getting on with the job. We had plenty of services. And being of my tradition (this was a high churchman speaking) *really helped, because the daily liturgy gave me a routine.*

- **Remember 'the inevitability of invasiveness'.**

  If you are feeling contaminated, with your difficult situation getting under your skin, taking over your life, involving distressing, abusive, violent and evil behaviour, make symbolic separations or 'cut-off' points in your life.

  I used to shower and change my clothes when I got home. It was a sign that my family and I were separate from all that was going on.

  When we realised that we were talking about it all the time, even last thing at night before we went to sleep, we knew we had to do something. So we decided we would only talk about it up to supper-time. Then the subject was banned.

For general safety

- **Avoid email communication where possible.**

  Once the send button has been clicked, it is uncontrollable.

  It made the whole thing so much more complicated. Everyone in the organisation suddenly knew something was going on. And the person who was critical of how I was handling the situation used it to lobby support – I decided not to email my responses but to go round and have conversations with people directly.

- **Delegate.**

  Ask someone else to act as go-between.

  When our daughter was so ill, some close friends took on being our mouthpiece to let people know how things were going. It helped us because we didn't have to tell the story over and over again and keep answering the phone, and it helped other people because they didn't have to worry about disturbing us.

When the situation broke, I rang my colleague and asked him to take over the evening service. He didn't need to know why.

- **Prioritise.**

  Others around you might see more clearly than you how you can do this.

- **Listen to someone whose judgement you trust.**

  When your adrenalin is flowing, your own judgement can become skewed. So check your decisions or opinions from time to time.

- **Find allies.**

  These are people who can help you protect yourself and others from your limitations.

Personal support

- **Support from whom?**

  Identifying and using personal support is a sign of wisdom and strength, not weakness.

  Use all the resources that are available to you.

  The regional minister put me in touch with someone who had been through a similar experience.

  I was glad of the peer supervision arrangement I had. He gave me valuable advice and provided a sounding board.

  I found someone outside the situation who didn't give me advice. I could just use her as a sounding board. This helped to generate ideas that helped me through the situation.

  There were one or two friends, who were far enough away for me to be able to swear, relax, laugh, and share my anger with.

- **Support from senior personnel.**

  The response of the senior person in your organisation who has authority is really important. If there is little support from senior management, take the initiative by requesting support or explore alternative options, rather than wait in frustration.

It made a big difference when my boss asked me not just about the facts but also 'how are you in all this?'

The project leader was really on my side . . . he felt genuine concern and understanding.

- **Support from colleagues and staff.**

  Supportive personal encouragement is likely to be lacking, but it boosts energy levels and outlook if it comes.

  My staff team were consistently even-handed in their approach to me and the person who was causing me so much grief. They were right to take this line, but it felt irrationally unfair and I felt unsupported. I wanted them to acknowledge how awful it was for me.

  However, the same minister continued, *at a meeting, when the subject was being discussed again, one person articulated their confidence in my leadership through this period. It was very important to me to hear this.*

- **Support from family and friends.**

  Experience and expectations are very different when it comes to family support. Responses varied from, *'I deliberately said very little about the situation to my wife and nothing at all to the kids. They all had their own life in the church. They didn't need their church relationships to be confused by knowing about this;'* to, *'I could not have got through that period without being able to offload on my wife.'*

It's worth asking yourself, 'In what way do I look to my husband/wife/family/friends for support?' And, where possible, check whether they agree with you.

When the difficult situation is in the public arena

- **Be sure to 'Use all the resources that are available to you'.**
  Double check that you have thought of all those within and outside your organisation who can give professional support.

- **Be on your guard when connecting with other professionals.**
  A group adrenalin can foster a false sense of importance; the salacious details of a difficult situation can be unnecessarily repeated in the disguise of briefing; 'experts' aren't always helpful; crisis managers don't prevent a lot of disorganisation; professional carers can be competitive in their caring for those at the centre of a difficult situation.

- **Be sensible – take advice before responding to the media.**
  At least say, 'I'll ring you back in ten minutes.'

- **Be resigned to the fact that you can't exit from the public arena.**

- **Be clear about your particular roles and responsibilities – and stick to them.**
  Consult with someone you trust before changing your mind, no matter what others say.

- **Be able to answer these questions:**
  Who is responsible for: the perpetrator? the victim? the organisation? the other people in the organisation?

- **Be expecting misunderstanding and criticism.**
  Difficult situations can lead to opposing reactions in organisations.

  Some people thought he was innocent and others believed he was guilty. Everyone wanted me to talk about it, which I wouldn't. So I was in the wrong with most people.

  There were different reactions when he came out of prison – some left the church, others were in denial, and others expected a public statement of remorse. I had to find a way of managing the different attitudes.

(Two different ministers who had sex offenders in their congregations.)

- **Be aware of your role in any Drama Triangles (see above).**

  To see what roles you are playing, draw out some triangles and discuss it with a colleague.

Talking about it

- **Essential talk**

  It is essential to find someone who can act as a sounding board for thinking straight and making good decisions.

- **Essential talk**

  It is essential to make good decisions about communication, within the organisation and publicly; use the ansaphone as a way of keeping control of the process and not being bounced into a decision or a reaction that you might regret.

- **Optional talk**

  It is optional to find someone who can let you unload, without needing to edit what you say.

- **Random talk**

  It is likely that you will be approached at any time by people who will ask you (nosily or caringly) about what's happening.

  Use honest but general phrases ('It's being hard work – it's very challenging – thank you for your concern – please pray for everyone involved – I am fairly exhausted', etc.). If you give too much detail, you will use up precious emotional energy.

- **Talk with your partner**

  If you are going to talk with someone you live with, decide when and even where you are going to discuss it. Don't talk late at night or in your bedroom – having your bedroom 'invaded' by the perpetrators or victims of the situation is probably not a good idea.

In church contexts

- **Remember that, although you are the minister, you are not God.**

- **Remember that, although you are not God, others will expect you to be.**

  You see yourself as 'just an ordinary person', but others probably don't see you like this. As minister, you will already be on the receiving end of others' expectations, projections and assumptions, for good and ill. Sometimes this is right – e.g. the need for a leader to take a certain amount of unfair criticism without cracking. Sometimes this is disabling – e.g. when the congregation leave responsibility for one another's well-being entirely to the minister and blame her when she fails to deliver.

- **Remember self-awareness and self-regulation will stand you in good stead.**

- **Remember normal habits might not work.**

  e.g. regular time off, transparency in management, keeping the peace between groups.

Paying attention to the whole person

As a leader during a difficult situation, you will be maintaining a 'non-anxious presence'[474] which helps to reduce other people's anxiety. This is demanding work. These tips for paying attention to your self can help.

---

474 This phrase is used to describe what a mediator offers in conflict transformation work. It provides a succinct summary of what a good leader can offer during a difficult situation.

- **Notice** what you are thinking *and* what you are feeling.

  These can help you understand and respond to the situation.

- **Stay** in your body – listen to it.

  Aches in head, stomach or back will give you clues about the stress you are carrying. Don't ignore these – even acknowledging that they are there will help.

- **Acknowledge** the discomfort of experiencing conflicting emotions and thoughts.

- **Be kind** to yourself.

  Stay connected – with yourself and with others.

- **Take account** of just how much the emotional energy you are expending is taking out of you. The incident is likely to take its toll. Remember how teachers are often ill in the first week of their holidays!

  It was still very vivid long afterwards.

  I couldn't understand why I felt so low the summer after it had all happened.

- **Be prepared** for the long haul –

  whatever your difficult situation, it is likely to take much longer than you anticipate.

- **Look** for a way of processing the experience later when there's opportunity.

  Writing about it was very helpful.

Conclusion

I have written about several principles of self-care in the course of this chapter. Far from being self-indulgence, self-care is both necessary and godly. A certain amount of self-awareness is helpful. Even under time pressure it is worth taking a step back, probably with the help of someone else, to assess both the situation and yourself, before you make swift decisions. Dealing with a difficult situation will probably take more out of you than you would think possible – emotionally, physically, mentally and spiritually. Make allowances for a recovery period when the repercussions of your exhaustion will go on making an impact.

Much of this applies anyway to us all as we face the normal challenge of finding a sane and deep Christian path in our multi-demanding organisations. When you hold a managerial or leadership role, you owe it to your staff, colleagues or congregations as well as to yourself, your family and friends, to be as fit as you can be to deal with these demands competently and safely. So it is particularly important to find a way of applying some of these principles when an out of the ordinary difficult situation arises.

Further reading

Dr Ruth Fowke has written very accessible short books that look at the issues of stress and Christian faith – e.g. *The Last Straw* (Eagle, 2000).

Daniel Goleman's *Emotional Intelligence* (Bloomsbury, 1996) is the classic on the importance of taking whole-person responses seriously.

Any book by Robert J. Wicks will be helpful: *The Resilient Counsellor* (Oxford University Press, 2008) is for counsellors and mental health professionals and contains wise advice for all managers and clergy who find themselves in stressful situations. *Bounce: Living the Resilient Life* (Oxford University Press, 2010) is another readable and practical guide.

For those working in churches and other Christian organisations, the Alban Institute, an American publisher, has an excellent range of books on 'practical knowledge in leadership and congregational life' – www.alban.org/books

CHAPTER TWELVE

Early Relationships

Jocelyn Bryan

In the beginning, when God created human beings, God declared, 'It is not good that man should be alone.'[475] While it is true that human beings are innately social, their ability to thrive being dependent on their relationships with others, it is also the case that some relationships are profoundly damaging to our well-being. The behaviours described in this book have a negative impact on relationships. They cause anxiety and distress, and may lead to enduring psychological problems in the lives of others, quite apart from their impact on those who act out these behaviours.

In this chapter, I explore the significance of our early relationships for our psychological and social development. From before our birth, we participate in a relationship with our mother. We are dependent on her and others for our survival throughout our childhood. Unsurprisingly, for centuries the influence of these early relationships on both our physical and psychological development has been recognised. But what is the extent of this influence, and what contribution might the nature and quality of early relationships make to the development of some of the behaviours and psychopathologies described in this book? Drawing on insights from developmental psychology, I will explore the significance of our early relationships for our subsequent psychological and social development, and also reflect on how this might inform our response to the challenging behaviours described in this book. But first it is important that we place early relationships in the context of the significance of the human relating we enact throughout our lives.

---

475   Genesis 2:18.

Human relationships

The human need for relationships is irrefutable.[476] Relationships are essential for our survival, development and well-being. We are inherently social beings and relationships are important at every stage of our lives. Relatedness is a fundamental characteristic of what it means to be human, and a basic human need. We need to be in a relationship with others. If we are alone for a long period of time it causes us distress, or at the very least we have to devise robust coping mechanisms to endure our isolation from other human beings. It is through our relationships that we experience care, love, encouragement, happiness, compassion and other life-enriching experiences and emotions. But the converse is also true. In our relationships we can experience abuse, jealousy, anger, fear, oppression and other negative emotions. Some relationships can cause so much damage to psychological well-being and functioning that a person never fully recovers. For example, the legacy of an abusive relationship may have an enduring effect on subsequent relationships both emotionally and sexually. It can also manifest itself in difficult behaviours, personality disorders and addictive behaviours. Chapter 1 on child sexual abuse describes these cycles of damage and their impact on victims, which includes many mental health problems such as phobias, depression and manic episodes, and obsessive-compulsive disorders.

It is obvious that our relationships have a profound effect on us and on how we experience life. They inform our understanding of who we are and how we make sense of others and what happens to us. We learn from others how to respond to the myriad experiences and situations that make up our daily lives. Relationships are essential for our development; we need each other to grow and flourish in life. But some relationships are more significant for our development than others. The primary relationship in our early years is with our parents or caregivers. This relationship shapes us profoundly. But as we become more independent, peer relationships, close friends and the relationship we may have with a partner also become significant influencers. Over the course of our lives, the pattern of relationships in our social networks often comes to consist of a

---

476 See Bryan, J. (2016). *Human Being: Insights from Psychology and the Christian Faith*. London: SCM Press, pp. 132–56.

few major relationships which are present for a large part of our lives, and other relationships which are more transitory and are associated with particular episodes or periods in life. These might include school friends, work colleagues or friends associated with a particular place of residence. But at every stage of life, relationships are of indisputable significance to our well-being and functioning in the world.

The chapters in this book describe behaviours which can all have a negative impact on relationships. They describe the devastating consequences of domestic and sexual abuse, and of bullying. Chapter 6 on 'Dealing With Difficult Behaviours' explores the way particular behaviours manipulate others, causing them to feel inferior, threatened or frustrated. Alcohol, gambling, sexual addiction and internet pornography severely damage existing relationships, often leading to an irretrievable breakdown of trust. All of these behaviours can contribute to the break-up of relationships with significant others, and can eventually result in social isolation as well as considerable psychological distress.

The symbiotic nature of human relationships means that, in all relating, negative or positive outcomes can impact upon both the person who acts out the behaviour and those who experience it. No one goes unaffected. But the negative consequences of some behaviours and ways of relating are greater than others, and this is the case with the difficult behaviours described in this book. During our early development, we are more vulnerable to the influence of negative and dysfunctional relationships than we may be at other times in our lives. Many developmental psychologists suggest that, in our early years, our patterns of relating form the psychological foundation of the assumptions we make regarding our future relationships. This chapter examines the psychological evidence for this and how it can help us to understand why some people behave in ways that are damaging both to themselves and to others.

The significance of early relationships

The belief that our early experiences are important – if not critical – for our subsequent psychological development has been prevalent for a number of centuries. William Wordsworth considered that 'the child is father of the man',[477] and the famous quote attributed to the Jesuits to 'give me a child for the first seven years and you may do what you like with him afterwards' betrays the belief that our experiences in childhood are the principal influences on our behaviour and personality in adulthood. This suggests that as children we are more malleable than at any other time in our lives and we retain the effects of these early relationships for an indefinite period.

At the core of our early experiences is the relationship we have with our parents or caregivers. This relationship has been the subject of considerable psychological research, questioning the extent to which we can predict behaviour patterns in adulthood from our knowledge of the parent/child relationship and other significant relationships in early life. But we need to be cautious and not exaggerate the claims regarding the lasting impact of these relationships. Not every child who experiences a neglectful or a dysfunctional parent-child relationship is destined to experience behavioural and psychological problems in adulthood. The interaction of nature and nurture and the ongoing development of personality and self-regulatory systems is complex, and falls far short of being fully understood. We have to be aware of the limits of this influence, but at the same time recognise that patterns of relating become deeply embedded as they are often reinforced over years. Hence, our knowledge of childhood experiences can make a considerable contribution to our understanding of why someone might engage in many of the difficult behaviours discussed in this book.

Sue Gerhardt argues that 'human beings are open systems permeated by other people as well as plants and air and water. We are shaped by other people as well as by what we breathe and eat.' Furthermore, she believes that the influence of relationships leaves its 'biggest mark in infancy'.[478] As babies, we learn not only to manipulate objects, move around, chew and eat solid foods, but we also experience and learn about emotions: what causes different feelings and how to deal with them. This is part of the process of learning to organise our experience and make connections between events, responses and emotions. Parents and caregivers who respond to their babies in predictable ways,

---

477 Wordsworth, William. 'My Heart Leaps Up When I Behold'. In *The Oxford Book of English Verse*, ed. by Helen Gardner. (1972). Oxford: Clarendon Press, p. 502.
478 Gerhardt, S. (2004). *Why love matters: how affection shapes a baby's brain*. Hove, Sussex: Routledge, p. 10.

help them to make these connections and regulate their behaviour in accordance with them. For example, when a baby cries and her mother responds with a calming voice and rocks her into a quieter state so that she feels comfortable again, the baby notices this repeating sequence over time and learns that when she cries her mother will pick her up and comfort her. These behaviour/response patterns shape our knowledge of what we can expect from other people; they are the way we learn about relationships and influence the way we relate to others throughout our life.

John Bowlby[479] described the relationship between a parent and infant as an attachment relationship and suggested that the need for this type of relationship continues into adult life, especially when we are feeling vulnerable or face a difficult, challenging situation. It is at these times that we seek out family and close friends for support and reassurance. We are emotionally attached to these people by a strong social tie, and they provide a sense of safety and security for us, mirroring the original relationship we experienced in the parent/child relationship in early life. Hence this attachment bond by its very nature has an enduring impact on us and the way we respond to our social world and form relationships within it.

Attachment theory and early relationships[480]

At the age of two months, a baby demonstrates a preference for the face and the voice of their primary carer. In other words, the attachment bond is already beginning to form. By eight months, the bond is much stronger. There are obvious evolutionary benefits from the establishment of this bond which is essential for the infant's survival and development but, although the bond is innate, its quality varies considerably. Often this bond is described as a bond of love and is associated with warmth, care, security and affection. But this is not always the case. In some instances, the bond exists but the relationship between the carer and infant is characterised by neglect, inconsistent or erratic responses from the parent, and very little affection. John Bowlby was one of the first psychologists to research the significance of this bond and its influence

---

479   Bowlby, J. (1969). *Attachment and Loss. Vol 1, Attachment*. New York: Basic Books.

480   See also Bryan, J. (2016). *Human Being: Insights From Psychology and the Christian Faith*. London: SCM, pp. 139–50 for discussion of early relationships, attachment theory and parenting.

into adult life. He, and others such as Mary Ainsworth,[481] built on the psychoanalytic movement and provided some scientific evidence for the idea that our early relationships are more relevant to our development than had been previously accepted.

The importance of the attachment bond for Bowlby was its evolutionary function.[482] Through the bond the infant is protected by the carer and their chances of survival increase. The bond is established by the parent's natural concern to protect and care for their infant and exemplifies our predisposition to form deep, loving, enduring relationships. Bowlby postulated that human love has an evolutionary purpose because the success and maintenance of such long-term relationships is a source of happiness and satisfaction in life. We flourish when we experience love.

In the early years of life, the attachment bond's main function is to provide safety and a secure base from which the infant can explore the world. It enables the infant to feel safe to develop the skills and intellectual abilities necessary to manage and negotiate the demands of adult life. But Bowlby went beyond the bond's role in the facilitation of intellectual and skills development to postulate that the parent/child relationship provides the prototype for all loving relationships. He proposed that the relationship establishes a pattern or model from which we learn to anticipate how others will respond to us, and how best to interact with them in order that our physical and psychological needs be fulfilled. Hence, when this bond is ruptured, dysfunctional or abusive, it may have a serious impact on our subsequent close relationships. The main legacy of Bowlby's work can be summarised in the notion that our experience of all other relationships in our lives is influenced by this primary early relationship. It is as if it acts as a lens or template by which other relationships are interpreted. Bowlby called the template an Internal Working Model (IWM).[483] Shaver and Rubinstein developed this idea further and named it an internalised template of love.[484]

---

481 Ainsworth, M.D.S. (1973). The development of infant-mother attachment. In Caldwell, B.M. and Ricciuti, H.N. (eds). *Review of Child Development Research* (Vol 3). Chicago: University of Chicago Press.
482 Bowlby, J. (1988). *A Secure Base.* New York: Basic Books, p. 81.
483 Bowlby, J. (1959). Separation Anxiety. *International Journal of Psychoanalysts* 61: 1–25.
484 Shaver, P.R. and Rubenstein, C. (1980). Childhood attachment experience and adult loneliness. In *Review of Personality and Social Psychology* (Vol.1, pp. 42–73). Beverley Hills, CA: Sage.

The IWM is, in effect, our personal representation of our social world and the way we expect other people to respond to us. It is constructed directly from the patterns of behaviour we have experienced in the way people respond to our needs and feelings. How we answer such a question as 'do other people comfort me and help me feel better when I am distressed, or do they disappoint and hurt me?' has even been found to have a neurological impact at the level of the biochemistry and structure of the brain.[485] It seems that our repeated experiences of relationships become generalised and integrated into our neural pathways, acting as a guide to our subsequent relating. This learning is then used to anticipate how others might respond to us in close relationships. So, for example, an infant whose parents are responsive, caring, and enable them to feel safe and secure will build up an IWM which includes trust in others and self-confidence. On the other hand, an infant who experiences an insecure attachment will incorporate rejection, negligence and uncertainty from others into their IWM, which in adult life may contribute to their low self-esteem, vulnerability and loneliness.[486]

Mary Ainsworth extended Bowlby's work, and in her groundbreaking study she examined the role of security in the attachment bond by focusing on how the infant responded to the presence of a stranger when the parent (in this case the mother) was present or absent. It is important to note that the attachment bond is not only a source of security. If the child is separated from their parent or frightened, when a stranger appears the closeness of the bond may become a source of anxiety. In other words, the separation might be more stressful because of the strength of the attachment bond. This dynamic tension between security and anxiety was investigated in the famous Strange Situation study.[487] The quality of the attachment bond between the parent and infant was tested by gradually increasing the stress on the infant as a stranger approached them and their parent left them and then returned. Four types of infant behaviour were identified from the study:

---

485 Gerhardt, S.(2004). *Why love matters: how affection shapes a baby's brain.* Hove, Sussex: Routledge, p. 211.
486 Shaver, P.R. and Rubenstein, C. (1980). Childhood attachment experience and adult loneliness. In *Review of Personality and Social Psychology* (Vol.1, pp. 42–73). Beverley Hills, CA: Sage.
487 Ainsworth, M.D.S., Blehar, M., Waters, E. and Wall, S. (1978). *Patterns of Attachment.* Hillsdale, NJ: Erlbaum.

- **Secure Attachment:** This infant explores the room when alone with her mother who acts as a secure base. She may be upset by separation, but greets her mother when she returns and is outgoing with the stranger when her mother is present.

- **Resistant Attachment or Insecure Attachment:** This is described as ambivalent attachment. The infant is quite anxious and will not explore even when her mother is present which suggests she is not a secure base. However, the infant becomes very distressed when her mother leaves, demonstrating separation anxiety and possible doubt about whether or not her mother will return. But when the mother returns, the infant is ambivalent and may show resentment and anger towards her mother. The infant is wary of strangers even with her mother present. The researchers describe this infant as one who appears to want attention but is uncertain whether she will receive it.

- **Avoidant Attachment:** The infant seems uninterested in exploring and does not show distress when separated from her mother and even avoids contact with her when she returns after their separation. She is wary of strangers and will avoid or ignore them. There is an apparent emotional distance between the infant and mother and she seems to deny her need for affection.

- **Disorientated Attachment:**[488] This infant appears confused as to whether to approach or avoid her mother. Following separation, when her mother returns she may freeze or seem stunned. There is no consistent or coherent pattern for regulating her negative emotions and she even appears frightened of her mother.

Ainsworth also observed the mothers with their children at home and, unsurprisingly, found responsive warm mothers had children who were more securely attached. Mothers who were unresponsive and aloof were

---

488   Added later by Hesse, E. and Main, M. (2000). Disorganised infant, child and adult attachment: Collapse in behavioural and attentional strategies. *Journal of the American Psychoanalytical Association* 48: 1097–127.

more likely to have avoidant children who had learned that they could not expect help and support from their mothers. Finally, the resistant children were most likely to have mothers who were erratic and inconsistent in their behaviour towards them. The children's experience of their mothers' responses was that their efforts to gain attention worked sometimes but not always.

These examples of the infant's experiences of how mothers or primary caregivers respond to them constitutes significant relational learning which is captured in the IWM and expressed in subsequent relationships. For example, if the attachment bond with my mother was insecure, ambivalent and anxious, and as any attempts I made to form an intimate affectionate relationship were ignored, then my IWM will lead me to interpret others as uninterested in me and my well-being. I also might well be suspicious of anyone who attempts to develop a close relationship with me, or I may be over attention-seeking in my attempts to develop an intimate relationship. Hence the behaviour of my mother towards me has had a significant effect on the way I form social relationships and on my emotional experiences in later life. However, it is important to note that, although the IWM is thought to be relatively stable after the first year of life, it can be changed by both positive and negative subsequent close relationships.

Tizard studied late-adopted children to explore what changes might be possible.[489] Her work suggested that there was a possibility for positive outcomes despite the little opportunity these children had to form attachment bonds early in life due to the large number of different carers in the institutions they came from. The children studied were admitted to an institution in their early weeks of life and subsequently adopted at an age ranging from 2 to 7 years. At this point they had their first opportunity to form attachments. Tizard carried out subsequent assessments at ages 8 and 16 years. She found that most of the children soon began to show real affection for their new parents and this quickly developed into a close emotional bond. Even those who had been in institutional care the longest were assessed as deeply attached to both of their adoptive parents. This might well

---

489   Tizard, B. (1977). *Adoption: A second chance*. London: Open Books; Hodges, J. and Tizard, B. (1989). Social and family relationships of ex-institutional adolescents. *Journal of Child Psychology and Psychiatry* 30: 77–98.

be explained by the responsiveness of the adoptive parents who were described as highly motivated and devoted a great deal of time and effort to their adopted children. But this bore fruit and there was no indication that the prolonged emotional deprivation in the early years had necessarily led to an affectionless character in the children or that a lack of close relationships in infancy results in an inability to form these kinds of relationship later on.

However, there were some negative effects. First, the children found difficulty in relating to adults outside the family. At 8 years they were described as being over-friendly and even affectionate to strangers, and although this was less of a problem at age 16, they still tended to be more inclined to seek adult approval and attention than a control group. There were also difficulties in their relationships with their peers. The adopted children tended to be less popular and less likely to have a special friend; they were more quarrelsome and also were reported to bully other children more often than the control group. All of this suggests that, even though family relationships were satisfactory, relationships outside the family were indeed negatively affected by their early attachment experiences.

Parenting

Early relationships are characteristic of the style of parenting adopted by the parent which reaches beyond the nature of the attachment bond. Attitudes and approaches to parenting vary between contexts as well as being influenced by family, societal attitudes and practices and cultural factors. A child growing up in South East Asia or Central Africa will experience a very different parenting style from one being brought up in the UK. Much of the research available has been based on parenting in the United States of America or a Western European context. Much of the research has been criticised for focusing on the practices of parents and giving little if any attention to the role and influence of the infant in the process. But in more recent years this has changed. Parenting is now acknowledged to involve a dyadic or triadic relationship between a child and one or two parents which exists in a system of mutual emotional influence. The infant is no longer viewed as a passive receiver of parent practices, but as an active participant in the relationship, with the behaviour of both the parent and the infant having an impact on each other. Hence, when a parent is feeling angry this will surely influence the way they respond to the demands of their child and will consequently affect the response of the infant to the parent. Likewise, when the infant is feeling very irritable then this will affect the way the parent responds to her. Just as parents assert influence on their infants, infants are understood to assert influence on their parents, and have some agency from the first months of life. This first relationship in which an infant participates is a dialogical relationship, involving a system of mutual influence that effects change in both the parent and the infant.

One of the most widely cited works on parenting styles is Baumrind's model of four styles which assesses children's behaviour in relation to their parents' actions.[490] But as already noted, his work fails to take into account any influence the child might have on the style adopted by the parents. However, the taxonomy outlined below continues to be influential, with its combination of the dimensions permissiveness/restrictiveness with warmth/hostility to produce four styles which have been correlated with a number of subsequent behaviours in children, adolescents and adults.

- **Authoritarian Parenting** (high restrictiveness and high hostility): characterised by the assertion of parental power and a detached attitude.

- **Permissive Parenting** (high warmth/high permissiveness): characterised by love and affection and only limited control.

- **Authoritative Parenting** (high warmth and achievement demands/high permissiveness with firm control): characterised by firm control but in non-punitive manner and encouragement of verbal give and take and respecting the child's own wishes.

- **Rejecting-neglecting Parenting** (high hostility/high permissiveness): characterised by a disengaged style. They are neither responsive nor demanding and not supportive; rejecting or neglecting the child.

---

490 Baumrind, D. (1971). Current patterns of parental authority. *Developmental Psychology* 4: 1–103, also cited in Bryan, J. (2016). *Human Being: Insights From Psychology and the Christian Faith*. London: SCM, pp. 147–8.

Interestingly, Baumrind's research revealed that the children's behaviour, associated with the various parenting styles, persisted through childhood and into adolescence. It also provided evidence that the most competent and self-regulated adolescents tended to have authoritative parents.[491] Clearly, there is a relationship between the style of parenting and the nature of the attachment bond, but this work provides further evidence of how early patterns of relating have a considerable impact on a child's subsequent social development, social competence and behaviour in other areas, such as self-regulation.

Parenting does not take place in a vacuum. We grow up in a particular social context and are embedded in a network of relationships. Some of these relationships also have a significant impact on the nature and quality of our attachment bonds and subsequent development; for example, those we have with grandparents, siblings, other carers and peers. Our web of relationships forms the social context of our early lives in which we are exposed to different models of relating and behaving. Family life is at the heart of the social context in our early years. It is where we learn to behave according to established family patterns and the cultural and social norms of our society. In what is known as the process of socialisation, we also learn about emotions and how to regulate them according to the prevailing protocols of our family and the various social worlds we inhabit. From very early on, we have to learn how to cope successfully with the continuous stream of experiences, and to self-regulate our emotional responses and our behaviour in response to it. Our parents or caregivers act as modifiers and models in this psychologically complex process of self-regulation.

Emotional development, self-regulation and early relationships

The family creates the primary emotional climate in which we develop. The relationships within it set an emotional tone which has consequences for a child's emotional development. If the relationship between the parent and infant is hostile or punitive, it leads to avoidant attachment, and there is evidence of this resulting in aggression later in life,

---

491   Baumrind, D. (1991). The influence of parenting style on adolescent competence and substance use. *Journal of Early Adolescence* 11: 56–95.

especially in boys.[492] An infant may also develop avoidant attachment in a family context where there is conflict between parents, and anger is expressed both verbally and physically. In each of these hostile contexts, an infant develops an IWM which includes the assumption that other people will be unresponsive or hostile towards them in their distress or need for empathy. They feel helpless and abandoned as well as angry and frustrated, which might even lead to a state of chronic anger. Unsurprisingly, this has a negative effect on their relationships with others who experience them as angry and aggressive.[493] However, not all infants express their anger towards their parents, and this can lead to them resorting to avoidant coping strategies as a way of reducing their emotional pain. These strategies might entail numbing their feelings or repressing or denying their anger.[494] The unpredictability of care may also cause these infants to fear being left alone and have an increased sense of vulnerability. It is a fear that continues throughout childhood and into adulthood, and may lead to psychosocial problems throughout their lives.[495]

Gerhardt claims that '[i]n effect, antisocial behaviour is a learned response to antisocial parenting'. When there is no secure attachment bond, there is no positive emotional buffer for the parent to draw on as the infant grows into a toddler and needs to learn to behave in socially acceptable ways. Rather, the infant has already established defensive strategies to cope with their expectation of being treated severely and being punished. In this emotional economy they have little to lose when they rebel and are defiant towards their parents. Furthermore, Gerhardt states that these experiences influence the development of the infant's brain, affecting the right brain. They are also imprinted in the child's neural pathways so that they are predisposed to interpret

---

492 Renken, B., Egeland, B., Marvinney, D., Mangelsdorf, S. and Sroufe, A. (1989). Early childhood antecedents of aggression and passive withdrawal in early elementary school. *Journal of Personality* 57(2): 257–81. Quoted in Gerhardt, S. (2004). *Why love matters: how affection shapes a baby's brain*. Hove, Sussex: Routledge, p. 174.

493 See Bowlby, J. (1973). *Attachment and Loss. Vol 2: Separation*. London: Pimlico, cited in Weinfield, N.S., Sroufe, L.A., Egeland, B., Carlson, E. (2008). Individual differences in infant-caregiver attachment: Conceptual and empirical aspects of security. In Cassidy, J. and Shaver, P.R. (eds). *Handbook of attachment: Theory, research, and clinical applications*, 2nd edition (pp. 78–101). New York: Guilford Press.

494 Gerhardt, S. (2004). *Why love matters: how affection shapes a baby's brain*. Hove, Sussex: Routledge, p.174.

495 Bowlby, J. (1973). *Attachment and Loss. Vol 2: Separation*. London: Pimlico, cited in Weinfield, N.S., Sroufe, L.A., Egeland, B., Carlson, E. (2008). Individual differences in infant-caregiver attachment: Conceptual and empirical aspects of security. In Cassidy, J. and Shaver, P.R. (eds). *Handbook of attachment: Theory, research, and clinical applications*, 2nd edition (pp. 78–101). New York: Guilford Press.

the behaviour of others as antagonistic or aggressive even when this was not the intent.[496]

However, there remains considerable debate as to how much aggressive and antisocial behaviour is due to style of parenting and how much can be explained by a genetic predisposition. Certainly, infants differ in their temperaments and the dialogical nature of the relationship should not be ignored. Every infant is a unique human being who has a particular level of tolerance and responsiveness to the external world and to their bodily experiences such as physiological pain and physical discomfort. Hence, the infant's and the parent's temperaments and the nature of their interaction should be taken into account in any attempt to ascertain a causal relationship between parental style and infant behaviour.

A significant goal for developing positive social relationships is knowing when it is appropriate to express our feelings and what is the appropriate intensity or degree of expression. In other words, we have to learn where, when and how we might express our anger and frustration when a friend has let us down. The family is the primary context where a child learns about both emotional expression and emotion regulation. Parents, in particular, model when emotions should be repressed or masked or on occasion accentuated. From birth we are the emitters and recipients of emotions. Emotions provide a window on our minds and the minds of others and have a considerable influence on personal well-being and social relationships. They are also related to our sense of self. Self-conscious emotions, such as pride, shame and guilt, are deeply enmeshed in our personhood and concern how we respond to ourselves and others. Our early relationships form the foundation of our emotional development and can leave a legacy of a vulnerability to emotion-related problems in later life.

Very early in life, before they are able to talk, infants can identify facial and vocal expressions of emotion and make connections between actions and emotions.[497] As early as 5 months, an infant can recognise

---

496   Gerhardt, S. (2004). *Why love matters: how affection shapes a baby's brain*. Hove, Sussex: Routledge, p. 175.
497   See Thompson, R.A. and Lagattuta, K.L. (2005). Feeling and Understanding: Early Emotional Development. In McCartney, K. and Phillips, D. (eds). *Blackwell Handbook of Early Childhood Development*. Blackwell Publishing.

the difference between some negative facial expressions of emotion and positive ones.[498] They also respond positively to happy approving vocalisations and negatively to angry prohibition vocalisations, even when they are spoken in their non-native language.[499] Thompson and Lagattuta comment that '[c]ontrary to a tradition that has viewed young children as simple emotion thinkers . . . contemporary scholarship highlights that young children have surprisingly complex emotion concepts'. Our emotions have a biological basis, and, consequently, during these early years when there is rapid development in the brain and the nervous system, it is unsurprising that our first relationships have a considerable influence on our emotional development. What we witness and experience in our early years and our conversations about emotions (both our own and others) make a significant contribution to the development of a sophisticated understanding of emotion.

As we have already established, emotional well-being is determined by the sensitive responsiveness of the parent to the infant's emotional signals predominantly expressed as smiling or crying, and their supportive responses during stressful experiences as well as everyday routines.[500] These positive responses associated with a secure attachment enable the infant to begin to regulate their developing emotions and psychobiological stress systems. This was confirmed by Gunnar and Donzella who found that, in stressful situations, an infant's physiological arousal to stress was buffeted by the parent being present (when the relationship included secure attachment).[501] The infant looks to their parent or someone they trust for guidance when they face threatening, confusing or upsetting situations. They cope well in these circumstances when the adult is reassuring in response to their emotional cues and supports and guides them in their efforts to cope.[502] A considerable body of evidence now suggests that parental responsiveness and a secure attachment

---

498 Bornstein, M.H. and Arterberry, M.E. (2003). Recognition, discrimination, and categorization of smiling by 5-month-old infants. *Developmental Science* 6: 585–99.

499 Fernald, A. (1996). Approval and disapproval: Infant responsiveness to vocal affect in familiar and unfamiliar languages. *Child Development* 64: 657–74.

500 Cassidy, J. (1994). Emotion regulation: Influences of attachment relationships. In Fox, N.A. (ed.). The development of emotion regulation and dysregulation: Biological and behavioral aspects. *Monographs of the Society for Research in Child Development* 59 (2–3, Serial No. 240): 228–49.

501 Gunnar, M.R. and Donzella, B. (2002). Social regulation of the cortisol levels in early human development. *Psychoneuroendocrinology* 27): 199–220.

502 Nachmias, M., Gunnar, M., Mangelsdorf, S., Parritz, R.H. and Buss, K. (1996). Behavioral inhibition and stress reactivity: The moderating role of attachment security. *Child Development* 67: 508–22.

are notably significant for positive emotional growth and emotional resilience in stressful situations.

It is not only the responsiveness of parents or caregivers in the early relationship that matters, but also the models of emotional expression to which the infant is exposed in the home. The behaviour of parents helps the infant to learn acceptable forms of expression and self-control, especially for specific situations such as when there is conflict. In Chapter 6, on dealing with difficult behaviours, the role of social learning was discussed in relation to the emotion of anger. At a very early age, infants learn how negative emotions such as anger are to be dealt with. In particular, they learn from their parents whether these disturbing emotions are to be confronted and resolved or repressed and ignored. Thompson and Laguttuta comment that '[p]arents . . . provide salient examples of when emotions must be masked, muted, or accentuated. These types of parental behaviours foster in children more generalised styles of responding to the emotions of others (e.g., in sympathetic, avoidant, dismissing, denigrating, or other ways) and the capacity to adapt their emotional reactions to widely varying circumstances.'[503]

Parents also model the impact of conflict on relationships and the degree to which conflict strains or damages a relationship.[504] The home can be a volatile place. There is considerable evidence that young children exposed to domestic violence are more likely to show symptoms of depression and anxiety, as well as aggressive behaviours and symptoms of post-traumatic stress disorder.[505] This is also true for those who have been maltreated.[506] Inevitably, these psychological problems can lead to difficulties in other relationships. However, although the risk of psychological problems increases in these and other threatening or traumatising situations, it is important to note that many children do not develop serious problems. With the provision of good social support and other resources for coping, good outcomes can be achieved and sustained.

---

503 Thompson, R.A. and Lagattuta, K.L. (2005). Feeling and Understanding: Early Emotional Development. In McCartney, K. and Phillips, D. (eds). *Blackwell Handbook of Early Childhood Development*. Blackwell Publishing. Blackwell Reference Online. 8 August 2016.
504 Cummings, E.M. and Davies, P. (1994). *Children and marital conflict: The impact of family dispute and resolution*. New York: Guilford.
505 See Evans, S.E., Davies, C. and DiLillo, D. (2008). Exposure to domestic violence: a meta-analysis of child and adolescent outcomes. *Aggression and Violent Behavior* 13:131–40.
506 Jungmeen, K. and Cicchetti, D. (2010). Longitudinal pathways linking child maltreatment, emotion regulation, peer relations, and psychopathology. *Journal of Child Psychology and Psychiatry* 51(6): 706–16.

Shame – a self-conscious emotion

Thompson and Lagattuta cite the development of knowing that people direct their emotions towards other people, objects or an event at the age of 9 to 12 months, as marking a major transition in our understanding of emotions. They also suggest that the development of 'secondary intersubjectivity' which is 'sharing knowledge or emotions about people outside the [child/caretaker relationship]' marks the child's early ability to understand other people's mental states. It is the beginning of their empathetic understanding of what others might need, think, feel and intend.[507]

A characteristic of many of the behaviours described in this book is a lack of empathy. Despite often acknowledging that their behaviour is damaging to others and their own well-being, many people continue to be abusive, resist support in curbing their addiction and act out difficult behaviours. There is considerable evidence that empathy is also linked to secure attachment and emotional regulation in children.[508] Many of the behaviours discussed in this book show both a lack of empathy and an inability to effectively regulate negative emotions, especially feelings such as anger and shame.

Once an infant has reached 20 months or so, they begin to show evidence of self-awareness and self-understanding. Among a number of things, they recognise themselves in a mirror, refer to themselves, describe themselves by their gender and become interested in how they are judged by others.[509] This increase in self-awareness is accompanied by the self-conscious emotions of pride, guilt and shame. An example of an infant feeling proud might be that, when they succeed in a task, they look to and smile at an adult and draw attention to their success. When adults disapprove of their behaviour, an infant experiences sadness, discomfort or distress, which then progresses into feelings of shame or guilt. During the ages of 4 and 5 years, as self-understanding continues, children also begin to describe themselves by their psychological attributes – e.g. I am shy, scared, sad.[510]

---

507 Thompson, R.A. and Lagattuta, K.L. (2005). Feeling and Understanding: Early Emotional Development. In McCartney, K. and Phillips, D. (eds). *Blackwell Handbook of Early Childhood Development*. Blackwell Publishing. Blackwell Reference Online. 8 August 2016.

508 Panfile, T.M. and Laible, D.J. (2012). Attachment Security and Child's Empathy: The Mediating Role of Emotion Regulation. *Merrill-Palmer Quarterly* 58(1): 1–21.

509 Ibid.

510 Ibid.

Schore believes there is a causal relationship between the kind of parenting and a child's management of shame and recovery from shame. Furthermore, he links this with the development of narcissistic personality disorder which he suggests is derived largely from the poor regulation of shame.[511] Shame depends not only on self-awareness, but also requires an awareness of an external standard by which any behaviour is evaluated. For children, this initially comes from their parents.

Children, like adults, are particularly sensitive to the expectations placed on them by those who matter to them, most likely their parents. It is from their parents that they learn what is and is not acceptable. In most instances, this is learned from how parents respond to their behaviour in the form of disapproval which ranges from verbal comments in the form of a 'telling off', to the withdrawal of attention or enforced temporary separation and, in some cases, physical punishment. The impact of this on the child is stressful and unpleasant. They may feel humiliated. But, most significantly, their relationship with their parent is ruptured, and accompanying this intense emotional experience the infant also experiences a physiological response in the form of a surge of cortisol.[512] Evidence suggests that the length of time a child remains in this hypoaroused, stressful state is important for their ability to regulate and manage their feeling of shame later in life.[513] It is vital that the relationship between the parent and child is repaired before 'the feeling of continuity of the good relationship is lost'. The child needs to re-experience the warmth of the relationship with their parent so that their stress is relieved and they can regulate their psychological and physiological state back to normal. If they remain in a prolonged state of distress without any effort on the part of the parent to re-establish their previous relationship, this influences their brain development: particularly the frontal lobes which are responsible for emotion regulation and the development of complex emotions such as shame.[514]

---

511 Quoted in Gerhardt, S. (2004). *Why love matters: how affection shapes a baby's brain.* Hove, Sussex: Routledge, pp. 157–9.
512 Gerhardt, S. (2004). *Why love matters: how affection shapes a baby's brain*, p. 158.
513 Schore, A.N. (1998). Early shame experience and infant brain development. In Gilbert, P. and Andrews, B. (eds). *Shame: Interpersonal Behaviour, Psychopathology and Culture.* New York/Oxford: Oxford University Press, pp. 57–77.
514 Ibid., p. 72.

The socialisation process in our early years normally involves this pattern of disruption and repair to the parent-child relationship. The management of the stress response of the infant to make a transition from their intense experience of negative emotions in response to disapproval, to the re-establishment of positive affect is an important task for the parent. The pattern of these 'shame transactions' which are acted out throughout our childhood are stored in the IWM and, depending on whether these experiences are associated with secure or insecure attachment, they can result in an enduring disposition to shame. Parents who find it difficult to regulate their child's behaviour and indeed their own behaviour are more likely to be inclined to leave their child in a distressed state for too long. This poor regulation can also manifest itself in teasing or humiliating their child when they are feeling ashamed, or responding inappropriately to their child's anger, causing an escalation of their feelings. Over time, these parents run the risk of their child losing confidence in their relationship with them and its basic goodness. Schore suggests that these impairments in the parent-child relationship can lead to future impairment in the ability to regulate feelings of shame, which may in turn lead to psychopathological problems.[515] It is interesting to note how this provides another example of the way repeating patterns evolve from this primary early relationship. The caregiver's poor emotional regulation negatively influences attachment security and impedes the infant's development of strategies to cope and regulate their own emotions, which may then lead to difficult behaviours and the possibility of future psychological problems.

Concluding reflections on the psychology of early relationships

There is little doubt that early relationships are important, but we need to be wary of making excessive claims. There is considerable evidence that an insecure attachment can lead to behavioural and psychological problems in later life, but this is not the case for every child who experiences neglect, abuse or institutional care. Likewise, not every child who experiences a disrupted childhood will be unable to provide

---

515   Ibid., p. 67.

secure attachment for their own children. Quinton and Rutter tested the assumption that a deprived child will become a neglectful and depriving parent.[516] They found that the children who had spent most of their early lives in institutional care were, as adults, less sensitive and supportive towards others, and not as warm in their relationships as the comparison group of parents they used in their study. However, it should be noted that there was a considerable amount of variability in the group. The path we take through our lives and our psychological development does not rest entirely on our early relationships. Other experiences can counteract negative ones, and many of us experience significant turning points[517] in our lives which can have considerable implications for our future lives and subsequent relationships. For those who have suffered adversity and neglectful parenting, certain decisions can become significant turning points – for example, whether they stay on at school, which friendships they make, who they marry, or even whether they join a church. These life choices explain some of the variation in the links between childhood and early relationships, and subsequent adult behaviour and psychological well-being. Experiences can change us at any time in our lives for better or for worse.

Another important consideration in the developmental research is the family context and how explanations of the influence of early relationships and experiences need to take into account the complex interaction of a number of factors which are operating in the social context of the family. Schaffer notes that abused children tend to come from particular kinds of families, characterised by marital conflict, insensitive parenting, poverty and some degree of social isolation.[518] Every one of these factors has some link with psychological and social difficulties for children. However, a lot of the early literature attributed these outcomes to the abuse itself, and did not take into account the negative context in which the abuse took place. Other studies have shown that in malfunctioning families where there is no child abuse

---

516 Quinton, D. and Rutter, M. (1988). *Parental breakdown: The making and breaking of intergenerational links.* Aldershot: Gower.

517 Rutter, M. (1996). Transitions and turning points in developmental psychopathology: As applied to the age span between childhood and mid-adulthood. *International Journal of Behavioral Development* 19: 603–26.

518 Schaffer, R.H. (2000). The early experience assumption: Past, present, and future. *International Journal of Behavioral Development* 24(1): 5–14.

there are still severe long-term negative effects on the children.[519] The main issue is that throughout childhood this context does not change. Adverse negative and insecure relationships continue within the family and, as is so often the case, negative experiences become the precursors to yet more negative experiences. This means that, even though the IWM constructed during these years may not be a completely closed system, the reinforcement of negative patterns of relating maintains the expectations and response patterns which the child has learned from their early attachment experiences. In the case of abused children, their IWM is likely to include a negative model of self, reinforced by feelings of shame and a profound lack of trust in others.

The centrality of love

In the report, *A Good Childhood: Searching for Values in a Competitive Age*,[520] the authors make the following comment:

> The report is not ashamed to put **love** at the centre of the child's needs – and the adult's too: love not as a warm feeling alone, but as long-term commitment to someone else's well-being as something that matters profoundly to one's own well-being.[521]

Earlier they state that '[c]hildren need above all to be loved. Unless they are loved they will not feel good about themselves, and will in turn find it difficult to love others. The basic need is for an enduring emotional tie to at least one specific person.'[522]

The research described in this chapter provides a great deal of evidence in support of this statement. The first relationship creates an attachment bond which is a product of parental love and the mutual exchange of responses between the parent and the infant. In time this creates the template of love. Central to this relationship are warmth and sensitivity to the infant's needs. It requires unconditional love which

---

519 Fergusson, D.M. and Lynskey, M.T. (1997). Physical punishment during childhood and adjustment in young adulthood. *Child Abuse and Neglect* 21: 617–30.

520 Layard, R. and Dunn, J. (2009). *A Good Childhood: Searching for Values in a Competitive Age*. London: Penguin Books.

521 Ibid., p. 174.

522 Ibid., p. 15.

bears all the characteristics that St Paul identifies in the great hymn of love in 1 Corinthians chapter 13.

Jesus identified the greatest commandment as "'You shall love the Lord your God with all your heart, and with all your soul, and with all your mind." This is the greatest and first commandment. And a second is like it: "You shall love your neighbour as yourself.'"[523] Love is at the heart of the gospel. It is the sacrificial love of God which offers us the hope of salvation. It is God's overwhelming love for creation which sustains it. It is God's unconditional and intimate love for each of us that gives us a deep sense of self-worth. Human love begins with God's love. We love because we are loved. 'We love because he first loved us.'[524] The psychological evidence overwhelmingly supports this. If we do not know love, if we have no experience of the warmth, sensitivity and sympathy of another person to our needs, then our template of love is corrupted, distorted or marred. This has implications not only for our relationships with others and our self-relating, but also for our relationship with God. Our early attachments can have a profound influence on our spirituality. Hence, our early relationships and their embodiment of the warmth of love are essential for our psychological and spiritual well-being. Without love we are not only deeply scarred and our personhood diminished, but we lose the capacity to love others, may diminish them and possibly cause them to suffer.

Conclusion

Children want and need love more than anything else – and so do adults. In the Church's ministry, there is an imperative to mirror and embody the love of Christ. The Church as the Body of Christ is called to be a community of love which builds up each of its members in love. But as we have seen in this chapter, we can only love if we are loved and surrounded by loving relationships that model the true nature of love to us.[525] If we have not experienced the affirmation and acceptance which comes with being loved, then we will be impaired in our ability to love,

---

523   Matthew 22:37-39.
524   1 John 4:19.
525   Bryan, J. (2016). *Human Being: Insights from Psychology and the Christian Faith.* London: SCM Press, p. 155.

trust and value others. Instead, we envisage them as untrustworthy and possible sources of distress. These experiences can also have a negative impact on our relationship with God. To feel accepted and loved by God is a difficult step for someone with an insecure attachment. The challenge for our church communities is to be places of love, acceptance and belonging where corrupted templates of love can be renewed and realigned through new and transformational experiences of love.[526]

---

526 Ibid., pp. 155–6.

CHAPTER THIRTEEN

Self-Regulation[527]

Brendan Geary

This book has been written to provide information on a range of difficult behaviours which people may find themselves dealing with at home, or in work, church or pastoral situations. As well as creating a space of compassion for those whose behaviour can be described in any of the preceding chapters, it is also hoped that this book can offer strategies in order to respond better to the individuals concerned. Perhaps more importantly, the book also highlights ways of caring for ourselves, as outlined in Alison Moore's chapter. In this chapter, we seek to offer insights that have been developed regarding self-regulation, i.e. how we can manage our own emotions and behaviour, particularly when dealing with behaviours that we find irritating or provocative, or which challenge our own capacity to maintain perspective. Baumeister and Tierney conclude that 'Most major problems centre on failure of self-control.'[528] There is growing awareness of the importance of self-regulation in a range of areas of life. For example, Kegan and Lehay, in a book on organisational leadership and management, ask the following question:

> How does our aversion to loss – threats we may feel about losses of status, control, predictability, affection, respect and the like – incline us to cognitive distortions that cloud our judgment and lead us to poor performance as managers of people or managers of money?

Their conclusion is that 'In all cases we are managing only one thing: ourselves.'[529] Kegan and Lehay demonstrate that work cultures where

---

527 I am grateful to Professor Emerita Joanne Marie Greer of Loyola University in Maryland who read this chapter, made corrections, and offered valuable suggestions regarding the text.

528 Baumeister, R.F. and Tierney, J. (2011). *Willpower: Rediscovering our greatest strength*. London: Allen Lane, p. 2.

529 Kegan, R. and Laskow Lehay, L. (2016). *An everyone culture: Becoming a deliberately developmental organization*. Boston, MA: Harvard Business Review Press, p. 176.

people are more transparent, more vulnerable and able to hear and work on feedback are healthier, and promote human and organisational development.

In this chapter, we will try to answer the question of how we can be assertive and not reactive in our dealings with behaviours that are problematic. We ask what we can learn about ourselves from the science of self-regulation that will help us to respond in ways that are effective, and that support our Christian values of care for others and care for ourselves.

Exploring assumptions

Before continuing, it is important to say something about the assumptions that underlie a great deal of research in this area, which is undertaken for the most part with 'normal' people in 'normal' settings. The concepts and strategies outlined in this chapter refer to people born with average bodily endowment, who have received average, 'good enough'[530] mothering, and who have been raised in an environment which was not affected by war, natural disasters, or other traumatic events.

The research on self-regulation brings us directly into the psychologically murky waters of the 'nature – nurture' debate.[531] The pendulum of opinion has swung different ways on this issue throughout the history of psychology. There is currently ongoing research in the area of genes and individual differences. Elaine Fox, an experimental psychologist and neuroscientist, wrote that 'It is the environment around the gene that influences whether a gene will be read or not' and concluded: 'It's not so much the genes you are born with that count, but which of those genes end up being expressed and which remain silent.'[532]

Some children are born with birth defects or genetic abnormalities. As well as affecting their opportunities in life, these may also lead to

---

530   This phrase was developed by W.R.D. Winnicott (1896–1971), an important child psychiatrist.

531   The psychologist, Oliver James, argues persuasively about the importance of nurture in the development of the person. See *Not in your genes: The real reason children are like their parents*. London: Vermilion, 2016. People who write on twin studies, on the other hand, often argue for the influence of what we have inherited from nature which influences our development. Research has not to this date identified a gene that explains differences in psychology.

532   Fox, E. (2012). *Rainy brain, sunny brain*. London: Arrow Books, pp. 123–4.

teasing or bullying by other children. In recent years, more attention has been paid to conditions such as attention deficit disorder (ADD), attention deficit hyperactivity disorder (ADHD), dyslexia, dyscalculia, Asperger syndrome and autism. Such conditions can have a significant effect on the life opportunities and behaviours of those affected. Other children may grow up in chaotic or 'toxic' families, with experience of abandonment or abuse, or experience war or natural disasters, leading to heightened anxiety as a result of their traumatic and destabilising experiences. Walter Mischel, who designed the 'marshmallow test', which will be discussed later, noted that 'When pre-schoolers have an experience with a promise maker who fails to keep his promise, not surprisingly they are much less willing to wait for two marshmallows than to take one now.'[533] It is important not to blame people for the limitations or traumatic events that they experience in life, but rather to provide strategies that can lead to more fulfilling lives and better relations with other people. Being judgemental can only compound difficulties; being compassionate opens doors to communication and healing.

One way that we can make a difference is to intentionally choose to behave in ways that promote well-being in churches and workplaces. Christine Porath, who has done research on incivility and problematic work cultures, wrote as follows:

> Research has shown that responses to threat, humiliation, loss, or defeat – all commonly associated with incivility – are significantly influenced by genetic makeup. Perhaps as a result, the most effective way to reduce the costs of incivility is to build a culture that rejects it.[534]

We cannot change other people's genetic make-up or their personalities, but we can actively contribute to cultures that discourage rude, uncivil or bullying behaviours.

---

533   Mischel, W. (2014). *The marshmallow test: understanding self-control and how to master it.* London: Corgi Books, p. 73.
534   Porath, C. (Fall, 2016). An antidote to incivility. In How to work with toxic colleagues, selected articles from HBR, *Harvard Business Review,* pp. 116–20.

Self-regulation

Self-regulation is concerned with our ability to monitor our thoughts, feelings and behaviour, and how we make and implement decisions which will help us to achieve our goals and promote our long-term well-being. It sounds rather simple, but in fact this issue has been the rock on which so many good intentions have perished. The absence of self-regulation has been the source of many mistakes, regrets and self-defeating behaviours by people down through the centuries. The gospel parable of the wise and foolish virgins[535] is a case study in self-regulation; saving limited resources for when they will be needed, rather than squandering them when they are unnecessary.

Self-regulation involves my ability to have control over my mental processes – to concentrate and stay focused on an important task. This becomes crucial when applying oneself to a task like learning a foreign language, especially learning vocabulary and mastering grammar. It is also important in studying for exams, mastering technique for a musical instrument, the skills involved in crafts like painting, sculpture or mechanical operations, or some of the intricacies of computers, for those of us who do not take to these things easily or quickly. Self-regulation is also important when interacting with people whose behaviour is challenging or generates stress for other people in our family, workplace or church.

Self-regulation involves controlling impulses and developing the ability to resist temptations. It often involves overriding something that is innate, such as the desires to eat, drink, have sex or avoid exertion. If a hungry animal is offered food, it is likely that it will eat it unless prevented from doing so. Also, if it is the time to mate and a partner is available, then an animal is unlikely to stop on account of other considerations. Human beings, on the other hand, have the potential to desist from behaviours, delay gratification of their desire, or choose an alternative course of action. For example, human beings need to eat in order to survive, yet most people try to avoid excessive eating, partly because it is unhealthy, while some people abstain from food, or certain foods, due to religious convictions or moral values (vegetarians and vegans). Self-regulation requires that we do something different

---

535 Matthew 25:1-13.

from what we have learned (as when sensitivity tells us to monitor our behaviour in new groups until we see what behaviour is acceptable), change our motivation (for example, when a man, having become convinced of feminist values, seeks opportunities to promote equality rather than dominate conversation in social situations) and habits (for example, if you are used to having a glass of white wine when you return from work every day and decide that this is not something you want to continue, then it requires effort to *not* pour yourself a glass of wine). Self-regulation can also involve choosing to do something that is unpleasant or painful, like exercise, in pursuit of a long-term goal of being fit and healthy.

Self-regulation is, all things being equal, one of the keys to success in life.[536] In particular, it is crucial in helping us to identify and achieve our goals, or, if faced with failure, to know when to persist, and when to readjust and choose other goals. In order to achieve our goals we usually have to forfeit other opportunities and pleasures that offer themselves to us or which can distract us.

Goals, of course, are not simple. Easy goals carry less personal reward, and more demanding goals – which require more self-regulation – have a higher pay-off. Ideally, you should aim for a goal that is within your level of competence and relates to your proven capacity to fulfil tasks. This is something that most of us learn in the course of life. There are, however, some people who predictably promise more than they can – or ever – deliver. There is a price for this, as people learn to avoid them, or they set themselves up for failure and frustration, with a lot of wringing of hands and feedback from angry or disappointed people.

The nature of self-regulation

It is clear that self-regulation – or the ability to self-regulate – is crucially important. It accounts for the great variety of human behaviours, and has a key role in moderating social relationships. Human beings are social creatures, and we need to learn to adjust our behaviours in order to gain acceptance from other people who are members of the groups which we seek to be part of. People with many of the behaviours

---

536   Baumeister, R.F., Leith, K.P., Muraven, M. and Bratslavsky, E. (1998). Self-regulation as a key to success in life. In Pushkar et al. (eds). *Improving competence across the lifespan* (pp. 117–32). New York: Plenum.

described in this book, related to addiction, abuse, anger or violence, often have great difficulty regulating their behaviour, or feel that they cannot have their needs met without recourse to these self-defeating or socially unacceptable behaviours.

Most people do not like negative feedback. Once we hear criticism, receive the cold shoulder or experience rejection, we can either become defensive or process the information and change (though, sadly, many people persist in behaviours that cause problems to themselves and others). Kegan and Lahey, writing about work cultures that value feedback and a capacity to share vulnerabilities, note that, when triggered, people 'take care of themselves by fighting or fleeing'.[537] We also have the ability to desist from impulsive behaviours that have appeal as they might allow us to discharge an unpleasant feeling, but which, we know, will not be in the best interests of ourselves or others. This is the case with people who manage to resist the impulse to be physically or verbally abusive or violent. What holds us back? Given the satisfaction that we would get in retaliation or dominance, something is required to stop us in our tracks. That 'something' involves self-regulation; an ability to see a bigger perspective and decide that the immediate need we experience can be managed, tempered, changed in some way. It is common to hear people – especially children – say, 'I couldn't help it.' Evidence proves the contrary; we often do stop ourselves. What is the nature of the 'something' we use to prevent ourselves from doing things we might regret, or to do things that are unattractive but which we believe are for our ultimate benefit?

Roy Baumeister, a social psychologist, has given considerable thought to this question. He concludes that self-regulation is a skill and a strength. He suggests that, like a skill, it is something that can improve with practise. This is supported by groups such as Alcoholics Anonymous which exist to help people to change a self-defeating behaviour – in this case, drinking alcohol. The first stages of withdrawal are clearly the most difficult, but once new patterns have been established and the person's self-image shifts to one that is without alcohol (or gambling or whatever) then the capacity to continue desisting presumably becomes

---

537   Kegan, R. and Laskow Lehay, L. (2016). *An everyone culture: Becoming a deliberately developmental organization*. Boston, MA: Harvard Business Review Press, p. 93.

stronger, and the ability to identify situations where there might be temptation becomes stronger too.

Self-regulation also appears to be a bit like a muscle and, like all muscles, it becomes stronger with exercise but also requires periods of rest. Baumeister, in an ingenious series of experiments, has shown that if people try to resist a temptation for a period of time, then their capacity to resist other temptations diminishes rapidly afterwards. It appears that trying to resist temptation in one area of our lives (e.g. eating chocolate) will limit our capacity to self-regulate in other areas of our lives. It is notable, for example, that when students are facing exams, parents and others who live with them accept that other duties and pro-social habits, such as keeping a room clean, are likely to be abandoned for the duration of the exams.[538] It appears that the energy expended in the final week before the exam can make it difficult to continue self-regulating in other spheres of life.

Baumeister also points out that the time of day at which we are most tired is late evening. If his hypothesis is correct, then after a day of self-regulation – at work, study, managing family, interacting with colleagues, censoring opinions, dealing with frustrations, making decisions and so on – people are likely to feel tired, and the store of self-regulatory energy will be depleted. He offers as evidence the fact that most violent and impulsive crimes are committed between 1.00 a.m. and 2.00 a.m., diets are most often broken late in the evening and sexual acts that people later regret are most likely to happen late in the day. He accepts that many of these behaviours will be compounded by the use of alcohol, but again, most people regulate their use of alcohol during the day because of its adverse consequences on behaviour, and relax in the evening when they have fewer responsibilities and can look forward to a night's sleep before resuming their commitments and the activities that require regulation.[539]

Self-defeating behaviours

Something that has puzzled psychologists is people's propensity to do things that undermine their goals and which are self-defeating. People who behave in ways that are self-defeating have plans and goals, and want to succeed, but they often go about this in ways that create the opposite effect or which undermine themselves. At the root of many of the things that can go wrong is some kind of trade-off that pursues a short-term end over a long-term goal. The most prevalent example is procrastination.

Procrastination

People who procrastinate choose to do another activity rather than the one which they claim is their priority. There are some people who 'live dangerously' by, for example, playing computer games well into the night before an assignment is due, or agreeing to demands that leave no margin of error for another commitment. Procrastinators will argue that they work best under pressure, and also benefit from the extra time to do other things (have fun). This is a tempting justification. Research, however, showed that procrastinators persistently achieved less academically at the end of a semester than those who studied conscientiously, and that they were not as healthy as those who managed their time without rushing at the end to meet deadlines.[540] (This was measured by recording the number of visits to the student clinic.)

Self-regulation and emotion

The piece of the jigsaw that has been missing from our discussion so far is emotion. It should be clear from what has been written above that self-regulation plays a key role in helping us to achieve happiness, though it can require that we delay an immediate benefit for a long-term good. None of us wants to experience negative emotions, and one of the reasons we have unpleasant emotions is to give us information that tells us to do something to change our situation, in the way that pain is our body's way of communicating with us that something needs attention or is not functioning as it should. While this is an effective mechanism, there are some things that require pain, discomfort, or at least an ability to tolerate frustration, which we know are in our long-term interests. For example, anyone who learned to touch type on an

---

540 Baumeister, R.F., Leith, K.P., Muraven, M. and Bratslavsky, E. (1998). Self-regulation as a key to success in life. In Pushkar et al. (eds). *Improving competence across the lifespan* (pp. 117–32).

old manual typewriter will remember the pain and discomfort when trying to use the little finger. The same goes for the acquisition of any skill, or decision to persevere with an arduous or unpleasant task. We need to override the message from our brain telling us to stop as this is painful and unpleasant.

This becomes problematic when people experience intensely unpleasant feelings, especially if there is internal pressure to behave in a way that promises to change the person's feeling – to make them feel better. Research on feelings and risk-taking behaviour has shown that when people feel bad, they are more likely to undertake high-risk behaviour in the hope that the pay-off will lead to them feeling better.[541] Negative feelings appear to lead to risky decisions, and positive feelings make people risk averse. When people are experiencing a good mood, there is too much to lose to indulge in a high risk. When people are in a bad mood, however, or are angry or stressed, they are more likely to opt for a high risk with the promise of some reward or improvement in mood, even though the chances of the rewarding stimulus are significantly lower, and there is increased danger of a negative or self-defeating outcome. It appears that when people feel bad, and are emotionally aroused, they are likely to do something risky and self-defeating.

People who are addicted to alcohol or gambling indulge in their addiction in the hope of feeling better. The chapters on addictions in this book have shown that addictions are complex realities, involving brain mechanisms, life history, genetics, personal circumstances and social factors. However, the motivation to drink, eat, smoke, have sex, gamble or take a drug can be triggered by an unpleasant feeling, which may include physical symptoms. Once the drug is taken or the behaviour acted upon, then, in the short term, the negative feelings will be assuaged and the person will feel better. Michael Sayette suggests that lapses are essentially attempts to regulate negative feeling states. In that sense, self-regulation *is* emotion regulation.[542]

---

541 Baumeister, R.F. and Heatherton, T.F. (1996). Self-regulation failure: An overview. *Psychological Inquiry* 7(1): 1–15.

542 Sayette, M.A. (2004). Self-regulatory failure and emotion. In R.F. Baumeister and Vos, K.D. (eds). *Handbook of self-regulation: Research, theory, and applications* (pp. 447–65). London: Guilford.

This is also true in situations where someone feels outraged or frustrated and turns to violence. When people are angry, and there is either a slow build-up or a sudden change of feeling, then an angry outburst or action can help to discharge the feeling and help the person to return to a less volatile and unpleasant feeling state. It appears that when men resort to violence against their partners it is often because they feel frustrated at the lack of words to express their emotions. They feel increasingly frustrated – and perhaps ashamed of not being able to express themselves – and resort to violence to bring this unpleasant feeling state to an end.[543] It has also been shown that improved self-control is related to a reduction in domestic violence.[544] Martin Seligman offers the following simple conclusion: 'Thoughts about trespass drive anger; thoughts about loss drive sadness; thoughts about danger drive anxiety.'[545]

The capacity to manage the emotion of anger is important for people who interact with a range of difficult behaviours. An impulsive angry outburst may relieve the build-up of emotional pressure, but seldom leads to a change of behaviour. This is not to say that there is no place for anger. Anger often effectively communicates a message that the person has crossed an important boundary and puts down a marker which establishes a limit. Unfortunately, some behaviours do not change as a result of appropriately expressed anger, and consequently the expression of anger may be counter-productive. It is in these circumstances that people need to learn other strategies.

When you feel bad, you have more to gain and less to lose, and therefore the high-risk option seems appealing. One of the problems with emotional distress is that it appears to lead to impulsive behaviour, presumably in the hope of getting rid of the unpleasant feeling quickly. This does not only relate to addictions and anger. It can also operate when someone feels unhappy, excluded or slighted and says something sarcastic or belittling. It is not likely to gain the person many friends, but at least they have the satisfaction of wounding someone else or getting attention – even for being 'bad' – which may feel better than

---

543 Clare, A. (2000). *On men*. London: Chatto & Windus, p. 47.
544 Baumeister, R.F. and Tierney, J. (2011). *Willpower: Rediscovering our greatest strength*. London: Allen Lane, p. 137.
545 Seligman, M. (2011). *Flourish*. London: Nicholas Brealey Publishing, p. 167.

being ignored or not being able to change their bad mood. Those who are familiar with transactional analysis will remember that people often prefer a 'bad' stroke to no stroke at all (a stroke meaning attention).[546] Most of us have the experience of wishing we had held our tongue in a social situation, and some people never seem to learn that certain comments are not appropriate. This may represent poor judgement, or a failure at self-regulation. It is likely that the decision to speak was done in the hope of feeling better, either by wounding someone or amusing others, which would generate social approval. Sadly, these things can backfire.

Emotional distress seems to lead to making quick choices, where the ability to interrupt the sequence of thought leading into action becomes reduced. Matthieu Ricard wrote that 'Our emotions can manipulate us and lead us into error.'[547] The old advice to count to ten when angry has a lot of merit. It appears that angry people who were asked to stop and think before acting on their anger tended to reject long-shot options in favour of low-risk options.

Delayed gratification and will power

Some people are able to monitor their own behaviour, reflect on what is happening, devise new strategies and adhere to them. However, this kind of regulation of emotion and behaviour is not easy. Two researchers framed the question well:

> What makes it possible for some people to give up their addictions, to resist the temptations that threaten their cherished values and goals, to persist in the effort, to maintain their relationship, to overcome the more selfish motivation and take account of other people – in short, to exert 'willpower'? And why do others seem to remain the victims of their own vulnerabilities and biographies?[548]

---

546 Harris, T.A. (1967). *I'm OK – You're OK*. London: Pan, pp. 42–51.
547 Ricard, M. (2003). *Happiness*. London: Atlantic Books, p. 131.
548 Mischel, W. and Ayduk, O. (2004). Willpower in a cognitive-affective processing system. In Baumeister, R.F. and Vos, K.D. (eds). *Handbook of self-regulation: Research, theory, and applications* (pp. 99–129). London: Guilford, p. 107.

Walter Mischel undertook a famous series of experiments which were elegant in their simplicity. In the experiment, four-year-old children who had chosen two cookies or little treats that they would like and would prefer to a smaller treat (for example, one cookie) were placed in a room with an adult. They were then told that the adult had to leave. If they waited until the adult returned they would receive the reward they preferred, but if they wanted to receive the lesser treat they could ring a bell and the adult would return at once, enabling them to have the treat. The longest they would have to wait would be 20 minutes. The results of this experiment, which was carried out over many years, demonstrated that those who were able to wait demonstrated higher levels of academic achievement and competency in a range of personal, cognitive and social skills. The children who demonstrated effortful control at four years of age demonstrated greater levels of achievement in later life, including avoidance of cocaine addiction.[549]

What affected the choices the children made? The children had different temperaments, different physical development histories, and different family backgrounds. They also had different cortisol levels, an indication of sensitivity to stress. One factor contributing to chronically high cortisol levels is poor quality caregiving. (This will be discussed further in the next section.) It appears that the choice of whether or not to delay was dependent on what expectations the child had, especially whether or not they trusted that the promise of the better reward would be forthcoming, how they felt about the immediate treat in front of them or the better reward that required waiting, and how much they valued the reward they would have to wait for. In other words, is it worth it, and do I believe that I will get it if I wait? It also depended on whether or not the child believed that s/he had the inner resources to hold off, which is called a self-efficacy belief. Those who decided to take the immediate reward were involved in what is called 'temporal discounting', which means that the longer we have to wait for something the less we are inclined to value the thing we are waiting for.

What kinds of strategy helped those who chose to wait? Before exploring this question, it is necessary to introduce the concepts of 'hot'

---

549 Mischel, W., Shoda, Y. and Rodriguez, M.L. (1989). Delay of gratification in children. *Science* 244: 933–8; Mischel, Walter. (2014). *The marshmallow test*. London: Corgi Books.

and 'cool' systems in the brain. Cool systems are thinking processes that slow us down. They generate reasoned, goal-oriented behaviours. The hot system is related to our emotions, and sends messages full of urgency, which seek an outlet in action or expression. This system facilitates speedy processing and can be useful in situations where we feel threatened. It tends to be impulsive, rather than reflective. It is important to be able to access both systems, and allow them to interact with each other. Self-regulation requires input from the cool system, especially when we feel under pressure, have a strong desire, feel attacked, slighted, provoked or are tired. The hot system is activated under stress; unfortunately, at the time when we need the cool system the most, it tends to shut down. 'It is an ironic aspect of will power and human nature that the cool system is most difficult to access when it is most needed.'[550]

Returning to our question, there are a number of things which appear to help people who find it difficult to regulate their behaviour or their feelings. The first is the ability to focus on the hoped-for reward, which appears distant, rather than focusing on the pressure felt in the immediacy of desire, anger, urge or indignation. The second is the ability to distract oneself, by consciously thinking of something else. (One strategy is to think of a humorous situation, as it is difficult to be angry and laugh at the same time.) Walter Mischel found that children who deliberately thought about the future reward activated the cooling system in the brain, which helped them to delay their desire to have their reward, whereas those who focused on the desired reward in front of them had a harder time waiting. One lesson to be learned from this is to remove oneself from situations that are likely to undermine the ability to self-regulate, as when we are faced with the thing we desire or which has aroused us in some way, our feelings intensify, passions escalate, and the ability to think in a cool way is undermined.

Self-regulation also requires a capacity to be flexible, and to stand back from situations before rushing to judgement. When problems arise in interpersonal conflicts, it has been shown that remaining trapped in one's own point of view is a barrier to overcoming problems and finding

---

550 Mischel, W. and Ayduk, O. (2004). Willpower in a cognitive-affective processing system. In Baumeister, R.F. and Vos, K.D. (eds). *Handbook of self-regulation: Research, theory, and applications* (pp. 99–129). London: Guilford, p. 110.

a solution. People who can be flexible (cool system) and avoid giving too much control to their feelings (hot system) tend to have better outcomes.[551] Once people have learned new strategies, it is important to use them regularly so that they become automatic. For example, if someone is prone to frustration, and has a tendency to take this out on airport workers, telephone representatives, other drivers or shop assistants, it may be necessary to remember that venting at someone at this level will seldom solve the problem. The person could then tell themselves that making a scene will only aggravate people who will be less inclined to be helpful, that this will frustrate the person's long-term goal of getting redress or assistance, and that the emotional cost is not worth what can be achieved at this stage. These all reflect the various tactics mentioned above. The first time this happens will be difficult but, with practise, the person should be able to develop the skills to put these strategies into action automatically.

Some people, of course, are more emotionally reactive than others. It has been noted that children who are highly emotionally reactive, and who have poor strategies for activating their internal 'cooling' system, are more prone to have difficulties with other children. People who can access these cooling strategies – looking to the long term, distracting themselves, reframing problems, removing themselves from highly charged situations – are more likely to live happier and more fulfilling lives. This involves being able to manage our emotions, and not to be managed by them.

Developing emotional resilience

It has already been mentioned that people differ in terms of personality, temperament and background. It was also mentioned that the high cortisol levels that contribute to stress can be related to the effects of parenting. At this point, we will turn attention to the critical first months and years of life, when the foundations for emotional resilience and the skills needed for self-regulation are acquired. The emotional template which we bring with us into adulthood is laid down and developed in our childhood. It develops through a process of interaction

---

551 Arriaga, X.B. and Rusbalt, C.E. (1998). Standing in my partner's shoes: Partner perspective taking and reactions to accommodative dilemmas. *Personality and Social Psychology Bulletin* 24: 927–48.

with our caregivers – our parents – who influence significantly the way we will deal with our needs, and help us to establish the patterns that will become our default responses during adulthood. Anyone who has looked closely at a baby will be aware of the amount of gazing that happens between babies and adults. The babies follow their mothers, and the mothers follow their babies. It is a two-way process, with each influencing the other. Mothers (caregivers) learn how to soothe their babies, they mirror their actions and noises, rock them to a steady rhythm, gently bring their voices down to regulate anxiety and bring their baby to a calmer state, or stimulate them to a happier state by engaging them with eyes which are dilated and sparkle. These behaviours enable the baby to feel comfortable again.

Babies need caregivers who behave in predictable ways, who are present and available, who can help the baby to regulate feelings which at times may feel overwhelming. This enables babies to tolerate uncomfortable feelings, as they are not yet able to accomplish this themselves. This support enables physically healthy babies to tolerate discomfort beyond the limits of what they could presently tolerate on their own. Most babies who receive this regular attentive response will grow up being able to manage their emotions, and will feel in control of their emotional lives. The adequately responsive mother has a lasting effect by triggering the release of brain chemicals that soothe and reduce stress levels via the management of cortisol. Babies cannot manage their own cortisol, so they need adults to help them to regulate the effects of this hormone. Gradually they get used to the feeling of distress and know that they can trust others to help them to manage this. In time they learn how to self-soothe. Ordinarily, children who grow up in chaotic or emotionally unavailable families will have high levels of cortisol. Children of alcoholics or children with depressed caregivers are usually affected in this way.

Not everything related to cortisol is bad, however. A disapproving face, for example, will release cortisol. Children need to learn how to understand the message being communicated through disapproval and adjust their behaviour accordingly. This becomes important around 18 months to 3 years as the baby needs to learn the limits of behaviour as it begins to learn to crawl and move around. It also has to learn to be respectful and sensitive to the needs of others – the capacity to empathise with others. Disapproval leads to the feeling of shame, which raises the cortisol levels. This is a necessary part of social development, as it helps the baby to internalise moral standards. Too much cortisol, however, is damaging, and leads to children who become stressed very easily. The mother's task is to help the baby to recover from negative feelings by offering reassurance, and, in time, helping the child to verbalise their feelings so that they can use words in future as their way to express internal states and to resolve conflicts. 'Emotions are first and foremost our guides to action.'[552] As we saw earlier in this chapter, if a person does not know how to regulate their emotions, then emotions *become* actions. It is during the first four years of life that a child learns how to manage their emotions.

It is worth mentioning the phenomenon of children with abnormally low cortisol. This often happens in children who are exposed to emotional, physical or sexual abuse, or neglect. It appears that the cortisol receptors 'switch off', and the child becomes immune to stress. Bruce Perry gives a good example of this in his book, *The boy who was raised as a dog*. He tells the story of a boy called Leon whose mother, Maria, belonged to a large Mexican family. When her first child, Frank, was born, she had lots of help from her extended family to help her to raise her first son, who turned out to be normal and emotionally healthy. When Leon was born, her husband moved to the United States to work. She was alone at home and Leon cried a lot. She did not know what to do, so she left him in his crib and took Frank for walks. Maria was mentally limited in some ways, and it did not occur to her that this would be distressing for Leon. Over time, Leon became very quiet, and never cried. Sometimes his mother paid attention to him and sometimes his father did, but the care was inconsistent. Bruce Perry continues:

> An environment of such intermittent care punctuated by total abandonment may be the worst of all worlds for a child. The brain needs patterned, repetitive stimuli to develop properly. Spastic, unpredictable relief from fear, loneliness, discomfort and hunger keeps a baby's stress

---

552 Gerhardt, S. (2004). *Why love matters*. London: Routledge, p. 33.

system on high alert . . . what he learned was that the only person he could rely on was himself.[553]

Leon went on to rape and kill two adolescent girls when he was 16 years of age. This tragic story highlights some of the points made at the beginning of this chapter about the importance of not judging people who have not had the 'normal' benefits of good enough parenting, or who have been raised in non-supportive, toxic or traumatic environments. Sadly, people with abnormally low levels of cortisol often become bullies, use aggression to solve problems, and may have antisocial personality disorder.

Interventions

Can anything be done to help people who have poor self-regulation skills, or are they doomed to be emotionally limited as a result of their pasts? The concept of emotional intelligence has shown itself to be useful in this context.[554] Educators, therapists and psychologists are now trying to promote and encourage the acquisition of emotional intelligence, particularly among children. If deficits in this area are recognised at an early age, then the earlier an intervention is made, the better.

Forty years ago, Marjorie Boxall, a psychologist, set up the first 'nurture group' in a school, in order to create a safe place where children from disrupted or stressful backgrounds could have a space to catch up emotionally and learn the social and emotional skills that they needed to be able to integrate with the other students, and then to benefit from school and move on to have worthwhile lives. This approach has now been copied and there are over 1,500 nurture groups – mostly in primary schools – throughout the United Kingdom.[555] They have been shown to have a significant impact on the behaviour and well-being of these children, and also to have a positive impact on the discipline and achievements of other children in the school. According to Hilary Wiles, a study undertaken in the 1990s showed that 83% of children who participated in a nurture group were later successfully reintegrated

---

553   Perry, D.B. and Szalavitz, M. (2006). *The boy who was raised as a dog.* New York: Basic Books, p. 113.
554   Goleman, D. (1996). *Emotional intelligence: Why it can matter more than IQ.* London: Bloomsbury.
555   https://senmagazine.co.uk/articles/articles/senarticles/nurturing-support. Retrieved 14 May 2016.

into mainstream classrooms.[556] These groups are particularly helpful for children who are unable to work with others, have poor negotiation skills, or who withdraw. One of the techniques that is taught is 'square breathing': 'breathing in for four, counting for four and then breathing out for four'. This helps children to calm and soothe themselves. Once they have acquired this skill they can apply it in many situations in their often difficult lives.

This approach is supported by Stephen Briers, a psychologist who has written a book for parents, based on these principles.[557] He said that 'Children who are emotionally literate, who demonstrate a high capacity for empathy, and have social problem-solving skills, tend to be protected from all manner of mental health problems.'[558] Briers emphasises the importance of helping children to talk through their emotional experiences, but emphasises even more the value of listening. Counselling can also be helpful to children.

These initiatives and resources show that it is possible to help children who have difficulty managing their emotions. The skills which are learned in these years, through good parenting, nurture groups or counselling programmes, can help them to learn how to manage their emotions better and develop an ability to self-regulate in other areas of their lives. As has been shown, people who have an ability to self-regulate benefit in a range of ways, have a better chance of achieving their personal, social, academic and professional goals, and are better at avoiding the traps of self-defeating behaviours.

Strategies

What kinds of strategy have people developed to help them to manage their feelings and improve their general well-being? Larsen and Prizmic, in a helpful chapter, have outlined the various approaches that people use to change and lessen the intensity of (mostly negative) feelings.[559]

---

556   Wiles, H. (6 September 2007). From wayward to mainstream in months. *The Independent, Education section*, p. 6.
557   Briers, S. (2008). *Superpowers for Parents: The Psychology of Great Parenting and Happy Children*. Essex: Prentice Hall Life.
558   Williams, H. (4 October 2008). Interview with Stephen Briers. *The Saturday Guardian, Family Section*, p. 3.
559   Larsen, R.J. and Prizmic, Z. (2004). Affect regulation. In Baumeister, R.F. and Vos, K.D. (eds). *Handbook of self-regulation: Research, theory, and applications* (pp. 40–61). London: Guilford.

- *Distraction and avoiding rumination.* According to research, this is the most frequently used strategy. People can watch TV, listen to music, spend time on a hobby, work or read. Others focus on the future when the problem will be solved. It seems to work in the short term – especially by avoiding rumination, which leads to repeating the negative thoughts that lead to and reinforce the negative feelings – but does not appear to work in the long term, as the previous mood and thoughts tend to return.

- *Venting and catharsis.* People vent to rid themselves of tension. It certainly appears to be the case that expression of sadness allows for relief; however, it appears to have the opposite effect with anger, as it leads to an increase in the feeling of anger.

- *Suppression.* This involves inhibiting the expression of an emotion. This may work in the short term, but can lead to other problems if used continually. In some social situations it may not be possible, wise or acceptable to express an emotion, and suppression may be the only available strategy. The problem with suppression is that the emotion may be expressed indirectly through displacement on to the wrong target, e.g. a man who takes out his anger on his family rather than on his boss or customers.

- *Cognitive reappraisal (reframing).* People who can find meaning in adversity or see an opportunity in a problem tend to have positive outcomes, especially in terms of living at peace with themselves. This has good long-term outcomes, and helps to reduce negative feelings.

- *Downward social comparison.* It seems that people feel better if they can compare their lot favourably with someone else's – for example, someone in a situation where there are fewer resources, supports or opportunities. This helps them to put their problem in perspective and stops them dwelling on it and whining, which others tend to find unpleasant.

- *Planning to avoid problems in the future.* This involves learning from a mistake, difficult situation or problem, and putting our 'problem-solving' hat on. For example, if I don't like my job I can either talk to the boss to change aspects that I am unhappy with, or change jobs. Staying and complaining will not lead to feeling better.

- *Self-reward and thinking about or doing pleasant actions.* This approach is associated with reducing depressive feelings. It has been shown that people who have lots of pleasant experiences tend to be less depressed or stressed.

- *Exercise, relaxation, eating.* Moderate exercise has consistently been related to increasing positive feelings. This also boosts energy, which can be used for purposeful or worthwhile enterprises, which will also be rewarding. Eating sweets and watching lots of TV does not appear to help people to feel better in the long run.

- *Meditation.* There has been considerable research on the positive effects of meditation. Even taking time for 'one-minute meditation' appears to help people to manage stress better.[560]

- *Socialising, and seeking comfort, help or advice.* Researchers continually find that people who are happy have lots of friends and satisfying relationships. Being able to tell your story to a friend enables you to 'frame' it and make sense of it. It may also help you to laugh at yourself.

- *Withdrawal, isolation and being alone.* This appears to be most helpful when people are angry, as it provides a space to cool down. It is not clear if this is the best strategy when feeling sad or depressed.

- *Gratitude.* A considerable body of research has been published which suggests that 'counting your blessings' deliberately and regularly helps to improve well-being and can also have health benefits.[561]

- *Helping others and acts of kindness.* This has been related to happiness. Presumably, it enables people to take a larger

---

560 Boroson, M. (2008). *The one-minute master.* London: Random House.
561 Emmons, R.A. and McCullough, M.E. (2003). Counting blessings versus burdens: An experimental investigation of gratitude and subjective well-being in daily life. *Journal of Personality and Social Psychology* 84: 377–89.

perspective and distracts them from their own sufferings, while helping them have a sense of satisfaction and purpose.

- *Humour and laughter.* 'Laughter is the best medicine' is certainly true. In particular, self-deprecating humour, where we can laugh at ourselves, seems to bring about improvements in well-being and facilitates ease in social situations. People with a sense of humour cope better with the adversities of life and appear to have enhanced immune systems.

It appears that cognitive reappraisal, socialising with friends and focusing on feelings are the most frequently used strategies and also, apparently, the most effective. Many of these strategies involve taking distance from an event, remembering a long-term goal, seeing a different perspective[562] (which is partly how humour works) and actively doing something to remove ourselves from a situation which is causing us to feel bad. Meditation appears to be particularly effective, and brings us to the final section: self-regulation and spirituality.

Spiritual development

Religious traditions have all recognised the need for self-regulation in the lives of their members, particularly those who dedicate their lives to ministry or the spiritual path. The words 'self-discipline' and 'asceticism' will be familiar to people who are interested in spiritual growth. Andrew Louth points out that the word 'asceticism' is derived from the Greek word 'askeo' which means 'to train' or, literally, 'to work with materials'.[563] In this case, the material is the self. This is consistent with Baumeister's conclusion that self-regulation is the moral muscle which enables people to live purposeful, regulated lives, and that it can be strengthened with use and practise.

Self-control was already encouraged in New Testament writings. St Paul, for example, tells his followers that 'Any bitterness or bad temper or anger or shouting or abuse must be far removed from you – as must every kind of malice.' He encourages them: 'Be generous to one

---

562 Wicks, R.J. (2014). *Perspective: The calm within the storm.* Oxford: OUP.
563 Louth, A. (2005). Asceticism. In Sheldrake, P. (ed.). *The New SCM Dictionary of Christian Spirituality.* London: SCM.

another, sympathetic, forgiving each other as readily as God forgave you in Christ' (Ephesians 4:31, 32).[564] St Paul asks his listeners to exercise restraint in some aspects of their lives and to cultivate virtues in others. The Christian tradition recognises that this is unlikely to happen unless people make choices in their attitudes and behaviours that will bring them into conformity with these values. The process of acquiring these virtues and curbing unchristian behaviours is no different from what is involved in self-regulation. There is an ancient Christian tradition that framed asceticism in terms of battling against demons, which is probably the same internal experience known by those who struggle against ill-temper, a tendency to take offence easily, poor judgement in humour, the tendency to procrastinate, addictions or self-defeating behaviours. Louth points out that monastic tradition framed self-discipline in terms of sensitivity to other people with whom one lived, especially putting up with their failings, and curbing one's own will for the sake of the community.

Roy Baumeister also points out that the well-known 'Seven Deadly Sins' of Christian spirituality all reflect failures of self-control in various ways. He writes:

> The sin of gluttony is a failure to control one's impulses and desires, especially for food. The sin of sloth (laziness) means lacking the self-discipline to do one's work. The sin of anger or wrath means acting in a hostile manner and possibly failing to control one's feelings. Sins of lust involve giving in to sexual impulses and desires. Sins of envy involve wanting what other people have and possibly trying to take them for oneself. Greed is also a failure to control one's appetites, desires, and impulses. The last sin, pride, is less obviously a failure of self-control, but in practice it too often means indulging one's impulses to feel superior to others and to claim special privileges and entitlements for oneself. Society works better if people restrain all these feelings and impulses.[565]

---

564   The New Jerusalem Bible. (1985). Darton, Longman, & Todd.
565   Baumeister, R. (2005). *The Cultural Animal*. Oxford: OUP, p. 338.

Christian spirituality has often presented the Seven Deadly Sins in terms of the potential damage that these sins do to the soul of the individual Christian. It is interesting to note that Baumeister's primary focus is on the effect these sins have on the fabric of society.

Modern writers in the Catholic and reformed traditions also highlight the need for self-discipline in the spiritual life. Richard Foster's well-known and highly regarded book, *Celebration of Discipline*, brings together the various insights and practices in the Christian tradition that have been seen to be helpful or necessary in living the Christian life. He groups them under three headings:

1. The inward disciplines: meditation, prayer, fasting and study.

2. The outward disciplines: simplicity, solitude, submission and service.

3. The corporate disciplines: confession, worship, guidance and celebration.

Foster writes that these disciplines are needed to bring us to a place of depth in our knowledge and experience of God. He recognises that, if we leave our spiritual development and fidelity to the principles and practices of our faith to the times when we feel like it, we will not advance very far and will probably give up, feeling discouraged. Ricard wrote: 'A spiritual dimension, whether religious or not, helps us to set goals in life, and promotes human values, charity, generosity and openness.'[566]

Robert Wicks, a psychologist and spiritual writer, takes this further and says that it is not possible to remain healthy in ministry unless we build certain practices – disciplines – into our lives. In a book chapter on 'the stress of spiritual ministry', he writes that certain steps are necessary to improve our well-being:[567]

1. an honest prayer life;

2. balance in one's schedule;

---

566 Ricard, M. (2003). *Happiness*. London: Atlantic Books, p. 180.
567 Wicks, R.J. (1995). The stress of spiritual ministry: Practical lessons on avoiding unnecessary distress. In Wicks, R.J. (ed.). *Handbook of Spirituality for Ministers*. New York: Paulist, pp. 249–58.

3. self-nurturance;

4. healthy intimacy with others;

5. the ability to deal with negative emotions;

6. the ability to put failure in perspective.

Some of these recommendations should be familiar from what has been written above about strategies for managing our feelings and living more healthily. Wicks continues by offering the following simple steps to maintain what he calls 'pastoral focus':

1. To promise at least two minutes of silence and solitude each morning to centre yourself **no matter how late you got up or busy you are.**

2. Several times each day to reflect on the presence of God in your life.

3. To read sacred Scripture at least once a week for five or ten minutes for no ulterior purpose or goal, so that God remains a real concrete presence in your life rather than a vague entity.

4. To speak about your faith and spiritual journey either formally (spiritual direction) or informally (with a spiritual companion).

It is clear from these authors that self-control, self-discipline and asceticism have their place in the spiritual life, and that the principles of cultivating them are no different from what is being recommended in the first part of this chapter.

Before concluding this section, it is worth noting that Foster talks about 'celebrating' discipline. He sees discipline as a positive force in people's lives, as it leads to depth, spiritual growth, fidelity to the gospel, sensitivity to others, and a sense of care for the planet we live on through living simply and avoiding greed and excess. Similarly, the section of *The Catechism of The Catholic Church* which mentions asceticism comes under Article 3 *On Freedom*, in the section on Life in the Spirit.[568] These various sources assure believers that discipline

---

568 *The Catechism of the Catholic Church.* (1994). Geoffrey Chapman, section 1734.

is not designed to restrict the Spirit and make people miserable, but rather to open up a richer life through the practice of the virtues. What all of these writers and traditions share is a conviction that, if we only did these things when we felt like it, we would make no progress in the spiritual life, and our interactions with others would be marked with less sensitivity and generosity.

Conclusion

This chapter has focused on the issue of self-regulation and its relationship with our emotions, partly to help in understanding strategies that can be of help to people who struggle to regulate their feelings, desires and behaviours, and partly to offer insight and support to those who interact with people whose behaviour is difficult and challenging in a range of ways. Researchers have become fascinated by ways in which people change, maintain or regulate their behaviour. They have also been puzzled by the ways in which people's behaviours do not always promote their interests or help them to achieve their goals – in other words, ways that people defeat themselves. The conclusions that have been drawn from this research are similar to what has been learned from centuries of wisdom passed down by spiritual writers in the various Christian traditions. The message is clear: in order to live a happy, wholesome, spiritual life, we need to attend to our feelings, learn how to live with ourselves, build disciplines and practices into our lives to protect us from overwork, our underdeveloped shadow side, our weaknesses and failings, and the temptation to believe that we can manage on our own.

Whether our issue is addiction, procrastination, holding our tongue or putting into practice a time for regular prayer, the principles of self-regulation, and how we listen to our emotions, but not allow ourselves to be mastered by them, are the same. 'To do anything, the self has to keep its own inner house in order, such as by organising its actions towards goals, avoiding swamps of emotional distress, obeying laws, and internalising society's standards of good (both moral and competent) behaviour.'[569] Our feelings exist to provide vital information to help us to

---

569 Baumeister, R.F. and Vos, K.D. (2004). Preface. In Baumeister, R.F. and Vos, K.D. (eds). *Handbook of self-regulation: Research, theory, and applications* (p. xi). London: Guilford.

survive and live well. However, while they can work well in emergencies, they are not the best guide in all circumstances. A well-regulated life – and not a life without passion, which has its place – requires attending to the hot emotional systems, but also to the cool thinking systems. Growth in self-regulation and related skills can improve our own lives and equip us better to manage situations where the behaviour of others can be difficult, destabilising or challenging.

Self-regulation: Recommended Reading

Baumeister, Roy F. & Tierney, John. (2011). *Willpower: Rediscovering our greatest strength.* London, UK: Allen Lane

Mischel, Walter. (2014). *The marshmallow test; Understanding self-control and how to master it.* London, UK: Corgi Books.

Ricard, Matthieu. (2003). *Happiness: A guide to developing life's most important skill. London,* UK: Atlantic Books.

Wicks, Robert J. (2010). *Bounce: Living the resilient life.* O.U.P.

Wicks, Robert J. (2014). *Perspective: The calm within the storm.* O.U.P.

CHAPTER FOURTEEN

Practical Theology[570]

Alan Bartlett

What is 'theology'?

Even this weekend, I found myself listening to a political discussion on the radio, and one of the speakers said: 'we must not get lost in the theology of this issue'. The speaker was not talking about real theology – the relationship of God to the issue in question. Rather, he meant that we must not get lost in minutiae or fantasy, inward-looking conversation or obsession with fine judgements of right and wrong. In other words, 'theology' has become a metaphor for irrelevant, introverted and inappropriate talk – as opposed to mature, well-grounded, proportionate and action-creating discussion.

> Laurie Green in his classic book, *Let's Do Theology*, opens with a lament which is heard again and again in the life of the Church, from surveys of preaching to responses to official church reports:
>
> I am often struck by the church notice board slogan which reads, 'Christ is the Answer'.
>
> I suspect that many would be prompted to respond, 'Yes, but does
> the Church know what the question is?'[571]

This is a tragedy. It is partly, of course, a product of the Church's obsession with internal arguments – and the obsessive nature of these arguments – but it also results from the Church's amateurism when talking about real life. The Church (and I write this essay as an English Anglican priest) is heard as not just believing impossible things but

---

570　My specific debts to colleagues and students are acknowledged below, but it is crucial to say at this stage that any of my insights into Practical Theology owe everything to my work on the Master's and doctoral programmes delivered in Durham by the (then) theological colleges – Cranmer Hall, Ushaw College and the Wesley Study Centre – in collaboration with the University Department of Theology and Religion. Three particular colleagues, Fr Chris Hughes, the Revd Dr Roger Walton and Dr Jocelyn Bryan have been very influential in this work and in my education.

571　Green, L. (2002). *Let's Do Theology* (London and New York: Continuum first pub. 1990, 2002 reprint), p. 1.

trying to connect them to real life in crass ways. I hope this book is a good example of how the Church can reclaim the language of 'theology', so that it becomes what it should always have meant: serious conversation about the relationship between God and the real lives of 'ordinary' human beings. And this is purposeful serious conversation, because it is about helping people to find methods and resources which will enable genuine encounters with God in the midst of the reality of everyday living, and further, to reflect on real life and these divine encounters so as to enable wiser living. This is Practical Theology. This book is Practical Theology.

Practical Theology

You will have noticed common patterns in the essays in this book. They all begin with careful professional attention to the reality of human experience. (By 'professional' I mean disciplined, accountable to some set of objective standards – both academic and corporate – and reliable.) We might be personally unused to starting theological conversation with experience, but it has become a mainstream way of doing theology. We might also be unused to this sort of professional human sciences discussion in church documents, though it exists quite widely.[572] I want to suggest that this way of doing theology is just as theological as the classic way, of beginning with Scripture and Tradition and then 'applying' it to our lives, and more strongly, that it is in fact essential for the life and mission of the modern Church and the society in which we are set. Christians cannot comment on the relationship of God to human situations unless they have informed themselves about the reality of these situations.

Often the reality of these situations is part of the experience of Christians themselves. While it might be possible to read this book as if difficult experiences happen to people outside the Church, the truth is that Christians are not immune, for example, from addictive problems. Part of the difficulty when doing this sort of theological work is enabling Christians to talk about, in appropriate contexts of course, their real experiences as opposed to the Christian image.

---

572 Note as just one example the careful research which is included within the ecumenical report *Faithful Cities* (Peterborough: Methodist Publishing House; London: Church House Publishing, 2006).

But even if the experience is not something which I, as a Christian, have experienced myself, I can still be enabled to understand it, when it is empathetically presented in a disciplined way. I wonder, were you surprised as you read this book? Were you surprised by the description of gambling? Not just by the extent of gambling, but by the way gambling addictions can be related to other experiences in a person's life? By the way in which gambling becomes a mechanism for finding psychological relief and so by the way in which gambling becomes addictive? Or were you shaken by the description of the extent of domestic violence and how it needs to be understood against the background of the long history of unequal gendered relationships between men and women? Or, to look at that from another angle, were you surprised by the way Christian theology has often been used to justify what now seems utterly abhorrent behaviour? Coming to understand that sad fact is part of our Christian task of coming to understand this very painful human experience.

One of my own frequent experiences, when working with students in Practical Theology, is that the first deep point of learning comes from beginning to understand an issue in all its reality and complexity. 'So that's what it's really like!' This comes not just from hearing about the experiences but also from beginning to analyse them and place them in a conceptual framework.

The Pastoral Cycle

A frequently used model for this way of doing theology is the 'pastoral cycle'.[573]

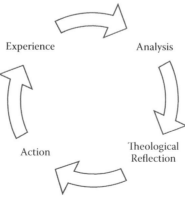

Experience

Analysis

Action

Theological
Reflection

---

573 Still the classic in this field is Ballard, Paul and Pritchard, John. (2006). *Practical Theology in Action* (2nd edition). London: SPCK. The Pastoral Cycle is not without its critiques, because it can feel artificial – see P. Ward – but it remains the most commonly used method of Practical Theology.

We start with an experience. It can be a crisis experience when something has gone wrong or it can be a routine experience which we want to understand better. Often it is an experience which feels slightly at odds with our understanding of how the world, and God, ought to be. In Practical Theology, we pay careful attention to this experience, to make sure that we have really seen and heard what happened and then we try to understand it by putting it into a wider framework. For example, in the essay on 'difficult people', we first see what such people do and how they impact on others. Then we try to understand this behaviour. Here we normally use tools from other disciplines, in this case psychology, to help us to understand that these are not just individual or random behaviours but can be 'explained' in terms of people's life experiences or the pattern of their personalities and relationships. This is the 'analysis' section of the Pastoral Cycle.

We then find ourselves trying to make sense of this theologically, and exploring our Christian beliefs and values to help guide our actions. At this point, there is often a dialogue. Our response to, for example, a 'difficult person' may be either to try to love them out of their woundedness – because Jesus taught us to 'love our neighbour' and even our 'enemy' – or it may be to try to help them to change by telling them the 'truth in love'. As you will see from the essay, either of these actions could produce the opposite reaction to the one intended by the caring Christian. And then we may find ourselves slipping back into being just pragmatic: we ignore or sideline or sack the 'difficult person' because they are a nuisance. Or we may find ourselves being 'super-spiritual' and praying for certain forms of miraculous healing and behaving unrealistically while we wait for this prayer to be 'answered'. Whereas the question we ought really to be asking ourselves is: 'What would it mean to care Christianly for such a person, with wise and professional insight?' For example, as Christian Practical Theologians we might ask, 'What can we honestly and realistically hope for as "redemption" for such a person?'

I need to stress here that the theological section of the Pastoral Cycle is very demanding: it is demanding because we are firing questions at Scripture and Tradition and not wanting to get simplistic answers – because that would be at odds both with real life and with the professionalism with which the rest of our Practical Theology work has been done. But it is also demanding because, while we are trusting that Scripture and Tradition will have true and wise things to say about real human beings, it is not always easy to discern this wisdom. For example, as part of our answer to the question about 'difficult people', we would have to ask what Scripture and the Tradition say about caring for deeply wounded or even mentally unwell people, but also how these ideas make sense in the twenty-first century when our understanding of human nature has moved on beyond, say, ancient beliefs in demon possession or the four 'humours'.

Finally, we resolve on the action we will take in the situation. But of course, once we begin to plan the action, and even more as we implement it, we will have new experiences to analyse and reflect on, so the process kicks in again. (In fact, the Pastoral Cycle is better described as the Pastoral Spiral but we will stick to the original phrase because it is so widely used.) This Cycle is used by Practical Theologians. But it is also used by all sorts of other professionals and carers.[574] Its objective is to train 'reflective practitioners' – that is, people who have learned to look carefully at a situation and then to analyse it before taking action, and then to review their action.

Good Practical Theology

But how do we do good – that is, reliable and wise – Practical Theology? I often find myself saying to students: 'keep your theology on hold until you have some understanding of the issue in question'. This sounds strange to, for example, young ordinands but it is crucial, though it needs careful explanation. Any one of us can fall into the bad habit of making snap judgements. But we can be particularly prone to this if we have strong opinions in an area or if it is an area of human experience about which we are ignorant or indifferent. For a variety of reasons, I have no understanding of the excitement of gambling. Therefore I need to be alert to my tendency to make simplistic moral judgements – 'just tell them to stop!' A sharper example is in the area of our response to those who commit child abuse. We assume that we know what we are talking about and that the explanation (and remedy) is clear and simple.

---

574 See the classic book Schon, D.A. (1991). *The Reflective Practitioner: How Professionals Think in Action.* Aldershot: Ashgate.

This is hugely reinforced if we have strong theological convictions – for example, about the nature of sin and of God's response to it. Therefore, we 'see' the people involved and the issue in a certain way, because we come to it, to use a familiar metaphor, with a strong set of spectacles. But we may be wrong. We may be at risk of misinterpreting actions or words because we are so sure of our interpretation. Therefore we need to be careful to stop and check. As my father-in-law, who had worked in industry as well as in the Church, said often: 'There are always simple answers to complex questions. They're just normally wrong!'

A good metaphor for Practical Theology is a set of traffic lights.[575] The first light is red. It warns us to stop and look. 'Do not proceed until you have looked, because you may have an accident.' Each of the essays in this book asks you to stop and look first, before you come to a judgement. Again, this may feel unnatural, especially if we are 'people of action' or if the situation is pressing. The red light requires us to stop the forward motion until we are safe to proceed. This is a spiritual as well as an intellectual discipline.

Another way of describing this is to use a longstanding Roman Catholic model of Practical Theology, whose origins lay in the difficult context of struggles in post-WWI Belgian industry. It is: 'See. Judge. Act.'[576] Cardinal Cardijn trained his Young Christian Workers to learn to look first. What are the economics of this industry? What are the causes of the high numbers of industrial injuries or the endemic unemployment? This will lead us on to asking deeper questions. Where does the power lie in this situation? Why does the power lie there? Is this balance of power unchangeable (as we are often told)? Are there alternatives? I believe very strongly that we must see and understand first, and then the theological thinking will be talking directly to the world as it is, not to some idealised or sanitised version. The best examples of Practical Theology are those which have thought with such clarity about human experiences that they have crystallised the issues which are at stake. What is the 'what-is-ness' in this situation? Then, we can take these issues to our theology and begin the search for insight. Notice how the essays on addiction have to wrestle with the question of

---

575   I am deeply indebted to my colleague, the Revd Dr Stephen Cherry, formerly Director of Training in the Diocese of Durham, for sharing this image with me and for giving me permission to share it in print.

576   See http://www.ycw.ie/resources/see-judge-act-resources-2/ for a modern exposition of this.

what addiction is, before they can find the best theology to illuminate the issue. This is good Practical Theology.

I need to make two important qualifications to my argument at this point. First, while we restrain the introduction of theological insights at the beginning of a Practical Theology process, we acknowledge that the reason we care about an issue in the first place is because of the love of God in Christ, embodied in who we already are as Christian human beings within the Church. I am shaken by the stories of abuse because my conscience has already been sensitised by God in my creation and in the Church. Second, we must recognise that even 'objective' analyses of human situations have values embedded deep within them. When we, as Christians, draw on the insights of, for example, psychology when understanding a situation, we need to do so alert to the values which are assumed in that discipline. Psychology is a huge and varied discipline but some elements within it have been critical of, or even hostile to, religious belief and, at its worst, there can be a sort of reductionism which 'explains away' theological understandings.[577] How do we as Christian theologians evaluate the account being given of the human beings in this situation by this other discipline? Therefore, even at the analysis stage in the process of Practical Theology, we find the flow of questions flowing in both directions.

An improved version of the Pastoral Cycle has been developed by Emmanuel Lartey which includes these insights.[578] Notice how there is a real dialogue between the experiences, the analysis with the human sciences, and the theological values and insights.

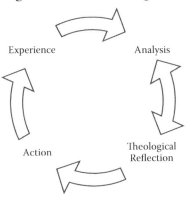

Experience

Analysis

Action

Theological Reflection

577 For a good way into this particular area see Watts, F., et.al. (2001). *Psychology for Christian Ministry.* London: Routledge.

578 Lartey, E. (2000). Practical Theology as a Theological Form. In Woodward, J. and Pattison, S. *The Blackwell Reader in Pastoral and Practical Theology.* Oxford: Blackwell, p.132. I have simplified Lartey's version by omitting his 'situational analysis of theology' and by using my own terminology.

Nonetheless, I need to repeat my warning to be wary of importing explicit theology too early into the process because of the risk of seeing real life through rose-tinted or indeed grey-tinted spectacles, depending on our own theological presuppositions!

Theology in Practical Theology

So what then is the role of 'theology' in this Practical Theology? We have already noted that the reason we wish to think about an issue may be that, because of our Christian faith, we care about those being damaged. Or it may be that the real-life experiences are jarring with our sense of how things 'ought to be' in our God-made world? This is the point in the cycle when we work most explicitly in theological terms. And here the traffic light is on amber, warning us to stop and think, to ponder actively, and then to get ready, to prepare to engage the clutch so that we can move on. It is a good metaphor for this phase in Practical Theology because it is about an anticipation to move – it is not waiting and watching for its own sake! – but it still requires patient attention. It remains a spiritual as well as an intellectual discipline.

Another question. One of our former students in Durham was a Professor of Economics before he trained to be an Anglican priest. He approached Practical Theology with a degree of caution, perhaps used to hearing church leaders utter platitudes about complex economic issues. So he used to ask us, regularly: 'What added value is theology bringing to this conversation?' As I might put it: 'Do we need to say something specifically Christian about this issue – or not?' And the essays in this book may have made you ask that question. Several of them provide clear and reliable accounts of the human experiences and offer wise practical responses, without having to draw much on overt Christian values. We might wish to say, theologically, that this reflects the presence of the Wisdom of God in the world[579] and that some of the values of care for the Other and of justice, which are now so deeply rooted in Western society, have their own deep roots in the

---

579   This opens up a rich theological theme. As the *Logos* (Word) of God, Christ is present in the work of creation [John 1:3; Colossians 1:15], as is the Spirit of God [Genesis 1:2]. Both *Logos* and Spirit shape human beings into the image of God [Genesis 1:27]. Part of the expression of this is human conscience [Romans 2:14-16]. For examples of how this is explored and justified theologically and then related to human life see Barton, S. (ed.). (1999). *Where shall Wisdom be found?* Edinburgh: T&T Clark, especially the essay by Colin Gunton.

Christian faith. But it remains the case that we may be asking ourselves, a little anxiously: 'But have Christians got something distinctive to say about this issue?'

I think they often have, but these insights are often at the big-picture level rather than in the detail. Reading these essays, I noted again and again reference to the *values* which Christians bring to discussion of human life. For example, in the essay on sexual addiction, we were reminded that it is *not* the Christian way to fear or despise human sexual activity. Part of the sub-discipline of theology which is called theological anthropology is the study of what it is to be a human being as understood within a Christian framework. The authors of this essay, and I agree with them, argue that loving and pleasurable sexual activity can be part of the God-given-ness of human nature. Therefore, there is an assumption that it is worth the effort to redeem human sexual activity, when it has become distorted, because it is part of God's good creation. We will return to the discussion about the 'cash value' of theological convictions such as 'Creation' shortly.

But, I can imagine a thoughtful reader beginning to furrow her brow at this point. Because it has not always been the case that Christian theologians have argued for the positive value of human sexuality. Indeed, for hundreds of years it seems to have been the case that human sexual desire was treated as inherently dangerous by the Church. One of the main consequences of the Fall – so it was argued – was that human desire became corrupted and human sexual desire most of all. It was always tainted with concupiscence:[580] that is, the power of the senses – in traditional language, the 'flesh' – was out of the control of the mind and of the spirit and so *certain* to lead human beings into actual sin.[581] While modern study of human psychology has reinforced the potential for human sexuality to become distorted, it has sharply warned us that inappropriate language of 'sin' can be one of the most potent sources of distortion. In other words, what happens at this stage

---

580   When confronted by a technical theological term like this, it is very helpful to use a good theological dictionary, such as the *Oxford Dictionary of the Christian Church* (3rd edition, 1997), Oxford: Oxford University Press. Theological terms such as this are excellent ways of both summarising and also opening up complex theological discussions. It is good to become familiar with them because – despite our wariness of jargon – they in fact enable us to talk with clarity about the variety of Christian understandings.

581   See chapter 3 of Bartlett, A. (2004). *Humane Christianity*. London: Darton, Longman and Todd.

in the Practical Theology process is that the questions which real-life experiences, and the analysis of them, have thrown up are taken to Scripture and Tradition and often trigger new insights. This can feel challenging, even disturbing and subversive. Certainly, part of the experience of the Church in the last 200 years has been that many of its long-accepted tenets about human beings have been challenged by allowing previously unheard voices to speak – for example, the voices of abused women.

I want to explore this issue of the challenge of Practical Theology a little further, before turning to a more positive account of the value of the classic Christian theological disciplines.

Practical Theology as challenge

Several years ago, one of our younger single male Anglican ordinands had been very moved by his experiences during a hospital placement about the pastoral care of parents who had suffered a stillbirth or neo-natal death. While this was outside his own personal experience, he had researched the issue carefully. He had developed some knowledge of the background medical and psychological realities; of the extent of the problem (through some statistical work) and also of its social reality (e.g. which sort or type or class of person is most likely to suffer this trauma); and, crucially, of what it feels like to go through this experience (through conversation and wider reading). In so far as it was possible, he had developed a good empathetic understanding of this experience.

He was then confronted with the issue of understanding it theologically. This raised huge issues about the providence of God. But the point at which he was most 'stuck' was when he turned to the Bible for insight and in particular for resources to use in the liturgical pastoral care of people caught up in these circumstances. He was attempting this in a seminar with fellow students. After some increasingly frustrated conversation, one of the group blurted out: 'The Bible is not much help in this area.' By this, the person meant that biblical texts about the death of neo-natal babies often expressed very different understandings about the meaning to be given to such tragic events. They might, for example, be seen as a divine judgement.[582] In this interpretation the

---

582 See 2 Samuel:12 for the account of the death of David and Bathsheba's first child.

child had no rights of its own, its fate was entirely determined by the sins of its parents, and especially its father. Crudely speaking – and it is a simplistic stereotype – children in the Old Testament were seen as the property of their parents, especially of their fathers. This is a deeply patriarchal account of human life, written in a deeply patriarchal society.[583] So the group had to confront the challenge posed to classic Judaeo-Christian faith in the providence of God by the tragic death of these babies, but also to some ancient Judaeo-Christian understandings of the status of the neo-natal. These are different sorts of challenge, but both are important. The question of suffering and a God of love remains one of the main causes of disbelief in our society. But the latter perception – that our scriptures are archaic and unhelpful – is increasingly common and is raised precisely by exploration of this sort of human experience in dialogue with our scriptures.

We will return to the issue of hermeneutics – that is, the study of how a text is interpreted – in a moment, but here I want to pause on the challenge to the Church raised by Practical Theology. Especially when Practical Theology is done in a Western theological context, it can feel as if the agenda is entirely one of challenge. So Bible and Church are portrayed as hierarchical, patriarchal, homophobic and so on. These debates need to be handled with care, of course, and crass sloganeering is often insensitive to the complexities and surprises in Scripture and Tradition. There is much good news in both, as we will describe soon. But it remains the case that modern (postmodern?) critiques of Scripture and Tradition are exposing deep problems in the life of the Church.

I will give an example by making a personal comment on the impact of Practical Theology on my doctrine of the Church. Much ecclesiology – the study of the doctrines about the Church – is highly conceptual. It portrays an idealised Church essentially defined by its relationship

---

583 This is not the place for an extended study of this issue but interested readers might explore: Trible, P. (1984). *Texts of Terror.* Philadelphia: Fortress; or Countryman, L.W. (1988). *Dirt, Greed and Sex.* Philadelphia: Fortress; or Hays, R.B. (1997). *The Moral Vision of the New Testament.* Edinburgh: T&T Clark. For examples of creative use of biblical materials with people who have experienced a stillbirth or neo-natal death, see The Compassionate Friends: Support for bereaved parents and their families, www.tcf.org.uk and also the Stillbirth and Neonatal Death Society (SANDS), www.uk-sands.org. Psalm 139 is one of the most popular and beautiful passages read, for example, at memorial services but it is just worth noting the double-edged nature of this psalm. The baby in the womb is 'wonderfully made' and known by God but the real baby is, of course, not so wonderfully made as to survive. And the psalm is about God's omniscience, omnipresence and indeed judgement. It surely needs careful handling in this very painful circumstance.

to selected theological norms. So the Church is 'the Body of Christ'. Such language can disguise the reality of local and wider church life and give a spurious cover to, for example, oppressive actions by the Church done in the name of Christ. Part of the gift of Practical Theology to the Church is to help the Church to look at itself honestly. The Church is both a supernatural and an all too human institution. I believe in the practical fallibility of the Church.[584] Thus, at a micro-level, I have seen Practical Theologians deploy to great effect the tools of group dynamics and social psychology to analyse the reality of local congregational life.[585] It is all very well to believe in, for example, the central importance of either the local congregational meeting (for Baptists) or the role of the local 'vicar' (for Anglicans) in church life but, unless we understand how these institutions and people actually work, we will make plans based on fantasies. And on a broader scale, it is, I fear, simply the case that serious study of the churches' history reveals not just occasional problems but rather *systematic* error and abuse. History and Practical Theology force Christians to take account of these ugly realities when doing their ecclesiology and when imagining and planning the life of the modern Church. In other words, and to go back to the version of the Pastoral Cycle offered by Lartey, Practical Theology changes our theology.

Practical Theology and the Bible

We have already explored some of the complexities of using the Bible in Practical Theology, but in this section I would like to push the questions further. (What is said of the Bible in this section could, with some changes, also be said of how tradition can be used within Practical Theology.) You may already have noticed how often the Bible is cited in the essays in this book and how some texts have become dominant in how we conceive of modern Christian mission – for example, Luke 4:18, 19. There are two important issues to be addressed when we bring the Bible explicitly into the theological element of Practical Theology: hermeneutics and purpose. We will look at them in turn.

---

584   This is NOT a comment on the nature of the Church's authority, or of any of the organs of the Church's life. For discussion of that in an Anglican-Roman Catholic perspective, the reader is referred to ARCIC. (1999). *The Gift of Authority. Authority in the Church III.* London: Catholic Truth Society.

585   See Savage, S. (2006). On the analyst's couch: Psychological perspectives on congregations and clergy. In S. Croft (ed.) *The Future of the Parish System.* London: Church House Publishing.

Hermeneutics is the discipline of thinking about how we read any text, especially any ancient text and in particular the Bible.[586] To summarise a very extensive and complex discussion, hermeneutics teaches us that the first step in the process of reading the Bible is to enter as fully as possible into the world of the biblical text. This requires us to do textual study (what is the text?) and historical-critical study (how does our understanding of the history of the text help us to understand its meaning?) as well as linguistic study (what do the words mean and what is the *genre* of the text and so how should we hear it?), and thus to ask what is the overall meaning of the text – its exegesis. But this is only the first part of the task.

The second part is to recognise our own assumptions, conscious and unconscious, about what is true, and thus about what is true in any given passage of Scripture. For example, modern people do not believe in a three-decker universe (this could be variously described but one version of this belief is that there is an underworld below us, the world of planet earth which we inhabit, and a further heavenly world above this). We so clearly do not believe this that we do not even notice that we are editing it out of our reading of Scripture. This is a simple example but there are many more weighty examples which bear much more sharply on the issues raised in Practical Theology: the relationship of mind, body and spirit in a human being; the nature of sin; the character of God. Good biblical study will enable us to see more clearly where our world overlaps with the world of Scripture and where it is different.

This then leaves the most difficult task, which is to answer the question of how our world *should* relate to the world of Scripture. Christians have always lived with this tension because the Christian version of the Bible includes material explicitly setting aside significant sections of the Hebrew Scriptures (the 'Old' Testament). Crudely speaking, for example, Christians do not accept the food laws in the Torah as still being relevant and to be obeyed. So Christians always operate with a strong hermeneutic when reading the Bible. Often, we only realise this when we are confronted by those who interpret the Bible differently.

A simple example: during my theological training, my wife and I went to Nigeria. Helen does not wear a hat to attend church. This

---

586 An excellent way into this complex discussion is Briggs, R. (2003). *Reading the Bible Wisely*. London: SPCK. Also Davis, E.F. and Hays, R.B. (eds). (2003). *The Art of Reading Scripture*. Grand Rapids, MI and Cambridge: Eerdmans).

scandalised some of our Nigerian hosts and, try as I might, I could not convince them that the command for women to cover their heads [1 Corinthians 11] was a culturally specific command only relevant to first-century Corinth (if that is indeed what it was . . .). We were clearly liberalising and backsliding Westerners – though this was implied with great graciousness! But what was more intriguing were the questions from the younger wives in the women's fellowships, asking how we had been married for six years but had no children? It was a birth control question and sprang from an incipient rebellion against the older tradition (hermeneutic) which regarded regular child-bearing as an inevitable and divinely ordained part of married life. This was practical hermeneutics.

So, when we bring the Bible into conversation with real life, we must do so alert to the meaning of Scripture (and how we ascertain that) but also to the potential gap between the scriptural world and ours, and how we bridge that gap.

This opens up a further area of discussion: the purpose with which we are approaching Scripture. This might be thought to be a strange question. Surely we go to Scripture for guidance, indeed for authoritative guidance? But this assumption shortcuts a discussion both about how God is heard through Scripture and about the nature of Scripture itself.

As an Anglican, I am only too aware of the painful difficulties of hearing God speak in Scripture. In a Communion where different modes of interpretation are leading to different ethical decisions and thus to potential schism, the question of how we interpret Scripture wisely is very pressing. One point on which Anglicans are, more or less, agreed is that we have to be self-aware and mature as we handle the Bible. As I have written elsewhere:

> Fundamentally, whilst the classic language of Anglicanism often refers to the Bible as the 'Word of God', this always sits over against the deeper assumption that the 'Word' is Christ . . . the phrase 'the authority of the Bible' should be understood as shorthand for 'the authority of the triune God, *exercised through* scripture'.[587] It is a relational,

---

587 The Lambeth Commission on Communion. *The Windsor Report*. (2004). London: Anglican Communion Office, para.54, p. 27. *Italics original.*

dynamic and transformative not a fixed, restrictive and legalistic understanding of the nature of scriptural authority. God 'speaks' and 'does' as the Bible is 'heard' and 'lived', in keeping with his whole mission: people and situations being brought to new life.[588] *God is primary.*[589]

This conviction about both the authority of Scripture and the necessity of our self-awareness and modesty when we expound it is closely connected to our understanding of the character of the Bible itself. This is not to return to the old arguments about 'inerrancy' – every word in the Bible is literally true – but rather to note the diverse and sophisticated way in which the Bible itself speaks, as well as the diverse and sophisticated ways in which we approach it. This has been explored in a very rich way by Professor David Ford.[590] He describes five different 'moods' of faith, which can also be read as five different moods in which Scripture speaks and within which we hear it speak:

Indicative mood or tense – 'it is or is not' – which affirms or denies. This is a theology of the blessing (and judgement) of God which affirms and confirms the identity of what is good, and denies and bounds what is not true. I interpret this as Scripture helping us to clarify 'what is good and true and beautiful' in a situation. It is partly a theology which sees Scripture as helping us to make good judgements.

Imperative of command and obedience – 'do this or do not do this'. This is Scripture/Faith requiring (life-giving) obedience to divine command. This is the mode in which Scripture is often presented (and resented). I am sure Ford is right to make it only one mood of Scripture but I would also argue that it is a mode of Scripture which we cannot, and in fact do not, ever lose, whatever our theological perspective.

Interrogative that questions, probes, tests and suspects – 'why is it like this, does it have to be?' Ford sees this as a divine testing of the human.

---

588 See Wright, N.T. (2005). *Scripture and the Authority of God.* London: SPCK, pp. 22–3.
589 Bartlett, A.B. (2007). *A Passionate Balance.* London: Darton, Longman & Todd, p. 91. *Italics original.*
590 Ford, D. (2007). *Christian Wisdom.* Cambridge: Cambridge University Press, pp. 5, 45–51.

I would want to add to this the human interrogative of the divine; as is best exemplified in the biblical tradition of Lament. I read this as a dialogue, not one-way traffic.

Subjunctive – exploring the possibilities of what might be – 'what if?' This is the least definite and the most playful of the moods, best characterised by the parables. It opens up new insights but without an inappropriate definiteness. 'Perhaps?' 'What if?' Partly because so many of the areas explored in Practical Theology are so new and partly because of the hugely complex nature of the task itself, I think that Practical Theology is best conceived of as an 'is it?' rather than an 'it is' discipline. We conduct theological thought experiments. This mood is both essential for Practical Theology and meshes well with this discipline, but it should be felt as a spur to further thinking and also a gentle goad to action, rather than navel-gazing!

The optative of desire – 'I wish'. This is the mood which expresses desire, longing, hope. Practical Theology is rooted in a desire to see human beings helped, healed, renewed. It is a discipline that grows out of the passion for change. This mood of Scripture incites this desire and gives it assurance that it meshes with divine desire.

These 'moods' relate closely to how we handle Scripture in Practical Theology.[591] Sometimes, as you will have noticed in the essays, people are making simple connections between their real-life experience and Scripture. This is partly a way of affirming the relevance of faith to real life, of making connections between their own spiritual identity and experience with this real-life experience, and partly the beginning of the journey of making conceptual sense of what is happening.

Some other essays have tried to extrapolate certain themes from Scripture. So the essay on alcohol addiction draws heavily on the Pauline sense of the divided self and how this encapsulates part of the human condition, as it is also understood by the human sciences. Here, both

---

591   In this section I am drawing very heavily on a seminal article by my colleague Walton, Roger. (2003). The Bible and Theology in Theological Reflection. In the *British Journal of Theological Education* 13(2). See also Ballard, P. and Holmes, S. (eds) (2005). *The Bible in Pastoral Practice*. London: Darton, Longman & Todd; and Bennett, Z. (2013). *Using the Bible in Practical Theology*. Farnham: Ashgate.

the human experience and the biblical material have been systematised and conceptualised, and this makes it easier for them to converse with each other. In other words, we look to Scripture for a framework to shape our thinking and relate this to the framework we have developed through the human sciences so that together they say: 'This is how it is!'

Then there is another mode of approaching Scripture, which is to look for authoritative judgements. I used to be very sceptical about 'proof-texting' from the Bible (quoting a verse to prove a point), until I realised that I do it too! There are some issues of which I am so convinced, that I rejoice that Scripture speaks with clear-cut authority: for example, the belief, widely found in Scripture, that God is especially on the side of the poor and weak and vulnerable. This is Scripture in imperative mood. 'Do it!'

In other essays, questions have been fired into Scripture, trying to provoke an answer. This is my interpretation of the interrogative mood. Can we really find good news for abused women in the 'patriarchal' Bible? (We can, and will return to the finding of good news for such women in a moment.) But this poses the question: 'Where is God in this mess?' This is closely linked to the more subjunctive mood which asks, both of God and of human beings, 'but does it have to be this way?' It invites us to try experiments of seeing the situation differently, of conceiving of God's interaction with a situation differently.

But above all, many of the essays have searched the Scripture for signs of hope; both for models of how to access power for transformation and also for reassurance that it can be done. Think of the essays which explored different aspects of addiction and how they portray where hope is to be found and trusted. Hence the frequent citing of Luke 4 where Jesus talks of his mission to bring liberation. This is Scripture as a means of bringing hope into a situation: both hope in the short term and a wider, eschatological (end of time) sense. 'It will be so.' This is Scripture enabling us, with faith, to connect with the action of God in the world. It is the mood of Scripture which drives us back into action.

Practical Theology and confidence in Christian Theology

One of the reasons I am an enthusiast for Practical Theology, as opposed to other branches of theology, is that the results connect closely to real life and, indeed, they actively help real people. In this book, we have examples of Christian people wrestling with very difficult issues and finding resources in their Christian faith which help to *illuminate* the situation they are in and to *resource* them in facing these situations.

In this section of my essay, which is part of our extended reflection on the place of theology in Practical Theology, I want to do two things. First, to note the areas where Christian theology gives us explanatory power and also personal, communal and spiritual resources to deal with difficult situations, and then to note briefly the theological areas which the essays in this book have revealed as being in need of further attention.

In one sense it is not difficult for us, in the modern West, to feel a sense of the value of human beings or to be worried about the future of the planet. One of the joys of Practical Theology is to realise how often the Church 'got there first' (though it often did not recognise it!). Without getting lost in the minutiae of debates about the 'how', the early chapters of Genesis provide us with a rich and imaginative account of the created order and of humanity's place within it. The nightmare has been the abuse of the concept of human 'dominion', but the good dream is the picture of the value and purpose of the created world alongside humankind, with humankind as its pinnacle. This gives Christians a very strong basis on which to do ecological theology. More, there is so much in the little phrase 'in the image of God'. It enables us to explore, subjunctively, what it is to be a human being. This has often been seen in purely spiritual or intellectual terms, but more recent thinking stresses the embodiedness, democracy and gender inclusivity of this phrase.[592] Of course we have to be careful not to project on to Scripture our own contemporary desires – back to hermeneutics – but it is also the case that we may be able to see new things in Scripture, to which earlier generations, because of their different social patterns, were blind.

This rich mine of theological possibility is also present in another central Christian doctrine, the Incarnation. Again, the modern Church is enriching this doctrine as it stresses the valuing of *physicality* which is implicit in the Incarnation. God took 'flesh' and made it his own. This

---

592   Bartlett, A. (2004). *Humane Christianity*, pp.12–23; and Middleton, J.R. (2005). *The Liberating Image*. Grand Rapids, MI: Brazos Press).

enormous valuing of humankind, in its embodiedness, is a weighty theological resource when struggling with social problems which tend to devalue human beings. This is theology in an indicative as well as an optative mood.

Conversely, even the doctrine of sin, which has been used to shortcut, for example, so many Christian discussions of human behaviour – 'he is a sinful drunkard, lecher, bully, etc.' – in fact has the capacity to help us to illuminate human experiences.[593] The sense of trappedness which is such a deep part of human self-destructive behaviour is also, of course, part of the doctrine of sin. 'I do not understand my own actions. For I do not do what I want, but I do the very thing I hate' [Romans 7:15]. The essays in this book may make us cautious about throwing the word 'sin' too quickly, for example, at addictive problems but they may also have reminded us of the addict's need for grace, for help, to enable them to break out of their trappedness. Further, the Christian understanding summed up in the word 'sin' may help us to be realistic about systemic failures, about the fallibility even of the good agencies, and about the sheer horror of some aspects of human behaviour. To answer an earlier question, an understanding of 'sin' is a concept and a reality which the Christian theologian does bring to the table, adding specific value to a discussion.

However, if Christian theology has much to contribute by way of insight into real human life, this aspect of theology remains relatively underdeveloped. In comparison with the shelves of books on the doctrine of the Trinity, serious and well-integrated theological discussion of what it is to be a human being (Christian theological anthropology) remains sparse.[594] Studies such as this book, which will enable, indeed force, theologians to face the reality of human life when thinking about human-ness, are crucial for this work to be accomplished.

Practical Theology and *praxis*

And so we turn at last to the green light. As Marx wrote (*Theses on Feuerbach*, 1845, thesis 11): 'the philosophers have only interpreted the

593 See the very sophisticated exploration of this in McFadyen, A. (2000). *Bound to Sin*. Cambridge: Cambridge University Press.
594 An interesting counter-example is the work of the Church of England's Doctrine Commission. (2003). *Being Human*. London: Church House Publishing.

world, the point is to change it'. The purpose of Practical Theology is to make a difference in real life. All of the essays in this book are written by people who are involved in making a difference and you are reading this book, in part, because you too want to make a difference. Practical Theology is an engaged discipline. In the words of the old joke, the contribution you make to Practical Theology is more like the contribution of the pig than of the chicken to a full English breakfast. You are fully committed! This can make Practical Theology a little suspect. It appears to lack the detached objectivity of other theological disciplines. But as the Liberation Theologians have taught us, there are no neutral disciplines or detached studies in a world of unjust suffering. Practical Theology is refreshingly honest about the real contexts in which we study and think.

It is also refreshingly honest that we do not think and study as detached minds. The wrestling we do with the painful issues which we confront in this book does need to be done in a disciplined way. Emotive thinking and discussion is distracting and even dangerous. But conversely, we also know that real-life decisions are shaped by our processes of rumination, of deep inner reflection. We have noted several times that Practical Theology requires us to stop and look and that this is a spiritual activity. It was the slogan of the ancient Church that 'the one who prays is a theologian' (Evagrius). Thinking and talking about these issues in prayer and conscious of the presence of God does change how we approach them. Notice the role of a holistic theological approach to the human self which characterises the essay on 'self-care'. This is not to say that prayer will always give us the 'right answers' . . .

Another way of discussing this is to use the language of 'wisdom'. Modern ethical discussion has moved away from a narrow focus on the rights and wrongs of individual issues, to discussion of how we become the sort of people who have been shaped to be wise people, who are likely to make good decisions in the midst of the muddle of real life.[595] Prayer and a disciplined spiritual life should help us to be the sort of people who can make wise decisions.

An apparently very different way of conceiving of the task of Practical Theology is to describe it as reflective *praxis*. In other words,

---

595   See, for example, Wells, S. (2004). *Improvisation: The Drama of Christian Ethics*. London: SPCK.

it is value-shaped reflection on value-driven action.[596] While one of the temptations of Christian ministry can be to try to impose conceptual convictions on to complex real-life situations, another is to slither into pragmatism. One of the ways to avoid this is consciously to ask the theological questions: 'Why am I acting in this way and where is God in this situation?' Even if Christian insights and outcomes are not always so very different from those of a non-Christian (and we have already touched on why that may be the case and why that can be acceptable), they must nonetheless be held within a wider Christian theological framework if they are to make sense as Christian *praxis*. So as Christian practitioners we ask, 'Why is it right to continue to attempt to care for sex offenders?' as well as 'What understandings and practices need to be in place if this care is to be realistic?' These are both theological questions.

Practical Theology and Jesus

We all know that the answer to every Sunday School question is 'Jesus!' I want to finish this chapter with a final encouragement. Even if the Church has often had dirty hands, we can go back to the example of Jesus of Nazareth with confidence, because of our confidence in the doctrine of the Incarnation. And even if we still have to ask hard hermeneutical questions about how we translate the teaching and example of Jesus into our world, as Christians, we have been captivated by the beauty of his life. For me, it is the heart of why I continue. And Jesus was a fine Practical Theologian: looking carefully at the experiences of those around him (he was enraged at the real hypocrisy of the religious élite); using language and concepts with which his listeners were deeply familiar (from agriculture or the home); and above all allowing his own experiences to reshape his vision. It seems to be the case that Jesus initially conceived of his mission being to the People of Israel but was so taken by the faith of Gentiles that he came to see that his mission was to them too.[597] As St John said, Christians are called to '*do* the truth' [1 John 1:6]. Jesus did it. So do we.

---

596 For a thorough exploration of the meaning of *praxis* see Graham, E. (1996). *Transforming Practice*. London: Mowbray.

597 See, for example, the Syro-Phoenician woman in Mark 7:24-30, or the God-fearing Centurion (Matthew 8:5-13 and Luke 7:1-10).

Books for further reading

Ballard, P. and Pritchard, J. (2006). *Practical Theology in Action,* 2nd edition. London: SPCK.

Bartlett, A., Hughes, C. and Walton, R. (2009). *Real God, Real World.* London: SPCK.

Graham, E., Ward, F. and Walton, H. (2005 & 2007). *Theological Reflection*: Vol.1. *Methods* and Vol. 2. *Sources.* London: SCM.

Ward, P. (2008). *Participation and Mediation: A Practical Theology for the Liquid Church.* London: SCM.

A very useful journal is *Practical Theology*, formerly *Contact*. Readers who wish to become involved in the further study and delivery of Practical Theology should consider joining the British and Irish Association for Practical Theology [BIAPT]: www.biapt.org. BIAPT membership includes a subscription to *Practical Theology.*

For reference see: Miller-McLemore, B.J. (ed.) (2012). *The Wiley-Blackwell Companion to Practical Theology.* Chichester: Wiley-Blackwell.

CHAPTER FIFTEEN

Concluding Reflections

Jocelyn Bryan and Brendan Geary

'Why do people behave the way they do?' is a persistent question which underlies the behaviour patterns described in this book. Why do some people bully others, struggle with addiction, mismanage their aggression or their sexual desires and fantasies, while others manage and regulate their behaviour in ways which enable them to establish and sustain positive relationships which are supportive and fulfilling? There is no simple answer to this question. However, studies in developmental and personality psychology have begun to make significant contributions to our understanding of the factors which influence and shape our patterns of thinking, feeling and behaving, and to show how these factors contribute to the individual differences which we engage with daily in our relationships.

The nature/nurture debate

There is a genetic effect in all behaviour. Biology is a significant factor in determining behaviour, but genetic and non-genetic influences are not entirely separable. The chapters which have examined aggressive and violent behaviour have described the gender differences in these behaviour patterns and the relationship between aggression and the male hormone testosterone. However, these biological factors, though important, influence aggressive behaviour through an interplay between the genetic make-up of the person and the different environments, and of the nurturing the person experiences.

Several studies have supported the interaction between nature and environment in particular behaviour patterns. In both antisocial behaviour and depression, the effect of adverse environments is most influential on those individuals who have been identified as genetically susceptible to these behaviours. Conversely, these adverse environments

441

have least impact on those who are not as genetically vulnerable. [598] We all respond to situations differently even when we share a common environment such as the home. In families it is evident that the environment itself is experienced differently by each child, not only because of their different genetic make-up but also because of the way their parents relate to them due to gender differences, birth order differences and the daily sequence of life events which are unique to that particular child. This goes some way to explaining why one member of a family may react violently when frustrated and another manage their anger in a different way, or why one child in the family copes better with a crisis than another.

The research in the development of personality has significance in helping to predict those who are at risk of developing psychopathologies (mental health problems) by identifying those features of environments which are associated with psychopathological outcomes when a child is developing. In a number of the chapters in this book, the behaviour issues addressed are not categorised as psychopathological but they are psychological disorders which may be associated with some of the environmental factors below, which an adult experienced as a child:

- Persistent discord and conflict, particularly when it involves scapegoating or other forms of focused negativity directed towards an individual child. This has been identified as associated with some forms of passive aggressive behaviour.

- Lack of individualised personal caregiving involving continuity over time. This is often associated with institutional upbringing, and leads to difficulty in establishing and sustaining relationships because of its effect on developing secure attachments and self-esteem.

- A lack of reciprocal conversation and play, which is important for the development of social skills.

- A negative social ethos or social group that fosters maladaptive behaviour patterns. [599]

---

598   Rutter, M. (2002). Nature, nurture, and development: From Evangelism through science toward policy and practice. *Child Development* 73(1): 3.
599   Ibid.: 8.

This area of research has significantly increased our knowledge of how human psychological development during childhood can predict behaviour patterns in adulthood. These predispositions have been seen in a number of areas, such as early hyperactivity leading to later antisocial behaviour,[600] early conduct problems associated with a predisposition to substance use and abuse, and this in turn leading to later depression.[601] However, the underlying processes and causes of these effects are not yet fully understood. The research indicates the importance of both our genetic make-up and environmental experience in shaping our behaviour. Understanding how these factors interact and the relative contribution of each in the formation of how we think, feel and behave, and how our unique personalities develop is still a long way off. But when we encounter challenging behaviour in a person, the context of their development as a child and any genetic predispositions they carry must be recognised as having significance in our understanding of them.

Socialisation

One significant process which is part of the nurturing experience of children is socialisation. This is the process by which we acquire behaviour patterns that are acceptable in the society in which we live. The challenging and difficult behaviour patterns discussed in this book can be seen as problems of socialisation. Behaviours which others find difficult or problematic and are offensive or damaging to others are indicative of problems with socialisation. The main agents in this process during development are parents who teach their children the social and cultural norms of behaviour. However, alongside the acquisition of behavioural norms, parents also engage in the process of the socialisation of emotions and this is one of the most important aspects of family life.

The nurturing family context is the primary formational unit in which the child learns about social living. The effect of the changing structure of family life and the increased complexity of the

---

600 Rutter, M., Giller, H. and Hagell, A. (1998). *Antisocial behaviour by young people.* New York: Cambridge University Press.

601 Rutter, M. (2002). Substance use and abuse: Causal pathways considerations. In Rutter, M. and Taylor, E. (eds), *Child and Adolescent Psychiatry* (4th edition). Oxford: Blackwell Scientific, quoted in Rutter, M. (2002). Nature, nurture, and development: From Evangelism through science toward policy and practice. *Child Development* 73(1): 12.

relationships within families on child development has received a great deal of attention. However, it seems that, from a child's point of view, a family can take a variety of different forms and still function as a secure base for healthy development.

The relationship between the family context and aggression, conduct disturbance and delinquency is supported by a considerable body of evidence. The significant factors linked to these behaviour patterns are:

- Family discord and disruption

- Weak family relationships

- Criminality in other members of the family (parents and siblings)

- Ineffective discipline and supervision.[602]

All these contribute to a weakening of the socialisation process. Patterson notes that four aspects are particularly significant:

- A lack of house rules, so that there are no clear expectations of what is and is not acceptable.

- A lack of parental monitoring, so parents are not adequately informed of the children's behaviour and emotions and therefore are not able to respond appropriately.

- A lack of effective contingencies, which results in parents shouting and nagging. Praise and punishment are inconsistent and not adequately differentiated.

- A lack of techniques for dealing with crises or problems. Conflict leads to tension and dispute. Resolution is difficult to achieve or not attained.[603]

It appears that problematic behaviour patterns associated with aggression may well be linked to the nurturing and social learning that was experienced by the adult in childhood. Models of aggressive

---

602 Rutter, M. and Rutter, M. (1993). *Developing Minds* (p. 176). London: Penguin.
603 Patterson, G.R. (1982.) *Coercive family process*. Eugene, OR: Castalia, quoted in Rutter, M. and Rutter, M. (1993). *Developing Minds* (p. 176). London: Penguin.

behaviour as an appropriate and acceptable way of dealing with frustration, interpersonal difficulties or other relationship problems are learned and transferred to different contexts and situations. This is also associated with the finding that physical abuse predisposes an individual to aggressive violent behaviour. Hence we can conclude that the effect of parental modelling and the parental role in the socialisation process are significant factors in our understanding of repeating patterns of violent and aggressive behaviour in adulthood.

Motivation and social cognition

Both our environment and our biology are aspects of life over which we have limited influence or control. The view of the person as a passive victim of unconscious impulses and responses, resulting from both biological processes and past experience, or the person as a passive respondent to changing environmental events, was called 'reciprocal determinism' by Bandura.[604] This was criticised for failing to take into account the role of our brains in interpreting the situation we are faced with and then making a conscious decision regarding our response. We select our behavioural responses from a vast range of possibilities. We decide what to do when faced with a particular situation. This decision is based upon a range of factors, including the memories we have of similar situations in the past, our motives and goals, and our emotional state. Not all behaviour is processed in this way. There are occasions when we respond instinctively or impulsively. Learning to control and manage our impulses is a significant challenge and in cases of abuse and violence, the inability to do this leads to significant damage to others. However, it is undoubtedly true that people's behaviour patterns are influenced by their interpretation of the situation in which they find themselves and in which they choose how they will respond. People are responsive to situations, and also construct situations and influence them. They select the situations they engage with as well as being shaped and influenced by them. Likewise, they influence the behaviour of others as well as being influenced by the behaviour of others. Hence we need to take into account how a person processes

---

604 Bandura, A. (1999). Social cognitive theory of personality. In Pervin, L.A. and John O.P. (eds). *Handbook of Personality: Theory and Research* (pp. 154–96). New York: Guilford.

and interprets events, which includes their predictions of likely outcomes. This influences their choice of a course of action which will be determined by whatever goal they have in mind.

This represents a view of the person as someone who has expectations and beliefs, competences and skills and sets personal goals, and seeks to explain why people behave as they do in these terms. This is known as social cognitive theory and it offers an explanation of behaviour in terms of the different ways individuals perceive situations and how this influences their responses; so one person might be threatened by a situation and another excited by it, simply because they interpret the situation in different ways. Behaviour is also influenced by the individual's perception of his or her ability to cope with a situation. If we feel insecure and uncomfortable we behave in a very different way from a situation where we feel in control and are confident about the outcome. An important application of this theory is cognitive behaviour therapy which seeks to enable a person to change his or her interpretation of situations and other people's response to them and so influence behaviour patterns and emotional responses. By controlling our mental processing of situations and events, we can change our behaviour.

Another significant factor in social cognitive theory is the effect of the goals we set for ourselves in situations. These depend on what is significant to a person at the time, what opportunities are available and their perceptions of what they can cope with and achieve. The chapters on addictions illustrate how a person's behaviour is directed by his or her desire or goal to change their emotional state or achieve a particular outcome. Hence, those who gamble set themselves the goal of the next win and this is accompanied by the incentive of the thrill which goes with the risk-taking involved. Likewise, the sex addicts seek to relieve negative feelings about themselves by engaging in the sexual acts which they find pleasurable. In instances of aggressive and violent behaviour, the goal of asserting power and superiority over another is achieved through bullying behaviour and in some situations this manifests itself in physical violence. Achieving the goal one has set contributes to self-esteem, which is another recurrent theme in this book. The tendency to maintain, protect and enhance self-esteem by striving to achieve a sense of success and avoid failure is one of the defining characteristics of human nature and a significant motive in determining behaviour patterns, whether problematic or congenial to the person's well-being. Each of the issues discussed in this book is related in some way to self-esteem and a person's self-perception.

Self-Esteem

Self-esteem concerns the self-evaluation or judgement about personal acceptability and worthiness to be loved, which carries with it pleasant or unpleasant feelings. It is related to the perceived views of the person by important others in his or her life.[605] It is a personal judgement of worthiness.[606] This sense of worthiness is developed through our relationships with others and by comparing ourselves with others. When we receive acceptance and praise, our sense of self-worth increases and when we experience rejection and criticism our sense of self-worth is diminished. Crocker and Park suggest that we are selective in the things which we allow to affect our self-esteem.[607] For one person, being attractive, having lots of friends and being competent at a particular skill is significant for his or her self-esteem, while for another person it could be winning at sport, being in a stable marriage and gaining promotion in his or her job. They call these 'contingencies of self-worth'. The effects of events, circumstances and relationships on self-esteem are determined by a person's interpretation of the event and its relevance to the person's contingencies of self-worth. There is an obvious link between personal goals and these contingencies of self-worth. When we achieve one of our goals our self-esteem increases, and when we fail, or our attempts are thwarted, our self-esteem is lowered. Positive, high self-esteem is associated with good social relationships and personal fulfilment. The way people respond to threats to their self-esteem or behave when their self-esteem is lowered is often associated with mental health issues, personality disorders and problematic behaviour. Both the avoidant personality disorder and the narcissistic personality disorder can be seen to be related to self-esteem issues.

The avoidant personality suffers from chronic extreme low self-esteem. Socially, they are awkward and have difficulty forming social

---

605 McGrath, J. and McGrath, A. (2001). *Self-esteem: The Cross and Christian Confidence* (p. 33). Leicester: IVP.
606 Pervin, L.A and John, O.P. (2001). *Personality: Theory and Research* (8th edition, p. 184). New York: Wiley.
607 Crocker, J. and Park, L.E. (2003). Seeking: Construction, maintenance and protection of self worth. In Leary, M. and Price Tangney, J. (eds). *Handbook of Self and Identity*. New York / London: Guilford Press.

relationships. They find criticism and rejection very difficult to cope with and see others as superior and critical of them. Their thinking and interpretation of others is distorted so that, if someone is positive and accepting of them, they think that this person does not really know them. They avoid social situations and have a fear of rejection which they experience as anxiety in the few relationships they have. In contrast, the narcissistic personality feels special and superior and this affects the way he or she relates to others. This may be a strategy for defending a very fragile low self-esteem or evidence of an inflated level of self-esteem.[608]

The issues examined in this book reflect the ways in which people respond when they feel their self-esteem is threatened. One defence strategy is to avoid situations where failure is an anticipated outcome. In passive aggressive behaviour patterns, the avoidance of conflict is a significant factor in this behaviour pattern, especially if any expression of anger is seen as weakness, or conflict resolution is viewed in terms of a win/lose outcome. Another strategy when the situation cannot be avoided is to lower their expectations of the possible outcomes, thereby avoiding being disappointed by failure. This defensive pessimism is often a way of managing anxiety. However, this can be particularly difficult to manage in teams.

Baumeister identifies self-handicapping as a strategy which may increase a person's chance of failure by deliberately taking alcohol or drugs or procrastinating, and then attributing any poor performance to the self-induced handicap rather than personal ability.[609] The excuses offered in passive aggressive behaviour for failing to meet deadlines may be a manifestation of this strategy, directing blame away from oneself and on to external factors.

Of particular interest is the evidence which suggests that people respond to threats with anger and hostility and frequently lash out at others.[610] This is especially relevant in cases of domestic violence. The assumption that domestic violence is associated with low self-esteem in the perpetrators has been challenged by the lack of evidence to

---

608   McGrath, J. and McGrath, A. (2001). *Self-esteem: The Cross and Christian Confidence* (pp. 54–5). Leicester: IVP.
609   Baumeister, R.F. (1998). The self. In Gilbert, D.T., Fiske, S.T. and Lindzey, G. (eds). *Handbook of Social Psychology: Vol 2* (4th edition, pp. 680–740). New York: McGraw-Hill.
610   Baumeister, R.F., Smart, L. and Boden, J.M. (1996). Relation of threatened egotism to violence and aggression: The dark side of high self-esteem. *Psychological Review* 103: 5–33.

conclusively support this. Instead, the notion of threatened egotism provides a plausible explanation. We are used to hearing people speak of low self-esteem, with the implication that we should be working towards high self-esteem. However, it may be more helpful to think of self-esteem as a continuum, with mature self-esteem being situated between low and inflated self-esteem. Inflated self-esteem, which is related to inflated egotism, is the source of a different set of problems, which often lead to violent behaviour. People like to think well of themselves, and generally react defensively to criticism.

If we take the case of domestic violence, for example, it is often suggested that male abusers must suffer from low self-esteem, and that the violence in some way restores their sense of maleness and power. It is perhaps more likely that men in violent relationships suffer from inflated self-esteem, and that perceived criticism from their female partner – nagging, silence, withdrawal of affection, refusal to provide whatever the man feels is necessary, e.g. sexual contact – can lead to the man's sense of himself being threatened. The man then has a choice: he either accepts the lower evaluation of himself or discredits the threat. Violence is often a way of discrediting the threat and re-establishing self-esteem.

This suggests that threatened high self-esteem is the cause of the violent aggressive behaviour rather than low self-esteem. In this case, the man's belief in his superiority is threatened by his wife's superiority on some important dimension in their relationship. This makes him feel insecure, and he experiences threatened egotism which leads to him acting violently towards her. The cause of the violence is the threat posed to the man's belief in his own superiority. This can also explain the behaviour of hostile aggressives whose threatened egos are expressed in anger and hostility when their plans are frustrated or challenged by others. Aggression is a response to fragile egotism which is characterised by a positive but vulnerable self-esteem. In spite of this behavioural response increasing the likelihood of rejection by others, the frustration experienced by the threat, particularly if it is experienced as unfair or unreasonable, triggers the aggressive response. Hostile aggressives also adopt the strategy of focusing on the shortcomings of others when their self-esteem is threatened. They blame and ridicule others in order to inflate their own self-esteem by making comparisons with the negative evaluation they make of others.

Genuine, or mature, self-esteem is a true sense of self-worth and self-respect and an acceptance of one's strengths and weaknesses.[611] However, the findings suggest that, instead of focusing on attaining this, people behave in ways that suggest that they are naturally defensive and unwilling to acknowledge their weaknesses and shortcomings. It appears that the desire to maintain, enhance and protect self-esteem may lead to behaviours which detract from the ability to form and maintain caring relationships and may also damage physical and mental health.[612] The behaviours people adopt in response to threats to self-esteem, such as blame, anger, antagonism, aggression, avoidance and withdrawal,[613] reduce rather than enhance their chances of fulfilling their need for positive relationships. In addition, fluctuations in self-esteem are also associated with poor mental health – in particular, depression and a number of personality disorders. There is also a relationship between self-esteem and the adoption of behaviours which have a negative impact on physical health, such as drinking alcohol, smoking and eating disorders.

To conclude, the idea that our sense of our self-worth is bound up with our appearance, achievements and what we do is a pervasive feature of our culture and environment. The goal of protecting, maintaining and increasing our levels of self-esteem is a major factor in our behaviour patterns. This pursuit can have a damaging effect on relationships and on our physical and mental health, especially when self-esteem is threatened. This applies equally to those who have a low and an inflated level of self-esteem, as shown above. In each of the issues addressed in this book, self-esteem is a significant factor in the explanation of the behaviour under examination.

Self-defeating behaviours

A number of the subjects dealt with in this book could be viewed as self-defeating behaviours. The cost to individuals of addictions, for example, often leads people to wonder why people begin to use drugs.

---

611   Rosenberg, M. (1979). *Conceiving the self.* New York: Basic Books.

612   Crocker, J. and Park, L.E. (2003). Seeking: Construction, maintenance and protection of self worth. In Leary, M. and Price Tangney, J. (eds). *Handbook of Self and Identity* (pp. 304–5). New York/London: Guilford Press.

613   Baumeister, R.F. (1998). The self.

The consequences of alcohol abuse or drug addiction can be devastating, leading to damage to health, broken relationships, significant financial loss if not poverty (which can lead to involvement in crime), with consequent damage to oneself and others. Other behaviours, such as bullying, may appear to benefit the perpetrator but, even here, there are costs in terms of social relationships and self-worth, as society does not publicly condone bullying. Difficult people also suffer in various ways as a result of their behaviour. How do we account for these behaviours? Roy Baumeister, who has written extensively on this topic, identifies two key factors: threatened egotism and self-regulation failure. He adds that they are both related to emotional distress. Threatened egotism was discussed in the section on self-esteem. We will look now at self-regulation failure.

Self-regulation failure

Self-regulation (or self-control) is described as the ways in which we change our own responses, which can involve our thoughts, feelings and behaviours.[614] Many of the issues dealt with in this book relate to a failure of self-regulation: addictions, use of violence, sexual abuse, socially difficult behaviour, bullying. It has been suggested that success in life is a 'matter of being able to live with oneself and other people'.[615] From this perspective, these individuals are not making a success of their lives, which is one of the reasons they demand our attention. What then, does self-regulation involve? Baumeister outlines the following:[616]

- Affect regulation

- Control over our mental processes

- Managing our impulses

- Setting and reaching our goals

- Delay of gratification.

---

614   Baumeister, R.F. (1997). Esteem threat, self-regulatory breakdown, and emotional distress as factors in self-defeating behaviour. *Review of General Psychology* 1(2): 145–74.

615   Dolores Pushkar, quoted in Baumeister, R.F., Leith, K.P., Muraven, M. and Bratslavsky, E. (1998). Self-regulation as a key to success in life. In Pushkar et al. (eds). *Improving Competence across the Lifespan*. New York: Plenum.

616   Baumeister, R.F. and Heatherton, T.F. (1996). Self-regulation failure: An overview. *Psychological Inquiry* 7(1) : 1–15.

The subject of addictions is vast and there has been considerable research into the causes of the various addictions, the characteristics of addictive behaviour and the personalities of addicts. However, one thing that all addictions appear to have in common is a desire to change the person's emotional state. Alcohol relaxes people and disinhibits behaviour (even though it also acts as a depressant). Cigarettes stimulate, but, as a consequence of eliminating the craving that accompanies nicotine addiction, also lead to feelings of relaxation, when the unpleasant feelings associated with withdrawal are removed. People who are addicted to internet pornography often use this to distract themselves from boredom, tiredness or loneliness, and become addicted to the excitement that internet sexual involvement provides. Some people can spend hours surfing sites to find more stimulating images, connect with more attractive partners, or find other dates. Sex addicts use sex partly to change negative feelings into pleasurable ones, while child abusers pursue sexual contact with children for a range of reasons, one of which is emotional satisfaction. Gamblers appear to become involved in gambling partly as it distracts them from problems that they face in their lives, as well as the thrill involved in hoping for the next big win. Bullies, presumably, feel a sense of superiority when they belittle, humiliate or exclude their victims, and violent men experience release of tension when they assault their partner, which brings a feeling of relief. In all of these cases, the behaviour has a mood-altering effect which is rewarding in the short term, even though it may result in poor consequences in the long term.

Another aspect of self-regulation is our ability to control our mental processes. This is the foundation of cognitive behavioural therapy, which is the therapeutic approach favoured with most of the problems outlined in this book. Sex offenders and addicts, for example, are taught in group therapy how to identify the triggers that lead to their abusive or addictive behaviour. These include negative mood states. Rather than seek the substances or behaviours that lead to loss of control or damage to another person, the individuals are taught how to identify the trigger and to take aversive action. This is the foundation or the approach known as relapse prevention.[617] Clearly, the earlier in the relapse

---

617   Marlatt, G. and Gordon, J.R. (eds). (1985). *Relapse prevention.* New York: Guilford Press.

chain that thinking and behaviour are changed, the more effective the outcome. The same is also true of violent behaviour in general, as the ability to stop and think, and deliberately change our thinking can lead to more socially acceptable and self-beneficial behaviour.

There is little we can do to change our impulses and attempting to control them can often lead to internal stress and tension which is not always healthy or helpful. Self-regulation involves acknowledging our impulses but refusing to give in to them. For example, a man may feel angry with his partner but that does not have to lead to violence. He can walk away, talk himself down or attempt to listen to his partner. This involves awareness of the impulse with a decision to behave in a different way. The same is true of addictions.

Self-regulation can fail because of underregulation or misregulation. Underregulation happens when we fail to make the effort to change a response that will lead to a more positive outcome. So, for example, a person who is dependent on alcohol may know from experience that regulating how much alcohol he or she drinks feels outside of his or her control. Walking in thinking 'I'll just have one drink', may be an example of underregulation, since the person is unlikely to be able to limit the amount of alcohol consumed and walk out of the pub sober. Similarly, if a person who is addicted to internet pornography switches on his computer late at night, he is setting himself up to fail, as it only takes three clicks to find stimulating images. Misregulation involves efforts at changing which do not bring about the desired result – for example, using alcohol to change how we feel, leading to a hangover and social, relational, financial and health problems. There are healthier ways to change how we feel, and part of life is learning how to tolerate uncomfortable feelings.

Our goals are also related to self-regulation. If we want to live in harmony with others, while respecting ourselves, then this precludes behaviours that will lead to alienation from others or feelings of shame, embarrassment or guilt. It is important to set goals that are appropriate and manageable, so that we are not setting ourselves up for failure.

Lastly, it has been noted that people who can delay gratification are often more successful in life. Those who cannot tolerate frustration are more likely to react precipitously or give in to temptations. Baumeister describes self-control as a 'moral muscle' which gets depleted if overused.

It is interesting to note, for example, that more violent and impulsive crimes, or sexual acts that people later regret, happen in the very early hours of the morning than at other times.[618] It is suggested that, after spending all day regulating our lives in various ways, our supply of self-control may be used up. This is often compounded by the use of alcohol, which both relaxes and disinhibits behaviours we might avoid when not under its influence. It would also appear to be the case, though, that this 'moral muscle' can be strengthened with practise and regular use, so, for example, attempting to give up alcohol, gambling, cigarettes or other addictive substances or behaviours may be more successful after various attempts, as the person learns from each attempt until success is finally achieved. This is reflected in the Motivational Interviewing approach to changing health behaviours, where it is accepted that relapse is part of recovery.[619] If people could accept that a lapse is a single mistake and not a catastrophe, then they could return to their attempted change of behaviour. Unfortunately, the combination of pleasure, relief from the stress of abstaining and the feelings of failure involved often leads to complete collapse rather than picking themselves up and starting again.

Negative moods

Negative moods are often involved in the various behaviours discussed in this book. Research has shown that when people experience negative mood states, especially when they are aroused as a result of feeling angry, embarrassed or frustrated, they are prone to making high-risk decisions. When people are not aroused and feel well, they are inclined to take low risks. In a sense, it is when people have little or nothing to lose (or feel that way) that the high risk with the promise of a big (emotional or financial) pay-off is more attractive. Inevitably, this leads to self-defeating outcomes, and, with gamblers, substance abusers or sex offenders, outcomes that can jeopardise the well-being of others.

Men and women can be addicted to sex, gambling, alcohol, nicotine, or any other substance, in order to help change their mood. It is also well known that part of the addictive process is the withdrawal effects

---

618 Baumeister, R.F. and Heatherton, T.F. (1996). Self-regulation failure: An overview. *Psychological Inquiry* 7(1): 3.

619 Miller, W.R. and Rollnick, S. (2002). *Motivational Interviewing: Preparing People for Change* (p. 213). London: Guilford Press.

of not having the substance (or experience). In order to maintain the same level of satisfaction, more of the drug is required. Biologically, addictions activate two different systems in the brain: the pleasure system and the reinforcement system. The pleasure system ceases to function while the reinforcement system continues to demand the substance or behaviour that leads to the neural changes to which the body has become accustomed.[620] Usually, this involves increases in the neurotransmitters of serotonin and dopamine, which lead to feelings of happiness and well-being. Once the body has learned that a behaviour or substance provides a shortcut to increased pleasure, it is difficult to change without experiencing the unpleasant sensations and feelings that are described as withdrawal symptoms.

Gender

Another important issue reflected in the topics dealt with in this book concerns the differences between men and women. Addictions can affect men and women, and there are female sex offenders and women who bully. However, there are important differences in these areas,[621] and in the area of violence, as Lesley Orr has pointed out in her chapter on domestic violence. For examples, men are 40 times more likely to kill another man than a woman is likely to kill another woman.[622] Anthony Clare noted that in domestic violence disputes women were twice more likely to be injured than men and much more likely to be victims of repeated attacks than men.[623]

Some people have argued that aggression is innate in men and that speed, courage and aggression were useful in the evolution of men to ensure the provision of food, and in the competition for mates to guarantee reproduction. However, Clare argues that, while aggression may be innate, malice is not. He quotes a researcher who examined the issue of male violence and concluded that biology is clearly important, but is not the sole factor. Social issues, such as deprivation, inequality, injustice, overcrowding, poverty and cultural attitudes, also play

---

620 Carlson, N.R. (2005). *Foundations of Biological Psychology*. London: Pearson.
621 Ciarrocchi, J.W. (2002). *Counseling problem gamblers* (p. 16). London: Academic Press; Center for Substance Abuse Treatment. (1994). *Practical approaches in the treatment of women who abuse alcohol and other drugs*. Rockville, MD: Department of Health and Human Services, Public Health Service.
622 Daly, M. and Wilson, M. (1988). *Homicide*. New York: Aldine de Gruyter.
623 Clare, A. (2000). *On men*. London: Chatto & Windus.

their part, as well as psychological factors, especially lack of affection, inconsistent or absent parenting, severely dysfunctional families, and gender stereotypes. This is discussed in the chapter on adult bullying. It also helps to explain the kind of people who resort to violence that are described by Michael Fitzsimons in his chapter on violence in the workplace.

In the chapter on child abuse, it was noted that not all sex offenders are men. Research on female offenders identifies three types:[624]

1. Women who abuse with a male

2. Women who sexually abuse teenage boys

3. Women who sexually abuse prepubescent children.

Women who abuse with men are often in emotionally dependent relationships and act partly out of fear. The second group are often involved in unsatisfactory marriages and believe they have fallen in love. It appears that they can benefit from therapy as they are helped to work through their own emotional issues and confront the reality of the emotional and power imbalance in the abusive relationship. As with male offenders, they often become involved with emotionally needy adolescent males. The third category often comprises adolescent girls or women who were victims of abuse or emotional deprivation themselves. The gender issue is clearly important when dealing with this group as it is not appropriate to generalise from the experience of male offenders.

The same is true of bullying. It was suggested in the chapter on adult bullying that men tend to use direct aggression while women use indirect aggression. It has been suggested that one of the significant differences between men and women is that men tend to be better at constructing and dealing with systems (a system is anything that takes inputs and delivers outputs, such as a computer, a machine, or weather patterns). Women tend to be better at empathising, which involves an ability to read the mind of another person, and to predict a range of possible outcomes rather than only one possible outcome.[625]

---

624 Hunter, J.A. and Matthews, R. (1997). Sexual deviance in females. In Laws, D. Richard and O'Donohue, W. (eds). *Sexual Deviance: Theory, Assessment, and Treatment* (pp. 465–80). New York: Guilford Press.

625 Baron-Cohen, S. (2003). *The Essential Difference*. London: Penguin.

This is important, for bullying as direct aggression usually involves an unpleasant consequence that relates to the behaviour. Indirect aggression, on the other hand, requires an ability to read the mind of the other. A policy of exclusion, for example, or removal from an email list, is a more strategic behaviour, where the consequences may not be immediate or even visible, than a straightforward insult, harangue, or sexual approach.[626]

One of the other significant differences between men and women relates to verbal ability, particularly in the area of articulating and expressing emotions. Men often feel ill-equipped to explain how they feel and this may be particularly galling if a female partner is belittling or critical. This involves a threat to the man's power and status. Lacking an ability to express their feelings, many men will resort to violence. Anthony Clare suggests that men's comparative inarticulacy compared to women's, particularly when trying to express their feelings, is a factor that contributes to male violence. Men often feel frustrated and resort to violence because they claim they cannot express their feelings in any other way. At the same time, men can also be verbally aggressive and intimidating.[627]

Women's speech is more cooperative and focused on establishing relationships. Men's speech, on the other hand, is more competitive. Women are better at negotiating and articulating the perspective of the other and at taking turns. Men, on the other hand, want to dominate to make sure that their perspective is heard. It can be more difficult, in work situations, to deal with a man who is aggressive, as he may lack the skills to listen, see the perspective of others, or negotiate.[628] High status men often have better language skills as well as access to levers of power and influence, which they can use to achieve their goals.

Boundaries

Another important issue that emerges in the subjects dealt with in this book is that of boundaries. People with healthy boundaries know where their world ends and the world of the other begins. Bullies, and people who resort to violence, intrude on the personal boundaries of others

---

626 Ibid.
627 Clare, A. (2000). *On men* (p. 47). London: Chatto & Windus.
628 Baron-Cohen, S. (2003). *The Essential Difference*. London: Penguin.

in ways that cause fear, and possibly damage, to the victim or his/her reputation. People with problems of addictions often trespass on the boundaries of others, in terms of finance, relationships or contractual obligations. But they also cross personal boundaries in terms of self-worth or morality. Part of the wisdom of the 12-Step tradition, which emerged out of Alcoholics Anonymous and has since been copied or adapted by other self-help groups, is the need to take a fearless self-inventory and to make amends to people who have been hurt or offended by the actions of the addict.

Healthy living requires an ability to know one's personal limits and how to respect the lives of other people. The various issues that are dealt with in this book all involve problems in terms of boundaries. Child abusers do not respect the physical, emotional, sexual and legal boundaries of the child. They allow their own needs to take precedence. Addicts in the grip of their addiction will sacrifice significant relationships and self-respect in pursuit of the 'fix', be it emotional or sexual. Bullies push uninvited into the living and work spaces of others to humiliate or belittle for personal satisfaction, or to appear powerful or clever in the eyes of others. Part of the responsibility of managers or clergy is to ensure that the rights of others are respected and that difficult people do not trespass on or interfere with the work of others.

Religion and well-being

The subjects dealt with in this book relate to mental health and violent or difficult behaviours. People who exhibit these problems or behaviours are unlikely to be satisfied with their lives, even if some of their behaviours bring them momentary feelings of pleasure or happiness. There has been considerable research in recent years into the relationship between religiousness and life satisfaction. Diener and Myers cite research from the United States and across 14 Western nations which suggests that 'Happiness and life satisfaction rise with strength of religious affiliation and frequency of worship attendance.'[629] They note that religious people are less likely to become delinquent or indulge in other non-social behaviours. They are more likely to be happily married, be physically healthier and live longer. They are slightly less vulnerable

---

629   Diener, E. and Myers, D.G. (1995). Who is happy? *Psychological Science* 6: 10–19 (p. 16).

to depression and report higher levels of well-being. They also note that highly spiritual people were twice as likely as other people to say they were 'very happy'. They report that the best predictors of well-being in the elderly were good health and participation in religion. They also report that those with a strong faith returned to positive levels of well-being more quickly after suffering a major loss.

One area of religiousness that has been the subject of reasonably thorough investigation is Gordon Allport's distinction between intrinsic and extrinsic religiousness.[630] Intrinsic religiousness 'is religion as a meaning-endowing framework', whereas extrinsic religiousness is defined as the 'religion of comfort and social convention'. [631] When extrinsics[632] and intrinsics are compared, intrinsics appear healthier on measures of well-being, internal locus of control and anxiety. Intrinsics also scored lower on factors labelled egocentric sexuality and restlessness, which could be related to use of sex as a coping mechanism and poor impulse control in people with addictions or those who have difficulty managing anger.

This research suggests that there are benefits for people who hold a sincerely held faith and a pattern of regular church attendance, and numerous studies have linked spirituality to well-being. The sense of being connected to something larger than oneself, which is labelled transcendence, is also seen as life enhancing. Spirituality has long been considered an important part of recovery for people caught in addictions. Similar research has also been done with sex offenders and pathological gamblers.[633]

The authors of the various chapters in this book have offered a section entitled 'A Christian Response', in order to offer insights from the perspective of Christian faith. The research that has been presented in this section also suggests that religious faith, religious practices and spirituality can help those whose behaviour is problematic, self-

630 Allport, G.W. (1954). *The Individual and his Religion: A Psychological Interpretation.* New York: Macmillan.

631 Donohue, M.J. (1985). Intrinsic and extrinsic religiousness: Review and meta-analysis. *Journal of Personality and Social Psychology* 48: 400–19.

632 Alker, H.A. and Gawin, F. (1978). On the intrapsychic specificity of happiness. *Journal of Personality* 46: 311–22.

633 Ciarrocchi, J.W. and Deneke, E. (2004). Happiness and the varieties of religious experience: Religious support, practices, and spirituality as predictors of well-being. *Research in the Social Scientific Study of Religion* 15: 235–62.

defeating or difficult, to manage their lives better, be more respectful of others, and live with more personal satisfaction.

Positive Psychology

When Martin Seligman became the President of the American Psychological Association in 1998, he chose to talk about two subjects in his presidential address. The first was ethnopolitical conflict. He expressed a hope that it would be possible to train psychologists to better 'understand, predict and even prevent' such tragedies, and to help people to recover from them.[634] His second topic concerned what he called 'A new science of human strengths'. Seligman said that psychology had a great deal to say about mental disorders, repairing damage to human beings (healing), and about how people survive in difficult, adverse situations, but that it had little to say about what makes life worth living and how to live a more positive, meaningful life. His presidential address, along with his own research, teaching and writing, have helped to bring about the sea change that he hoped for, and have given significant impetus to the movement known as positive psychology.

Positive psychology was already making an impact when the first edition of this handbook was published in 2008. In this revised edition, we want to note some important developments that have taken place regarding resilience, recovery from trauma and distress, how to respond to difficult behaviours, and how to help those affected by such behaviours to develop resilience and strength.

Recent developments

There have been a number of initiatives in recent years that show promise in bringing healing to people who have mental health problems or who have been affected by trauma. The therapeutic approach known as Eye Movement Desensitisation and Reprocessing (EMDR) continues to be used to treat a range of mental health problems that have often seemed difficult to treat. There is research evidence which shows that this approach can be helpful for adult survivors of sexual

---

634 Seligman, M.E.P. (August, 1999). *American Psychologist*. President's Address.

abuse, including abuse by clergy.[635] There have also been advances in the treatment of people whose behaviour is problematic for themselves, their families or colleagues, and can be experienced as difficult or even criminal. In the chapter on child sexual abuse there was reference to the Circles of Support and Accountability, which originated in Canada and have now been established in other countries. The Good Lives[636] model of treatment also offers a combination of support and challenge to people who have perpetrated sexual abuse. Motivational Interviewing continues to be used to support people with a range of addictions. It has also been applied to support people who need to change aspects of their behaviour to improve their physical or mental health.[637]

In recent years, the positive psychology movement has had a significant impact on both psychology and counselling. In the following sections we outline some of the key ideas that have developed in this area which have particular relevance to the topics and themes presented in this book. We have chosen to focus on new understandings about positive emotions, resilience, post-traumatic growth, neuroplasticity and mindfulness.

Positive emotions

Martin Seligman wrote that positive psychology has three pillars:[638]

1. The study of positive emotion

2. The study of positive traits, especially strengths, virtues and abilities, e.g. optimism, empathy, intelligence and spirituality

3. The study of positive institutions such as democracy, strong families, voluntary organisations, charities and churches.

The chapters in this book are concerned with difficult situations and behaviours that result from and give rise to negative emotions: fear, anxiety, depression, anger and so on. Difficult behaviours can lead to feelings of frustration, fear, avoidance, exasperation, distress and

---

635 Farrell, D., Dworkin, M., Keenan, P. and Spierings, J. (2010). Using EMDR with survivors of sexual abuse perpetrated by Roman Catholic priests. *Journal of EMDR Practice and Research* 4(3): 124–33.

636 http://www.goodlivesmodel.com/

637 http://www.motivationalinterviewing.org/

638 Seligman, M.E.P. (2002). *Authentic happiness* (p. xiii). New York: Free Press.

discouragement in those who deal with them as managers or pastoral workers. Seligman writes that the pursuit of happiness, in terms of pleasure and gratification, is not sufficient. Positive emotion that arises from achievement, the exercise of virtue, and the pursuit of meaningful goals is more likely to make a significant difference in our lives in terms of our well-being and life satisfaction.

The study of emotion has led to an understanding of the purpose of negative emotion. Seligman suggests, for example, that:

- Thoughts about trespass drive anger

- Thoughts about loss drive sadness

- Thoughts about danger drive anxiety.[639]

Using this model of understanding, the purpose of positive emotions was not immediately clear. Barbara Fredrickson, who has studied positive emotions, has concluded that, where negative emotions lead us to narrow our perspective to focus on a particular goal, positive emotions broaden and build resources for future well-being, and that they have two main functions:

- **Undoing** the effects of negative emotions

- Triggering an **upward spiral** that can build the foundations for further positive emotional experiences

In these ways, positive emotions expand our feeling repertoire and create space for more positive experiences. They also help to build a buffer against adverse experiences in life.[640]

Gratitude, joy, optimism, empathy and other positive emotions, traits and abilities build resilience, friendship and love, and lead to better health and lasting achievements.[641] Seligman recommends that people keep a gratitude journal, noting things for which they are grateful each night. He writes that soldiers who did this reported health benefits,

---

639   Seligman, M.E.P. (2011). *Flourish* (p. 167). London: Nicholas Brealey Publishing.
640   Werdel, M.B. and Wicks, R.J. (2012). *Primer on posttraumatic growth* (pp. 99–100). New Jersey: John Wiley and Sons.
641   Seligman, M.E.P. (2002). *Authentic happiness*, p. 43.

improved sleep and relationships, and that they performed better in their jobs.[642] If soldiers in conflict situations experience these positive effects from such a simple exercise, how much more might it be the case for ordinary people who are often dealing with stressful or discouraging situations at home or at work?

Feelings have a contagious effect. Seligman quotes research that shows that the closer someone lives to a person who is lonely or depressed, the higher the likelihood that these will also be lonely or depressed. The good news is that happiness is more contagious than loneliness or depression. This has implications for everyone, but especially for people in leadership or management roles, whose emotional disposition can have a significant effect on other people, especially in situations where difficult behaviours can have a negative influence on a group.[643] Seligman writes that 'positive emotions build the cathedrals of our lives'.[644]

Post-Traumatic Growth

Television and the media have been bringing news and images of disasters, wars, terrorism, abusive situations, and extraordinary human suffering into our lives for decades. As a result of these media reports, many of us are familiar with the word trauma and its effects. In recent years, there has been greater awareness of the impact of war, shock, sudden deaths and explosions and horrific incidents on military personnel and aid workers. This has led to the diagnosis of post-traumatic stress disorder (PTSD) which can involve heightened experiences of anxiety, long-lasting depression, emotional flatness, hyper-vigilance and intrusive thoughts and nightmares. In the years after the Vietnam War, the United States Veterans' Medical System became a laboratory for the study of PTSD and its effects, along with the seeming intractability of the condition.

Psychological trauma is the result of a disruption in a person's assumptive world – that is, the person's worldview has been turned upside down and their sense of safety has been shattered because of an unexpected event or situation which was beyond their ability

---

642 Seligman, M.E.P. (2011). *Flourish*, p. 171.
643 Ibid., p. 146.
644 Seligman, M.E.P. (2002). *Authentic happiness*, p. 257.

to cope.[645] This was certainly true for the 18-year-old soldiers who fought in Vietnam, and it has been true of other military personnel who have been involved in conflicts since that time. Martin Seligman has become interested in post-traumatic growth, making use of the insights from positive psychology to build resilience in individuals and giving them the tools to prevent them suffering from post-traumatic stress.[646] He has worked with the US military to help personnel build mental toughness, develop their personal strengths and strengthen their relationships. This has involved building resilience and, in the process, providing the resources to prevent PTSD from taking hold. He points out that optimism is a major contributor to growth, and that building mental resilience should enable soldiers to grow professionally and in their personal lives, as well as building a buffer against the effects of traumatic situations.[647]

Werdel and Wicks note that meaning-making is a significant part of post-traumatic growth. The person who has suffered trauma needs to reappraise their life goals and the nature of the stressor. Many people experience 'adversarial growth' in the aftermath of a traumatic experience.[648] Counsellors and psychologists can help people rebuild their lives after traumatic incidents, though this is a long process which requires time for healing to take place. Werdel and Wicks note that spirituality and spiritual practices have been shown to have a positive impact in the recovery process after traumatic experiences.[649] They discuss the importance of forgiveness, but stress that the primary motivation for forgiveness is to set oneself free from the effects of rumination on a painful event or from holding a grudge.[650] There is good research evidence on the beneficial effects of forgiveness. There may be valid moral reasons to offer forgiveness to another, but from a psychological perspective the key beneficiary is the person who chooses to forgive, who can then let go of the hurt and anger, and move on with their lives. When painful feelings are heard, there is often a lessening of

---

645 Janoff-Bulman, R. (1992). *Shattered assumptions: Towards a new psychology of trauma.* New York: The Free Press.
646 Seligman, M.E.P. (2011). *Flourish*, pp. 101–25.
647 Ibid., p. 170.
648 Werdel, M.B. and Wicks, R.J. (2012). *Primer on posttraumatic growth.* New Jersey: John Wiley and Sons, p. 15.
649 Ibid., p. 168.
650 Ibid., pp. 145–58.

the intensity of the sadness and distress that the person is experiencing, leaving room for the experience of positive emotions, which, as we have seen, can build resources for a more resilient and worthwhile future.

Research on post-traumatic growth has shown that trauma can be turned into growth. Writers often quote Nietzsche who wrote: 'What does not kill me makes me stronger',[651] and that would appear to be the case regarding what has been learned with the recent developments in the area of post-traumatic growth. In *Bounce*, his popular and insightful book on resilience, Wicks writes:

> It is not the amount of darkness in the world that matters. It is not even the amount of darkness in ourselves that matters. It is how we stand in the darkness that makes all the difference in how we lead our lives in ways that positively impact others as well as ourselves.[652]

The chapters in this book deal with many situations where we confront darkness: abuse, addiction, interpersonal violence, bullying and so on. Developments in recent years suggest that there are positive ways forward for people who are affected by these behaviours. The positive psychology movement has developed knowledge, insight and interventions to support resilience and growth, especially after traumatic and distressing experiences. As Wicks has written, how we stand in the darkness is more important than the amount of darkness that we experience.

Neuroplasticity

Elaine Fox, an experimental psychologist and neuroscientist, wrote that until the 1980s it was commonly held that brain circuits were only malleable at a young age.[653] Recent research has demonstrated that there is more plasticity and malleability in the brains of adults than was previously recognised. Brain processes are not set in concrete, but are, in fact, more fluid than previously thought. It has been shown, for

---

651   Seligman, M.E.P. (2011). *Flourish*, p. 159.
652   Wicks, R.J. (2010). *Bounce*. Oxford: OUP, p. 164.
653   Fox, E. (2012). *Rainy Brain, Sunny Brain*. London: Arrow Books, p. 134.

example, that the parts of the brain that deal with fear and pleasure are particularly capable of change. Psychologists have made use of exposure and reconditioning to help people recover from phobias, and this has been applied, for example, to people who have a fear of flying. The cognitive approach to psychotherapy helps people to identify cognitions (thoughts) that lead to emotions that cause distress. It has been shown that if we change our cognitions we can reshape our brains, improve our emotional well-being and behave differently.

People who are pessimistic or afraid, often operate from negative biases in their view of the world. If it were possible to change people's biases then it might be possible to change their perspective, leading to more positive emotional experiences, improved social behaviour and healthier relationships. Fox provides research data on cognitive bias modification (CBM) that suggests that people with addictions can be helped to avoid addictive choices, by helping them override a dangerous thought. This intervention has been shown to be effective for alcohol abuse, social anxiety and depression.[654] More research is necessary in order to be confident about the efficacy of this approach. Such research holds out the possibility of finding ways to modify pessimistic outlooks, with the resultant change in well-being for individuals. The reality of neurogenesis (generation of new cells) can offer possible ways forward for degenerative illnesses like Parkinson's or Alzheimer's.[655]

Mindfulness

One of the major growth areas in mental well-being in recent years has been in the promotion of mindfulness. Mindfulness can be helpful for those who are dealing with difficult behaviours, as part of their own self-management. Current mindfulness training in the fields of mental and medical health emerge from centuries-old religious practices used to help people to develop awareness and contact with the God of their understanding. Mindfulness as referenced in the context of mental and medical treatment is a non-sectarian, secularized practice that focuses on healing both the mind and the body.[656]

---

654 Ibid., pp. 155–62.

655 Ibid., pp. 133, 137, 162.

656 James Walsh, PhD, author of the chapter on Gambling Addiction, contributed the section on mindfulness. Dr Walsh is a trained Mindfulness practitioner with many years' experience as a counsellor who successfully integrates mindfulness into his work as a therapist. See www.jamesmwalshpastoralcounseling.com

Mindfulness is a state of mind, a way of relating to all of experience, whether that experience is perceived as positive, negative or neutral. When mindful, one is aware of the activity of body and mind, in the present moment, bringing a non-judgemental acceptance to all that is perceived. There are many formal definitions of mindfulness that reflect the traditions from which they are drawn (generally, either religious or psychological traditions), but in the current climate of mindfulness-based psychological and medical treatments the definition most frequently cited is from Jon Kabat-Zinn:

> Mindfulness is the awareness that emerges through paying attention on purpose, in the present moment, and non-judgmentally to the unfolding of experience moment to moment.[657]

Kabat-Zinn developed the first mindfulness-based treatment (Mindfulness-Based Stress Reduction [MBSR]) at the University of Massachusetts Medical School in 1979, with a primary focus on pain management. Since then there have been thousands of articles published in peer-reviewed journals examining the impact of mindfulness-based treatments. Mindfulness-based treatments now target any number of psychological problems including anxiety, depression, addiction and a variety of physical disorders that are caused or worsened by stress.[658] A review conducted in 2013 of extant literature concerning outcome research that studied mindfulness, found 2,876 articles in peer-reviewed journals, dissertations and books.[659] Clearly, mindfulness has become a mainstream treatment modality in the mental health field.

While mindfulness training has been found to be helpful in relieving many problems, particularly stress-related problems, it is important for counsellors to understand how mindfulness can be

---

657   Kabat-Zinn, J. (2003). Mindfulness-based interventions in context: past, present, and future. *Clinical Psychology: Science & Practice* 10(2): 144–56.

658   Baer, R. (2016). Assessment of mindfulness and closely related constructs: Introduction to the special issue. *Psychological Assessment* 28(7): 787–90.

659   Khoury, B., Lecomte, T., Fortin, G., Masse, M., Therien, P., Bouchard, V., Chapleau, M.A., Paquin, K. and Hofmann, S.G. (2013). Mindfulness-based therapy: A comprehensive meta-analysis. *Clinical Psychology Review* 33: 763–71.

used in a therapeutic milieu. Following Germer, Siegel and Fulton's (2013) conceptualisation,[660] counsellors should first receive hands-on training for themselves to develop their own mindfulness practices (e.g. meditation skills) in order to become a mindful therapist. Mindfulness skills have been demonstrated to increase therapist presence and capacity for accurate empathy,[661] which are key elements in any type of psychotherapy. With deepening of the counsellor's personal mindfulness practices, psychotherapy can become mindfulness-informed, meaning that the principles (e.g. radical acceptance, present moment focus) and vocabulary (e.g. 'skilful means', 'noticing', 'making space for pain') of mindfulness practice get incorporated into therapeutic conversations. Finally, with sustained practice and specialised training, counsellors can begin to do mindfulness-based therapy, in which participants commit to learning mindfulness as a skill taught (usually in group settings) by the counsellor-instructor.

As mentioned above, there have been thousands of studies of the effects of mindfulness on psychological and physical problems. The most studied application of mindfulness has been MBSR. A standardised review of MBSR (and Mindfulness-Based Cognitive Therapy [MBCT], a closely related programme) found that mindfulness training significantly improved depressive symptoms, anxiety, stress, quality of life, and physical functioning.[662] Another programme derived from MBSR, Mindfulness-Based Relapse Prevention (MBRP), has been shown to be highly efficacious in addiction treatment. In a 12-month longitudinal study, a research team at the University of Washington found that MBRP produced clinically and statistically significant improvements in outcome over and above Treatment as Usual.[663]

---

660 Germer, C.K., Siegel, R.D. and Fulton, P.R. (2013). *Mindfulness and Psychotherapy*. New York: Guilford Press.

661 Bruce, N.G., Manber, R., Shapiro, S.L. and Constantino, M.J. (2010). Psychotherapist mindfulness and the psychotherapy process. *Psychotherapy Research, Theory, Practice, Training* 47(1): 83–97.

662 Gotink, R.A., Chu, P., Busschbach, J.J.V., Benson, H., Fricchione, G.L. and Hunink, M.G.M. (2015). Standardised mindfulness-based interventions in healthcare: An overview of systematic reviews and meta-analyses of RCTs. *PLOS One* found at http://journals.plos.org/plosone/article?id=10.1371/journal.pone.0124344

663 Bowen, S., Witkiewitz, K., Clifasefi, S.L., Grow, G., Chawla, N., Hsu, S.H., Carroll, H.A., Harrop, E., Collins, S.E., Lustyk, M.K. and Larimer, M.E. (2014). Relative efficacy of mindfulness-based relapse prevention, standard relapse prevention, and treatment as usual for substance use disorders: A randomized trial. *JAMA Psychiatry* 71(5): 547–56.

Generally, mindfulness has been demonstrated to have moderate to strong effects in the treatment of psychological and physical illnesses.

The key to integrating mindfulness into treatment is the personal mindfulness practice of the counsellor. Mindfulness is not an intervention *per se*. Rather, it should be understood as a way of being that helps define counsellor presence and, when incorporated into the therapy session by a mindful therapist, a mindfulness-informed therapist, or in formal mindfulness training, helps the client to develop a mindful way of being in the world.[664] But counsellors should be cautious about teaching mindfulness without an established personal practice and appropriate training in mindfulness-based interventions. Mindfulness practices can be difficult at first for clients with psychological or physical illnesses, and mindfulness teachers must have personal experience with the sorts of difficulty that arise, particularly the flooding of emotions that one may feel when meditation becomes deep and lengthy. In the moment of client suffering that is fully experienced by both client and counsellor, where appropriate, the bond of authenticity is strengthened as the counsellor can say 'I, too, have suffered' and can then guide the client through his/her emotional pain. After hours spent in meditation and contemplation, the mindful therapist is well equipped to handle these challenges.

Conclusion

Why do people behave as they do? This book has attempted to analyse some complex, difficult and challenging behaviour patterns. Each human being is unique in both biology and experience. The interaction between our nature and our nurture, and the underlying processes involved in determining how we think, feel and behave, continue to be the focus of significant research which has far-reaching implications for applications in genetics and in finding effective intervention and treatment programmes which it is hoped enhance psychosocial development for those who are at risk. Our unique personalities develop throughout our life span and are characterised by our emotional

---

664 Bruce, N.G., Manber, R., Shapiro, S.L. and Constantino, M.J. (2010). Psychotherapist mindfulness and the psychotherapy process. *Psychotherapy Research, Theory, Practice, Training* 47(1): 83–97; Germer, C.K., Siegel, R.D. and Fulton, P.R. (2013). *Mindfulness and Psychotherapy*. New York: Guilford Press.

and behavioural responses. Emotion management and self-regulation have important implications for our own behaviour and well-being. Developments in psychology and counselling offer approaches to treatment that can help those who are motivated to manage negative emotions better, improving the quality of their lives and resulting in less distress and potential damage to the lives of others.

About the Contributors

Alan Bartlett is an Anglican priest. He is currently the Clergy Development Advisor for the Diocese of Durham, having just finished nine years as Vicar of St Giles' Durham and Priest-in-Charge of Sherburn and Shadforth. Before that he was the St John's College Director of the Durham Doctor of Ministry programme, involved in the teaching and supervision of Practical Theology and still teaches in the areas of Practical Theology and Anglicanism. Previously he was a curate in West Newcastle and a youth worker in Bermondsey. He is married with two adult children. He has published on Christian Spirituality (*Humane Christianity*, 2004) and Anglican Theology (*A Passionate Balance*, 2007) and is now writing a book on being a vicar.

Jocelyn Bryan is Academic Dean at Cranmer Hall, St John's College, Durham and an Anglican Lay Reader. She teaches Psychology and Christian Ministry, Sexuality, Gender and Christian Ministry and Practical Theology. Her PhD is in psychology, for which she studied ageing and memory. Her research interest is in the interface between psychology, theology and Christian ministry and she has published *Human Being: Insights from Psychology and the Christian Faith* (2016), and chapters on adolescence, human sexuality, ageing and a variety of pastoral issues. She is editor of the online journal *Theology and Ministry*. Jocelyn is married and has three adult children.

Mark Brouwer is a pastor, writer, and speaker. He serves as the pastor of Loop Church in Chicago, IL. He is also the director of Renew Resources, which provides teaching and support for people who want to help others, but struggle with stress, overwhelm, discouragement or addiction. He is the editor of the sexualsanity.com blog, and the creator of an online support programme for people in recovery from sexual addiction: *The Recovery Journey* (recoveryjourney.com). He is author of the forthcoming *Not So Overwhelmed: spiritual solutions for changing the world without wrecking your life*. Mark and his wife Charlene live in Chicago, and have two grown-up sons.

The Reverend Professor Christopher Cook is Professor of Spirituality, Theology & Health in the Department of Theology & Religion at Durham University and an Honorary Minor Canon of Durham Cathedral. Chris worked in the psychiatry of substance misuse for over 25 years. He is now Director of the Project for Spirituality, Theology & Health at Durham University. He is President of the British Association for the Study of Spirituality. His books include *Spirituality, Theology and Mental Health* (2013) and *Spirituality and Narrative in Psychiatric Practice: Stories of Mind and Soul* (eds Cook, Powell & Sims, 2016).

Michael Fitzsimons. Having worked in community and youth work settings, services for homeless people and prisons, Fr Michael Fitzsimons is now a priest of the Archdiocese of Liverpool. He currently serves at the Parish of St Wilfrid, Widnes. He is also Chair of Trustees at Nugent, the official caring services charity of the Archdiocese which is one of the oldest and most diverse charities in the northwest of England.

Brendan Geary F.M.S. is the Provincial of the Marist Brothers' Province of West Central Europe. He is a UK, HCPC Registered Clinical and Counselling Psychologist. He was the Director of Human Formation at Ushaw College, former Seminary for the North of England (2004–09). He has published numerous book chapters and articles, and has given workshops and retreats in areas related to psychology, human development, sexuality, ministry and spirituality, in Europe, Africa, Australia, and in Latin and Central America. He is co-editor of *Sexual Issues: Understanding and advising in a Christian Context* (Kevin Mayhew Ltd, 2010), and *The Dark Night of the Catholic Church* (Kevin Mayhew Ltd, 2011) on the clergy sexual abuse crisis.

Tracey Hume is a Methodist Minister in Gateshead. Prior to training for ministry, she spent 17 years as a special educational needs teacher and advisory teacher. For 4 years she was a specialist advisory teacher for autism across County Durham, developing strategies for children on the spectrum in a range of educational settings. Tracey is passionate about those who are often marginalised in society and, as part of her Master's degree studies, she developed a range of Autism-Friendly Churches materials and wrote her dissertation on the challenges of reading and comprehending the Bible for people with Asperger syndrome. Tracey's eldest son has Asperger syndrome which has given her insight and inspired her passion for this area of research.

Mark R. Laaser is the President and Founder of Faithful & True and the host of *The Men of Valor Program*, Faithful & True's online radio show. Dr Laaser is recognised as a leading authority in the field of sexual addiction and healthy sexuality, with over 29 years of recovery experience. He has written 15 books on the subject of sexual addiction, including *Healing The Wounds of Sexual Addiction, Becoming a Man of Valor, Taking Every Thought Captive, 7 Principles of Highly Accountable Men* and the recently released *The Fight of Your Life* (Destiny Image, 2016) with Dr Tim Clinton. Dr Laaser lectures around the world and teaches at colleges, universities, religious organisations and treatment centres. He holds a PhD from the University of Iowa and a divinity degree from Princeton Theological Seminary.

Bex Lewis is passionate about helping people engage with the digital world in a positive way, where she has more than 20 years' experience. Trained as a mass communications historian, writing the original history of the poster *Keep Calm and Carry On,* she is Senior Lecturer in Digital Marketing at Manchester Metropolitan University and Visiting Research Fellow at St John's College, Durham University, with a particular interest in digital culture, and how this affects the third sector, especially faith organisations, voluntary organisations, and behavioural campaigns. She is Director of social media consultancy Digital Fingerprint, and author of *Raising Children in a Digital Age* (Lion Hudson, 2014) which has been featured in a wide range of publications and programmes, including *The One Show, BBC News, Steve Wright in the Afternoon,* the *Daily Telegraph,* and the *Church Times.*

Bill Macgregor is a retired police officer with degrees in History and Law. He is an independent researcher in those disciplines and has contributed to publications in both fields. He is interested in the wider implications of social media use on the internet, particularly for its ability to facilitate abusive behaviour. He is married and lives in Glasgow with his wife and family.

Alison Moore started out teaching English literature, but from the 1980s she broadened that fascination and respect for people's stories into working in counselling, training, facilitating, supervising, conflict transformation, writing and spiritual direction. Roles have included working for Relate as counsellor and trainer and as Adviser in Pastoral Care and Counselling for the Anglican Diocese of Durham, where she ran the Counselling Service and provided consultancy and support to clergy and churches. She now has a varied freelance life. Where she can, she tries to be a good 'translator' of impenetrable technical language, whether therapeutic or theological! She is married with four adult sons, three daughters-in-law and an expanding band of grandchildren.

Lesley Orr is a historian, writer and activist, currently based at the University of Edinburgh Centre for Theology and Public Issues (CTPI) and previously at Scottish Women's Aid, where her task was to coordinate national education and training for the Scottish Government's Strategy to Address Violence Against Women. She initiated the pioneering *Gender justice and violence: feminist approaches* course at Queen Margaret University Edinburgh, and is a member of the teaching team. Lesley has a longstanding commitment to challenging gender inequality, abuse and violence against women – in Scotland and internationally – and has written extensively on these issues in relation to Christianity, faith communities and wider society. Lesley has worked in local Women's Aid groups, campaigning, transnational networks, advocacy and education. Under CTPI auspices, she coordinated an action-research project: *Out of the Shadows: Christianity and Violence Against Women in Scotland*. She has extensive experience in third sector and church initiatives to address gender-based violence, was consultant to the World Council of Churches Decade to Overcome Violence 2001–2010, and won Action for Children Scotland's 'Woman of Influence' Award, 2012. Lesley is engaged in Scottish initiatives for active citizenship and is a member of the ecumenical Iona Community.

James Walsh is a Pastoral Counsellor working in private practice in Wilmington, Delaware, USA. He is a Licensed Professional Counsellor of Mental Health. After retiring from his full-time faculty position at Wilmington University, he continues to teach graduate courses on the topics of Humanistic Counselling and Mindfulness-Based Counselling. He has been an International Certified Gambling Counsellor-II since 2001, working with compulsive gamblers and their families, and has published research on gambling and spirituality. He is married and has two adult children.

Index

Index of Authors